6th EDITION

Infants & Toddlers

CURRICULUM AND TEACHING

6th EDITION

Infants & Toddlers

CURRICULUM AND TEACHING

LINDA WATSON ■ TERRI SWIM

THOMSON

DELMAR LEARNING

Australia Brazil Canada Mexico Singapore Spain United Kingdom United States

THOMSON

DELMAR LEARNING

Infants and Toddlers, Curriculum and Teaching, 6th Edition
Linda Watson and Terri Swim

Vice President, Career Education Strategic Business Unit:
Dawn Gerrain

Director of Learning Solutions:
John Fedor

Managing Editor:
Robert L. Serenka, Jr.

Senior Acquisitions Editor:
Erin O'Connor

Product Manager:
Philip Mandl

Editorial Assistant:
Alison Archambault

Director of Production:
Wendy A. Troeger

Production Manager:
Mark Bernard

Content Project Manager:
Karin Hillen Jaquays

Technology Project Manager:
Sandy Charette

Director of Marketing:
Wendy E. Mapstone

Channel Manager:
Kristin McNary

Channel Manager:
Scott A. Chrysler

Marketing Specialist:
Erica S. Conley

Art Director:
Joy Kocsis

Cover Design:
Rose Design

For permission to use material from this text or product, submit a request online at http://www.thomsonrights.com Any additional questions about permissions can be submitted by email to thomsonrights@thomson.com

Library of Congress Cataloging-in-Publication Data

Douville-Watson, Linda.
  Infants & toddlers : curriculum and teaching.—6th ed. / Linda Douville-Watson, Terri Jo Swim.
      p. cm.
  Includes bibliographical references and index.
  ISBN 1-4180-1662-4 (alk. paper)
  1. Child care—United States. 2. Infants—United States. 3. Toddlers—United States. 4. Child development—United States. 5. Family day care—United States. I. Swim, Terri. II. Title. III. Title: Infants and toddlers.
  HQ778.63.D68 2007
  362.71071—dc22
                                    2007005386

NOTICE TO THE READER

Contents

PART **Establishing a Positive Learning Environment . . .137**

Preface

This revised, expanded, and updated edition was developed by Terri Jo Swim with the intention of guiding the reader through the acquisitions of skills necessary to provide high-quality care for infants and toddlers in any educational setting. Information based on current theories and research, as well as standards for infant/toddler teacher preparation, are reflected throughout the book. We provide appropriate caregiving and educational techniques along with activities for groups of very young children and the individual children within those groups. Early childhood educators, administrators, advocates, and parents will find practical information that can be put to immediate use to promote the highest-quality care and education possible for all children.

Text Organization

Part I. Infant and Toddler Development and Caregiver Preparation

This section presents an overview of the history, theories, and research in the fields of child development and early childhood education, including new information on brain development, to prepare the reader as a professional educator who possesses the skills necessary to effectively meet the developmental and learning needs of infants and toddlers. Chapter 1 provides both historical and current overviews of environmental, social, cultural, and governmental influences in child care. Chapter 2 sets a standard of care and presents theories and definitions of development, learning, and teaching, as well as how these can be applied to enhance the development and care of infants and toddlers. Chapter 3 creates a framework for growth and development in four major areas from birth to 36 months. Chapter 4 presents the master tools of caregiving: Attention, Approval, and Attunement as a model of conscious caregiving, combining practical principles and techniques from current theories and research in the field. Chapter 5 describes specific knowledge bases that professional educators acquire through informal and formal educational opportunities. One such knowledge base involves the appropriate assessment of children. This chapter, then, focuses on various observational tools for tracking development and learning, and how to use the data as the groundwork for other aspects of your work.

Part II. Establishing a Positive Learning Environment

Four chapters provide the reader with details about how to create appropriate environments for very young children. Learning environments include not only attending to the physical arrangement by carefully selecting equipment and materials but also the socio-emotional and intellectual climates created among adults and children. Chapter 6 utilizes key components of the Reggio Emilia approach to infant/toddler education as the foundation for creating a caring community of learners. Respectful and effective communication and guidance strategies are outlined for your use. Chapter 7 is devoted to communication strategies that are appropriate when creating reciprocal relationships with family members and colleagues. Family situations that may require additional support from you, your program, or community agencies are presented. Chapter 8 covers components of high-quality and developmentally appropriate indoor and outdoor learning environments from the teachers' and children's perspectives and presents common safety issues for children. Chapter 9 presents practical techniques for designing the intellectual environment. Curriculum—both routine care times and planned learning experiences—must be specially designed to enhance the development and learning of all children in your care, including children with special needs.

Part III. Matching Caregiver Strategies and Child Development

Seven developmental levels are defined within the age range of birth through 36 months, and tasks, materials, and specific activities to enhance development are provided in chapters 10 through 16. Developmental Profiles and Prescriptions are provided to establish the structure within which specific activities are accomplished, so that the caregiver maintains a constant awareness of goals and growth in the major areas of development. This practical section provides specific techniques, activities, and solutions to many of the common problems confronted in the growth and development of infants and toddlers.

Major Revisions in the Sixth Edition

The sixth edition of *Infants and Toddlers: Curriculum and Teaching* is the result of a new working relationship with a seasoned professional in early childhood education. Terri Jo Swim joined as an author on this text and has worked diligently to create a newly updated edition. Building from the strong foundation of previous editions, she updated, reorganized, and otherwise completed the revisions for the text. While notable differences set apart this edition, points of continuity remain. For example, in the sixth edition of *Infants and Toddlers: Curriculum and Teaching* the child continues to be, rightfully so, at the center of care and education. Defining infants and toddlers as engaging, decision-making forces within their environments sets a tone of excitement and enthusiasm. No longer can we afford to agree with the description of toddlerhood as the "terrible twos." Rather, we need to embrace the image of the child as capable, competent, and creative. Doing so opens a number of educational options that were before unavailable. While the three *As* continue to guide our conceptualization of competent caregiving, the theories and research used to explain them have been expanded and updated. Results of research on brain development and attachment behaviors, for example, have been included as foundations for this textbook. In addition, incorporating key components of the high-quality infant-toddler and preschool programs in Reggio Emilia, Italy, has improved our understanding of what developmentally appropriate practice looks like in action. Respecting children, designing the physical, social, and intellectual environments, building partnerships with families, and planning individually appropriate curriculum are all components that are discussed throughout this edition. Major content revisions in this edition also include the following:

- Chapters 1 and 2 have been expanded to include information on brain development, attachment theory, and Lev Vygotsky's sociocultural theory. Practical applications of developmental theories for early childhood programs now include family grouping, continuity of care, and the primary caregiving system.
- The section on "Children with Special Needs" in Chapter 2 was broadened to cover even more issues that might affect children in your care.
- Chapter 3 provides more information about cultural diversity, especially regarding resolving conflict with family members over issues such as toilet learning.
- Chapter 4 improves our understanding of the three As (Attention, Approval, and Attunement) by enlarging and expanding the theories and research used in their application. The contemporary theories discussed in Chapter 1 serve as the foundation for this explanation.
- In Chapter 5, "Acquiring Knowledge" now includes information about early child care and education, partnerships, and advocacy. A discussion of the impact of teacher education on quality care and education has been added to further your understanding of why teachers need to view themselves as lifelong learners. Issues surrounding observation and assessment, especially tools for this purpose, are also incorporated.
- Chapter 6 provides a new focus on creating a positive socio-emotional environment by building relationships with infants and toddlers on the basis of your *image of the child*. Strategies for communicating and guiding the behavior of very young children have been reorganized and expanded in this chapter.
- Forming reciprocal relationships with family members and colleagues is the theme of Chapter 7. The section called "Family Situations Requiring Additional Support" was relocated to this chapter and updated to improve your understanding and valuing of family diversity.
- Principles for designing the physical environment from the teachers' and children's perspectives are explored in Chapter 8.

- Chapter 9 converges the information in chapters 1–8 to explain how to create the intellectual environment for infants and toddlers. Curriculum—routine care and planned learning experiences—for very young children that meets the individual needs, interests, and abilities of each child is highlighted.
- Issues related to cultural diversity are emphasized, and specific strategies for appreciating and celebrating cultural identities and differences are included.
- A clearer focus has been placed on providing care to infants and toddlers with special needs.

Instructional Features

- Chapter overviews, objectives, and a specific chapter outline are provided for each chapter.
- New Key Terms used in each chapter are listed for easy reference, and important terms are presented in color.
- New case studies present real-life examples of the concepts and principles discussed in each chapter.
- Helpful Web sites are provided for every chapter.
- The Glossary has been expanded to cover definitions of new terms in child care and development.
- References, questions and experiences for reflection, and chapter review questions are provided at the end of each chapter.
- Sample Developmental Profiles and Prescriptions are provided for each age from birth to 36 months, and behavioral descriptions explaining the prescriptions accompany each.
- Numerous photos and illustrations are included throughout to illustrate the concepts and materials presented.
- A comprehensive Developmental Prescription of behavioral expectations for children from birth to 36 months for each of the four major areas of development is provided to assist the caregiver in establishing Developmental Profiles and Developmental Prescriptions for each child in care.
- The text is comprehensive so that you acquire the essential skills necessary to function at nationally accepted standards of quality.
- The level of the language used is easy to follow and offers practical examples for self-study by new caregivers-in-training.

We would welcome questions or discussions on any of the topics that are covered in the book.

Terri Jo Swim
swimt@ipfw.edu

Linda Douville-Watson
energynurse1@yahoo.com

Ancillaries

Instructor's Manual

The instructor's manual includes tools for facilitating learning, questions for generating discussion, and suggested projects for constructing knowledge for instructors of classes on infant and toddler care and development.

Computerized Test Bank

The computerized test bank comprises true/false, multiple choice, short answer, and completion questions for each chapter. Instructors can use the computerized test bank software to create sample quizzes for students. Refer to the CTB User's Guide for more information on how to create and post quizzes to your school's Internet or intranet server. Students may also access sample quizzes from the Online Resources™ to accompany this sixth edition of *Infants & Toddlers: Curriculum and Teaching*.

Online Resources™

The Online Resources™ to accompany the sixth edition of *Infants & Toddlers: Curriculum and Teaching* is your link to early childhood education on the Internet. The Online Resources™ contain many features to help focus your understanding of infants and toddlers.

 The Online Resources™ icon appears at the end of each chapter to prompt you to go online and take advantage of the many features provided.

You can find Online Resources™ at http://www.earlychilded.delmar.com

Acknowledgments

This sixth edition of *Infants and Toddlers: Curriculum and Teaching* would not have been possible without the influence, loyalty, and positive influence of the following very exceptional people.

To my parents and grandparents, thanks for intuitively knowing all about the three *As* when I was growing up. Special thanks goes to Danny and Randy for providing support, inspiration, and time to work throughout this project.

T. J. S.

A heartfelt thanks to Gerry Linton, Judean Frank, April Intrabartola, and Jennifer, beloved friends and exceptional colleagues. You are all indeed special. And to my children, Marcus and Milinda, who have grown up to be unique and caring adults whose involvement with infants, young children, and teens continues to pass along the true essences of the three *As*—Attention, Approval, and Attunement—to the future generations in their daily roles as caregivers and teachers.

L. W.

To Erin O'Conner, Chris Shortt, Philip Mandl, and the rest of the staff at Thomson Delmar Learning for continued support and guidance.

To the following reviewers of the *sixth* and previous editions, we thank you for your candid feedback and support:

Mary Cordell
Navarro College, Corsicana, TX

JoAnne D. Greata
Nova Southeastern University,
Fort Lauderdale, FL
Germanna Community College,
Locust Grove, VA

Berta Harris
San Diego City College, San Diego, CA

Janet Imel
Ivy Tech State College, Fort Wayne, IN

Tracy Keys
Kutztown University, Kutztown, PA

Tisha Bennett Sanders
Peabody College, Vanderbilt University,
Nashville, TN

About the Authors

TERRI JO SWIM, Ph.D., is an Assistant Professor and Program Director of Early Childhood Education at Indiana University—Purdue University in Fort Wayne, Indiana. She has been in the field of early childhood education for over 15 years. She has worked in private child care centers, university-based laboratory infant/toddler and preschool programs, and summer camps with children from birth to 13 years of age. Terri is the coauthor of *Creative Resources for Infants and Toddlers* (2nd ed.) with Dr. Judy Herr. Current research interests include infant-toddler and preschool curriculum, Reggio Emilia, documentation, and teacher education.

LINDA DOUVILLE-WATSON, M.P.S., R.N., is a Master's level nurse with 30 years of medical and child development and care experience. She is a trained CDA Representative. She has an appropriate practical approach, as well as respect for the child as an individual. She is past president of Workplace Childcare, Inc. and is responsible for designing and implementing award-winning turnkey corporate child care centers and managing staff development in New York and Maryland. She previously was an adjunct professor of psychology at Nassau Community College and Director of Early Childhood Intervention at the Warren Trauma Institute in New York.

Infant and Toddler Development and Professional Educator Preparation

Since publication of the previous edition, the information explosion in child development and caregiving has continued. As a result, early childhood educators need to learn more theories, principles, and skills to keep pace with the demands of their profession.

The new standards require that teachers learn to take good care of both themselves and the children, and to be aware of the needs of the child, the care setting, the family, the community, and society as a whole. This section provides the history and current trends in care, theories and principles of child development, and a structure and model of caregiving that helps prepare the caregiver for the challenging and rewarding profession of early childhood education.

This edition includes a new emphasis on science and new discoveries by researchers (for example, on brain development and attachment), as well as the influences these findings have on caregiver behavior when working with very young children. By closely observing and recording the behaviors of children, the child care specialist will create a powerful framework to use in caring for and educating infants and toddlers.

When you finish this section, you will have the knowledge and principles necessary to effectively care for and enhance the development of each child through your direct interactions. The following sections build on this base of knowledge to give you all the specific skills, techniques, strategies, and activities needed to confidently function as a professional.

CHAPTER 1

Looking Back to Move Forward

Foundations for Quality Infant and Toddler Care and Development

■ OBJECTIVES

After reading this chapter, you should be able to:

- Outline the major historical and current trends in early care and education.
- Compare historical and contemporary theories of child development.
- Justify how Bronfenbrenner's ecological systems theory can be used to explain current trends in early care and education.

■ CHAPTER OUTLINE

INTRODUCTION

What do people who work with young children need to know and what do they need to be able to do? Early childhood educators* have long debated these questions. For almost 100 years, people from all areas of the field and all corners of the world have gathered together to come to a consensus in answering these two key questions. Current research has helped early childhood specialists to clearly define a core body of knowledge, as well as standards for quality in both teacher preparation and in programming for young children. Scholarly research has validated what early childhood professionals have always known intuitively: the quality of young children's experience in early care and education settings is directly related to the knowledge, skills, and dispositions of the adults caring for them. Scientific evidence through the latest brain research clearly brings to light the importance of the "disposition" part of the equation in creating quality care and education for all young children, but most importantly in the care of infants and toddlers. This validation of our work allows us to more clearly assume an advocacy or leadership role in sharing this information with others.

For the past 75 years, the National Association for the Education of Young Children (NAEYC) has worked to develop standards for the educational preparation of early care and education teachers (Hyson, 2003) as well as the children's programs (accreditation). Many other professional organizations, such as NFCCA (National Family Child Care Association), NACCRRA (National Association of Child Care Resource and Referral Agencies), and Council for Professional Recognition, have articulated professional values and desired outcomes for both teachers and children. These standards provide the definition of quality and support for both young people and programs as they work to improve the quality of care and education for young children.

Recent brain research has provided evidence of the connection between early care and education and a baby's ability to develop the capacity to incorporate all of the skills that any human being has ever developed. The philosophical grounding of this text is supported by the findings that "warm, responsive care is not only comforting for an infant; it is critical to healthy development" (Shore, 2003).

A common theme in both the results of the brain research and in the standards mentioned previously is the importance of building strong, respectful, reciprocal relationships with infants, toddlers, and their families. Family members have much to tell us about their child(ren) in our care. Educators must come to understand quickly that the needs of the infants and toddlers are best met when partnerships are formed to support the clear, open exchange of ideas. Viewing infants, toddlers, and family members as competent, capable, and caring assists in promoting optimal development and learning for everyone involved. Today's theories and philosophies have evolved over time and have been influenced by both ancient and modern society and

---

*In this book, the terms *early childhood educator, teacher, caregiver,* and *primary caregiver* will be used interchangeably to describe adults who care for and educate infants and toddlers. Other terms, such as early childhood specialist, educarer, practitioner, staff, child care teacher, Head Teacher, Assistant Teacher, facilitator, or family child care provider, might also be familiar. The use of these four terms is not intended to narrow the focus of professionals discussed in this text or to minimize a particular title, rather the purpose is to provide some consistency in language.

thought. They are the direct result of the early childhood professionals and scientists of today building upon the theories of the past in order to better understand where we are today by understanding where we started from.

HISTORICAL INFLUENCES ON DEVELOPMENT AND CARE

Past Theories and Views

Before the Reformation in sixteenth-century Europe, little importance was placed on children or child care. Children were considered little adults cared for by the females in the family. With the Reformation and the Puritan belief in **original sin** came harsh, restrictive child-rearing practices and the idea that the depraved child needed to be tamed (Shahar, 1990).

The seventeenth-century Enlightenment brought new theories of human dignity and respect. Young children were viewed much more humanely. For example, John Locke, a British philosopher, advanced the theory that a child is a **tabula rasa**, or blank slate. According to his theory, children were not basically evil but were completely molded and formed by their early experiences with the adults around them (Locke, 1690/1892).

An important philosopher of the eighteenth century, Jean-Jacques Rousseau, viewed young children as **noble savages** who are naturally born with a sense of right and wrong and an innate ability for orderly, healthy growth (1762/1955). His theory, the first child-centered approach, advanced two important concepts still accepted today: the idea of **stages** of child development and the concept of **maturation**, which means a naturally unfolding course of growth and development.

During the late 1800s Charles Darwin's theories of **natural selection** and **survival of the fittest** strongly influenced ideas on child development and care (1859/1936). Darwin's research on many animal species led him to hypothesize that all animals were descendants of a few common ancestors. Darwin's careful observations of child behaviors resulted in the birth of the science of child study.

At the turn of the twentieth century, G. Stanley Hall was inspired by Darwin. Hall worked with one of Darwin's students, Arnold Gesell, to advance the **evolutionary theory** that child development is genetically determined and happens automatically. Hall and Gesell are considered founders of the child study movement because of their **normative approach** of observing large numbers of children to establish average or normal expectations (Berk, 1997). At the same time, in France, Alfred Binet was establishing the first operational definition of intelligence by using the normative approach to standardize his intelligence test, which is sometimes still used with young children (Siegler, 1992).

It was not until Sigmund Freud postulated his **psychoanalytic theory** of personality development in the early 1900s that child development and care became a legitimate discipline (1938/1973). For the first time, Freud explained that infants and toddlers are unique individuals, whose earliest experiences and relationships form the foundation for self-concept, self-esteem, and personality, and are the basis for why we experience life as adults the way that we do.

A proponent of Freud, Erik Erikson, expanded Freud's concepts into what became known as the **psychosocial theory** of child development. Erikson's theory, which is still used in child care today, predicted several stages of development, including the development of trust, autonomy, identity, and intimacy. How these stages are dealt with by child development specialists determines individual capacity to contribute to society and experience a happy, successful life (1950). Erikson's stages are presented in Chapter 2.

While Freud and his disciples greatly influenced the fields of child development and care, a parallel approach was being studied, called **behaviorism**. John Watson, who is considered the father of behaviorism, was influenced by a Russian physiologist named Ivan Pavlov and his scientific observations of animal **responses** to various environmental **stimuli** (Horowitz, 1992). In a historic experiment, Watson taught an 11-month-old named Albert to fear a neutral stimulus (a soft white rat) by presenting the rat several times accompanied by loud noises. Watson and his followers used experiments in **classical conditioning** to promote the idea that the environment is the primary factor determining the growth and development of children.

B. F. Skinner and coauthor Belmont expanded Watson's theories of classical conditioning to include his **operant conditioning theory** (1993). Skinner clearly demonstrated that child behaviors can be increased or decreased by applying **positive reinforcers** (rewards), such as food and praise, and **negative reinforcers** (punishment), such as criticism and withdrawal of attention.

During the 1950s, **social learning theories** became popular. Proponents of these theories, led by Albert Bandura, accepted the principles of behaviorism and enlarged on conditioning to include social influences such as **modeling**, **imitation**, and **observational learning** to explain how children develop (Grusec, 1992).

The theorist who has influenced the modern fields of child development and care more than any other is Jean Piaget. Piaget's **cognitive developmental theory** predicts that children construct knowledge and awareness through manipulation and exploration of the environment, and that cognitive development occurs through observable stages (Beilin, 1992). Piaget's stages of cognitive development have stimulated more research on children than any other theory, and his influences have helped child development specialists view young children as active participants in their own growth and development. Piaget's contributions are clear and have many practical applications for teachers.

Past Needs and Trends

Whereas cultural and social expectations for child care roughly follow historical theories and views of child development, specific social and cultural influences, including religion, governmental policy, war, and economic demands, have also affected the settings and approaches to child development and care.

Throughout history, the care and development of infants and toddlers has been the responsibility of the primary family unit and extended family, which often included members of the local community as well as blood relatives. Even in cultures where governmental or religious needs required older children to be taken away from the family for training or education, infants and toddlers remained with the women and girls of the home and community.

Before the Reformation, child care was primarily the responsibility of the women in the family unit. However, since social groups were small (for example, tribe, village, hamlet), children were often cared for by all the women of the community, and it was common practice for one family to take over care of another family's children whose parents had died.

With increases in world population and the emphasis on religious education brought about by the Reformation, the Church established orphanages and schools so that young children were cared for in institutional settings outside the family for the first time. In cultures in which the population remained small or in which religious training was not a major influence, the family remained responsible for early child development and care.

Until the beginning of the twentieth century, the only exceptions to family care were extreme situations such as war, famine, or epidemics, at which times infants and toddlers had to be cared for in groups because a large number of adults had died.

The industrialization of the major world cultures created a change in the social belief that only mothers should provide total care for young children. In the early twentieth century in the United States, fewer middle- and upper-middle-class mothers of infants and toddlers were in the workforce than are today. Mothers who worked in jobs to which they could not take their babies counted on older children, female relatives, or neighbors to care for their young. Professional child care settings as we know them today did not exist.

One factor that affected the number of working mothers was the prevalence of stereotyped male and female roles. The social norm was that the husband provided for the family's financial needs and the wife assumed all domestic responsibilities, including cooking, sewing, housework, and child care. Women who worked outside the home were often considered "out of place."

Another influence on the number of mothers with infants and toddlers who worked outside the home was the prevailing belief that only the mother could provide proper care for young children. A sibling or extended family member was thought to be an acceptable substitute for the mother, but the belief generally was that a nonrelative could not meet the needs of infants or toddlers for very long. The mother-child attachment was thought to be crucial, and it would be weakened if the infant were cared for primarily by someone else. The idea was that only the mother bonded well enough with her infant or toddler to meet the child's emotional needs. The two world wars brought more mothers into the workplace and changed the stereotype that only mothers could adequately care for young children.

Early research on child care was partly responsible for the social belief that only mothers could adequately care for young children. Since institutionalized infants and toddlers provided the most easily accessible population for child study, early research tended to concentrate on the effects of infant care by people other than the mother in hospitals and long-term care facilities. The results of this type of research generally found that the mother-child attachment was weakened in the situations studied (Bowlby, 1951; Goldfarb, 1943; Spitz, 1945).

A grandparent can share in caring for an infant.

CURRENT PERSPECTIVES ON DEVELOPMENT AND CARE

Current Theories and Views

New theories, research, and effective approaches to enhance the growth and development of young children are still being discovered. Among these exciting developments are discoveries in brain research and advancements in attachment, ecological systems, and sociocultural theories.

Innovations in noninvasive neuroscience technologies have begun to have a significant impact on our understanding of brain development (Acredolo & Goodwyn, 2000). It was once believed that nature, or the basic genetic makeup of a child, played a dominant role in determining both short- and long-term cognitive developmental outcomes. But now that new technologies allow for close examination of nurture, or environmental impacts, on the same outcomes, scientists have found that harmful, stressful, or neglectful behaviors early in life can affect the development of the brain, potentially leading to lifelong difficulties (Gunnar & Cheatham, 2003; Legendre, 2003; Morgan et al., 2002; cf. Johnson, 2003). The quality and consistency of early care will affect how a child develops, learns, and copes with and handles life. The more quality interactions you have with the children in your care, the more opportunities for positive development occur.

Attachment theory also examines how early care, especially relationships between adults and children, impacts later development. Bowlby (1969/2000), after observing children between the ages of one and four years in post–World War II hospitals and institutions who had been separated from their families concluded that "the infant and young child should experience a warm and continuous relationship with his mother (or permanent mother substitute) in which both find satisfaction and enjoyment" in order to grow up mentally healthy (p. 13). Relying heavily on **ethological** concepts, he proposed that a baby's attachment behaviors (e.g., smiling, crying, clinging) are innate and that they mature at various times during the first two years of life (Bowlby, 1958). The ethological purpose of these behaviors is to keep the infant close to the mother, who keeps the child out of harm's way (Honig, 2002). However, the quality of attachment is not just determined by the infant's behavior. The caregiver's responses to the attachment behaviors serve to create a foundation for their relationship to develop (see, for example, Oppenheim & Koren-Karie, 2002). Attachment history has been associated with emotional, social, and learning outcomes later in life (see Honig, 2002, and Thompson, 2000, for reviews) and has been very influential on classroom practices.

A recent theory of child development is the **ecological systems theory** developed by Urie Bronfenbrenner, an American psychologist. Bronfenbrenner (1995) has expanded the view of influences on young children by hypothesizing four nested structures that affect development (see Figure 1–1). At the innermost level is the **microsystem**, which comprises patterns of interactions within the immediate surroundings of the child. This system includes families, early childhood educators, direct influences on the child, and the child's influence on the immediate environment. The **mesosystem** is the next level of influence and includes interactions among the various microsystems. For example, family and teacher interactions in the child care setting represent connections between home and school that impact the child's development. The **exosystem** includes influences with which the child is not directly involved that affect development and care, such as parent education, parent workplace, and the quality and availability of health and social services. The **macrosystem** consists of the values, laws, resources, and customs of the general culture in which a child is raised. This theory has wide applications in understanding and categorizing the factors that affect child care.

A final theory that is finding application as the world becomes a cross-cultural community is the **sociocultural theory**. A Russian psychologist, Lev Semenovich Vygotsky, hypothesized that culture, meaning the values, beliefs, and customs of a social group, is passed on to the next generation through social interactions between children and their elders (1986). Those social interactions must be at the appropriate level for learning to occur. Adults must observe and assess each child's individual levels of performance as well as her assisted levels of performance on a given task in order to judge what supports (also known as scaffolding) are necessary for promoting learning (Berk & Winsler, 1995; Bodrova & Leong, 1996; Wink & Putney, 2002). Cross-cultural research has supported this theory through findings that young children from various cultures develop unique skills and abilities that are not present in other cultures (Berk, 1997).

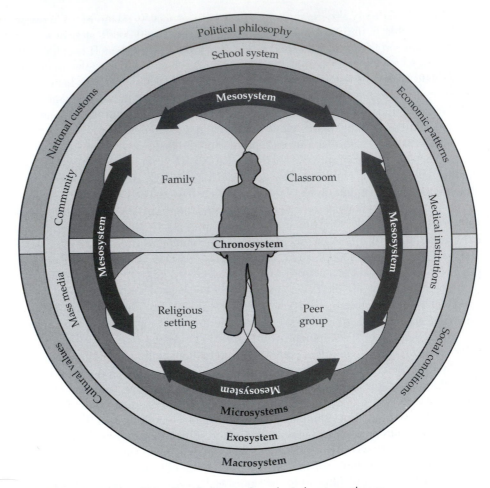

FIGURE 1–1 Model of Urie Bronfenbrenner's ecological systems theory.

It must be kept in mind that the United States is the world leader in the fields of child development and care, but we cannot assume that research findings on developmental skills and abilities from primarily Caucasian American children directly apply to other cultures outside, or subcultures within, the United States. Only through taking a world view of child care based on universal aspects of development will we be able to determine the skills, abilities, and practices that optimally enhance the growth and development of infants and toddlers all over the world.

Current Needs and Trends

Current child care trends considered in this section reflect the research being completed concerning brain development, attachment theory, and sociocultural theory. All of these trends are discussed within the framework of the ecological system of

Urie Bronfenbrenner (1995): microsystem, mesosystem, exosystem, and macrosystem. In this system, human relationships are described as bidirectional and reciprocal. *Relating* is the act of being with someone and sharing the same space and setting, expressing needs and accepting responsibility for interacting with each other.

The recommendation to respect children is also expressed by other authorities in child development such as Magda Gerber, who feels that one of the most important aspects of relating to infants is an adult's respect for the child as an individual. The educational leaders of the municipal infant, toddler, and preschool centers of Reggio Emilia have clearly communicated their beliefs about the rights of children, which include, among other things, the right to be held in high regard and treated respectfully. Similarly, previous editions of this text emphasize that the reader be mindful of positive intentions toward the child and engage in reflective, careful planning, resulting in good outcomes for both. Trends in the microsystem involve effects that adults and children have on each other. For example, an adult who consciously uses attention, approval, and attunement with children elicits a positive response from children. Any third party who is present may also be affected. How this person is affected is determined by whether or not the reciprocal relationship is positive or negative. If the people interacting are supportive, the quality of the relationship is enhanced. An example of how an early childhood educator can enhance an interaction as a third party is explained in detail later in the text.

The microsystem is the closest system to the child. It contains the child, the immediate nuclear family, and others directly relating to the child. There are more children in subsidized care in the United States, with many vastly different backgrounds, than ever before. By 2002, 11.6 million or 63% of the 18.5 million children under the age of five were in a regular child care arrangement (Johnson, 2005). These children have widespread cultural differences in customs, family structure, and parenting styles. Many come from culturally diverse homes with families who are learning to define their own traditions. For example, children experience living with one parent, two parents, grandparents and other extended family members. In addition, more and more children grow up experiencing poverty (see Table 1–1). Respectful, mindful teachers are necessary in all child care settings to promote interest, acceptance, and pride among children and families.

The mesosystem includes child care settings. In the past, it was thought that the immediate family (microsystem) had the greatest single impact on a child's life. However, with so many more people entering the workforce today, the need for child care is so great that this is no longer true. Many young children spend more waking hours with caregivers than they do with their primary families. While initially this was of great concern for many child development experts, they are no longer concerned as long as best practices are adopted by child care programs. Family grouping, continuity of care, primary caregiving, and creating partnerships with families are ways to minimize the effects on children of long hours away from family members.

Family grouping for infants and toddlers involves having a small number of children of different ages in the same classroom. Such living arrangements reproduce relationships that children naturally have in a home setting. For example, families often have siblings who are two or fewer years apart in age. Organizing the program so that

TABLE 1-1   FACTS AND FIGURES ON FAMILIES IN THE UNITED STATES WITH INFANTS AND TODDLERS

ALL INFANTS AND TODDLERS

There are about 11.6 million infants and toddlers in the United States. Every minute a baby is born to a teen mother.[a]

Infants and toddlers in this country are becoming increasingly diverse. In 2000, 15 percent were African American, 19 percent were Hispanic, and an additional 5 percent were nonwhite. The percentage of Hispanic young children has risen dramatically in recent years, up from 11 percent in 1987.

Increasing numbers of mothers caring for young children work either full time (31 percent) or part time (42 percent). Fifty-six percent of all mothers with children under age one work.

Almost three-quarters of the infants and toddlers of working mothers are being cared for by someone other than their parent; 40 percent are cared for in centers and family child care.

Infants and toddlers with working mothers spend an average of 35 hours a week in child care.

INFANTS AND TODDLERS IN POVERTY

Every 35 seconds a baby is born into poverty.[a] Forty percent of infants and toddlers are in families living below or near the federal poverty line (10 percent live in extreme poverty). Poverty, however, is related to race and ethnicity with African American and Hispanic infants and toddlers being three times as likely to live in poverty as young white children.

Most poor infants and toddlers live in families where at least one adult works. Nearly 60 percent of poor families rely exclusively on their earnings to support their families. When including those who receive public assistance in addition to their wages, the percentage of poor working families increases to 75 percent.

Fifty-nine percent of poor single mothers work either full or part-time.

Approximately two million low-income children—10 to 15 percent of the 15 million who are eligible for child care subsidies—are served monthly by Child Care and Development Funds (CCDF). Twenty-eight percent of these children are under three years old.

[a]Based on calculations per school day (180 days of seven hours each).

Sources: Infant and Toddler Project (retrieved December 19, 2005, from http://www.nccp.org/it_context.html#poverty) and Children's Defense Fund (2004) *State of America's Children,* retrieved December 19, 2005, from http://childrensdefense.org.

the six children who share the room vary in age from a very young infant (e.g., six weeks) to three years of age provides opportunities for interactions that are similar to those that may be found more naturally.

Attachment theory suggests that infants, toddlers, and adults need time to create positive emotional bonds with one another. Having the same teachers work with the same children for a three-year period is one way to promote strong attachments (Bernhardt, 2000; Essa, Favre, Thweatt, & Waugh, 1999; Honig, 2002; Miller, 1999). This type of arrangement is often referred to as *continuity of care.* As this term suggests, emphasis is placed on maintaining relationships for long periods of time. With older children, this is often referred to as *looping.* Continuity of care can appear in several different forms in practice. For example, a teacher and her group of children could remain in one classroom for the infant and toddler years, changing furniture, instructional tools, and supplies as needed to respond to the developing capabilities of the children. In contrast, a teacher and her group of children could move each year into a new classroom which already is equipped with age-appropriate furniture, supplies, and materials.

Another way to help adults bond with infants is to divide the work using a *primary caregiving system* (Kovach & De Ros, 1998). In this method, one teacher in the room is primarily responsible for half of the children and the other teacher is primarily responsible for the rest. While a teacher would never ignore the expressed needs of any infant or toddler, she is able to invest time and energy into coming to understand a smaller group of children and their families. Frequently, the primary caregiver is the person responsible for providing assistance during routine care times such as diapering, feeding, or napping.

Keep in mind that caregiving factors at the mesosystem level exert bidirectional influences. Of particular importance at this level is the relationship that teachers have with families. The transition between home and school should be smooth and continuous. The only pathway for achieving that is through *partnering* with families. Families are experts on their children. Recognizing, supporting, and utilizing this can significantly improve your effectiveness as a caregiver and educator. On the other hand, you are an expert on this time period—infancy and toddlerhood—given your vast experiences with numerous children of this age. Help each person bring his or her strengths to the relationship. Valuing each family's childrearing practices while helping them to understand child development is not only respectful but also part of your ethical responsibility (National Association for the Education of Young Children, 2005).

Another trend in the mesosystem of child care bears mentioning. Due to the many recent, highly publicized, violent acts by school-age children against peers, there has been renewed interest in violence among children throughout the United States. This interest can be a positive trend because social pressure to understand and stop the causes of violence among young children can result in better parenting and child care practices. Many movements against violence are aimed at the care of preschool-age children. For example, National Association for the Education of Young Children (NAEYC) has established ACT (Adults and Children Together) Against Violence, "a campaign in conjunction with the American Psychological Association and the Ad Council to teach young children positive, nonviolent ways to respond to conflict, anger, and frustration" (NAEYC, 2001). Teaching young children to become more emotionally intelligent instead of merely cognitively intelligent is one of the most important trends in child development and care today; a trend that will become even more important as people live closer together.

All of these factors at the mesosystem level have been shown to result in positive outcomes for children, families, teachers, and programs. Used in combination, the effects can be particularly strong. Our purpose in highlighting the relationships between the nested systems is to help you understand that the purpose of child care is not to replace familial influences on very young children but rather to enhance them.

The exosystem refers to social settings that do not contain the child but still directly affect the child's development, such as community health services and other public agencies. This structure manifests itself in the work of grassroots groups and professional organizations who lobby and advocate for quality child care services.

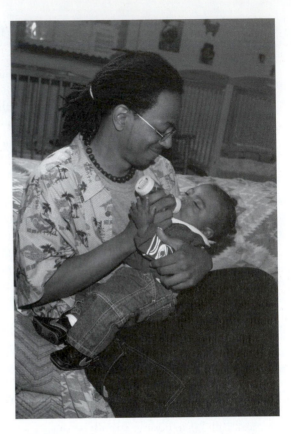

Infants, toddlers, and adults need time to create positive emotional bonds with one another.

Many local, regional, and national organizations stress child care advocacy that sets higher standards of care, along with education that touches each child in the community. The National Association for the Education of Young Children, for example, has created standards defining high quality early educational programs. The accreditation process, recently revised, is a way for programs to demonstrate they are providing exceptional care and educational experiences for young children. Hence, this organization, while a part of the exosystem, can directly impact the work of teachers in early education programs. Moreover, this association works with other agencies to advocate for best practices. To illustrate, they worked with the International Reading Association to create a position statement on learning to read and write, and they have an ongoing working relationship with the National Council for Accreditation of Teacher Education (NCATE) to create and monitor teacher preparation programs to ensure they achieve high standards for educating future professionals.

Being an advocate yourself might seem like an overwhelming task. However, each and every time you interact with family members, colleagues, and community members, you are a teacher-leader. Your dedication to engaging in and sharing professional knowledge and practices makes you an advocate for young children, families, and the early childhood profession.

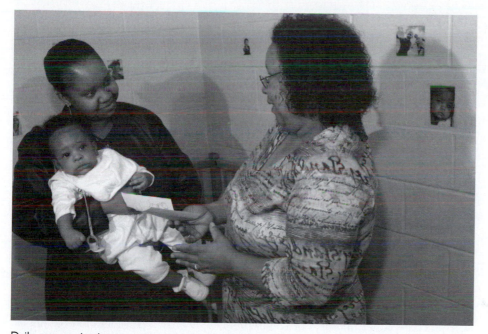

Daily communication promotes reciprocal relationships and professional advocacy.

Other social policies also are affected by the availability, affordability, and quality of care for very young children. The following current issues in development and care are discussed in depth in later chapters:

- child abuse and neglect
- homelessness
- divorce and its impact on the family
- children with special needs
- the impact of AIDS on the community
- adverse environmental factors
- education of early childhood educators

Next we turn to trends within the macrosystem, the most general level of Bronfenbrenner's ecological systems theory. The child is ultimately affected by decisions made at this level because the macrosystem consists of the laws, customs, and general policies of the social system (government). This is where the availability of resources (money in particular) is determined. The macrosystem structure of the United States went through a remarkable change in the late 1990s. This can be understood best by explaining the changes in welfare reform legislation.

In the late 1980s and early 1990s child care needs increased significantly in the United States. In response to this need, providers expanded existing centers and opened new ones. This expansion increased the need for new curricula, materials, teachers, and directors. Training programs centered their efforts on the quality of services offered to families and children and continued to raise the standard of child care with federal and state investments. Laws were later passed to emphasize moving people from welfare into the workforce.

In 2002, the federal budget for Early Head Start was $653.7 million for 708 programs. The money is used to provide a variety of services to low income families with children under the age of three and to poor pregnant women.

Vermont has a "Success by Six" Program, and North Carolina has instituted a flexible county program called "Smart Start." In the latter program, teachers, parents, doctors, nurses, child care providers, ministers, and businesspeople form partnerships to help young children and their families. Several states are trying to help educate parents about parenting; home visits by social workers or nurses are among the most successful.

Because of the emphasis on work, welfare reform placed significant stress on the existing system of early childhood services and caused broad ramifications for the quality, accessibility, and affordability of services for poor and working families. This raised concern about methods of monitoring quality in child care; the ability to compensate teachers and directors; and the ability of programs to support and respond to the family's changing roles. Richard Clifford, president of the NAEYC, asked in 1996, "Will the new pressures brought on by Welfare Reform continue to keep us from addressing our basic concerns about the quality of services offered to the youngest citizens of our country? . . . Will reform force a reduction in the standards of care provided all children to accommodate larger numbers of children?" The new law's consideration of "unpaid child care" positions as a viable alternative to employment had two repercussions: first, nonparents and substitutes, such as grandparents, family members, neighbors, and early childhood educators, were recognized as primary caregivers; and second, there was no mandate that everyone caring for children at any level be educated.

As a result, most professionals who had been working diligently to improve the minimal educational requirements for child care teachers demanded that their local governments raise training and care standards. This became necessary because many of the federally supported departments that funded and guaranteed these standards were no longer in existence. Good, affordable child care is not a luxury or fringe benefit for working families but essential brain food for the next generation.

VALUING CULTURAL DIVERSITY

As mentioned previously, child care settings are increasingly becoming more and more diverse. We cannot ignore these differences, but rather need to embrace and value them. It is important for the early childhood educator to accept the challenge to develop a cross-cultural curriculum that involves both parents and children, because many young families are just exploring their own cultural backgrounds.

Cross-cultural curriculum development fits into Vygotsky's theory of the dissemination of culture. He viewed "cognitive development as a socially mediated process . . . as dependent on the support that adults and more mature peers provide as children try new tasks" (Berk, 1997). A culturally rich curriculum encourages the recognition of cultural differences and helps young families connect with the traditions of their own heritage and culture.

Each person employed in early childhood education draws upon his or her own cultural model for behavior that is both relevant and meaningful within his or her particular social-cultural group. The knowledge and understanding that caregivers use with families is drawn primarily from two sources: their educational knowledge base and their personal experiences as family members and educators. Therefore, we need to recognize and continually re-examine the way we put our knowledge into practice. We need to develop *scripts* that allow us to learn more about the families' cultural beliefs and values regarding the various aspects of child rearing. In other words, we must create a method or sequence of events for getting to know each family. That way we can understand the family's actions, attitudes, and behavior, as well as their dreams and hopes for their child.

Consideration of cultural models can help us bring coherence to the various pieces of information that we are gathering about families and organize our interpretation of that information. Organizing and ongoing reflection upon what parents tell us about their strategies can help us discover their cultural model for caregiving, and then compare it with the cultural models that guide our own practice (Finn, 2003).

We caregivers recognize the richness and opportunity available to us in our work with families of diverse ethnic, racial, and cultural groups. We can learn the different ways that families provide care for their children when they are all striving toward similar goals—happy and healthy children who can function successfully within the family culture. We can use that knowledge to construct a cultural model of culturally responsive practice, designed to support families in their caregiving and assist them in meeting their goals for their children (Finn, 2003).

Bronfenbrenner's ecological systems theory assumes the interconnectedness of each person to others and examines the ways in which one system affects another.

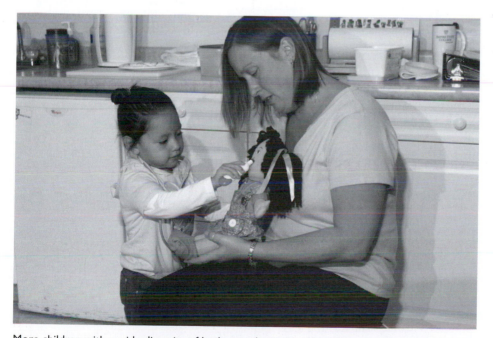

More children with a wide diversity of backgrounds are in early childhood education programs.

It recognizes the importance of respecting each individual's uniqueness and considers carefully the decisions made at every level that affect us all.

Transactional theories, such as Bronfenbrenner's, view care from the perspective of how the child interacts with and affects the environment (Sameroff, Seifer, Baldwin, & Baldwin, 1993). These theories help us understand that children are not passive recipients of whatever happens in their environment, but are very involved in influencing their environment and aiding their own development. It is important for the primary caregiver to understand that even newborns have a part in their growth and development. Infants' wants, needs, and desires must be respected.

To summarize, current trends in child care involve the bidirectional and reciprocal relationship between the child and his or her environment. Early childhood education programs now serve a wide diversity of backgrounds. As a result, there is an increased need for teacher education; parent education, including proper selection of care settings; innovative and child-centered practices such as continuity of care; effective use of resources; social and political advocacy for high-quality, affordable, and accessible care; and use of culturally diverse materials in child care curricula.

Take it as your individual responsibility to be aware of the power of your actions and their immediate and future impact on children. When you see that the early childhood educator also directly influences the family, community, and culture, you can truly understand the old African saying, "It takes a village to raise a child." This much quoted saying is a simple way to understand that Bronfenbrenner's term *bidirectional* describes the relationships that influence a child, occurring between mother and child, child and father, child and teacher, and that the influences go both ways.

■ KEY TERMS

attachment theory	infants	original sin
behaviorism	macrosystem	positive reinforcers
caregiver	maturation	primary caregiver
classical conditioning	mesosystem	psychoanalytic theory
cognitive developmental theory	microsystem	psychosocial theory
continuity of care	modeling	responses
curricula	natural selection	social learning theories
early childhood educator	nature	sociocultural theory
ecological systems theory	negative reinforcers	stages
ethological	noble savages	stimuli
evolutionary theory	normative approach	survival of the fittest
exosystem	nurture	tabula rasa
family grouping	observational learning	teacher
imitation	operant conditioning theory	toddlers

CASE STUDY

Trisha

Trisha works at the Little Folks Child Care Center as an assistant teacher while she attends classes at a local community college to earn her associate degree in early childhood education. She was surprised to learn that her center was using family grouping with continuity of care. Although she always knew that she had the same children from the time they enrolled until they were around three years of age, she did not know it was associated with a particular term or of such great educational value. Currently she assists the head teacher with caring for eight children who range in age from 8 weeks to 17 months. Like those in the rest of the program, this group of children is culturally diverse. Trisha has worked with parents, staff, and the children on cross-cultural issues; she always attempts to learn more about each culture represented in her room. As part of a course, she organized a tool for gathering information about child-rearing practices and used the results to individualize routine care times.

As she has learned new ideas, such as the primary caregiving system, accreditation standards, and Bronfenbrenner's ecological systems theory, she has assumed a more active role in the microsystem. She has repeatedly discussed with her director and lead teacher the need to reduce the number of infants and toddlers per classroom to six and to adopt a primary caregiving system. While they are enthusiastic about learning more about the primary caregiving system, they have not yet seriously considered cutting the class size by two children per room, due to financial concerns.

1. Provide two examples of how Trisha has, in her words, "assumed a more active role in the microsystem."

2. In what other systems does Trisha work? Provide examples for each system you identify.

3. What might be the added benefits of the center adopting a primary caregiving system when it is not possible for them to reduce the number of children in each room from eight to six?

■ QUESTIONS AND EXPERIENCES FOR REFLECTION

1. Which perspective from the section "Current Perspectives on Development and Care" do you think would most influence your behavior as a professional educator? Why?

2. Think about two or three experiences you had as a student in a high school or college setting. Explain those experiences by using as many of the four systems of Bronfenbrenner's ecological theory as possible. Consider bidirectional influences in your analysis as well.

3. Talk with a teacher who is currently working with infants and/or toddlers. What does she see as the most important issue she faces in her job? How does she address that issue? What additional support or information could she use to be more effective in addressing that issue?

4. What experiences did you have growing up with people who were different from yourself? Consider all of the ways in which people differ including, but not limited to, race or ethnicity, religion, ability, or sexual orientation. How did you react to those differences?

■ CHAPTER REVIEW

1. How have theories of child development influenced the care of young children both in the past and currently?

2. Select one theory from the past and one that currently influences the field. Compare and contrast them; in other words, explain how they are alike and how they are different.

3. Explain some of the current trends in early care and development.

4. How does the diversity of families in today's society influence early education programs and teachers?

■ REFERENCES

Acredolo, L. P., & Goodwyn, S. (2000). *Baby minds: Brain-building games your baby will love.* New York: Bantam Books.

Beilin, H. (1992). Piaget's enduring contribution to developmental psychology. *Developmental Psychology, 28,* 191–204.

Berk, L. E. (1997). *Child development* (4th ed.). Boston: Allyn and Bacon.

Berk, L. E., & Winsler, A. (1995). *NAEYC Research into Practice Series: Vol. 7. Scaffolding children's learning: Vygotsky and early childhood education.* Washington, DC: National Association for the Education of Young Children.

Bernhardt, J. L. (2000). A primary caregiving system for infants and toddlers: Best for everyone involved. *Young Children, 55*(2), 74–80.

Bodrova, E., & Leong, D. J. (1996). *Tools of the mind: The Vygotskian approach to early childhood education.* Upper Saddle River, NJ: Prentice Hall.

Bowlby, J. (1951). *Maternal care and mental health.* Geneva: World Health Organization.

Bowlby, J. (1958). The nature of the child's tie to its mother. *International Journal of Psychoanalysis, 39,* 350–373.

Bowlby, J. (2000). *Attachment and loss: Vol. 1. Attachment.* New York: Basic Books. (Original work published 1969).

Bronfenbrenner, U. (1995). The bioecological model from a life course perspective: Reflections of a participant observer. In P. Moen, G. H. Elder, Jr., & K. Luscher (Eds.), *Examining lives in context* (pp. 599–618). Washington, DC: American Psychological Association.

Clifford, R. M. (1996). Partnerships with children. *Young Children, 52*(1), 2.

Darwin, C. (1936). *On the origin of species by means of natural selection.* New York: Modern Library. (Original work published 1859)

Erikson, E. H. (1950). *Childhood and society.* New York: Norton.

Essa, E. L., Favre, K., Thweatt, G., & Waugh, S. (1999). Continuity of care for infants and toddlers. *Early Child Development and Care, 148,* 11–19.

Finn, C. D. (2003). *Cultural Models for Early Caregiving.* Washington, DC: Zero to Three.

Freud, S. (1973). *An outline of psychoanalysis.* London: Hogarth Press. (Original work published 1938)

Gnezda, M. T. (1996). Welfare reform: Personal responsibilities and opportunities for early childhood advocates. *Young Children, 52*(1), 55–58.

Goldfarb, W. (1943). The effects of early institutional care on adolescent personality. *Journal of Experimental Education, 12,* 106–129.

Grusec, J. E. (1992). Social learning theory and developmental psychology: The legacies of Robert Sears and Albert Bandura. *Developmental Psychology, 28,* 776–786.

Gunnar, M. G., & Cheatham, C. L. (2003). Brain and behavior interface: Stress and the developing brain. *Infant Mental Health Journal, 24*(3), 195–211.

Honig, A. S. (2002). *Secure relationships: Nurturing infant/toddler attachment in early care settings.* Washington, DC: National Association for the Education of Young Children.

Horowitz, F. D. (1992). John B. Watson's legacy: Learning and environment. *Developmental Psychology, 28,* 360–367.

Hyson, M. (Ed.). (2003). *Preparing early childhood professionals: NAEYC's standards for programs.* Washington, DC: National Association for the Education of Young Children.

Johnson, J. O. (2005, October). Who's minding the kids? Child care arrangements: Winter 2002. *Current Population Reports, P70–101.* Washington, DC: U.S. Census Bureau.

Johnson, M. H. (2003). Neuroscience perspectives: Development of human brain functions. *Biological Psychiatry, 54,* 1312–1316.

Kovach, B. A., & De Ros, D. A. (1998). Respectful, individual, and responsive caregiving for infants: The key to successful care in group settings. *Young Children, 53*(3), 61–64.

Legendre, A. (2003). Environmental features influencing toddlers' bioemotional reactions in day care centers. *Environment and Behavior, 35,* 523–549.

Locke, J. (1892). Some thoughts concerning education. In R. J. Quick, (Ed.), *Locke on education* (pp. 1–236). Cambridge, London: Cambridge University Press. (Original work published 1690)

Miller, K. (1999, September). Caring for the little ones: Continuity of care. *Child Care Information Exchange,* 94–97.

Morgan, B., Finan, A., Yarnold, R., Petersen, S., Rickett, A., & Wailoo, M. (2002). Assessment of infant physiology and neuronal development using magnetic resonance imaging. *Child: Care, Health & Development, 28,* Suppl. 1, 7–10.

National Association for the Education of Young Children. (2001). ACT (Adults and Children Together) Against Violence. *Young Children, 5,* 55.

National Association for the Education of Young Children. (2005, April). Position Statement. Code of ethical conduct and statement of commitment. Retrieved October 31, 2006, from http://www.naeyc.org/about/positions/pdf/PSETH05.PDF

Oppenheim, D., & Koren-Karie, N. (2002). Mothers' insightfulness regarding their children's internal worlds: The capacity underlying secure child-mother relationships. *Infant Mental Health Journal, 23,* 593–605.

Rousseau, J. J. (1955). *Emile.* New York: Dutton. (Original work published 1762)

Sameroff, A. J., Seifer, R., Baldwin, A., & Baldwin, C. (1993). Stability of intelligence from preschool to adolescence: The influence of social and family risk factors. *Child Development, 64,* 80–97.

Shahar, S. (1990). *Childhood in the Middle Ages* (C. Galai, Trans.). London: Routledge.

Shore, R. (2003). *Rethinking the brain: New insights into early development* (2nd ed.). New York: Families and Work Institute.

Siegler, R. S. (1992). The other Alfred Binet. *Developmental Psychology, 28,* 179–190.

Skinner, E. A., & Belmont, M. J. (1993). Motivation in the classroom: Reciprocal effects of teacher behavior and student engagement across the school year. *Journal of Educational Psychology, 85,* 571–581.

Spitz, T. (1945). Hospitalism: An inquiry into the genesis of psychiatric conditions in early childhood. *Psychoanalytic Study of the Child, 1,* 53–74.

Thompson, R. (2000). The legacy of early attachment. *Child Development, 71,* 145–152.

Vygotsky, L. S. (1986). *Thought and language* (A. Kozulin, Trans.). Cambridge, MA: MIT Press. (Original work published 1934)

Wink, J., & Putney, L. (2002). *A vision of Vygotsky.* Boston: Allyn & Bacon.

■ ADDITIONAL RESOURCES

Advisory Committee on Head Start Quality and Expansion. (1993). *Creating a 21st Century Head Start. Final report.* Washington, DC: Head Start Bureau, Administration on Children, Youth, and Families.

Douville-Watson, L. (2003). *Childcare's Coming of Age*. New York: Instructional Press.

Edwards, C. P., & Raikes, H. (2002). Extending the dance: Relationship-based approaches to infant/toddler care and education. *Young Children, 57*(4), 10–17.

Eliot, L. (2000). *What is going on in there? How the brain and mind develop in the first five years of life.* New York: Bantam Books.

Gallagher, K. C. (2005). Brain research and early childhood development: A primer for developmentally appropriate practice. *Young Children, 60*(4), 12–18, 20.

Gerber, M. (1989). *Educaring: Resources for infant educarers.* Los Angeles: Resources for Infant Educarers.

Grolnich, W. S., & Slowiacvek, M. L. (1994). Parents' involvement in children's schooling: A multi-dimensional conceptualization and motivational model. *Child Development, 65,* 237–252.

Lally, J. R. (Ed.). (1992). *Language development and communication: A guide.* San Francisco: Far West Lab.

Nash, J. (1997, February 3). Fertile minds [Special report]. *Time, 149*(5), 48–56.

■ HELPFUL WEB SITES

Association for Childhood Education International. Supports child-centered whole curriculum education from infancy through early adolescence. **http://www.acei.org/**

Better Brains for Babies. A collaboration of state, local, public, and private organizations dedicated to promoting awareness and education about the importance of early brain development in infants and young children. **http://www.fcs.uga.edu/ext/bbb/index.php**

Center for Law and Social Policy. Site provides current data on teenage pregnancy and child poverty. Also has downloadable resources. **http://clasp.org**

Children's Defense Fund. Provides national- and state-level statistics concerning children and families, especially poverty rates, educational attainment, incidences of violence. **http://www.childrensdefense.org**

Clearinghouse on International Developments in Child, Youth and Family Policies. Compares child, youth, and family policies in countries worldwide. **http://www.childpolicyintl.org**

Diversity Training University International. Distance learning courses that teach students to become diversity trainers who are capable of cross-cultural and multicultural teaching, training, and consulting. **http://www.dtui.com**

Early Head Start National Resource Center @ Zero to Three. A plethora of resources including, for example, articles and professional development opportunities. **http://ehsnrc.org**

Families and Work Institute. A nonprofit center for research that provides data to inform decision making on the changing workforce, changing family, and changing community. **http://www.familiesandwork.org**

National Center for Children in Poverty. Columbia University's Mailman School of Public Health site for national and state statistics concerning families and children in poverty. **http://nccp.org**

National Mental Health Information Center. Information for teachers and parents to use when talking with children about disasters. Some resources are in Spanish. **http://www.mentalhealth.org/cmhs/EmergencyServices/after.asp**

For additional infant and toddler resources, visit our Web site at
http://www.earlychilded.delmar.com

2

A Developmental Perspective on Educating Infants and Toddlers

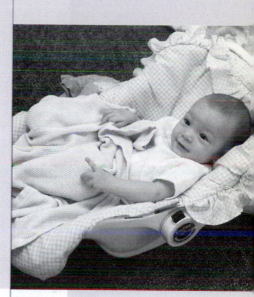

■ OBJECTIVES

After reading this chapter, you should be able to:

- Identify the four major developmental areas for assessment, and discuss how they differ from one another.
- Understand how to view the child after having done an assessment of developmental areas.
- Grasp the use of developmental profiles.
- Describe theoretical contributions for each developmental area.
- Understand the characteristics and care of children with special needs.

■ CHAPTER OUTLINE

- Taking a Developmental Perspective
- Four Major Developmental Areas
- Using a Developmental Profile
- Theoretical Contributions
  Physical Development
  Emotional Development
- Social Development
- Cognitive and Language Development
- Summary of Theoretical Contributions
- Children with Special Needs
- Case Study: Sasha

TAKING A DEVELOPMENTAL PERSPECTIVE

The structure of this book allows for the philosophy that the authors believe is most helpful in child care settings. The major contributions of early childhood theorists are presented within this structure. This philosophy, which follows a *Developmental Perspective*, states that every child has the capacity to develop *all* of the skills that any human being has ever developed. Unlike the tabula rasa theory of the past, which claimed that children are molded to parental or societal specifications, current research indicates that we bring to life all the potentials of our entire ancestry; all that it is possible for people to become is available in the potential of the newborn (Douville-Watson, 1988).

Of course, there are environmental factors that limit the realization of our full potential. A child born with a physical handicap such as brain damage will not realize as much potential in certain areas as a child born neurologically intact, and a child whose ancestry dictates adult height less than 5 feet will most likely not realize the potential to play professional basketball. However, within these limiting physical and environmental factors, every child has the potential for a fulfilling and productive life, depending on how well his or her needs and abilities are satisfied and challenged and to what extent the skills necessary to become a happy and successful adult are fostered by family members and caregivers.

A brief discussion of our developmental perspective applied to the four major developmental factors illustrates the functional value of approaching children in this way. Heredity largely dictates general physical qualities, such as height, body size, and hair color, but current research in neuropsychology and nutrition indicates that when one physical system is weak or injured, other systems compensate by becoming stronger, sometimes even taking over the functions of the weakened system. As mentioned in Chapter 1, much research has been conducted on brain development. One concept has received attention in recent years: **brain plasticity**, which means that when one part of the brain is damaged, other parts take over the functions of the damaged part. However, brain plasticity is bound by critical periods of development; after a critical period has passed, the brain is less able to compensate for damaged parts (Berk, 2000). What this means for a caregiver is that infants and toddlers are in the process of forming nerve pathways, and by providing them with the proper nutrition and experiences, we can enhance physical and neurological development.

In addition to being born with certain temperament traits, children are also born with unlimited potential for loving and intimate relationships, joy, happiness, and personal fulfillment. Research clearly indicates that the way the environment provides for children's needs and the manner in which caregivers interact with children determine the emotional and social intelligence adults exhibit. There is no such thing as too much love, approval, acceptance, or positive attention for infants and toddlers. By approaching each child with respect and unconditional regard, we help maintain the enthusiasm, curiosity, and loving nature that is present at birth and enables us to be fully human.

Approaching young children as being capable of unlimited growth establishes security, trust, confidence, and respect for the caregiver. When the caregiver maintains appropriately high expectations and regards children with the perspective that each individual can accomplish what he or she is motivated to do, children develop positive self-esteem and responsibility. The task of helping each child reach her or his own potential is a collaborative effort between the caregiver, the family, the community, and society.

FOUR MAJOR DEVELOPMENTAL AREAS

In this section we will examine the skill areas that are important in helping children develop to their full potential. These skill areas can then be put together in a graphic form developed by Watson called a Developmental Profile (1977). A Developmental Profile is a graphic picture of a child's development compared to age expectancies in four major developmental areas. Table 2–1 lists the four developmental domains important in human development. Assessment of each child in your care compared to age norms or expectations is necessary for you to promote optimal development (Watson, 1995).

USING A DEVELOPMENTAL PROFILE

Use the Developmental Prescription in Appendix A or another developmental hierarchy to evaluate which behaviors and skills the child can perform successfully and the point in the hierarchy at which the child can't perform higher-level behaviors (refer to Appendix B for Profile Construction). The last point at which the child performs with success is translated into an estimate of age in months indicating the level of development in that skill area. For example, in evaluating a 12-month-old in Area I (Physical), the Developmental Prescription in Appendix A for 8 to 12 months lists six behaviors under "Muscular Control, Trunk and Leg." If the child being observed can successfully perform the first three behaviors, his or her development is estimated to be 10 months (half of the age range between 8 and 12 months). Evaluate each child in all the skill behaviors of the age range in order to establish an average age level for each of the four developmental areas on the profile. Remember that these are average estimates of ages and not specific tests.

TABLE 2–1	DEVELOPMENT DOMAINS
AREA I	**Physical:** height, weight, general motor coordination, visual and auditory acuity, and so on
AREA II	**Emotional:** feelings, self-perception, perception of others related to self, confidence, security, and so on
AREA III	**Social:** interactions with peers, elders, and youngers, both one on one and in a group
AREA IV	**Cognitive/language:** reasoning, problem solving, concept formation, abstraction, imagination, verbal communication, and so on

Name: **Juan P.**
Date: **2/24/XX**

Date of Birth: **2/21/XX**
C. A.: **12 months 3 days**

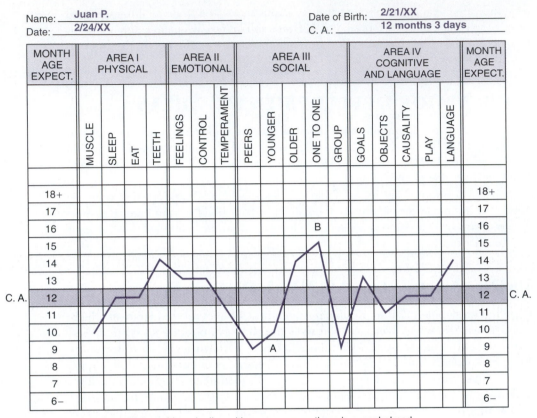

Notes: A = Juan has a little problem dealing with a group–sometimes is overwhelmed.
B = He responds very well to one-on-one adult attention.

FIGURE 2–1 Sample Developmental Profile.

Figure 2–1 graphically illustrates the assessment of a 12-month-old compared to age norms on a Developmental Profile. The heavy line at 12 months indicates Juan's chronological age (C. A.) and each point indicates his development in each of the four areas. To make up the points on the profile, specific skills under each area from the Developmental Prescription in Appendix A were evaluated. By comparing relative strengths and weaknesses, a program can be implemented to enhance his development (refer to Appendix B for instructions on Developmental Profile construction and Appendix A for specific age expectations). In the example, Juan is above his age in responding to adult attention and below age expectancy in interacting in a group. From this profile we can see that activities should be done to help Juan feel more secure in a group setting and to help him function more independently in one-on-one interactions. Since his language skills are good, talking to Juan while he is in a group might help.

A word of caution is in order here. Although needs and skills must be measured to provide a structure for promoting development, estimates of skill development are used only to determine goals and not to label children as better or worse, or ahead or behind. Development varies widely, especially for infants and toddlers, so you should assess needs and skill levels on an ongoing basis and be timely in changing your goals to keep up with the rapidly changing child. Development is a continuing process wherein people grow in the same direction at different rates.

THEORETICAL CONTRIBUTIONS

Using the framework of the four developmental areas, we can now examine how the brain works, as well as some major contributions theorists discussed in Chapter 1 have made toward supporting each child's development.

As mentioned in Chapter 1, new technologies have led to a better understanding of how brain development results from complex interactions between nature (i.e., genetic makeup) and nurture (i.e., environmental factors). Genes are responsible for the basic wiring of the human brain. The brain is a complex electrical system which is divided into three main parts; each is further divided into specialized regions with specific functions (McDevitt & Ormrod, 2007). Starting in the womb, the electrical activity of brain cells changes the physical structure of the brain, just as they will power learning after birth. Before age one, the infant's brain will produce trillions more connections than it can possibly use (Nash, 1997).

The newborn's brain is constantly taking in information available in the environment, utilizing all existing senses. The brain records these pieces of information, whether they are emotional, physical (sensory), social, or cognitive in origin. This information influences the shape and circuitry of the neurons, or brain cells. The more data taken in, the stronger the neuron connections and pathways are. A repeated behavior or the consistency of a behavior increases the chance of the pathway becoming strong. If there is not a consistent pattern introduced to the brain, the brain's job is to cut off the circuitry to that area, and the potential growth for a skill is significantly minimized. In fact, through competition the brain eliminates, or prunes, synapses that are seldom used and leaves a pattern of emotion and thought (Nash, 1997). Hence, the growth and strength of the brain are directly influenced by which neurological circuits are activated and the number of times they are used (Johnson, 1999).

Brain development during infancy is best promoted when caregivers are affectionate, consistent, responsive, and reassuring (McDevitt & Ormrod, 2007). Attachments between infants and adults (discussed in greater detail later in this section) help very young children to develop not only emotionally but also physically and intellectually. Responsive adults tend to provide infants proper nutrition, protect them from harm, soothe them when they are distressed, and talk about objects, patterns, or people who have attracted their attention (Eliot, 1999; Shore, 2003). Immersion in a language-rich environment that includes sign language can stimulate brain development. Using *Baby Signs* (Acredolo & Goodwyn, 2002), for example, can promote language, memory, and concept development. Signaling needs and desires through simple gestures enables very young children to take an active part in interactions and helps to diminish frustration. Signing has been used successfully with children of diverse abilities including those with autism and Down syndrome (Acredolo & Goodwyn, 2002).

Responsive caregivers assist very young children in dealing with strong emotions.

Unresponsive, harmful, stressful, or neglectful caregiving behaviors affect the development of the brain negatively. For example, children who experience unresponsive and stressful conditions, either in a home or child care setting, were found to have elevated cortisol levels (see Gunnar & Cheatham, 2003, for a review). Monitoring cortisol levels in children may help in creating interventions and prevent negative outcomes that are associated with high levels of cortisol in adults, such as anxiety disorders and cognitive disturbances (for reviews, see Gunnar, 2001, and Lupien & McEwen, 1997, respectively).

Thus, responsive caregiving by parents and teachers is a major factor in brain development. The adult role is critical because early experiences significantly affect how each child's brain is wired (Herr & Swim, 2002). Creating positive social, emotional, cognitive, language, and physical experiences all influence the development of a healthy brain (Acredolo & Goodwyn, 2000; Herr & Swim, 2002).

Physical Development

Systematic observations of behavior by Charles Darwin, Stanley Hall and Arnold Gesell, John Watson, and B. F. Skinner have resulted in an approach called **task analysis**, which, when applied to physical development, yields a developmental hierarchy from simple to complex patterns of physical movements. For example, careful observation of the physical movements required to stand erect reveals a hierarchy of behaviors, starting with the simplest arm and leg joint bending and building through a series of natural milestones, such as rolling over and crawling. Contributions from behavioral pioneers have shown that any behavior can be subjected to a task analysis, broken down into a hierarchy of steps from the simplest to the most complex behavior necessary to perform the goal.

The Developmental Prescriptions presented in Appendix A are examples of general task analyses for infants and toddlers in the four major developmental areas. By carefully observing a child's behavior, the caregiver can determine the highest step on the list the child can perform, and then "task-analyze," or determine the specific steps necessary to help the child move to the next level in the hierarchy. Chapter 4 provides specific tools to help adults promote development and reinforce children's successes with the three As: Attention, Approval, and Attunement.

Emotional Development

Erikson's psychosocial theory (1950) adds to our understanding of emotional development and the qualities children need to become happy and successful adults. Erikson defined eight psychosocial stages that humans experience throughout life. The first three are extremely important in the development of infants and toddlers.

1. *Basic trust versus mistrust*—Children learn to trust or mistrust themselves and the world during infancy depending on the warmth and sensitivity they are given. When infants are required to wait too long for comfort, or they are handled harshly and insensitively, they develop basic mistrust of themselves and others.

2. *Autonomy versus shame and doubt*—Once infants become mobile, a process of separation and individuation begins, eventually resulting in autonomy. Children need to choose and decide things for themselves. When caregivers permit reasonable free choices and do not force or shame children, autonomy and self-confidence are fostered.

3. *Initiative versus guilt*—When caregivers support a child's sense of purpose and direction, initiative in the form of ambition and responsibility is developed. When caregivers demand too much self-control or responsibilities that are age-inappropriate, children respond by feeling overcontrolled or guilty, or both.

Erikson's stages reveal how children develop the qualities that result in a happy, meaningful life. Activities based on the first three stages should be part of the daily curriculum, and the caregiver should help promote confidence, security, and trust in each child. Such purposeful practices are important, since successful resolution of the earliest stages is particularly vital to lifelong emotional development; the results of initial crises affect the outcomes of later stages.

Recent research on emotional development suggests that although all emotions are present at birth, our emotional reactions are learned through stages. The development of affective reactions and self-regulation of emotions appears to be the direct result of caregiving styles.

"What wires a child's brain, say neuroscientists—or rewires it after physical trauma—is repeated experience. . . . When the brain does not receive the right information—or shuts it out—the result can be devastating. . . . Emotional deprivation early in life has a similar effect" (Nash, 1997). For a more complete understanding of the development of emotions, refer to *The Organization of Emotional Life in the Early Years* (Sroufe, 1996).

Margaret Mahler's theory regarding separation-individuation and bonding and Daniel Goleman's theory of emotional intelligence are discussed in detail in Chapter 3. These theories help the caregiver to understand developmental patterns of the formation of **identity**, self-concept, self-esteem, and the skills necessary for a person to function effectively in the world.

Social Development

Contributions by numerous social learning theorists help us to understand how infants and toddlers develop relationships. The first relationships we have in the world with our parents and caregivers result in the formation of the self, which forms the basis for all future relationships.

William James (1890–1963) first identified two distinct aspects of the self: the I, or **existential self**, which is separate from the environment and other people and maintains continuous existence over time; and the **reflective self** or the "me" and the "not me," which perceives the physical, material, and relationship qualities of experience.

The emergence of **self-recognition** has been demonstrated in infants as young as nine months and appears to be present in the majority of 15-month-olds (Bullock & Lutkenhaus, 1990). Many theorists hypothesize that the development of self is rooted in a **sense of agency**; for example, awareness that our actions cause other objects and people to react in predictable ways (Pipp, Easterbrooks, & Brown, 1993). By two years of age, a sense of self is well established and toddlers express possession of objects with *me* and *mine* (Levine, 1983).

The opposite side of the coin from separation-individuation is presented in the widely accepted view of infant emotional ties to the caregiver in Bowlby's ethological theory of attachment (Bowlby, 1969/2000). According to this theory, the infant's relationship to the parent starts as a set of innate signals that keep the caregiver close to the baby and proceeds through four phases, as follows:

1. *The preattachment phase* (birth to six weeks) occurs when the baby grasps, cries, smiles, and gazes to keep the caregiver engaged.
2. *The "attachment-in-the-making" phase* (six weeks to eight months) consists of the baby responding differently to familiar caregivers than to strangers. Face-to-face interactions relieve distress, and the baby expects that the caregiver will respond when signaled.
3. *The clear-cut attachment phase* (eight months to two years) is when the baby exhibits separation anxiety, protests caregiver departure, and acts deliberately to maintain caregiver attention.

4. Formation of a *reciprocal relationship phase* (18 months onward) occurs when children negotiate with the caregiver and are willing to give and take in relationships.

Researchers measure attachment history for young toddlers using an experimental design called the Strange Situation. This experiment involves a series of separations and reunions. Four categories have been used to classify attachment patterns: secure, ambivalent/insecure, avoidant/insecure (Ainsworth, 1967, 1973) and disoriented/insecure (Hesse & Main, 2000; Main & Solomon, 1990). These attachment patterns have been found to be influenced by the type of caregiving provided and to result in different social outcomes for toddlers, preschoolers, and school-age children.

Infants' attachment styles have been found to correlate to sets of caregivers' behaviors. Regarding secure attachments, infants and caregivers engage in finely tuned, synchronous dances where the adults carefully read the infants' cues, see events from the infants' perspectives, and respond accordingly (Isabella & Belsky, 1991; NICHD Early Child Care Research Network, 1997; Oppenheim & Koren-Karie, 2002). More specifically, infants classified as securely attached tend to have caregivers who

- consistently respond to infants' needs.
- interpret infant emotional signals sensitively.
- regularly express affection.
- permit babies to influence the pace and direction of their mutual interactions (for reviews see Honig, 2002, and McDevitt & Ormrod, 2007).

In contrast, caregivers of insecurely attached infants tend to have difficulty caring for the infants (e.g., dislike physical contact, are inconsistent, unpredictable, insensitive, and intrusive) or are unwilling to invest energy in the relationship (Belsky, Rovine, & Taylor, 1984; Isabella, 1993; Thompson, 1998). In some instances the caregivers act on their own wishes rather than the infants' needs, while at other times, they respond to the infants' needs with irritability or anger. For children in the severest category of insecurity—disoriented—the caregivers can be addicted to drugs or alcohol or be severely depressed or otherwise mentally ill; they are unable to care for their own needs, let alone their children's. In one study, these caregivers were found to have experienced their own attachment-related traumas when they were children (Hesse & Main, 2000).

Attachment histories are important to early childhood educators because these childhood relationships set the foundation for later close relationships, especially those with peers. Securely attached children tend to be more independent, empathic, and socially competent preschoolers, especially in comparison to insecurely attached children (McDevitt & Ormrod, 2007). Supporting and complementing strong, positive parent-child attachment, then, can have long-term consequences (Puckett & Black, 2002).

In conclusion, caregivers should be very aware of factors that affect attachment security in young children. Sensitive caregiving that responds quickly to the child's signals and needs is the most important factor in supporting children's development. The findings from many studies clearly reveal that securely attached infants have primary caregivers who respond quickly to signals, express positive feelings, and handle babies with tenderness and sensitivity. The best principle for infant and toddler social development is probably that adults cannot be too "in tune" or give too much approval and affection; young children can't be spoiled. Your sensitive caring sets the basis for future relationships that young children will have throughout their lives.

Cognitive and Language Development

As mentioned in Chapter 1, the most widely applied theories of higher cognition are Piaget's cognitive developmental theory (Beilin, 1992) and Vygotsky's sociocultural theory (Rogoff & Chavajay, 1995). Later chapters detail several applications of these theories in child care settings, but some major principles from each theory are discussed here. According to Piaget, children construct knowledge through their interactions with materials in their environment. As a stage theorist, Piaget believed that children developed higher cognitive skills in a systematic manner through four stages: (1) sensorimotor, (2) preoperational, (3) concrete operational, and (4) formal operational. Children use **schemes**, or patterns of actions, to learn at each of these stages through the intellectual functions of adaptation and organization.

Adaptation involves using schemes that have direct interaction with the environment; for example, grasping and dropping an object over and over. **Accommodation** involves changing schemes to better fit the requirements of a task or new information. Thus, a child will change or alter his or her strategies to fit the requirements of a task. For example, banging on a hard toy will produce a noise. Yet, when faced with a soft toy, the child finds that banging is insufficient to produce a response. Squeezing might be tried instead. When children are in a familiar situation, they function by means of **assimilation**, which involves dealing with an object or event in a way that is consistent with their existing schemes (McDevitt & Ormrod, 2007). When children are in such situations, they are considered to be in the internal state called **equilibrium**. Their current cognitive schemes work to explain their environment. However, when faced with information that is contrary to their current schemes and understanding or placed in an unfamiliar situation, they experience **disequilibrium**. This internal mental state provides a motivation for learning because the children are uncomfortable and seek to make sense of what they have observed or experienced. "The movement from equilibrium to disequilibrium and back to equilibrium again is known as **equilibration**. Equilibration and children's intrinsic desire to achieve equilibrium promote the development of more complex levels of thought and knowledge" (McDevitt & Ormrod, 2007, p. 195, emphasis in original).

Another cognitive function through which schemes are changed is called organization, which takes place internally. **Organization** is a process of rearranging new schemes and linking them with other schemes to form a cognitive system. For example, a baby will eventually relate schemes for sucking, dropping, and throwing with new, more complex schemes of near and far.

Although many of the hypotheses of Piaget's theory have come into question after the advent of research demonstrating that infants and toddlers have many more cognitive skills than Piaget theorized (Rast & Meltzoff, 1995), the principles and stages defined by Piaget have functional value for the caregiver in supporting children in their cognitive development. Some additional contributions include discovery learning, awareness of readiness for learning, and acceptance of individual differences in learning rates.

Unlike Piaget, Vygotsky viewed cognitive development as an interaction between children and their social environment. For Vygotsky knowledge is co-constructed through social interactions. Cultural tools mediate and facilitate this construction of knowledge; the most important tool for humans is language because "Language is thought; language is culture; language is identity. . . . Denying language is denying access to thought" (Wink & Putney, 2002, p. 54). In Vygotsky's own words:

> Thought is not merely expressed in words; it comes into existence through them. Every thought tends to connect something with something else, to establish a relationship between things. Every thought moves, grows and develops, fulfills a function, solves a problem. (1934/1986, p. 218)

Vygotsky believed that, once language is developed, children engage in **private speech**; in other words, they talk to themselves as a means of self-guidance and direction (1934/1986). Recent research supports this view with findings that children who use more private speech show more improvement on difficult tasks than children who do not use much private speech (Berk & Spuhl, 1995). In addition, children use more private speech as tasks become more difficult (Berk, 1994), and children with learning problems use more private speech than do children with normal learning skills (Diaz & Berk, 1995).

Vygotsky hypothesized that higher cognitive processes develop from verbal and nonverbal social interactions. This is accomplished when more mature individuals instruct less mature individuals within their **zone of proximal development** (Wink & Putney, 2002). This term refers to a range of tasks that a child is ready to learn with the help of more skilled peers or adults. The zone of proximal development is established by assessing the child's individual level of performance and the child's assisted level of performance. The gap between these two levels is considered the "zone" (Wink & Putney, 2002). As a child is able to accomplish skills at the assisted level independently, the zone shifts upwards to the next skill to be addressed. Children adopt the language and actions of dialogues and demonstrations with adults into their private speech and then use those to guide and regulate their own actions. At least two other aspects of this process have found research support: intersubjectivity and scaffolding.

Intersubjectivity refers to how children and adults come to understand each other by adjusting their views and perspectives to fit the other person. **Scaffolding** involves changing the support given a learner in the course of teaching a skill or concept (Berk & Winsler, 1995; Bodrova & Leong, 1996; Wink & Putney, 2002). The more skilled person can utilize a number of instructional strategies to scaffold learning during a new, challenging, or complex task. Verbal encouragement; physical assistance; coaching; providing hints, clues, or cues; asking questions; and breaking the task into manageable steps are all strategies to assist in accomplishing the given task. As the learner starts mastering the new skills, the more skilled person withdraws instruction and praise in direct response to the learner's ability to perform successfully. Caregivers who effectively learn to use intersubjectivity and scaffolding help promote

Children make the language and actions of adults part of their private speech.

development, because children learn to use positive private speech and succeed more easily (Behrend, Rosengran, & Perlmutter, 1992).

A final aspect of Vygotsky's theory involves the use of **make-believe play** in higher cognitive development. Vygotsky believed that children who engage in make-believe play use imagination to act out internal ideas about how the world operates and to set rules by which play is conducted, which helps them learn to think before they act (Berk & Winsler, 1995). Recent research on preschoolers supports this concept since children who engage in make-believe and pretend play are found to be more flexible and advanced in their problem-solving and thought processes (Lillard, 1993).

As is evident from the above discussion, language plays a critical role in cognitive development from a Vygotskian perspective. Language is a tool for thinking (Bodrova & Leong, 1996; McDevitt & Ormrod, 2007). How do children come to acquire language skills for thinking and communicating? The easiest answer, of course, is through engaging in conversations with others. When adults and children talk with infants and toddlers, they provide examples of the four basic components of language: **phonology**, the basic sounds of the language and how they are combined to make words; **semantics**, what words mean; **syntax**, how to combine words into understandable phrases and sentences; and **pragmatics**, how to engage in communication with others that is socially acceptable and effective (McDevitt & Ormrod, 2007).

Infants begin to engage in verbal communication around four months of age, when they **coo** (or make repetitive vowel sounds). Around six or seven months of age, they begin to **babble** (or produce speech-like syllables such as *ba, ra*) using sounds from their native language. The first "real" word is typically spoken around the first birthday. For a while, toddlers will blend babble with a real word in what is called **jargon**. To illustrate, an infant says "tatata car bebe" while playing. The teacher might respond with elaboration by saying "You moved the car. You pushed it with your hand. It went bye-bye." In this case, the adult supplies words that help to explain what the child is experiencing; thus, encouraging the acquisition of other new words and facilitating the linking of two "real" words or **telegraphic speech**. Just as a telegraphic message omits words, telegraphic speech includes only the words vital to the meaning the toddler is trying to convey. By 36 months, most toddlers are able to clearly and effectively communicate their wants, needs, and ideas. (See Baron, 1992; Herr & Swim, 2002; and Snow, 1998, for more information on communicating with infants.)

Like other areas of development discussed in this chapter, optimal language development requires interactions with teachers, peers, and family members. Engaging in conversations about events as they happen supports and facilitates language development.

SUMMARY OF THEORETICAL CONTRIBUTIONS

1. **Brain Development.** Major advances in understanding the impact of environments and environmental factors have come about as a result of new medical technologies. Primary caregivers who demonstrate affectionate, consistent, responsive, and reassuring behaviors have been found to positively impact brain development for very young children.

2. **Physical Development.** Major contributions to behavioral psychology, starting with Darwin and continuing through current research, aid in the task analysis of physical movements and behavioral skills. Breaking down goal behaviors into their natural steps, starting with the behaviors the child can perform and proceeding to the goal behavior, provides the caregiver with a powerful tool to support children's development. When lots of positive attention, approval, and attunement are added, the caregiver can enhance the physical development of all children in care.

3. **Emotional Development.** Erikson's psychosocial theory supplies stages for the development of essential personality characteristics, such as trust, autonomy, and initiative. Caregivers can plan daily activities using Erikson's stages to help children remain unlimited in their happiness and personality development.

   Teaching young children to identify and express feelings accurately in ways that help them fill their needs and not hurt others is a goal every caregiver should have to help children grow up emotionally healthy.

4. **Social Development.** To apply principles for relationships and interactions, the caregiver must first understand the development of the self. William James first defined the existential (authentic) self and the reflective self (me

and not me). Bowlby's ethological theory helps the caregiver understand how infants and toddlers participate in relationships through his four stages of attachment. Findings from many studies demonstrate that warm, sensitive, conscious caregiver-to-child interactions are essential to set the basis for keeping children unlimited in all their future relationships.

5. **Cognitive and Language Development.** Piaget and Vygotsky have provided frameworks for understanding cognitive reasoning and development. From a Piagetian perspective, caregivers need to be aware of the schemes that infants and toddlers use to interact with the environment through adaptation, assimilation, and accommodation. Vygotsky gave caregivers the powerful principles of private speech; the zone of proximal development, including how adults and children come to understand each other through intersubjectivity and scaffolding; and the important role of make-believe play.

Regarding language development, infants enter the world communicating primarily through nonverbal communication, progress to cooing and babbling, produce their first word, and exit toddlerhood using language as a tool for thinking and interacting.

A comment on the narrowness of the information presented in this discussion is in order. There are entire bodies of research in each of the four developmental areas. The reader should understand that the scope of this text allows for only an overview of each area; numerous theories and research findings could not be presented in this brief review.

CHILDREN WITH SPECIAL NEEDS

All the theories, concepts, tools, and skills discussed in this book influence the care given to individual children. A developmental perspective is profoundly applicable. Caregivers who use their knowledge to identify needs in a child's development and suggest early interventions may observe a step-by-step, positive change in the child that is a direct result of their actions.

In virtually every community in the United States, early interventions for at-risk infants and toddlers are currently available (Guralnick & Bennett, 1987; Odom, Teferra & Kaul, 2004). Children who are considered at risk require specialized equipment, care, and curricula, and the child care specialist must learn how to care for children with special needs. Because it is impossible to cover all the special conditions and procedures necessary to care for at-risk children in one text, an overview of categories and characteristics is provided here. The first source of information should be the family. The partnerships you create should encourage the family members to freely exchange information with you. Contact the appropriate local and national associations and organizations for specific information on how to care for individual children with special needs, when necessary.

The following terms related to children with special needs come from Hardman, Drew, & Egan (2005):

- **disorder:** A disturbance in normal functioning (mental, physical, or psychological).
- **disability:** A condition resulting from a loss of physical functioning, or difficulties in learning and social adjustment that significantly interfere with normal growth and development.

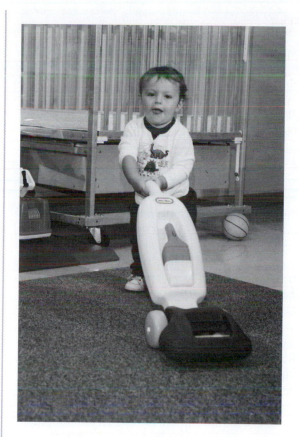

All children have the right to individualized, challenging curriculum that facilitates growth and development.

- **exceptional:** A term describing any individual whose physical, mental, or behavioral performances deviate so substantially from the average (higher or lower) that additional support is required to meet the individual's needs.
- **special education:** Specially designed instruction provided to children, at no cost to the parents, in all settings (such as the classroom, physical education facilities, the home, and hospitals or institutions).
- **early intervention:** Comprehensive services for infants and toddlers who are disabled or at risk of acquiring a disability. Services may include education, health care, and/or social and psychological assistance.

The following categories explain many of these children's special needs:

1. **Environmentally At-Risk Infants and Toddlers.** Children from socially and economically disadvantaged families are included in this category. Results from several studies reveal that the most effective interventions involve children attending day care and families receiving parent training on an ongoing basis. For more information, contact your local health department, department of social/human services, or community-specific organizations, such as an Early Head Start program.
2. **Biologically At-Risk Infants and Toddlers.** Some children experience central nervous system (CNS) damage, for example, from CNS infections, trauma, ingestion of toxins, and sustained hypoxia

(continued)

CHILDREN WITH SPECIAL NEEDS *(continued)*

(lack of oxygen). Research results on interventions ranging from special nursery settings and free nursing and medical care to infant stimulation by parents yield mixed results, with very short-term, positive effects. Interventions for this population appear to be more effective with parents than with children. For more information, contact the American Medical Association, your county health department, American Academy of Pediatrics, or local pediatricians.

3. **Children with Cognitive and General Developmental Disorders.** Some infants and toddlers exhibit delays in every facet of cognition, such as information processing, problem solving, and ability to apply information to new situations. Global delays in motor, language, and socioemotional areas are common with these children. They tend to reach milestones typically but at a much slower rate, with lower final levels of development, such as mental retardation, Down syndrome, and teratogenic damage. Research strongly indicates that early intervention programs prevent the decline in intellectual functioning found in mildly retarded children without intervention. Programs for moderately and profoundly retarded children are more effective with active parental participation and training, but overall they appear to be less effective than with mildly retarded infants and toddlers. For more information, contact the American Association on Intellectual and Developmental Disabilities, formerly the American Association on Mental Retardation, the local special education administration, or local chapters of specific associations such as the Down Syndrome Association.

4. **Children with Motor Disabilities.** Infants and toddlers with motor disabilities exhibit delayed motor development, retention of primitive reflexes, and abnormal muscle tone as the result of CNS damage or malformation. The three major disabilities that are accompanied by motor handicaps are cerebral palsy, myelomeningocele, and Down syndrome. Infants and toddlers with motor disabilities usually exhibit delays in other developmental areas as well because learning occurs through active exploration of the world. Research on interventions involving systematic exercise and sensory stimulation and integration indicate that early intervention can improve motor and sensory development and encourage parent support and acceptance. For more information contact the American Medical Association, American Academy of Pediatrics, and local chapters of specific organizations such as the United Cerebral Palsy Foundation.

5. **Children with Language and Communication Disorders.** Infants and toddlers who exhibit problems with the mechanics of speech (phonation, moving air from the lungs through the mouth, and articulation) have speech disorders, and children with problems using the rules of language (labeling or forming sentences) have language disorders. Results of studies on various kinds of interventions suggest that the course of communication disorders can be modified through early intervention. For more information, contact the American Association for Speech and Language, Association for Speech and Hearing, and local chapters of associations for speech and language disorders.

6. **Children with Autism.** Infants and toddlers with autism exhibit disturbances in developmental rates and sequences, responses to sensory stimuli, communication, and the capacity to relate appropriately to people, events, and objects. The incidence of autism in the general population is very low: four to five in every 10,000 births, but males substantially outnumber females (American Psychiatric Association, 2000; Hardman, Drew & Egan, 2005). Data on early assessment suggest that children as young as 18 months can be reliably diagnosed with autism, but that the tools fail to recognize the disorder in many toddlers who will later show clear symptoms of autism (Watson, Baranek, & DiLavore, 2003). Research on structured early intervention programs, which include

parents, has yielded highly encouraging results. For more information, contact the National Society for Children and Adults with Autism, the American Psychological Association, or your local psychological association.

7. **Children with Visual Disabilities.** Infants and toddlers who are blind or have low vision are found in approximately one out of 3000 births, with a wide range of severity and etiology. The most important consideration is visual efficiency, which includes acuity, visual fields, ocular motility, binocular vision, adaptations to light and dark, color vision, and accommodation. Research findings indicate that early intervention helps visually impaired infants and toddlers perform closer to typical developmental expectations. Interventions using a team approach, including parents, child care specialists, and other professionals, is more effective than individual treatment approaches. For more information, contact the National Society for the Prevention of Blindness, National Council for Exceptional Children, the local health department, and agencies for the blind or those with low vision.

8. **Children with Hearing Disabilities.** Hearing disabilities are classified by type (sensorineural, conductive, or mixed), time of onset (at birth or after), severity (mild to profound), and etiology. Research indicates that early intervention programs should include parent counseling, staff with training in audiology, staff with speech and language training, inclusion of sign language as a normal program component, the flexibility to help each family, and the inclusion of deaf adults as resources for children. For more information, contact the Council for Exceptional Children, local health department, and the National Association of the Deaf.

9. **Children with Fetal Alcohol Syndrome or Fetal Alcohol Effect (FAS/FAE).** Children with FAS/FAE were exposed to an adverse environmental agent, alcohol, during the periods of prenatal development. Children with FAS typically have growth delays, facial abnormalities, mental retardation, impulsivity, and behavioral problems (McDevitt & Ormrod, 2007). The difference between FAS and FAE seems to be the amount, frequency, and duration of alcohol consumed by the mother during the pregnancy. However, researchers and medical professionals do not know how much alcohol needs to be ingested to produce FAS instead of FAE. Because of the diversity of characteristics for these children, intervention programs tend to focus on specific aspects of the disability, i.e., cognitive disabilities.

10. **Children Who Are Medically Fragile.** A new subgroup of health disorders, referred to as medically fragile, has emerged in recent years (Hardman, Drew, & Egan, 2005). These individuals are at risk for medical emergencies and often require specialized support. For example, children with feeding tubes need highly trained individuals to provide necessary nutritional supplements. Other times medically fragile children have progressive diseases (e.g., AIDS or cancer) or episodic conditions (e.g., severe asthma or sickle cell anemia; Hardman, Drew, & Egan, 2005). Such disorders have an impact not only on the way the infant or toddler forms his or her own identity, but also how others see and treat him or her. Seeking information from families or community agencies/organizations can help to alleviate your concerns and educate the child's peers about the specific disorder, improving peer relationships (McDevitt & Ormrod, 2007).

11. **Children with Multiple Disabilities.** As defined by the Individuals with Disabilities Education Act (IDEA) federal regulations, many children experience multiple disabilities or concomitant impairments, meaning that they have more than one identified exceptionality. The particular combination causes such severe educational issues that the individual cannot be accommodated in special education programs designed solely for one of the special needs [34 Code of Federal Regulations 300.7(c)(7) (1999), as cited in Hardman, Drew, & Egan, 2005].

(continued)

CHILDREN WITH SPECIAL NEEDS *(continued)*

It is essential that early childhood educators not work in isolation when caring for children with special needs. When any of the conditions described here is suspected, the teacher must consult professionals who are trained to evaluate, prescribe for, and intervene with these children. In fact, every child care program should have medical and psychological services as a regular part of the evaluation and care of children. It is also important for each caregiver to network with other child development professionals in the area, such as psychologists, pediatricians, and speech and language therapists. Caregivers must be aware of community resources for children with special needs, since many families lack funding sources. Sometimes community groups or generous, qualified professionals donate their time and energy to ensure proper treatment for children with special needs.

The research on interventions with children with all types of disabilities strongly indicates that a team approach that includes parents, all caregiving staff, and specialized professionals, is necessary to promote optimal growth and development for children with special needs.

Given that a team approach is necessary, several new curricula have been established for infants and toddlers with special needs. The states of California, North Carolina, and Florida are among the nation's leaders in programs for infants and toddlers with special needs. For example, *The Carolina Curriculum for Infants and Toddlers with Special Needs,* by Johnson et al. (1991), offers strategies, activities, and techniques in all developmental areas. The early childhood educator should contact the department of education in these states to obtain specific information on the care of these children.

As late as 1970, most children with birth abnormalities or learning difficulties were cared for an individual basis with no formal procedures or laws to direct their care. Educational theories and principles that would later become *special education* were just beginning. A landmark law was passed in 1976 called the Education of All Handicapped Children Act. This law later grew in scope and purpose and became the Individuals with Disabilities Education Act.

Because this act was passed, children with special needs became entitled to appropriate public education regardless of their disability. The law provided that children should have the "least restrictive environment possible," which meant that all children would be registered in the same school district and special services would be provided as necessary.

Three- to five-year-olds were among the first to be served. Later, additional laws were passed to educate even younger children with special needs. One pediatrician, Dr. Cecilia McCarton, took exception to the accepted view that infants with special needs do not need special public assistance. She remembers that

> In the 70's, the usual practice was to make a diagnosis and then send the parents of these children back to their own communities for follow-up care. There was not a single place that offered a diagnosis, prescription for care and actual appointments with those supporting professionals necessary for follow up. Parents faced extremely frustrating situations, and most often were devastated to find no available people in their community to follow through with our suggestion. (1994)

In response to the need, Dr. McCarton developed one of the first comprehensive treatment centers in the United States. She conducted research on thousands of children with low birth weight and special anomalies. For more than 20 years, Dr. McCarton and colleagues at the Infant Health and Development

Program did much to advance research in the areas of underweight preemies and children with special needs, which is still used to inform educational practices today.

Functional Ability versus Actual Age

In the design of special education curricula, age and individual appropriateness have particular meanings. Children with special needs often function at a lower level in certain areas than their chronological age leads us to expect, so knowing the functional age of a child is essential for structuring and designing appropriate activities. Equally important is using attention, approval, and attunement as a way of communicating and meeting the child's needs.

As discussed above, curriculum development for children with special needs generally involves a didactic team approach. Specialists interact with each other on behalf of the child based on the type of special needs the child exhibits. Professionals work together to establish a functional age in each area of development, and priorities for care are set using Developmental Profiles and Prescriptions.

■ KEY TERMS

accommodation	existential self	scaffolding
adaptation	FAE	schemes
assimilation	FAS	self-recognition
babble	intersubjectivity	semantics
brain plasticity	jargon	sense of agency
coo	make-believe play	separation and individuation
disability	medically fragile	special education
disequilibrium	multiple disabilities	syntax
disorder	organization	task analysis
early intervention	phonology	telegraphic speech
equilibration	private speech	zone of proximal development
equilibrium	pragmatics	
exceptional	reflective self	

CASE STUDY   Sasha

Angelica, just over two years of age, is relatively new to Sasha's class of mixed-age infants and toddlers. She joined the class for part-time care (three days a week) about three months ago after she was formally adopted by her aunt (her biological mother's sister) and uncle. Angelica is now the youngest of three children. She is

(Continued)

CASE STUDY (continued)

obviously adored by her parents and siblings. Sasha is concerned because she is having difficulty forming a close attachment with Angelica in the child care setting.

Angelica has missed more than two-thirds of the days that she was scheduled to be at child care due to her illness, sickle cell anemia or SCA. This is an inherited disorder that profoundly affects the structure and functioning of red blood cells for African Americans (Hardman, Drew, & Egan, 2005). Angelica's disorder was identified at birth, yet is progressing at a rapid rate; she seems to be experiencing frequent and serious complications. Angelica misses school when she has to get partial-exchange blood transfusions. These treatments tend to cause her to throw up. In the last three months, she has needed eight such transfusions. After the last treatment, she had to be admitted to the hospital overnight because of dehydration. Angelica had only experienced three partial-exchange transfusions before being adopted.

When Angelica enrolled in her class, Sasha began to find out more about SCA and how she could best meet the toddler's needs. Her first source of information was Angelica's parents, of course, but they are just learning about this disorder as well. Next, she searched the World Wide Web, but found conflicting information and not much about partial-exchange blood transfusions and their side effects. She did discover that minimizing stress, fatigue, and exposure to cold temperatures can assist those with a history of SCA crises. So, while she has gained some information, Sasha is still nervous about working with Angelica.

1. What else can Sasha do to learn more about SCA? What other sources would you suggest?

2. Do you think that knowing more about SCA will help Sasha form a close attachment with Angelica? Why or why not? Given Angelica's family history, should Sasha be concerned about forming such an attachment with her? Why or why not?

3. What strategies would you suggest that Sasha use to help develop a strong attachment when Angelica is able to come to school?

■ QUESTIONS AND EXPERIENCES FOR REFLECTION _____

1. Copy the Developmental Profile Form in Appendix B and assess one infant and one toddler by establishing a complete profile for each using the Developmental Prescriptions in Appendix A.

2. Observe two children and take notes on the behaviors they exhibit during the period of one hour. Use the Developmental Prescriptions in Appendix A to determine a functional age for their behaviors.

3. Using the Developmental Prescriptions in Appendix A, task-analyze (write up the small steps) how you would help move a child's behavior from one developmental level to the next. For example, determine how you can help an infant move from "moves arms randomly" to "reaches" with arms.

4. Using the Developmental Prescriptions in Appendix A, work with one child to move him or her from one developmental level to the next for a particular behavior.

■ CHAPTER REVIEW

1. List differences between a *Developmental Perspective* and the tabula rasa theory of development.

2. Describe why needs at one level must be met before an infant or toddler can move to the next higher level.

3. Compare the behavior of two toddlers of the same age in the Social Area (one on one and in a group).

4. Image that you are working with a group of younger toddlers and that two of them have identified special needs. Explain each of their chacteristics and what you would need to consider when promoting their development.

■ REFERENCES

Acredolo, L. P., & Goodwyn, S. (2000). *Baby minds: Brain-building games your baby will love.* New York: Bantam Books.

Acredolo, L. P., & Goodwyn, S., with Douglas Abrams. (2002). *Baby signs: How to talk with your baby before your baby can talk* (Rev. ed.). Chicago: Contemporary Books.

Ainsworth, M. D. S. (1967). *Infancy in Uganda: Infant care and the growth of love.* Baltimore: Johns Hopkins University Press.

Ainsworth, M. D. S. (1973). The development of infant-mother attachment. In B. M. Caldwell & H. N. Ricciuti (Eds.), *Review of child development research: Vol. 3. Child development and social policy.* Chicago: University of Chicago Press.

American Psychiatric Association. (2000). *Diagnostic and statistical manual of mental disorders* (4th ed., text revision). Washington, DC: Author.

Baron, N. S. (1992). *Growing up with language: How children learn to talk.* Reading, MA: Addison-Wesley.

Behrend, D. A., Rosengran, K. S., & Perlmutter, M. (1992). The relation between private speech and parental interactive style. In R. M. Diaz & L. E. Berk (Eds.), *Private speech: From social interaction to self-regulation* (pp. 85–100). Hillsdale, NJ: Erlbaum.

Beilin, H. (1992). Piaget's enduring contribution to developmental psychology. *Developmental Psychology, 28,* 191–204.

Belsky, J., Rovine, M., & Taylor, D. G. (1984). The Pennsylvania Infant and Family Development Project, part 3. The origins of individual differences in infant-mother attachments: Maternal and infant contributions. *Child Development, 55,* 718–728.

Berk, L. E. (1994). Why children talk to themselves. *Scientific American, 271*(5), 78–83.

Berk, L. E. (2000). *Child development* (5th ed.). Boston: Allyn and Bacon.

Berk, L. E., & Spuhl, S. T. (1995). Maternal interaction, private speech, and task performance in preschool children. *Early Childhood Research Quarterly, 10,* 145–169.

Berk, L. E., & Winsler, A. (1995). *NAEYC Research into Practice Series: Vol. 7. Scaffolding children's learning: Vygotsky and early childhood education.* Washington, DC: National Association for the Education of Young Children.

Bodrova, E., & Leong, D. J. (1996). *Tools of the mind: The Vygotskian approach to early childhood education.* Upper Saddle River, NJ: Merrill Prentice Hall.

Bowlby, J. (2000). *Attachment and loss: Vol. 1. Attachment.* New York: Basic Books. (Original work published 1969).

Bullock, M., & Lutkenhaus, P. (1990). Who am I? The development of self-understanding in toddlers. *Merrill-Palmer Quarterly, 36,* 217–238.

Diaz, R. M., & Berk, L. E. (1995). A Vygotskian critique of self-instructional training. *Development and Psychopathology, 7,* 369–392.

Douville-Watson, L. (1988). *Family actualization through research and education: F. A. R. E.* (3rd ed.). New York: Actualization, Inc.

Eliot, L. (1999). *What's going on in there? How the brain and mind develop in the first five years of life.* New York: Bantam Books.

Erikson, E. H. (1950). *Childhood and society.* New York: Norton.

Gunnar, M. R. (2001). The role of glucocorticoids in anxiety disorders: A critical analysis. In M. W. Vasey & M. R. Dadds (Eds.), *The developmental psychopathology of anxiety* (pp. 143–159). New York: Oxford University Press.

Gunnar, M. G., & Cheatham, C. L. (2003). Brain and behavior interface: Stress and the developing brain. *Infant Mental Health Journal, 24*(3), 195–211.

Guralnick, M. J., & Bennett, F. C. (Eds.). (1987). *The effectiveness of early intervention for at-risk and handicapped children.* San Diego: Academic Press.

Hardman, M. L., Drew, C. J., & Egan, M. W. (2005). *Human exceptionality: School, community, and family* (8th ed.). Boston: Allyn and Bacon.

Herr, J., & Swim, T. J. (2002). *Creative resources for infants and toddlers* (2nd ed.). Clifton Park, NY: Thomson Delmar Learning.

Hesse, E., & Main, M. (2000). Disorganized infant, child, and adult attachment: Collapse in behavior and attachment strategies. *Journal of Psychoanalytic Association, 48*(4).

Honig, A. S. (2002). *Secure relationships: Nurturing infant/toddler attachment in early care settings.* Washington, DC: National Association for the Education of Young Children.

Isabella, R. A. (1993). Origins of attachment: Maternal interactive behavior across the first year. *Child Development, 64,* 605–621.

Isabella, R. A., & Belsky, J. (1991). Interactional synchrony and the origins of infant-mother attachment: A replication study. *Child Development, 62,* 373–384.

Johnson, M. H. (1999). Developmental neuroscience. In M. H. Bornstein & M. E. Lamb (Eds.), *Developmental psychology: An advanced textbook* (4th ed.). Mahwah, NJ: Erlbaum.

Johnson, N. M., Jens, K. G., Attermeier, S. M., & Hacker, B. J. (1991). *The Carolina curriculum for infants and toddlers with special needs* (2nd ed.). Baltimore: Paul H. Brookes.

Levine, L. E. (1983). Mine: Self-definition in 2-year-old boys. *Developmental Psychology, 19,* 544–549.

Lillard, A. S. (1993). Pretend play skills and the child's theory of mind. *Child Development, 64,* 348–371.

Lupien, S. J., & McEwen, B. S. (1997). The acute effects of corticosteroids on cognition: Integration of animal and human model studies. *Brain Research Review, 24,* 1–27.

Main, M., & Solomon, J. (1990). Procedures for identifying infants as disorganized/disoriented during the Ainsworth Strange Situation. In M. T. Greenberg, D. Cicchetti, & E. M. Cummings (Eds.), *Attachment in the preschool years.* Chicago: University of Chicago Press.

McCarton, C. (1994). An interview with a child. Bronx, NY: Beth Israel Hospital Information Center.

McDevitt, T. M., & Ormrod, J. E. (2007). *Child development: Educating and working with children and adolescents* (3rd ed.). Upper Saddle River, NJ: Pearson Prentice Hall.

Nash, J. (1997, February 3). Fertile minds: How a child's brain develops and what it means for child care and welfare reform [Special report]. *Time, 149*(5), 48–56.

NICHD Early Child Care Research Network. (1997). The effects of infant chid care on infant-mother attachment security: Results of the NICHD study of early child care. *Child Development, 68,* 860–879.

Odom, S.L., Teferra, T., & Kaul, S. (2004). An overview of international approaches to early intervention for young children with special needs and their families. *Young Children, 59*(5), 38–43.

Oppenheim, D., & Koren-Karie, N. (2002). Mothers' insightfulness regarding their children's internal worlds: The capacity underlying secure child-mother relationships. *Infant Mental Health Journal, 23,* 593–605.

Pipp, S., Easterbrooks, M. A., & Brown, S. R. (1993). Attachment status and complexity of infants' self- and other-knowledge when tested with mother and father. *Social Development, 2,* 1–14.

Puckett, M. B., & Black, J. K. (2002). *Student enrichment series: Infant development.* Upper Saddle River, NJ: Pearson Prentice Hall.

Rast, M., & Meltzoff, A. N. (1995). Memory and representation in young children with Down syndrome: Exploring deferred imitation and object permanence. *Development and Psychopathology, 7,* 393–407.

Rogoff, B., & Chavajay, P. (1995). What's become of research on the cultural basis of cognitive development? *American Psychologist, 50,* 859–877.

Shore, R. (2003). *Rethinking the brain: New insights into early development* (2nd ed.). New York: Families and Work Institute.

Snow, C. W. (1998). *Infant development* (2nd ed.). Upper Saddle River, NJ: Prentice Hall.

Sroufe, L. A. (1996). *The organization of emotional life in the early years.* Cambridge Studies in Social and Educational Development. New York: Cambridge University Press.

Thompson, R. A. (1998). Early sociopersonality development. In W. Damon (Editor-in-Chief) & N. Eisenberg (Vol. Ed.), *Handbook of child psychology: Vol. 3. Social, emotional, and personality development* (5th ed.). New York: Wiley.

Vygotsky, L. S. (1986). *Thought and language* (A. Kozulin, Trans.). Cambridge, MA: MIT Press. (Original work published 1934).

Watson, L. R., Baranek, G. T., & DiLavore, P. C. (2003). Toddlers with autism: Developmental perspectives. *Infants and Young Children, 16*(3), 201–214.

Watson, M. A. (1977). *Tests of group learning skills. Experimental edition.* Freeport, NY: Activity Records.

Watson, M. A. (1995). *WALDO developmental learning program.* Glen Cove, NY: Instructional Press.

Wink, J., & Putney, L. (2002). *A vision of Vygotsky.* Boston: Allyn & Bacon.

■ ADDITIONAL RESOURCES

Craik, F. I. M., & Tulving, E. (1975). Depth of processing and the retention of words in episodic memory. *Journal of Experimental Psychology: General, 104,* 268–294.

James, W. (1963). *Psychology.* New York: Fawcett. (Original work published 1890).

National Down Syndrome Society. (2001). *About Down syndrome.* New York: Author.

Stray-Gunderson, K. (1995). *Babies with Down syndrome.* Rockville, MD: Woodbine House.

■ HELPFUL WEB SITES

American Academy of Pediatrics (AAP). http://www.aap.org

American Psychological Association (APA). A wealth of information regarding psychology in all areas of inquiry. http://www.apa.org

American Speech-Language-Hearing Association. Hearing Treatment and Rehabilitation. Rockville, MD. This site provides a directory of audiologists and speech pathologists. http://www.asha.org/default.htm

Association for the Help of Retarded Children (AHRC). http://www.ahrc.org

Association for Psychological Science (APS). Schedules for conventions, teaching, research, and other information. http://www.psychologicalscience.org

The Creative Curriculum. Developed by Teaching Strategies, Inc., this curriculum focuses on how children learn, what children learn, the parent's role, the teacher/provider's role, and the physical environment. The curriculum can be matched to Head Start performance standards and CDA credential requirements. http://www.teachingstrategies.com/index.cfm

Frank Porter Graham Child Development Institute. Provides teachers and parents with educational resources for specific age groups including infants, one-year-olds, and two-year-olds, as well as children with special needs. http://www.fpg.unc.edu

Mayo Clinic. A wealth of information on a number of health-related issues. You can search the site for information on various topics such as sickle cell anemia. http://www.mayoclinic.com

Nanny's Place for Parents. Resources for parents-to-be and parents of small children and infants. http://www .moonlilly.com/parents/

National Center for Hearing Assessment and Management. http://www.infanthearing.org/

Psych Web. Psychology-related information for students and teachers of psychology. http://www.psychwww.com

United Cerebral Palsy. The leading resource on cerebral palsy. Phone: (800) 872-5827. http://www.ucp.org

For additional infant and toddler resources, visit our Web site at http://www.earlychilded.delmar.com

3

Birth to Thirty-six Months: Developmental Patterns

After reading this chapter, you should be able to:

- Define the differences between development and learning.
- Identify typical patterns of physical, emotional, social, and cognitive development between birth and thirty-six months of age.
- Understand how the development of each child differs from typical patterns of development.

DIFFERENCES BETWEEN DEVELOPMENT AND LEARNING

As with many unresolved questions in child development, entire books are written on the nature versus nurture controversy. Many authors contend that child development is the result of heredity and natural biological processes that are largely independent of learning and experience (nature), whereas many others argue that development mostly depends on learning (nurture) (Plomin, 1994). The best conclusion to date is that child development is a very complex process occurring through natural sequences and patterns that depend on learning and experience, among other processes (Berk, 2000; McDevitt and Ormrod, 2004).

For purposes of this book, **development** is operationally defined as general sequences and patterns of growth and maturity. Learning is only one process involved in development. Development follows a generally predictable sequence of behaviors that mark change from dependency on the environment to independence from the environment. To track development, specific behaviors common to an entire population are observed when they are first manifested or are consistently manifested. These behaviors are called **milestones**. We measure development of an individual child by comparing milestone behaviors with the large group that was used to establish what behavior is "normal" for that age.

Children grow in four major developmental areas in the same general sequences and patterns, yet each child is affected differently by social, cultural, and environmental influences. Children move through these developmental sequences at widely varying rates. The rate of development for each individual is dependent on many factors, including environmental experiences, culture, heredity, metabolism, and nutrition (Berk, 2000).

A major goal of this book is to help caregivers understand normal sequences and patterns of development and to become familiar with learning tools that enhance development in the four major developmental areas. To this end, the Developmental Prescriptions in Appendix A present general patterns of development from birth through three years of age and the construction of Developmental Profiles (Appendix B) provides a visual basis for understanding the development of individual children.

To fully understand the learning tools presented throughout this book, teachers must have a clear understanding of what is meant by learning. For purposes of this book, the authors define **learning** as long-term change in response to a stimulus resulting from practice or conscious awareness. This definition takes into consideration both overt behavioral changes in responses and more internal changes in perceptions resulting from practice or conscious awareness, or both. In other words, changes in a response to a stimulus can either be observable to another person (overt) or can occur internally without obvious change in observable behavior (internal). Much of the learning that occurs during the first three years of life is this internal type. Therefore, caregivers must consistently observe the child very carefully to understand how changes in responses create the perceptions, thoughts, beliefs, attitudes, feelings, and behaviors that constitute the young child's evolving map of the world. Since no two individuals have the same map of the world, the biggest challenge for early childhood specialists is to understand developmental patterns and determine how each child differs from expected patterns.

THE PART-WHOLE RELATIONSHIP

This chapter extends the theories, concepts, and principles presented in Chapters 1 and 2 to better understand the whole child. A necessary aspect of studying child development is to analyze the child's essential skills, abilities, and factors that must be understood individually before assembling them into a more meaningful and understandable whole. Patterns of development are discussed in each of four major Developmental Areas in this chapter: Physical, Emotional, Social, and Cognitive. Then, the integration of these four factors is discussed in terms of child behaviors and the interactions between children, caregivers, and family members. Once individual parts are understood, early childhood educators can apply the knowledge to competently care for the whole, living, breathing, and constantly changing child.

From the moment of birth, the child and the people around the child affect each other. This dynamic interaction is sometimes deliberate and controlled and sometimes unconscious behavior. Caregivers working with infants and toddlers plan many experiences for children. Simultaneous with these planned experiences are the thousands of actions that are spontaneous, that stimulate new actions and reactions and challenge both the child and the caregiver (Figure 3–1).

FIGURE 3–1   Children interact spontaneously with one another.

Magda Gerber (e.g., Gerber & Weaver, 1998) has established an approach and structure for child care that emphasizes the interaction between child and caregiver. This approach is illustrated through her "10 principles of caregiving."

1. Involve children in activities and things that concern them.
2. Invest in quality time with each child.
3. Learn the unique ways each child communicates with you and teach him or her the way you communicate.
4. Invest in the time and energy necessary with each child to build a total person.
5. Respect infants and toddlers as worthy people.
6. Model specific behaviors before you teach them.
7. Always be honest with children about your feelings.
8. View problems as learning opportunities and allow children to solve their own problems where possible.
9. Build security with children by teaching trust.
10. Be concerned about the quality of development each child has at each stage.

PATTERNS OF DEVELOPMENT IN FOUR MAJOR AREAS

In psychological assessments, human skills and abilities are separated into four major areas for evaluation. This evaluation structure provides an excellent format for understanding the development of infants and toddlers. Throughout this book, child development and care are discussed in terms of the following four major developmental areas in order:

1. physical factors
2. emotional factors
3. social factors
4. cognitive and language factors

At birth and even earlier, infants are already developing and learning. They are actively involved with themselves and the world. The child constantly interacts with the world, making adjustments in actions as information is processed and organized. When teachers understand their role and the interaction between development, learning, and experience, they can determine the child's present level of development, his or her potential next step, and the specific areas in which the child needs help. In other words, caregivers determine the children's zone of proximal development, which serves as the basis for high-quality care.

Physical Development

Physical development includes neurological, gross physical, sensory, teething, motor, and sleep and elimination development. Each of these is discussed below.

Neurological Development

The nervous system is responsible for communication among all body parts and ultimately with the environment. This section defines and familiarizes the reader with the major nervous system functions. Newborns are complex beings whose growth and development is closely related to the health and integrity of the nervous system, which is made up of the brain, the spinal cord, and nerve cells (neurons).

By the end of the eighth week of pregnancy the foundation for all body structures, including the brain and nervous system, is evident in the growing fetus. Nerve cells (neurons) store and transmit information. At birth the brain is packed with an estimated 100 billion neurons, many of which die due to lack of stimulation. However, each surviving neuron can make over 10,000 different connections to other cells over time (Beatty, 1995). Pathways and networks of neurons are formed that carry coded information from all body parts to the brain. The lower brain, called the brain stem, is the seat of emotion. The midbrain is responsible for regulating automatic functions, such as breathing, digestion, and alertness. Another part of the brain, called the cerebellum, regulates coordination and balance.

The cerebral cortex is what distinguishes our species as human. Considered the most important part of the brain, it is the slowest-growing and largest part of the brain. The cerebral cortex begins at around 12 months to organize and specify functions for neuron activity. Other parts of the brain continue to grow rapidly only through the second year of life, whereas the cerebral cortex continues to grow until the fourth decade of life. The nervous system is the "command center" for all the vital functions of the body.

At birth, the brain weighs 25 percent of an adult's, and by 24 months it has tripled its weight, being 75 percent of an adult's. This increased weight is due to specific brain cells, called glia, which consist of a fatty sheathing called myelin. Myelin is a substance that protects, coats, and insulates neurons, helping connect impulses from one neuron to another. These impulses are coded information lines that function like insulated electrical wires, carrying vital current to where it is needed in the body and brain. The myelin coating promotes the transfer of information from one neuron to another. It is a scientific fact and the basis of much study that neurons require environmental stimulation in order to grow. This fact is also of great importance for you—the parent, grandparent, teacher, guardian, or caregiver. It has been demonstrated that physiological changes occur within the nervous system of the child as he or she processes environmental information. Your individual input controls much of the information registering within the actual nerve cells of the child. Appropriate and meaningful contact with infants by the caregiver is vital to continued overall neurological growth.

As previously stated, the cerebral cortex is the largest structure of the brain and continues to grow well into adulthood. The cerebral cortex receives stimuli in the form of sensory information. Associations are formed between the thought processes and physical actions. Specific areas of the cerebral cortex control special functions, such as vision, hearing, and motor movement. Neurological development of these specialized areas follows a particular pattern as the development of the child progresses. Milestones for motor movement such as sitting, crawling, and standing are controlled by the cortex, and the cortex develops control of the head and chest before the trunk and legs.

To be a competent caregiver for infants and toddlers, it is important to recognize the impact you have on the child's neurological growth and to initiate activities that reinforce the natural sequences of behaviors that support healthy growth in all areas. You, the child's caregiver, directly affect neurological growth through the activities and interactions you provide during the first months and years of life. Caregivers have an enormously important opportunity to influence the basic structure of the child's developing neurological systems by presenting positive, appropriate activities to enhance growth and development (Herr & Swim, 2002).

Physical Growth

The brain grows from the inside out. The size of the head doesn't change as drastically as the weight of the head (i.e., the head weighs three times more at age two than at birth). This weight is caused by the growing density of the brain, due to developing neuron pathways. Motor neuron pathways apparently expect specific stimuli at birth. These pathways are called **experience-expectant**. The environment provides expected stimuli; for example, reflex sucking during breast-feeding is experience-expectant. Infant survival obviously depends on experience-expectant pathways. Another set of neuron pathways, called **experience-dependent**, seems to wait for new experience before activation. Specific experience-dependent cells form synapses for stable motor patterns only after environmental stimuli are repeated several times. When stimulation from the environment occurs in a consistent way, a stable pathway is created and physical changes occur in the nervous system. One of the human brain's greatest assets is this ability to change neurologically and behaviorally from experience, allowing us our unique flexibility and adaptability to the environment.

Human babies are different from any other species because they cannot stand immediately after birth and so cannot get themselves out of harm's way. However, the gestation process results in a complete person because if it took any longer, the head would be too big to safely complete delivery. The newborn's head is the largest part of the body and is usually born first. The circumference of the head increases by about three inches during the first eight months, and by two years of age the head is 90 percent of adult size (Lamb & Campos, 1982). At birth, the baby's head is not fused but has "soft spots" in the front and back. The back soft spot closes after a few months, but the front spot stays soft for almost two years.

Reflexes are the beginnings of more complex behavior. As the cerebral cortex develops rapidly in the first weeks of life, reflexes quickly change from involuntary reactions to purposeful, intentional actions that support the growing child over time.

Children usually gain body weight at an astounding rate during the first 12 months of life as long as they are physically nurtured and active, but children who are restrained from physical movement often gain weight at a slower rate. Height usually parallels weight, so children who gain weight slowly in the first three years also tend to grow in height slowly. The caregiver should be aware that there are large variations in the rate of physical growth in children under three years of age. Growth spurts and plateaus are normal for development of height, weight, activity levels, and so on, so the caregiver should keep careful records of physical milestones and consult with parents and health professionals on body development.

Hearing and Vision Development

Newborns respond to a range of sounds. They startle easily with sudden loud noises and become agitated at high-pitched noises. They turn their heads to locate sound and show interest in their caregivers' voices. Infants explore their own utterings and use their bodies and toys to play with sound.

Infants use their eyes from birth, although their vision develops relatively slowly. By the fourth month, coordination of both eyes can be observed. Four-month-old infants demonstrated looking preferences that were similar to adult preferences when given simple visual, black and white displays (Chien, Palmer, & Teller, 2005). They focus well with both eyes at a distance of 12 inches, which is the normal distance for breast-feeding. By age two, vision is around 20/80; full 20/20 acuity is not expected until they reach school age.

Teething

Infants usually begin growing teeth between four and eight months, but individuals vary widely in teething. New teeth erupt every month or so after the first one. Sometimes an emerging tooth causes an infant to be very fussy and irritable, while at other times a new tooth just seems to appear with no discomfort at all. Contrary to popular belief, diarrhea, fever, and other symptoms are not caused by teething (Nowak, 2002), so alert the family if these symptoms occur. Teething infants often drool profusely and like to bite things, using teething rings and anything else they can put in their mouths. When an infant seems to be in pain from teething, a cold teething ring provides both coldness and hardness for the child's gums. Never rub gums with an alcohol substance to relieve discomfort, and contact a dentist or medical specialist if pain persists.

The average age for having all 20 baby teeth is around 24 months. According to Nicolas Johniditis, D.D.S., "Parents and caregivers should treat a child's first teeth with great care because the mouth is growing and first teeth create space for second teeth. Good oral hygiene and dental practice like regular brushing and check-ups from the dentist can prevent unnecessary difficulty with second teeth" (2000).

Motor Development

One theory of motor development, called the dynamic systems theory, predicts that individual behaviors and skills of the growing infant combine and work together to create a more efficient and effective system. "Kicking, rocking on all fours, and reaching gradually are put together in crawling. Then, crawling, standing, and stepping are united into walking alone" (Hofsten, 1989). "Each skill is learned by revising and combining earlier accomplishments to fit a new goal. Consequently, different pathways to the same outcome exist, and infants achieve motor milestones in unique ways" (Berk, 1998).

Physical development occurs in a predictable order, starting from the head and chest and moving to the trunk and lower extremities. This directional growth is readily observable as the infant gains control of head, chest, trunk, and then legs to turn over. To crawl, the infant gains control of lower back and leg muscles; to walk, the infant gains

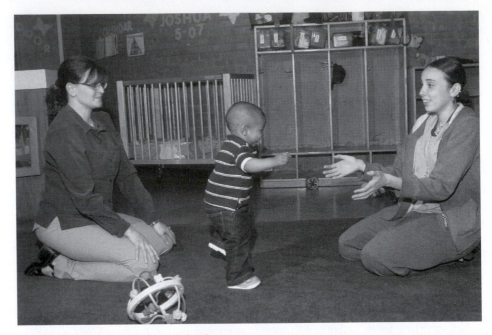

Walking is a milestone of physical development.

control of neck, shoulders, back, legs, feet, and toes. Infants develop control of their arm movements from erratic waving to accurate reaching. Hand control develops from accidentally bumping and hitting to purposefully touching. Reaching occurs first, with an open hand grip. Then the fingers develop, from reflexive pinching, grasping, and reflexive releasing to controlled opening and closing. Physical development involves both large movements, or **gross motor control**, and small muscle activity, **fine motor control**. Three areas of movement that are developed over the first three years are (1) stability, (2) locomotion, and (3) manipulation. *Stability* refers to sitting and standing upright; *locomotion* refers to crawling, walking, and running; and *manipulation* includes reaching, grasping, releasing, and throwing.

Gross motor development involves large movements through milestone achievements, such as crawling, standing, walking, and throwing. Fine motor development milestones involve smaller, more refined movements, like grasping and pointing. The progression of motor development is fairly uniform, but individual children vary within and between cultures in the age at which they develop both gross and fine motor skills. Milestones of development are essential for teachers to know. One of the teacher's most important tasks is to identify children who are not reaching the milestone markers within a specific range of time. Teachers should seek further professional assistance only when several motor skill areas are developmentally delayed.

Appendix A provides a somewhat detailed Developmental Prescription of motor skill milestones for infants through three years of age. At around six weeks of age, children begin to hold their heads steady and erect. By two months, infants lift their upper bodies by their arms and can roll from side to back. From three to four months, babies begin grasping palm-size objects and can roll from back to side. From six to eight months, they can sit alone and begin to crawl. Between eight and ten months, babies pull up to stand and perhaps play patty cake. At this time they begin to stand alone, and then begin to walk. From 13 to 16 months, children can build a tower of two cubes, vigorously scribble with a large crayon, and begin to walk with help upstairs. At around 20 to 24 months, toddlers begin to jump in place and kick objects. By 26 to 30 months, children begin to climb, stand on one foot, and have some interest in toilet learning. Usually at around 36 months, the child can jump and independently use the toilet.

As this general outline indicates, motor development is a progression from one milestone behavior to the next, based on successful integration of the previous behaviors and neurological maturity resulting from environmental experiences. Children who develop within the average range do not necessarily proceed through all of the developmental milestones or move in the exact sequence outlined in a specific Developmental Prescription. The challenge for the caregiver is to observe behavioral milestones and determine where individual children fall on the general scale of motor development. The caregiver should use a Developmental Prescription, perform careful observations of behavioral milestones, and clearly determine each child is compared to the normal expectations for the age range. By performing evaluations on a regular basis, caregivers can determine a child's areas of motor development that require specific tasks and activities to enhance development and areas in which he or she shows advanced development in motor skills.

Sleep and Elimination Development

The stages of sleep and wakefulness are described as states. A *state* is an organized pattern of physical responses that relates to arousal levels. A state can last minutes, many hours, or even years. Changing a young child's state from crying or sleeping to being calm or fully alert can be difficult at times because states are relatively stable in young children. The following states of arousal have been defined and carefully studied in young children (Wolff, 1993; Zeskind & Marshall, 1991):

Quiet sleep. Respirations are regular, eyes are closed and not moving, and the child is relatively motionless.

Active sleep. Muscles are more tense than in quiet sleep, the eyes may be still or display rapid eye movements (REM), breathing is irregular, and there are spontaneous startles, sucks, and rhythmic bursts of movement.

Drowsiness. Eyes open and close and there is increased activity, more rapid and regular breathing, and occasional smiling.

Quiet alert. Eyes are open, scanning the environment, the body is still, and respiration is more rapid than in sleep.

Active alert. The child is awake and has body and limb movements, although the child is less likely to attend to external stimulation and focuses eyes less often than in the quiet alert state.

Crying. Activity and respiration rate are elevated, and the child exhibits cry vocalization and a facial expression of distress.

Newborns sleep an average of 16 to 17 hours per day. Sleep periods range from two to ten hours. By three to four months, infants regularly sleep more at night than during the day, but night awakenings are common throughout infancy and early childhood (Anders, Goodlin-Jones, & Zelenko, 1998; Kleitman, 1963). Assist very young children with transitioning from waking to sleeping. Do so by providing dimmed light and quiet, soft voice tones. Hold and rock the child before she goes to sleep and make every effort to reduce stimulation. Then, because of the risk of sudden infant death syndrome, place the baby on her back on a firm mattress. *Do not* let the child sleep with a bottle.

A condition in which breathing momentarily stops is called sleep apnea (Hofsten, 1989). Short periods of apnea are normal during active (i.e., REM) sleep, but with some children these episodes are prolonged and more frequent. Infrequently, sleep apnea can become dangerous to a person's health because the period of not breathing becomes too long. Some research suggests that **sudden infant death syndrome (SIDS)** may be related to sleep apnea. SIDS is a tragic event in which a young child dies after going to sleep for a nap or at bedtime with no indication of having discomfort. Research on apnea in infants indicates that the baby's brain is not mature and therefore periods of instability occur. Since young children spend extensive periods in REM sleep, the instability of the nervous system may cause such extended apnea that the child stops breathing completely (Beatty, 1995). The incidence of SIDS is very low (two infants per 1000 births between one week and one year of age), but the American Academy of Pediatrics has found that infants who are placed on their backs to sleep have a lower incidence of SIDS (Stokes, 2001). As long as the child is awake and closely supervised, however, belly lying should be encouraged to develop chest muscles, which are important for normal development.

As children become more mobile and begin to crawl and walk, their sleep patterns change and they require less sleep. Children should still be encouraged to rest every day, and a well-planned child care program provides nap times that meet the individual needs for children under three years of age. A balance of structured physical activity and rest is essential for optimal physical and emotional development and growth.

Some babies accomplish toilet learning as early as six months of age, but there appears to be a moderate correlation between early forced bowel and bladder training and later emotional problems (Berk, 2000). The muscles that control bowel and bladder, called sphincter muscles, are usually not mature until after 18 months of age. Toilet learning requires the child to become aware of the sensations of the sphincter muscles and to control them until the appropriate time, when he or she relaxes the muscles to eliminate. This awareness first happens with larger muscles; control usually occurs first with bowel movements at around 24 months of age. However, children frequently do not learn to use the toilet independently until after three years of age. In fact, a child must be over four years old to be diagnosed as having encopresis, which is lack of bowel control, and must be over five years old to be diagnosed with enuresis, which is the inability to control urination (American Psychiatric Association, 1994).

When children are ready to start toilet learning, they practically teach themselves, with a little guidance and encouragement. The best approach to toilet learning is to provide specific feedback on success and avoid punishing or shaming for mistakes. The child should participate as much as possible for his or her age in cleaning up when mistakes are made. When you act as if a simple mistake was made, the child realizes that he or she can come to you for assistance.

Children frequently do not learn to use the toilet independently until after three years of age.

Diapers should always be changed when wet. With young children, it is common to have seven or eight changes within a 12-hour period. Some children may have several bowel movements per day, while others may have only one. If a child does not have a bowel movement each day, the family should be notified because constipation can be a problem in some cases. Diarrhea can also be a problem because of the possibility of rapid dehydration. As with other areas of physical development, accurate daily records should be kept on elimination and shared with parents. It is important to recognize that the child's family members are your partners in toilet learning.

All human relationships are bound to involve conflicts and disagreements. Toilet learning is an area ripe for such conflicts because it is accompanied by such a great deal of variability in cultural beliefs (Gonzalez-Mena, 2001; Gonzalez-Mena & Eyer, 2007). Cultural groups and individual families within those groups often have strong beliefs about when and how to assist with toilet learning. One family will start toilet learning at one year of age and another will wait until the child is "ready," while still another may not provide any formal assistance until the child is four years of age. None of these perspectives on timing is definitively correct or incorrect; they just reflect different belief systems. As a parent, member of a cultural group, and/or a teacher, you have beliefs about toileting also. Open communication and respectful listening are the beginning steps in addressing cultural conflicts, but they are not enough. You must be clear about your own views and the philosophy of the program so that you can truly listen and work toward solutions with the families. Issues like toilet learning will not be resolved in one conversation. Sustained dialogue is necessary for resolving the conflict (Gonzalez-Mena, 2001).

Emotional Development

Unlike most other warm-blooded species, human infants are totally dependent on the environment to supply their most basic needs. For independent physical survival, children are born nine months too soon because they require assistance for that amount of time before they can crawl and move independently within the environment. Therefore, a caregiver needs to create a safe and secure space for the physical and emotional survival of the child. A child should be provided with conscious care; be kept warm, fed, and stress-free; and should have his needs fulfilled quickly. Very young children should be touched, kept close to the chest, talked to, played soft music, and rocked. Children should be provided with appropriate transportation to move from one place to another safely; an ideal device is a baby carrier in which the infant is carried next to the chest.

A safe and secure child care center creates a positive learning atmosphere in which children feel secure in initiating responses to their environment based on interest and curiosity. Children should not be judged because they have great needs (Figure 3–2). When the child's emotional needs are met, he experiences a world that invites his participation.

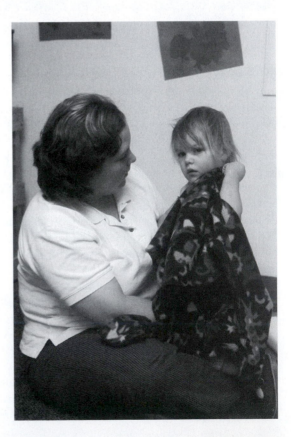

FIGURE 3–2 There are no bad children—only unmet emotional needs.

Evolution of Feelings

The most basic feelings on a physical level are pleasure and pain. It was once thought that newborns experience only these two general feeling states. However, anyone who has extensively cared for a young infant understands that infants experience and express the full range of human emotion from ecstasy to deep sorrow. Through active experience with their environment, babies quickly learn to repeat behaviors that result in pleasurable experiences and avoid, as much as they can, behaviors that result in pain. It sometimes appears that young children move through emotions rapidly. One minute a young toddler may scream, and the next moment jump into your arms and give you a hug. As the child grows older and cognitive and language skills develop, he or she can use words better to specify and describe many different feeling states.

During the first three years of life, the combination of traits present at birth, including physical size, health, and temperament, interact with pleasurable and painful experiences in the environment to form the growing child's personality. This section describes how security, trust, temperament, and bonding versus the process of separation-individuation combine to help form the child's perceptions of self, others, and the world. This model of the world is the basis for the enduring reactions and patterns people have throughout life—what we call personality.

Security and Trust

Positive emotional and behavioral traits can be enhanced by ensuring that the infant or toddler develops security and trust with caregivers. Consistent and appropriate behavior from the caregiver is necessary to provide security for the child. Consistent but inappropriate behavior or inconsistent but appropriate behavior has been shown to be detrimental to the development of security and trust.

The way to ensure consistent and appropriate caregiver behavior with children is to establish consistent routines and supply generous amounts of the three As of child care: Attention, Approval, and Attunement. Consistently responding to the needs of the child with warmth and respect will help develop security and trust in the child. Reading the infant's or toddler's cues as well as being able to take her perspective are necessary components in responsive caregiving (Oppenheim & Koren-Karie, 2002). Security develops largely from consistent responses to specific behaviors, and trust develops largely from acceptance and appreciation of the child (Greenspan & Pollock, 1989). This is reflected in policies that ensure a low infant:caregiver ratio. Early childhood educators need to be available to respond to the many needs of each dependent infant or toddler.

Children need reasonable expectations. To have these reasonable expectations you need to know (1) normal patterns of development and (2) each child's individual pattern of development. Because the sequence of development is similar among children, you have some guidelines for your expectations. A caregiver needs to know where each child fits within the range of development (Figure 3–3). If you expect children to accomplish things that are below or above them developmentally, you produce undue stress. For example, you can expect 30-month-old Mark to be able to hold a spoon in his hand, fill it with food, and usually get it up to his mouth. It is unreasonable

FIGURE 3–3   Children who feel secure are free to explore.

to expect nine-month-old Naomi to have that level of muscular coordination. Use of Developmental Prescriptions and Profiles is important. Consistent updating of developmental steps helps children establish security and trust, because they meet with success, mastery, and the three *A*s rather than stress, frustration, and rejection.

Young children's temperaments, feelings of self-esteem, and coping skills are important factors in their emotional development.

Temperament

Temperament has been defined as "the basic style which characterizes a person's behavior" (Chess, Thomas, & Birch, 1976). All children are born with particular temperaments. Temperament will influence what they do, what they learn, what they feel about themselves and others, and what kinds of interactions they have with people and objects.

Until recently research has suggested that temperament is stable and not very changeable by environmental influences (Kagan, Reznick, & Gibbons, 1989; Caspi & Silva, 1995). However, a growing body of research strongly suggests that child-rearing practices and other environmental factors can dramatically influence temperament

TABLE 3–1   BEHAVIORAL CATEGORIES OF TEMPERAMENT

BEHAVIORAL CATEGORY	EXTREMES	
	MORE	LESS
(1) Activity Level	Hyperactive—can't sit still	Lethargic—sedate, passive
(2) Regularity	Rigid and inflexible patterns	Unpredictable and inconsistent patterns
(3) Response to New Situations	Outgoing, aggressive, approaching	Withdrawing, timid, highly cautious
(4) Adaptability	Likes surprises, fights routine, dislikes structure	Dislikes change, likes routine, needs structure
(5) Sensory Threshold	Unaware of changes in light, sound, smell	Highly sensitive to changes in light, sound, smell
(6) Positive or Negative Mood	Feels optimistic	Feels negative; denies positive
(7) Response Intensity	Highly loud and animated, high energy	Highly quiet and soft; low energy
(8) Distractibility	Insensitive to visual and auditory stimuli outside self	Unable to focus attention, highly sensitive to visual and auditory stimuli
(9) Persistence	Persists until task completed	Gives up easily, doesn't try new things

during the first three years (Gunnar, 1998; Rubin, Hastings, Stewart, Henderson, & Chen, 1997).

Chess, Thomas, and Birch (1977) worked with hundreds of children and their parents to investigate how babies differ in their styles of behavior. The analysis of observations and interviews revealed nine patterns of behavior. Within each pattern they found a range of behaviors. Table 3–1 lists the nine categories and extremes of behaviors observed in each category. The behavior of most people falls somewhere between these extremes. Chess and her colleagues further collapsed the nine patterns into three basic types of temperament: flexible and easy, slow to warm up, and difficult.

The following descriptions further illustrate the extremes of some of these patterns.

ACTIVITY LEVEL. Ryan runs into the room, yells "Hi," and goes to the blocks. He stacks them quickly, they fall down, and he stacks them again and leaves them as they tumble down. He walks over to stand by Melba, the caregiver, who is reading a picture book to another child. Ryan listens a few minutes and then moves on to another activity. Ryan has a high activity level. He has always been very active. He kicked and waved and rolled a lot when he was a baby. His body needs to move. He becomes very distressed when he is physically confined with a seat belt in the car or must sit quietly.

Benjamin sits quietly on the floor playing with nesting cans. He stacks the cans and then fits them inside each other. He accomplishes his task with few movements: his legs remain outstretched; his body is leaning forward slightly but remains mostly still; he has the cans close to him so his arms and hands need to move only slightly. Benjamin has a low activity level. He was a quiet baby, not kicking his blankets off or twisting and turning often. He becomes distressed when he has to rush around to put away toys or quickly get ready to go somewhere.

APPROACH OR WITHDRAWAL AS A CHARACTERISTIC RESPONSE TO A NEW SITUATION. Jamol hides behind his mother as he enters the room each morning. He hides behind the caregiver whenever someone strange walks in the door. When others play with a new ball, he stands by the wall and watches. He leaves food he does not recognize on his plate, refusing to take a bite. Jamol is slow to warm up. He needs time to get used to new situations. Jamol is distressed when he is pushed into new activities. Telling him that a new ball will not hurt him or that the strange food is good for him does not convince him. When he feels comfortable, he will play with the new ball. He needs time and space for himself while he becomes familiar with a situation.

Carlos arrives in the morning with a big smile. He looks around the room and notices a new puzzle set out on the table. He rushes over to it, asking the caregiver about it and giggling at the picture. He takes the puzzle pieces out, puts some of the pieces back in and then seeks assistance from the caregiver. Carlos warms up quickly. He is excited about new situations and eager to try new experiences.

PERSISTENCE AND ATTENTION SPAN. Jesse takes the three puzzle pieces out of the puzzle. He successfully puts in the banana. He picks up the apple piece and tries to fit it into a space. When it does not fit, he drops the piece and leaves the table. Jesse moves on to a new experience when he is not immediately successful.

Clayton takes the three puzzle pieces out of the puzzle. He then turns and pushes and turns and pushes each piece until he has returned all three pieces to their proper places. Clayton persists with an activity even when it may be challenging or frustrating or takes a long time. When he completes his task, he expresses his pleasure with smiles and words.

Identifying each child's temperament as well as your own will help you to be an effective caregiver. Thomas and Chess (1977) suggest that the type of temperament a child has is less important to her overall functioning and development than the temperamental match she has with her caregiver. The adult-child **goodness-of-fit** model has been supported by research with families (Mangelsdorf, Gunnar, Kestenbaum, Lang, & Andreas, 1990; Paterson & Sanson, 1999) and early childhood educators (Churchill, 2003; De Schipper, Tavecchio, Van IJzendoorn, & Van Zeijl, 2004).

Consider the following example: Olaf is playing with blocks. The tall stack he built falls over, one block hitting hard on his hand. He yells loudly. Ray is playing nearby and also is hit by a falling block. He looks up in surprise but does not say anything. What will you as a caregiver do? What will you say? What is *loud* to you?

I did it! I finally made it to the top of the "mountain."

What is acceptable to you? Why is a behavior acceptable or not to you? Do you think Ray is *better* than Olaf because he did not react loudly? What you do and what you say to Olaf reflects your acceptance or rejection of him as a person, reflects whether you are able to help him adapt to his environment, and reflects your ability to adapt to the child.

Franyo & Hyson (1999) found that temperament workshops designed especially for early childhood teachers resulted in their gaining important knowledge about temperament concepts. However, there was no evidence that these workshops effectively increased the caregivers' acceptance of children's behaviors and feelings. Carefully reflecting about your and the children's temperament can assist you with identifying strategies to responsively and respectfully meet the needs of the children who are different from yourself and helping each child have "goodness of fit" with you.

Bonding and Separation-Individuation

A pediatrician from Vienna named Margaret Mahler wrote extensively about the importance of bonding between parent and child and the process called separation-individuation (Greenberg & Mitchell, 1983). Personality development, security, trust, and self-concept are all related to the attachment between infant and caregivers and how separation-individuation from caregivers is conducted and experienced by the child. Mahler's phases of the individuation process are valuable guidelines for caregivers of infants and toddlers to understand identity development. Mahler's four subphases of separation-individuation are as follows:

Subphase	Age
1. differentiation	four months to ten months
2. practicing	10 months to 15 months
3. rapprochement	15 months to 36 months
4. libidinal object constancy	36 months throughout childhood

The *normal autistic phase* occurs during the first few weeks of life, when time spent asleep exceeds time the baby is awake (Mahler, Pine, & Bergman, 1975). At three to four weeks, a maturational crisis occurs, in which the infant shows increased sensitivity to the external world and has a beginning awareness that the primary caregiver is an external object. During this normal symbiotic phase, the baby organizes experiences into good (pleasurable) and bad (painful) memories, which form the basis for identity.

At about four months, the separation-individuation phase begins, with some variations among individuals. From four to ten months, the *differentiation* subphase occurs, in which the baby begins to act in more self-determined ways and explores the caregiver (e.g., pulls hair, clothes). The baby also scans the world and checks back to the caregiver to discriminate "caregiver" from "other." The baby also develops skill in discriminating external from internal sensations. This discrimination forms the basis for self-awareness (self-concept) as opposed to awareness of object (anything other than self, including other people).

Once the baby becomes mobile at around 10 months, the *practicing* subphase begins. Because the baby can now move away from the caregiver, increased body discrimination and awareness of separateness from others manifest themselves. The child begins using the caregiver as an emotional and physical "refueling station"— moving short distances away and then returning for refilling. Think of yourself as a recharging station, a physically and emotionally rewarding place where children feel a sense of security and return again and again for energetic nourishment.

The child becomes excited by the world, the caregiver, and his or her own body and capacities to function. During this phase, the child concentrates on his or her own abilities separate from the caregiver and becomes **omnipotent** (not aware of any physical limitations). According to Mahler and colleagues (1975), the caregiver must be able to allow physical and psychological separation during this phase if the child is to establish a strong identity.

Between 15 and 18 months, the toddler enters the *rapprochement* subphase, where the sense of omnipotence (having no limits) is broken. What is wanted is not always immediately available, so the child experiences frustration, separation anxiety, and the realization that caregivers are separate people who don't always say yes. Often, children will alternate between clinging neediness and intense battling with caregivers at this stage because of these conflicting dependence and independence needs. Because of rapid language development during this period, the child struggles with gender identity, accepting "no," and the development of beliefs, attitudes, and values to add to the already formed self-concept.

Mahler's final subphase of *libidinal object constancy* starts around 36 months and involves developing a stable concept of the self (one that does not change), and a stable concept of other people, places, and things. Self-constancy and object constancy are comparable to Piaget's **object permanence**, the stage at which people and things continue to exist in the child's mind even when they aren't present. During this phase, it is crucial that the caregiver be available as a buffer between the child and the world while supporting and respecting the competencies of the growing child to separate and individuate without anxiety or fear. Three-year-olds truly believe that their make-believe is real. Playing with them with toys and puppets can elicit information from them on how they are doing emotionally.

Emotional Intelligence

Healthy personality development involves more than helping young children recognize their feelings, experience security and trust in others, enhance their positive temperament traits, and establish a healthy balance between attachment and separation-individuation. Daniel Goleman has provided the most concise and comprehensive view to date of the skills necessary for healthy personality development in his book entitled *Emotional Intelligence* (1996). In this book, Goleman reports that the usual way of looking at intelligence as consisting only of cognitive abilities is incomplete. Eighty percent of the skills necessary for life success are determined by what he calls **emotional intelligence**.

From an extensive research review, Goleman defined five *domains* that are learned early in life and are necessary for high emotional intelligence and healthy identity development. Consistent with all five domains, families and caregivers need to trust their basic instincts and use the three As (Attention, Approval, and Attunement) to promote the growth of emotional intelligence. Goleman's five domains are described next.

1. **Knowing one's emotions.** Recognizing a feeling as it happens, or **self-awareness**, is the keystone of emotional intelligence. The caregiver should start helping children at birth to recognize, experience, label, and express their feelings in healthy ways. Moreover, caregivers should also help young children develop the skills needed to observe their own thoughts, feelings, and behaviors. This self-observation is called **metacognition** by cognitive psychologists. Caregivers who give a lot of feedback and ask a lot of questions about children's thoughts, feelings, and behaviors help children develop metacognition.

2. **Managing emotions.** Handling feelings in a way that is appropriate to the situation is a skill that builds on self-awareness. Skills in soothing oneself and maintaining a balance between thoughts, feelings, and behavior are necessary to manage emotions. Caregivers need to help children with this process of self-regulation by providing a model of balance between rational behavior and expression of emotions. As Josephs points out in *Character Structure and the Organization of the Self* (1992),

"in identification with the other, one begins to treat oneself as one was treated by the other." As children acquire language, they also acquire the value system of beliefs and attitudes that form their conscience.

As caregivers help infants regulate their emotions, they contribute to the child's style of emotional self-regulation. For example, a parent who waits to intervene until an infant has become extremely agitated reinforces the baby's rapid rise to intense stress (Thompson, 1988). This makes it harder for the parent to soothe the baby in the future and for the baby to learn self-soothing (Berk, 2000). When caregivers validate children's wants and needs by supporting and helping the child fulfill the need expressed by a feeling, children internalize a positive approach to managing emotions, developing self-esteem, and regulating emotions.

3. Motivating oneself. Channeling emotions in the service of a goal is essential for paying attention, mastery, and creativity. Goleman refers to research on getting into the flow to illustrate how children can learn to balance thought and feeling and to behave in extremely competent ways (Nakamura, 1988). A basic attitude of optimism (the belief that success is possible) and self-responsibility appear to underlie the skill of getting into the flow (Csikszentmihalyi, 1990). Caregivers of young children and infants can observe flow in infants and toddlers. For example, when an infant becomes totally engrossed in exploring her hand or the caregiver's face, you can see that her cognition, perceptions, emotions, and behaviors are all intensely focused and coordinated in their joyful exploration. When a toddler is engrossed in exploring how a toy works, you can observe the coordination of thought, feeling, and behavior that reflect being in the flow.

Many researchers of motivation consider curiosity the primary human motivator. Infants and toddlers are naturally brimming with curiosity and the desire to explore. When caregivers help fulfill basic needs at physical and safety levels and respect the children as separate individuals with the ability to take some responsibility for their own experiences, children feel secure and are able to get into the wonderful flow of exploring both internal and external worlds.

4. Recognizing emotions in others. Empathy (sensitivity to what others need or want) is the fundamental relationship skill. Recent research in infant development has demonstrated that newborns exhibit empathy within the first two months of life. When an infant is in the same environment with another living being in pain, the infant will do whatever possible to comfort the other (Dondi, Simion, & Caltran, 1999; Zahn-Waxler, 1991). If it is true that empathy is present at birth, then insensitivity is learned from the environment. Styles of caregiving have a profound impact on emotional self-regulation and empathy as children grow. Caring, nurturing, and encouraging children results in children who remain empathetic toward others as they grow up (Eisenberg & McNally, 1993). On the other hand, care that is critical, negative, punitive, or aggressive results in children who rarely show signs of concern for others. Instead, they respond with fear, anger, and physical attacks (Klimes-Dougan & Kistner, 1990). Creating a positive learning environment promotes stability and fosters compassion.

Implications of this research for caregivers of young children should be obvious: insensitivity, negativity, or aggression directed at infants and toddlers results in children exhibiting those qualities toward themselves and others. Child care that is sensitive, positive, and nurturing results in children who exhibit those qualities as they grow up. Although empathy needs to be encouraged and modeled more than taught, the social and verbal behaviors involved in "loving thy neighbor as thyself" (not more or less than thyself) should be modeled and directly taught.

5. Handling relationships. The last domain of emotional intelligence involves interacting smoothly and demonstrating skills necessary to get along well with others. It may seem odd at first to suggest that infants and toddlers manage their relationships with others, but research indicates that infants as young as four weeks detect others' emotions through "emotional contagion" (Sullins, 1991), and imitate others' behaviors and expressions within the first three months. There is no question that the behavior of a baby elicits responses from caregivers. Many families even mark their child's first smile, step, word, and so forth with great celebration. Therefore, children learn very early in life that their behavior affects others, even though the conscious awareness that "When I do A, Mommy does B" doesn't come about until between 12 and 18 months. Goleman (1996, pp. 111–112) uses an example of a 30-month-old toddler to illustrate skills used to manage emotions in another person. Specific skills in working with others are spelled out later in this textbook, but it is important to understand here that development of these people skills occurs during the first years of life in the relationships with primary caregivers.

Very little research has been reported on how young children develop skills to manage emotions in others. Studies of the baby's contributions to their primary relationships involve the temperament research discussed previously and studies on **interactional synchrony** (Isabella & Belsky, 1991). This term is best described as a sensitively tuned "emotional dance" in which interactions are mutually rewarding to caregiver and infant. The two share a positive emotional state, and the caregiver usually "follows" and the infant "leads" in the dance. One study indicated that interactional synchrony occurs only about 30 percent of the time between mothers and babies (Tronick & Cohn, 1989). Caregivers need to learn how to establish rapport in this type of interaction with infants and toddlers, to enhance their emotional development and help them learn to manage their relationships.

To summarize, healthy self-concepts develop from young children being helped to recognize their feelings and the feelings of other people, establishing secure and trusting attachments with their caregivers, having their positive temperament traits supported, and having a healthy balance between bonding and separation-individuation. In addition, caregivers should understand the five domains of emotional intelligence and use strategies that enhance them.

Self-Esteem

Self-esteem can be defined as follows:

> the evaluation which the individual makes and customarily maintains with regard to himself: it expresses an attitude of approval or disapproval, and indicates the extent to which the individual believes himself to be capable, significant, successful, and worthy. In short, self-esteem is a personal judgment of worthiness that is expressed in the attitudes the individual holds toward himself. (Coopersmith, 1967, pp. 4–5).

Summarizing his data on childhood experiences that contribute to the development of self-esteem, Coopersmith wrote, "The most general statement about the antecedent of self-esteem can be given in terms of three conditions: total or near total acceptance of the children by their parents; clearly defined and enforced limits; and the respect and latitude for individual actions that exist within the defined limits" (1967, p. 236). It is important that children think they are worthy people. Coopersmith's three conditions for fostering self-esteem—acceptance, limits, respect—provide guidelines for caregivers.

ACCEPTANCE. Each child needs to feel accepted for who he or she is right now. Children need to feel worthy and appreciated. When early childhood educators focus on what children ought to be or what they may become, they communicate to children that they are not all right. What children build on for the future is their sense of being all right now. Caregivers can encourage children to demonstrate acceptance of other children.

LIMITS. Adults set boundaries on behavior to help infants and toddlers learn to live safely and acceptably in their world. Society has rules. Some are physical: play in the yard, not in the street (to keep from physical harm). Some are interpersonal: you play with your doll and Greta will play with hers (possession, ownership—temporary in this case).

The boundaries set for children must fit their developmental level and be observed consistently. For example, both Yolanda and Theresa have difficulty sharing, so the caregiver does not force one to share her airplane with the other. All the children have been told, however, that when someone is playing with a toy, no one else is to take it. Therefore, when Yolanda grabs the airplane Theresa is playing with, the caregiver reaches in to hold the airplane still while she reminds Yolanda about taking a toy someone else is playing with.

RESPECT. Ralphino is playing with a tractor. He must play with it in the space away from children building with blocks. Miss Jana watches him push his tractor around in a circle, push it under a chair and bring it out the other side, lift it to climb the side and seat of the chair and down the other side. Miss Jana allows Ralphino to explore with his tractor. He is not hurting the tractor or the chair as he moves the tractor under and over the chair. Miss Jana does not force Ralphino to be realistic, that is, to recognize that tractors don't really drive over chairs. She allows him to use his fantasies and explorations, encourages private speech, and uses scaffolding to help him learn about his world.

In general, research in the area of self-esteem has found that people who develop good self-esteem have learned and exhibit three specific skills:

1. People with good self-esteem assume responsibility for their own thoughts, feelings, and behaviors. **Self-responsibility** is the keystone to independence. It is accurate to state that the most important task of child care is to prepare children to function as healthy, autonomous individuals capable of providing for their needs in ways acceptable to society. Caregivers should help children take responsibility for their own wants and needs as is appropriate for their developmental level, while allowing dependency in areas in which they are not yet capable of providing for themselves. For example, learning to manage one's emotions and respond using non-aggressive strategies when a want cannot be immediately fulfilled is a developmental challenge that children face early in life (Fuller, 2001). Helping a child take as much responsibility as is age appropriate provides the child with a sense of mastery and overall successful emotional development.

2. People with good self-esteem are *sensitive* and kind toward other people. Although there are individual differences at birth, the sensitivity that children exhibit toward others later in life is clearly related to the quality of sensitivity, kindness, and respect they are shown in the first few years of life. Teachers need to interact with kindness and model empathy to help children respond to others in kind and considerate ways (see Lawrence, 2006). Caregivers who value kindness and empathy help children develop positive self-esteem later in life (Figure 3–4).

3. People with good self-esteem make *conscious positive statements* to themselves about their own value and self-worth (Kocovski & Endler, 2000). Infants and

FIGURE 3–4 Children learn good self-esteem from specific skills.

toddlers internalize the moral values, beliefs, and attitudes of the people in their environment. This becomes part of their personality. The infants and young toddlers adopt the attitudes, statements, and feelings that their caregivers direct toward them. When caregivers consistently direct affection, positive attention, approval, and respect toward young children, the child feels valuable, worthy, and proud. However, when caregivers are critical, angry, demanding, or judgmental toward children, the child learns guilt, anxiety, shame, and self-doubt.

Social Development

Normal patterns for social development are the result of our all-important relationships with our primary caregivers. The word *relationship* implies two entities: a person *relates* to another.

Relationship Development

During infancy and toddlerhood, respect for the child's physical and psychological boundaries is crucial to healthy social development. Because infants begin life unable to care for their physical being, it is necessary for caregivers to intrude on their physical boundaries to provide care. *Intrude* is used here because the baby has no choice in how the caregiver handles his or her body. When the caregiver respects the baby's body, the baby feels secure and loved. However, when the caregiver doesn't respect the baby's body and is rough or insensitive, he or she causes feelings of insecurity and physical pain (Freed, 1991).

Healthy relationships develop from positive attention, approval, and attunement.

FIGURE 3–5 Interactional synchrony is the basis for healthy relationships.

The same principle of respect holds true for emotional boundaries. When the caregiver respects the baby's feelings and provides a positive emotional connection, the baby feels secure. In contrast, anger, criticism, or ignoring the baby is disrespectful and results in insecurity and emotional pain. In the previous section on emotional development, handling relationships was discussed as one of the five domains of emotional intelligence. The skill of handling relationships requires that the caregiver manage her own emotions, demonstrate sensitivity to the child's feelings, and communicate in a way that creates interactional synchrony. To establish this finely tuned emotional dance, the caregiver must be aware of and respect the physical and emotional boundaries of the child and be aware of her own thoughts, feelings, and behaviors (Figure 3–5).

Children who have their physical and psychological boundaries respected learn to respect other people's feelings as well. As a result of being able to value their own wants and needs while being sensitive to other people, these children are able to establish, manage, and maintain healthy relationships with other people.

Once relationships are established with adults, the children use the acquired knowledge of how to treat others in their relationships with peers (Bowlby, 1969/2000). Yet, other developmental milestones facilitate peer interactions and relationships as well. For example, between 24 and 36 months the rapid language development of the toddler provides the basis for understanding the feelings of other people, using more words to express feelings, and active participation in managing relationships. As language increases, so does the toddler's more complete model of the social world. Active **self-talk** dialogues, make-believe play, and beliefs about the self, the world (including other people), and the self in relation to others are exhibited during this period (Gopnik & Wellman, 1994). By the time children reach school age, they have established a model of the world that includes self-concept, beliefs about the world (including other people), and a style of communication that influences how they will manage relationships with others.

Empathy Development

The research discussed in the previous sections suggests that sensitivity to the feelings of other people is present at birth and infants are motivated to comfort another person who is in pain. Since sensitivity is present at birth, it follows that insensitivity is learned. The caregiver should understand how children learn to be insensitive to feelings so that systematic instruction can be conducted to teach children a balance of sensitivity to their own needs and desires and those of other people.

It is interesting that a review of the English language reveals no single word that describes a healthy self-interest in having one's needs and desires fulfilled. On the other hand, words are available to describe lack of self-interest (*selfless*), too much self-interest (*selfish*), and a variety of words to describe lack of interest in other people (e.g., *insensitive, egocentric, narcissistic, aloof*). Since the skills necessary for emotional intelligence require balance between awareness of one's own needs and sensitivity to the feelings of other people, a term is required that accurately denotes a healthy amount of self-interest in fulfilling one's own needs, combined with awareness of the needs of other people.

The authors use the term **enlightened self-interest** to describe balanced awareness of one's own needs and feelings and the needs and feelings of other people. Enlightened self-interest is also the name of the philosophy on which the Constitution of the United States was founded. The makers of the Constitution accepted the philosophy that individuals are more motivated and work harder to fill their own desires than to fulfill the desires of a king, nation, or group, and it was out of this philosophy that American democracy was born (Bancroft, 1834).

For purposes of this book, enlightened self-interest means the skill of balancing one's own feelings and desires with the feelings and desires of other people. A child who learns to make other people's feelings important to the exclusion of his own feelings becomes a selfless victim living a life burdened with inappropriate responsibilities for other people. On the other hand, a child who learns to make his or her own feelings important to the exclusion of other people becomes a selfish manipulator who is insensitive and therefore alienated from intimacy with other people.

To understand enlightened self-interest, the caregiver must be aware of how insensitivity to the feelings of other people is learned. The basis of a person becoming insensitive to other people is physical and emotional pain created by the individual's life experiences. It is impossible to protect infants and toddlers from experiencing physical and emotional pain, no matter how sensitive and caring we are. Pain is a natural and normal life experience and is extremely valuable for our ability to stay alive and learn from experience. Just as athletes understand the saying "No pain: no gain" because muscles don't grow stronger unless they are taxed, most changes that produce growth cause some pain along with pleasure. A goal of a competent caregiver should be to help children remain at ease through their life experiences. Caregivers who try to protect children from all pain and keep them in a state of pleasure establish very unrealistic expectations for themselves and the children in their care.

However, infants and toddlers are emotionally vulnerable to painful experiences because of their lack of defenses. When a young child cannot escape a situation of persistent emotional pain, such as consistent abandonment, rejection, or adult anger, or a situation of chronic physical pain, such as physical or sexual abuse, **emotional detachment** can become severe and long-lasting. Emotional or physical trauma can also cause pathological detachment. Under these conditions, detachment from one's own feelings or the feelings of other people, or both, can cause permanent lack of self-awareness and insensitivity to the feelings of other people.

Another factor that helps determine infant and toddler empathy involves caregiver relationship style. Watson found three problematic parenting styles from research conducted on a test of parent competency called The National Parenting Scales (1996). Parents who exhibit a **controlling caregiver style** tend to discount and negate children's feelings and communicate in an insensitive manner, which causes emotional pain. Children often react by becoming angry and insensitive to the feelings of other people. Parents who exhibit a **detached caregiver style** often are not cognitively or emotionally involved enough with children to be aware of their feelings, so the children tend to become detached or angry with other people. Parents who exhibit a **selfless caregiver style** make the child's feelings important to the exclusion of their own, which often results in children becoming self-absorbed, guilt-ridden, and insensitive to the feelings of other people. A **healthy caregiver style** balances the feelings and needs of the child with those of the caregiver, resulting in a "win-win" rather than a "win-lose" relationship.

The development of empathy starts with the newborn being open to all stimulation from the body, mind, and environment, in which the most immediate need or stimulus take precedence. Infants cannot be selfish, so their empathy toward others is limited by how completely their own needs are fulfilled. For example, when a baby wakes up hungry in the middle of the night, she does not have the experience or awareness that her hunger is an inconvenience to her sleeping caregiver. However, when the child's basic needs are filled, she is able to be extremely curious, sensitive, and aware of other people. From this basic level, children progress to balancing their own feelings and needs with the feelings and needs of other people and become capable of intimate relationships with equal give and take. By the age of five or six, children who have experienced quality caregiving are capable of sophisticated, conscious discrimination of self from others in terms of thoughts, feelings, and behaviors.

Locus of Control Development: Self-Control and Self-Responsibility

Our culture expects individuals to behave in ways that are not harmful to themselves, other people, or the environment. These expectations are taught to infants and toddlers by their families, caregivers, and society. To live successfully with other people, children must learn to control their desires and impulses (self-control), and to take responsibility for themselves appropriately for their age and developmental abilities. The extent to which people perceive their lives as within their own control determines what is called **locus of control**. The word *locus* in this context means perceived location, so children who learn to take responsibility for themselves have an internal locus of control. Conversely, people who perceive their lives to be controlled by others have an external locus of control.

Throughout our discussions of emotional and social development, the cited research has repeatedly indicated that healthy emotional and social development are closely related to self-control and self-responsibility. For example, two domains of emotional intelligence are self-motivation and self-control, and good self-esteem requires self-responsibility. Therefore, understanding development of a healthy internal locus of control is essential for caregivers of young children.

Much research has been conducted on how young children develop morality, which is the basis for self-control. Current thinking is that children need to move beyond their family's perspectives and internalize from their own perspective that certain behaviors are right and wrong (Grusec & Goodnow, 1994). For infants and toddlers to internalize that certain behaviors are right and others are wrong for *them,* they must feel that they have the power to choose their own behavior. Unfortunately, many adults believe that they must control children's behavior in order to care for children and keep them safe. The fact that many families and other caregivers think that *they* control children's behavior may be largely responsible for many social problems created by people not taking responsibility for their own thoughts, feelings, and behavior. It is important to understand that it is the *perception* of control that adults have, and not actual control, that causes children to develop an external locus of control. Many parents and caregivers perceive themselves to be responsible for children's behavior when, in fact, they are neglectful in caring for and providing proper guidance for children.

The consistent emotional message communicated to children by adults who feel that they are responsible for the child's behavior is "You have no choice but to do what I tell you." Child psychologists and counselors observe external locus of control in many young children referred for behavior problems. As early as 18 months, children with "acting out" behavior typically cannot explain why they misbehave, but many express the belief that they are being controlled and made to do many things. On the other hand, the majority of children who do not act out inappropriately say that they can choose how to behave (Watson, 2001).

The question is how to respect children's choices and still provide the guidance and care they require to remain safe and healthy. Development of an internal locus of control requires that caregivers respect the right of young children to choose their behavior. Caregivers must also set clear and consistent positive consequences for appropriate behaviors and clear and consistent loss of positive consequences and application of negative consequences for behavior that is harmful to the child, another person, or the environment. Since children choose their behavior, they must be instructed directly in what positive consequences will follow when they choose to behave positively and what negative consequences will follow for choosing to behave negatively. When clear and consistent consequences are delivered to children, children quickly develop an internal locus of control (Mischel & Liebert, 1966).

Providing choices of what to clean up helps to develop responsibility and an internal locus of control.

Research on the effects of punishment reveals that children of highly punitive parents are especially aggressive and defiant outside the home (Strassberg, Dodge, Petitt, & Bates, 1994; Straus, 2001). Alternatives to harsh punishment that are more effective in developing an internal locus of control include redirection, problem-solving, a warm caregiver-child relationship, and explanations of consequences, including expectations for future behavior (Larzelere, Schneider, Larson, & Pike, 1996; Marion, 2007).

A final word of caution regarding self-control is important here. Many children develop an internal locus of control that is too strict and limiting of their thoughts, feelings, and behavior. Over-controlled children are likely to become obsessive-compulsive, overly anxious, fearful of making mistakes, or rigid and judgmental toward other people. To avoid development of over-control with children, keep the definition of misbehavior limited to behaviors that are clearly harmful to the child, another person, pet, or the environment. Never define thoughts or feelings as a misbehavior. Thoughts and feelings are *never* wrong, but how we express them may be harmful. These distinctions are essential for helping infants and toddlers develop a healthy internal locus of control.

From a review of the literature, it appears that healthy social development is related to secure attachment and trust in our primary caregivers, healthy identity development, and caregiver respect and sensitivity to children's physical and psychological

TABLE 3–2   MILESTONES FOR SOCIAL DEVELOPMENT: BIRTH TO 36 MONTHS

AGE	ACTIVITIES
Birth to 6 months	Fusing with mother evolves into basic self-discriminations Matches feelings and tones of caregiver Demonstrates empathy Exhibits interactional synchrony Social smile observed Shows happiness at familiar faces Gains caregiver attention intentionally
7–12 months	Exhibits self-recognition and discrimination from others Awareness of others' emotional signals Social referencing and self-referencing begins Imitative and parallel play
12–24 months	Exhibits possessiveness Self-conscious behavior with others observed Stranger anxiety common Dramatic increase in verbal interactions Beginning of cooperative play
24–36 months	Awareness that emotional reactions of others differ from own Increased vocabulary to express feelings Understands perspective of other people Evolving of belief structures and more complete model of self, others, and the world Start of active management of relationships with caregivers and peers

boundaries. Healthy social development involves children being aware of their own needs and desires and those of other people, as well as communicating verbally and nonverbally in ways that establish interactional synchrony with others. Infants and toddlers need help in developing an internal locus of control, self-control, and self-responsibility. Table 3–2 presents some of the major milestones for social development from birth through thirty-six months.

The Importance of Attachment

Fourteen-month-old Louise is walking in the yard carrying a small truck in her hand. She sees Randy, the caregiver, and squeals and giggles. She walks rapidly to Randy with arms up and a big smile on her face. Attachment is the special, close relationship between the child and a caregiver. Attachment provides security for small children as they encounter new social experiences in their world and form a model of themselves, relationships, and their environment.

Strong, positive attachment develops from looking into each other's eyes, touching, stroking, and cuddling. Interactional synchrony comes from rapid and consistent responses to the infant's cries and from the infant picking up on cues from the adult that the child has worth and is special. When the family member or caregiver responds quickly and appropriately to the infant's needs, such as providing food, holding, or comforting, the infant builds trust in that adult.

The relationships families and caregivers form with little children help to determine what relationships children will develop later in life. Strong, sensitive attachment has a positive influence on a child's confidence, self-concept, and self-esteem for the remainder of his or her life. Most research on caregiver-child relationships has examined infants with their parents. The findings from this research apply equally well to infant-caregiver relationships.

1. Infants need to establish emotional attachment with their caregivers. This attachment develops through regular activities such as feeding and changing diapers, cuddling, looking, and touching.

Caregivers should provide physical contact; learn the child's needs, schedules, likes and dislikes, and temperament; act in ways that comfort and stimulate interactions; and respond to the child's preferences.

As discussed in Chapter 1, when more than one caregiver is responsible for a group of children, a primary caregiving system can be used to divide the work and best meet the needs of the children. The primary caregiver works closely with family members to establish consistent routines and strategies for meeting the infant's needs. She can share her knowledge about the child's needs and preferences so that other caregivers can match their care to the child. Alternate caregivers should report observations about the child's behaviors to the primary caregiver. Thus, the primary caregiver has two main responsibilities: (1) to establish a special attachment with the child and (2) to gather, coordinate, and share information about the child with other caregivers and the family.

2. Each child needs to have a caregiver respond quickly, sensitively, and consistently to cries and cues of distress. The child then learns to trust the caregiver. When crying infants are left alone for several minutes before a caregiver responds, or when the caregiver responds quickly sometimes and leaves them alone sometimes, children are confused and have difficulty establishing a strong attachment because they cannot develop a strong sense of trust in the caregiver. Responding quickly to infant and toddler needs does not spoil the child. The most important task for an infant or toddler is to develop trust and a secure attachment to the caregiver. For this to occur, the caregiver must respond quickly, consistently, and sensitively to the child's needs.

3. Each child and his or her primary caregiver need special time together. This "getting to know you" and "let's enjoy each other" time should be a calm, playful time to relax, look, touch, smile, giggle, cuddle, stroke, talk, whisper, sing, make faces, and establish the wonderful dance of interactional synchrony. Sometimes this can be active time, including holding an infant up in the air at arm's length while you talk and giggle and then bringing the infant up close for a hug. Other times, this can mean very quiet activities, such as rocking, cuddling, and softly stroking in a loving way.

4. The caregiver must treat each child as a special, important person. Infants and toddlers are not objects to be controlled but individuals of worth with whom you establish a respectful, positive emotional relationship while providing for their physical, cognitive, and learning needs.

Cognitive and Language Development

Newborns use all their senses—listening, seeing, tasting, touching, and smelling—to learn about their world. This leads to young children thinking differently from adults. Adults are logical thinkers; they consider facts, analyze relationships, and draw conclusions. Young children are *prelogical* thinkers; their conclusions are based on their interactions with materials and people in their environment and perhaps on an incomplete or inaccurate understanding of their experiences. For example, two-and-a-half-year-old Ivan has made a tilting stack of blocks. When he places a small car on top of the blocks, the stack tumbles down. Ivan tells Mrs. Young that the car broke the blocks. Ivan does not understand gravity, the need to stack blocks straight up rather than at a tilt, and why the car's rolling wheels may have started the car's movement downhill. The object Ivan put on the stack just before it fell was the car, so as far as Ivan is concerned, the car broke the blocks.

Jean Piaget's research contributed significantly to the knowledge of cognitive development in young children. A brilliant young scientist, Piaget began his studies as a biologist. Later, listening to children respond to questions on an intelligence test, he became intrigued by their incorrect responses and the patterns of the children's verbal reasoning. Combining his scientific orientation, his knowledge of biology, and his experiences with the children's incorrect response patterns, Piaget began to study children's cognitive development. Piaget's clinical observation method included close observations of his own three young children as well as many other children in his extensive subsequent research. He observed what children did and wrote narrative descriptions, including the date, the participants, and the actions. Later, analyzing these detailed observations, he developed his theories of cognitive development. Piaget's (1952) approach is central to the school of cognitive theory known as *cognitive constructivism;* other researchers, known as *social constructivists,* such as Vygotsky and Bruner, have placed more emphasis on the part played by language and other people in enabling children to learn (Wood, 1998; Atherton, 2005).

Stages of Cognitive Development

Central to Piaget's theory is that there are stages of cognitive development; that is, four-month-olds are cognitively different from 24-month-olds. Piaget contended that the sequence of development is the same for all children. However, the age and rate at which it occurs differs from child to child.

Piaget's first two stages of cognitive development involve children between birth and three years of age. These stages, the sensorimotor stage and the beginning of the preoperational stage, are the aspects of cognitive development relevant to an infant and toddler curriculum. The **sensorimotor stage** starts at birth, when the baby explores self and the environment. Sensorimotor development involves the infant understanding his or her body and how it relates to other things in the environment (Piaget & Inhelder, 1969). The earliest form of thinking occurs during this stage, at approximately 18 months, and involves assimilation of sensorimotor cause and effect, called interiorized actions. There are three key aspects of this early age: (1) infants play an assertive role in their own development, (2) their knowledge base is acquired by means of their own actions in the environment, and (3) infants need moderate challenges to master the environment. For caregivers, tasks should be provided that challenge babies but are not beyond their ability to succeed. The three *As* represent a valuable tool to help children experience challenges they can meet successfully.

SENSORIMOTOR STAGE. The sensorimotor stage of cognitive development occurs from birth to about age two. Piaget identified six substages.

Substage 1 (birth to approximately 1 month)	*Reflex* Reflex actions become more organized. Directed behavior emerges.
Substage 2 (approximately 1–4 months)	*Differentiation* Repeats own actions. Begins to coordinate actions, such as hearing and looking.
Substage 3 (approximately 4–8 months)	*Reproduction* Intentionally repeats interesting actions.
Substage 4 (approximately 8–12 months)	*Coordination* Intentionally acts as a means to an end. Develops concept of object permanence (an object exists even when the infant cannot see it).
Substage 5 (approximately 12–18 months)	*Experimentation* Experiments through trial and error. Searches for new experiences.
Substage 6 (approximately 18–24 months)	*Representation* Carries out mental trial and error. Develops symbols.

PREOPERATIONAL STAGE. The early part of the preoperational stage is called the preconceptual substage and occurs from about two to four years of age.

The child can now mentally sort events and objects. With the development of object permanence, the child is moving toward representing objects and actions in his or her thinking without having to have actual sensorimotor experiences. Development and structuring of these mental representations is the task undertaken during the preoperational stage of cognitive development. Cowan (1978) outlined the preoperational stage as follows:

Preconceptual substage

Mentally sort objects and actions.

Mental symbols partly detached from experience.

Nonverbal classification
Graphic collections.

Focus on figurative properties.

Own interpretations.

Verbal preconcepts
Meanings of words fluctuate, are not always the same for the child.

Meanings of words are private, based on own experience.

Word names and labels are tied to one class.

Words focus on one attribute at a time.

Verbal reasoning
Transductive reasoning—from particular to particular.

If one action is in some way like another action, both actions are alike in all ways.

Generalizes one situation to all situations.

Reasoning is sometimes backward—from effects to causes.

Reasoning focuses on one dimension.

Quantity
How much?

Some, more, gone, big.

Number
How many?

More, less.

Space
Where?

Uses guess and visual comparison.

Up, down, behind, under, over.

Time
Remembers sequence of life events.

Now, soon, before, after.

COGNITIVE FUNCTIONS. Piaget identified processes and functions in thinking. When you solve a problem, you feel that you understand it. As discussed in Chapter 2, Piaget's theory included concepts such as equilibrium, disequilibrium, equilibration, assimilation, and accommodation. For Piaget, an infant who reaches or touches an object quickly develops *knowing*, an active process of co-construction between what there is to know and the child's motivation and actions. More complex forms of knowing develop out of simple behaviors such as sucking, mouthing, and touching, according to Piaget.

All people use these processes and functions—assimilation, accommodation, and equilibration—continually through life. For example, Shane is looking around and notices a ball on the floor. As he crawls to it, he bumps the ball so the ball rolls. He crawls to it again, picks up the ball, looks at it, licks it, and puts it down on the floor. Shane started out in seeming equilibrium; that is, he seemed settled and quiet. Something caused disequilibrium; that is, something stimulated him. Shane responded to seeing the ball. What he saw may match in some way what he has seen before in previous play with a ball. He may have assimilated some idea about the ball. When he bumped the ball and it rolled, he was presented with additional information about the ball that did not fit into his present concept. Therefore, through accommodation, he makes adjustments in his concept of "ball" to include the rolling movement. His disequilibrium is over, and he once again for an instant has attained equilibration, a sense of balance, of understanding his world.

COGNITIVE STRUCTURES. Shane's actions also show one of the structures of intelligence. Shane constructs concepts or schemas as his mind organizes or structures its experiences. The schema or concept of ball is constructed as Shane sees, touches, holds, and tastes a ball. When he sees the ball roll, that does not fit into his schema or structure of ball-ness. He continues to construct his knowledge of ball-ness by reorganizing his schema so that now rolling is included in ball-ness. Shane's schema of ball today is different from his schema yesterday, when he had not noticed a rolling ball. Individual experiences and behavior bring about changes in schemas.

KNOWLEDGE CONSTRUCTION. Young children construct knowledge about themselves and their world. They cannot copy knowledge, but rather must act on their own and construct their own meaning. Each of their actions and interpretations is unique to them. They see an object and construct thoughts about that object. Young children's thinking organizes information about their experiences so they can construct their own understanding.

TYPES OF KNOWLEDGE. Piaget identified three types of knowledge: physical knowledge, logico-mathematical knowledge, and social-arbitrary knowledge.

Physical knowledge is knowledge children discover in the world around them. Twenty-five-month-old Tommy kicks a pine needle as he walks in the play yard. He picks up the pine needle, throws it, and picks it up again. He drops it in the water tray, picks it up, and pulls it through the water. Tommy has discovered something about pine needles from the needle itself. Tommy uses actions and observations of the effects of his actions on the pine needle to construct his physical knowledge of pine needles.

Kamii and Devries have identified two kinds of activities involving physical knowledge: movement of objects and changes in objects. Actions to move objects include "pulling, pushing, rolling, kicking, jumping, blowing, sucking, throwing, swinging, twirling, balancing, and dropping" (1978, p. 6). The child causes the object to move and observes it rolling, bouncing, cracking, and so on. Kamii and Devries suggest four criteria for selecting activities to move objects.

1. The child must be able to produce the movement by his or her own action.
2. The child must be able to vary his or her action.
3. The reaction of the object must be observable.
4. The reaction of the object must be immediate (1978, p. 9).

A second kind of activity involves changes in objects. Compared to a ball, which when kicked, will move but still remain a ball, some objects change. When Kool-Aid® is put in water, it changes. Ann sees the dry Kool-Aid and observes that something happens when it is added to water. She can no longer see anything that looks like the dry Kool-Aid. She sees the water change color and can taste the difference between water without Kool-Aid and water with Kool-Aid in it. Her observation skills (seeing and tasting) are most important to provide her with feedback on the changes that occur.

Logico-mathematical knowledge is constructed by the child and involves identifying relationships between objects.

Andrea is in the sandbox playing with two spoons: a teaspoon and a serving spoon. She notices the spoons are different. Although they fit into her schema of *spoon*, she notices some difference in size. Thus, in relationship to size, they are different. At some time someone will label these differences for her as different or bigger or smaller than the other, but these words are not necessary for her to construct her concepts of sizes.

Social-arbitrary knowledge is knowledge a child cannot learn by him- or herself. It has been constructed and agreed upon by groups of people (Branscombe, Castle, Dorsey, Surbeck, & Taylor, 2003). This type of knowledge is passed on or transmitted from one person to another through social interaction. "Language, values, rules, morality, and symbol systems are examples of social-arbitrary knowledge" (Wadsworth, 1978, p. 52).

Chad is eating a banana. He bites it, sucks on it, swallows it, looks at the remaining banana, and squeezes it. All of these are concrete actions which help him construct his physical knowledge of this object. Then someone tells him this object is a banana. The name *banana* is social-arbitrary knowledge. It could have been called *ningina* or *lalisa*, but everyone using the English language uses *banana* to name that object.

In another example of social-arbitrary knowledge, Kurt follows Mrs. Wesley into the storage room. She sees him and says, "Kurt, go back into our room right now. You are not supposed to be in this room." Kurt did not make the decision that it is not permissible for him to be in the storage room; someone else decided and told him the rule.

PLAY. Play is the child's laboratory for cognitive trial and error and rehearsal for real-life problem solving. Children begin active pretend play between 18 and 24 months. As they rapidly develop symbols and interpretations and start to reason verbally, complex sequences of play are executed. For example, two-year-olds might play "cooking," using blocks and sticks for food and utensils. From basic themes, children develop more complex strategies, perhaps using water and sand to explore measurement while learning about textures, temperatures, smells, and liquidity. Table 3–3 presents levels of exploratory and pretend play. Play develops from simple mouthing and touching objects to extremely abstract activity, in which materials are substituted and transformed to make up a complete story with beginning, middle, and end.

TABLE 3–3   LEVELS OF EXPLORATORY AND PRETEND PLAY

1. **Mouthing:** Indiscriminate mouthing of materials

2. **Simple manipulation:** Visually guided manipulation (excluding indiscriminate banging and shaking) at least 5 seconds in duration that cannot be coded in any other category (e.g., turn over an object, touch and look at an object)

3. **Functional:** Visually guided manipulation that is particularly appropriate for a certain object and involves the intentional extraction of some unique piece of information (e.g., turn dial on toy phone, squeeze piece of foam rubber, flip antenna of toy, spin wheels on cart, roll cart on wheels)

4. **Relational:** Bringing together and integrating two or more materials in an inappropriate manner, that is, in a manner not initially intended by the manufacturer (e.g., set cradle on phone, touch spoon to stick)

5. **Functional-relational:** Bringing together and integrating two objects in an appropriate manner, that is, in a manner intended by the manufacturer (e.g., set cup on saucer, place peg in hole of pegboard, mount spool on shaft of cart)

6. **Enactive naming:** Approximate pretense activity but without confirming evidence of actual pretense behavior (e.g., touch cup to lip without making talking sounds, touch brush to doll's hair without making combing motions)

7. **Pretend self:** Pretense behavior directed toward self in which pretense is apparent (e.g., raise cup to lip; tip cup, make drinking sounds, or tilt head; stroke own hair with miniature brush; raise phone receiver to ear and vocalize)

8. **Pretend other:** Pretense behavior directed away from child toward other (e.g., feed doll with spoon, bottle, or cup; brush doll's hair; push car on floor and make car noise)

9. **Substitution:** Using a "meaningless" object in a creative or imaginative manner (e.g., drink from seashell; feed baby with stick as "bottle") or using an object in a pretense act in a way that differs from how it has previously been used by the child (e.g., use hairbrush to brush teeth after already using it as a hairbrush on self or other)

10. **Sequence pretend:** Repetition of a single pretense act with minor variation (e.g., drink from bottle, give doll drink, pour into cup, pour into plate) or linking together different pretense schemes (e.g., stir in cup, then drink; put doll in cradle, then kiss good night)

11. **Sequence pretend substitution:** Same as sequence pretend except using an object substitution within sequence (e.g., put doll in cradle, cover with green felt piece as "blanket"; feed self with spoon, then with stick)

12. **Double substitution:** Pretense play in which two materials are transformed, within a single act, into something they are not in reality (e.g., treat peg as doll and a piece of green felt as a blanket and cover peg with felt and say "night-night"; treat stick as person and seashell as cup and give stick a drink)

Source: J. Belsky & R. K. Most. (1981). From exploration to play: A cross-sectional study of infant free play behavior. *Developmental Psychology, 17,* 630–639.

Language Development

Most babies are able to screen out many sounds that are not useful in understanding their native language by the age of six months (Polka & Werker, 1994). Between six and twelve months of age, babies are usually able to recognize familiar words in spoken passages (Jusczyk & Hohne, 1997). These findings suggest that infants begin to discriminate, associate, and analyze the structure of words and sentences before nine months of age!

Adults unconsciously conduct what is called **child-directed speech** with babies. This means that adults automatically adjust their tone, volume, and speech patterns to capture and sustain focal attention from the baby (Moore, Spence, & Katz, 1997). Almost as soon as the baby starts to use words, caregiver speech changes to more information, directions, and questions rather than child-directed speech (Murray, Johnson, & Peters, 1990).

Communication begins with infants both verbally and nonverbally. Newborns initiate interaction by making eye contact, and by four months they gaze in the same direction as the caregiver (Tomasello, 1999). It is important for caregivers to label and describe things that the baby visually attends to because this significantly enhances language development. In contrast, caregivers who interrupt or restrict the baby's focal attention and activities impede language development (Carpenter, Nagell, & Tomasello, 1998).

The next level of language development, vocalization, begins with the baby cooing and progresses to babbling. When a caregiver copies or mimics the baby's vocalization, the child can attend to the sounds that the caregiver makes as well as engage in turn-taking: the baby vocalizes, the caregiver vocalizes in return and waits for a response, and the "conversation" continues. Games such as patty-cake help babies to interact actively and even initiate turn-taking interactions (Bruner, 1983).

Gestural communication begins between nine and twelve months, when the baby touches or holds objects while making sure the caregiver notices and gives attention, or the baby directs the caregiver to do something by pointing or gesturing (Fenson et al., 1994). When the caregiver labels and describes what the baby is holding or gesturing at, language development is enhanced. By the beginning of the second year, verbalization of words and phrases is associated with gestures to communicate accurately. As vocabulary increases and becomes more descriptive, gestures decrease toward the end of the second year (Namy & Waxman, 1998).

You read about baby signing in the previous chapter. This technique has proven to be a wonderful way to prepare youngsters to successfully conquer the challenges of communication and is considered by many to be a method that enhances learning. The authors found that their Baby Sign alums outperformed their non-baby signing peers by a very impressive margin on the WISC III, a universal test to measure language (Acredolo & Goodwyn, with Abrams, 2002).

The many aspects of more complex speech development, such as grammar and semantics, are beyond the scope of this text. It must suffice to say that young children quickly learn the rules of speech governing their native language and are proficient by around six years of age. Teachers enhance children's language development by labeling, describing, mirroring, and actively engaging the child in conversations.

■ KEY TERMS

child-directed speech	double substitution	enactive naming
controlling caregiver style	emotional detachment	enlightened self-interest
detached caregiver style	emotional intelligence	experience-dependent
development	empathy	experience-expectant

fine motor control	memory	self-esteem
functional-relational	metacognition	self-responsibility
goodness of fit	milestones	self-talk
gross motor control	object permanence	selfless caregiver style
healthy caregiver style	omnipotent	sensorimotor stage
interactional synchrony	physical knowledge	social-arbitrary knowledge
learning	pretend other	substitution
locus of control	pretend self	sudden infant death syndrome (SIDS)
logico-mathematical knowledge	self-awareness	

CASE STUDY   Marcus

You should now have a working knowledge of normal patterns of development in each of the four areas for children under the age of 36 months. To test your understanding, decide if Marcus is advanced, behind, or at age level in the following evaluation summary.

Marcus, who is 24 months old, is in child care from 7:30 a.m. to 4:00 p.m. five days a week. An evaluation of his development in each of the four major areas revealed the following observations.

Physical Factors. Marcus is 36 inches tall, weighs 35 pounds, has 20/20 vision, and can focus and track across a line of letters fluidly. He has all 20 baby teeth, can stand on one foot and hop, and is interested in toilet learning. He can throw a ball with each hand and use a fork to eat.

Emotional Factors. Marcus clings to his caregiver much of the time and shows anxiety at the presence of strangers. He is compliant and follows directions when he feels secure, but he can become whiny when he does not receive enough individual attention. He has difficulty understanding his feelings or soothing himself. When not involved with his caregiver or other children, Marcus has difficulty being at ease.

Social Factors. Marcus has some difficulty determining what things are his, and he cooperates with other children only when he has the full attention of his caregiver. He is easily emotionally hurt by other children

and cannot defend himself when other children take advantage of him. He is not often able to be sensitive to the feelings of other children. Although his language skills are sufficient, Marcus screams rather than uses words when other children bother him.

Cognitive Factors. When he feels secure, Marcus is curious, explores his environment, and gains a lot of physical knowledge. Although he has some difficulty interacting with peers, he participates in active, creative pretend play and exhibits a logical sequence in the stories he makes up. He uses double substitution in play and understands four- and five-direction sequences.

1. Determine if you think Marcus is advanced for his age level, at age level, or below age level for each area of development. Explain how you drew each conclusion.

2. In which of the four areas is it most difficult for you to make an assessment of Marcus? What additional information did you want? Why?

3. If you decided that Marcus is (1) advanced in physical development, (2) below age expectations for emotional and social development, and (3) at age level in cognitive development, then you have a good working understanding of typical, or universal, patterns of development. If not, explain how your answers were different. What information did you attend to and why?

■ QUESTIONS AND EXPERIENCES FOR REFLECTION

1. During the children's alert play time observe two children of different ages between birth and three years, focusing on one area (physical, emotional, social, or cognitive). Write down everything each child does and says for five minutes.

   Make a chart to compare the behaviors, using the following as a guide:

Child:	Age:	Child:	Age:
Area:		Area:	
Behaviors		Behaviors	

2. Observe one child between birth and three years of age interacting with one adult. List the behaviors each uses to get and maintain the other's attention.

	Initial Behavior	Response
Child		
Adult		
Child		
Adult		
Child		
Adult		

3. Define emotional intelligence.

4. How do children learn from relationships? What role will you as caregiver play in this process?

5. Which of the three basic types of temperament do you respond most easily to? Why? What do you need to do to learn to respond caringly to the other two types?

■ CHAPTER REVIEW

1. How can you apply Margaret Mahler's separation-individuation substages?

2. Discuss the implications of conscious care as if you were a teacher talking to family members.

3. Temperament is an important issue. What factors influence these classifications most?

4. How does a child's emotional IQ influence her relationships with others?

5. Name the major milestones for motor development from birth to three years of age.

6. How is toilet learning a complex developmental accomplishment?

7. What three skills do children need to have good self-esteem?

8. Explain why caregivers should establish interactional synchrony with children.

9. Discuss Piaget's stages of cognitive development in terms of activities with two-year-olds.

■ REFERENCES

Acredolo, L. P., & Goodwyn, S., (with Douglas Abrams). (2002). *Baby signs: How to talk with your baby before your baby can talk* (Rev. ed.). Chicago: Contemporary Books.

American Psychiatric Association. (1994). *Diagnostic and statistical manual of mental disorders* (4th ed.). Washington, DC: Author.

Anders, T. F., Goodlin-Jones, B. L., & Zelenko, M. (1998). Infants' regularity and sleep-wake state development. *Zero to Three, 19*(2), 5–8.

Atherton, J. (2005). Piaget's developmental theory. Retrieved March 12, 2005, from http://www.learningandteaching.info/learning/piaget.htm

Bancroft, G. (1834). *History of the United States of America, from the discovery of the continent.* New York: Appleton and Co.

Beatty, J. (1995). *Principles of behavioral neuroscience.* London: Brown and Benchmark.

Berk, L. E. (1998). *Child development* (4th ed.). Needham Heights, MA: Allyn and Bacon.

Berk, L. E. (2000). *Child development* (5th ed.). Needham Heights, MA: Allyn and Bacon.

Bowlby, J. (2000). *Attachment and loss: Vol. 1. Attachment.* New York: Basic Books. (Original work published 1969).

Branscombe, N. A., Castle, K., Dorsey, A. G., Surbeck, E., & Taylor, J. B. (2003). *Early childhood curriculum: A constructivist perspective.* Boston: Houghton Mifflin.

Bruner, J. S. (1983). The acquisition of pragmatic commitments. In R. M. Golinkoff (Ed.), *The transition from prelinguistic to linguistic communication* (pp. 27–42). Hillsdale, NJ: Erlbaum.

Carpenter, M., Nagell, K., & Tomasello, M. (1998). Social cognition, joint attention, and communicative competence. *Monographs of the Society for Research in Child Development, 63*(4), 1–174.

Caspi, A., & Silva, P. A. (1995). Temperamental qualities at age three predict personality traits in young adulthood: Longitudinal evidence from a birth cohort. *Child Development, 66*, 486–498.

Chess, S., Thomas, A., & Birch, H. G. (1977). *Your child is a person: A psychological approach to parenthood without guilt.* New York: Penguin Books.

Chien, S. H., Palmer, J., & Teller, D. Y. (2005). Achromatic contrast effects in infants: Adults and 4-month-old infants show similar deviations from Wallach's ratio rule. *Vision Research 45*(22), 2854–2861.

Churchill, S. L. (2003). Goodness-of-fit in early childhood settings. *Early Childhood Education Journal, 31*, 113–118.

Coopersmith, S. (1967). *The antecedents of self-esteem.* San Francisco: W. H. Freeman.

Cowan, Philip A. (1978). Piaget with feeling: Cognitive, social, and emotional dimensions. New York: Holt, Rinehart and Winston.

Csikszentmihalyi, M. (1990). *The psychology of optimal experience* (1st ed.). New York: Harper & Row.

De Schipper, J. C., Tavecchio, L. W. C., Van IJzendoorn, M.H., & Van Zeijl, J. (2004). Goodness-of-fit in center day care: Relations of temperament, stability, and quality of care with the child's adjustment. *Early Childhood Research Quarterly, 19*, 257–272.

Dondi, M., Simion, F., & Caltran, G. (1999). Can newborns discriminate between their own cry and the cry of another newborn infant? *Developmental Psychology, 35*, 418–426.

Eisenberg, N., & McNally, S. (1993). Socialization and mothers' and adolescents' empathy-related characteristics. *Journal of Research on Adolescence, 3*, 171–191.

Fenson, L., Dale, P. S., Reznick, J. S., Bates, E., Thal, D. J., & Pethick, S. J. (1994). Variability in early communicative development. *Monographs of the Society for Research in Child Development, 59*(5), 1–189.

Franyo, G. A., & Hyson, M. C. (1999). Temperament training for early childhood caregivers: A study of the effectiveness of training. *Child & Youth Forum, 28*, 329–349.

Freed, A. M. (1991). *T. A. (transactional analysis) for tots.* Torrance, CA: Jalmar Press.

Fuller, A. (2001). A blueprint for building social competencies in children and adolescents. *Australian Journal of Middle Schooling, 1*(1), 40–49.

Gerber, M., & Weaver, J. (Ed.). (1998). *Dear parent: Caring for infants with respect.* Los Angeles: Resources for Infant Educarers (RIE).

Goleman, D. (1996). *Emotional intelligence: Why it can matter more than IQ.* New York: Bantam Books.

Gonzalez-Mena, J. (2001). *Multicultural issues in child care* (3rd ed.). Mountain View, CA: Mayfield.

Gonzalez-Mena, J., & Eyer, D. W. (2007). *Infants, toddlers, and caregivers* (7th ed.). New York: McGraw-Hill.

Gopnik, A., & Wellman, H. M. (1994). The "theory" theory. In L. A. Hirschfeld & S. A. Gelman (Eds.), *Mapping the mind: Domain specificity in cognition and culture.* Cambridge, UK: Cambridge University Press.

Greenberg, J. R., & Mitchell, S. A. (1983). *Object relations in psychoanalytic theory*. Cambridge, MA: Harvard University Press.

Greenspan, G., & Pollock, G. (1989). *The course of life*. Madison, CT: International University Press.

Grusec, J. E., & Goodnow, J. J. (1994). Impact of parental discipline methods on the child's internalization of values: A reconceptualization of current points of view. *Developmental Psychology, 30*, 4–19.

Gunnar, M. R. (1998). Quality of early care and buffering of neuroendocrine stress reactions: Potential effects on the developing human brain. *Preventive Medicine, 27*, 208–211.

Herr, J., & Swim, T. (2002). *Creative Resources for Infants and Toddlers* (2nd ed.). Clifton Park, NY: Thomson Delmar Learning.

Hofsten, C. Von. (1989). Motor development as the development of systems. *Developmental Psychology, 25*, 950–953.

Isabella, R. A., & Belsky, J. (1991). Interactional synchrony and the origins of infant-mother attachment: A replication study. *Child Development, 62*, 373–384.

Johniditis, N. (2000). *Youth teeth* (information pamphlet). Locust Valley, NY: Nicholas.

Josephs, L. (1992). *Character structure and the organization of the self*. New York: Columbia University Press.

Jusczyk, P. W., & Hohne, E. A. (1997). Infants' memory for spoken words. *Science, 277*, 1984–1986.

Kagan, J., Reznick, J. S., & Gibbons, J. (1989). Inhibited and uninhibited types of children. *Child Development, 60*, 838–845.

Kamii, C., & Devries, R. (1978). *Physical knowledge in preschool education: Implications of Piaget's theory*. Englewood Cliffs, NJ: Prentice Hall.

Kleitman, N. (1963). *Sleep and wakefulness*. Chicago: University of Chicago Press.

Klimes-Dougan, B., & Kistner, J. (1990). Physically abused preschoolers' responses to peers' distress. *Developmental Psychology, 67*, 599–602.

Kocovski, N. L., & Endler, N. S. (2000). Self-regulation: Social anxiety and depression. *Journal of Applied Biobehavioral Research, 5*(1), 80–91.

Lamb, M. E., & Campos, J. J. (1982). *Development in infancy*. New York: Random House.

Larzelere, R. E., Schneider, W. N., Larson, D. B., & Pike, P. L. (1996). The effects of discipline responses in delaying toddler misbehavior recurrences. *Child & Family Behavior Therapy, 18*, 35–37.

Lawrence, D. (2006). *Enhancing self-esteem in the classroom* (3rd ed.). London: Paul Chapman Educational Publishing.

Mahler, M. S. (1975). The psychological birth of the human infant. In *Selected papers of Margaret S. Mahler*, Vol. 2. New York: Basic Books.

Mahler, M. S., Pine, F., & Bergman, F. (1975). *The psychological birth of the human infant: Symbiosis and individuation*. New York: Basic Books.

Mangelsdorf, S., Gunnar, M., Kestenbaum, R., Lang, S., & Andreas, D. (1990). Infant proneness-to-distress temperament, maternal personality, and mother-infant attachment: Associations and goodness of fit. *Child Development, 61*, 820–832.

Marion, M. (2007). *Guidance of young children* (7th ed.). Upper Saddle River, NJ: Pearson Prentice Hall.

McDevitt, T. M., and Ormrod, J. E. (2007). *Child development: Educating and working with children and adolescents* (3rd ed.). Upper Saddle River, NJ: Pearson Prentice Hall.

Mischel, H. N., & Liebert, R. M. (1966). Effects of discrepancies between observed and imposed reward criteria on their acquisition and transmission. *Journal of Personality and Social Psychology, 3*, 45–53.

Moore, D. S., Spence, M. J., & Katz, G. S. (1997). Six-month-olds' categorization of natural infant-directed utterances. *Developmental Psychology, 33*, 980–989.

Murray, A. D., Johnson, J., & Peters, J. (1990). Fine-tuning of utterance length to preverbal infants: Effects on later language development. *Journal of Child Language, 17*, 511–525.

Nakamura, J. (1988). Optimal experience and the uses of talent. In M. Csikszentmihalyi, & I. S. Csikszentmihalyi (Eds.), *Optimal experience: Psychological studies of flow in consciousness* (pp. 150–171). Cambridge, UK: Cambridge University Press.

Namy, L. L., & Waxman, S. R. (1998). Words and gestures: Infants' interpretations of different forms of symbolic reference. *Child Development, 69*, 295–308.

Nowak, R. (2002). When a baby is teething, that means they are . . . well, simply teething. *New Scientist, 176* (2365).

Oppenheim, D., & Koren-Karie, N. (2002). Mothers' insightfulness regarding their children's internal worlds: The capacity underlying secure child-mother relationships. *Infant Mental Health Journal, 23*, 593–605.

Paterson, G., & Sanson, A. (1999). The association of behavioural adjustment to temperament, parenting and family characteristics among 5-year-old children. *Social Development, 8*, 293–309.

Piaget, J. (1952). *The origins of intelligence in children* (M. Cook, trans.). New York: International University Press.

Piaget, J., & Inhelder, B. (1969). *The psychology of the child*. London: Routledge and Kegan Paul.

Plomin, R. (1994). Nature, nurture, and social development. *Social Development, 3*, 37–53.

Polka, L., & Werker, J. F. (1994). Developmental changes in perception of non-native vowel contrasts. *Journal of Experimental Psychology: Human Perception and Performance, 20*, 421–435.

Rubin, K. H., Hastings, P. D., Stewart, S. L., Henderson, H. A., & Chen, X. (1997). The consistency and con-comitants of inhibition: Some of the children, all of the time. *Child Development, 68*, 467–483.

Stokes, I. (2001). The role of inheritance in behavior. *Science, 248*, 183–188.

Strassberg, A., Dodge, K., Petitt, G. S., & Bates, J. E. (1994). Spanking in the home and children's subsequent aggression toward kindergarten peers. *Developmental Psychopathology, 6*, 445–461.

Straus, M. A. (2001). New evidence for the benefits of never spanking. *Society, 38*(6), 52–60.

Sullins, E. S. (1991). Emotional contagion revisited: Effects of social comparison and expressive style on mood convergence. *Personality and Social Psychology Bulletin, 17*, 166–174.

Thomas, A., & Chess, S. (1977). *Temperament and development*. New York: Brunner/ Mazel.

Thompson, R. A. (1988). On emotion and self regulation. In R. A. Thompson (Ed.), *Nebraska Symposium on Motivation: Vol. 36. Socioemotional development* (pp. 367–468). Lincoln: University of Nebraska Press.

Tomasello, M. (1999). Understanding intentions and learning words in the second year of life. In M. Bowerman & S. Levinson (Eds.), *Language acquisition and conceptual development*. Cambridge, UK: Cambridge University Press.

Tronick, E. Z., & Cohn, J. F. (1989). Infant-mother face-to-face interaction: Age and gender differences in coor-dination and the occurrence of miscoordination. *Child Development, 60*, 85–92.

Wadsworth, B. J. (1978). *Piaget for the classroom teacher*. New York: Longman.

Watson, M. A. (1996). *The national parenting scales, experimental edition*. New York: Instructional Press.

Watson, M. A. (2001). *Mood disorders in young children*. C. E. U. course lecture. Wheaton, MD: American Healthcare Institute.

Wolff, P. H. (1993). *Behavioral and emotional states in infancy: A dynamic perspective*. Cambridge, MA: MIT Press.

Wood, D. (1998). *How children think and learn: The social contexts of cognitive development* (2nd ed.). Oxford: Blackwell Publishing.

Zahn-Waxler, C. (1991). The case for empathy: A developmental review. *Psychological Inquiry, 2*, 155–158.

Zeskind, P. S., & Marshall, T. R. (1991). Temporal organization in neonatal arousal: Systems, oscillations, and de-velopment. In M. Weiss, & P. Zelago (Eds.), *Newborn attention: Biological constraints and the influence of experience* (pp. 22–62). Norwood, NJ: Ablex.

■ ADDITIONAL RESOURCES

Ball, J., & Pence, A. (1999). Beyond developmentally appropriate practice: Developing community and culturally appropriate practice. *Young Children, 54*(2), 46–50.

Belsky, J., & Most, R. K. (1981). From exploration to play: A cross-sectional study of infant free play behavior, *Developmental Psychology, 17*, 630–639.

Douville, L. (1994). *3A's of Child Care: Attention, Approval, Affection.* Bayville, NY: Instructional Press.

Douville-Watson, L. (1994). *F. A. R. E. Family Actualization through Research and Education.* Bayville, NY: Instructional Press.

Douville-Watson, L. & Watson, M. (1998). *Child accountability programs.* Anaheim, CA: National Association for the Education of the Young Child.

Dunn, M., Mutuku, M., & Wolfe, R. (2004). Developmentally and culturally appropriate practice in the global village: The Kenya Literacy Project. *Young Children, 59*(5), 50–55.

Hyun, E. (1998). *Rethinking childhood: Vol. 3. Making sense of developmentally and culturally appropriate practice (DCAP) in early childhood education.* New York: P. Lang.

Lynch, E. W., & Hanson, M. J. (2004). *Developing cross-cultural competence: A guide for working with children and their families* (3rd ed.). Baltimore: Paul H. Brookes.

Moore, G. A., Cohn, J. F., & Campbell, S. B. (1997). Mothers' affective behavior with infant siblings: Stability and change. *Developmental Psychology, 22*, 317–326.

Piaget, J. (1954). *The construction of reality in the child* (M. Cook, trans.). New York: Basic Books.

Zahn-Wolff, P. H. (1966). *The courses, controls, and organizational behavior in the neonate.* Madison, CT: International Universities Press.

■ HELPFUL WEB SITES

Association for Childhood Education International. Supports child-centered whole curriculum education from infancy through early adolescence. http://www.acei.org/

Early Childhood Educators Web Guide. Links to Web sites on child development, cultural diversity, discipline, and guidance. http://www.ecewebguide.com/

Human Services Research Institute (HSRI). Develops policies and undertakes research, development, and evaluation projects. http://www.hsri.org/

Migrant and Seasonal Head Start Quality Improvement Centers (MHSQIC). Nationwide programs and technical assistance. Provides appropriate state-of-the-art responsive training. http://www.mhsqic.org/

Ministry of Women and Child Development. Department of the government of India that deals with child development issues. This site serves as an example of how other nations create policies and procedures for addressing issues related to child development from birth through age six. http://www.wcd.nic.in/

For additional infant and toddler resources, visit our Web site at
http://www.earlychilded.delmar.com

The Three As: The Master Tools for Child Care

INTRODUCTION

Have you ever heard the cry of a troubled newborn that sends ripples down your spine? Ask any new parents in the first few nights of adjusting to family life what their baby's cry feels like to them. Instinctively, humans feel the distress almost as if the cry reaches the very fiber of our being. The response is almost universal: do whatever is necessary to soothe, calm, and reassure the fragile infant. Once the goal of comforting is achieved, the experience is a sense of triumph like no other. How do we respond so quickly? What lost memory motivates us to take such sudden action? Could it be that we re-experience our own sense of utter aloneness, a vibration so familiar and so foreboding that every cell wishes to quiet the call?

Teaching the concepts of the three As—Attention, Approval, and Attunement— has been a passion for the authors for many, many years. The lifelong effects of positive, consistent, and conscious infant and toddler care have been understood by child development and early childhood experts for a long time. A working premise of this book is that what you do with children matters. Positive intention coupled with responsiveness to developmental characteristics makes a profound difference in the lives of children.

Children give back what they are given during early childhood. They return kindness, stability, consistency, and caring as they grow up and relate to other people in the schools, their workplace, and in their own families. As previously discussed in the section on neurological development, the quality of your caring, including actions, verbal messages, voice tone and tempo, and secure handling, helps create the nerve pathways that determine each child's perceptions and models of the world. Your interactions with young children help determine how each child will eventually perceive himself or herself—as worthy, unworthy, capable, hopeful, or hopeless.

Caregivers have a mission that is monumental in nature. Your daily movements, efforts, and attitudes affect the very fiber of each child; no position in society is more important. The three As are the master tools that ensure that your effect on children is positive and productive. There is no better way to provide quality care than a wonderfully soothing dose of consciously administered attention, approval, and attunement.

The abilities to understand and fulfill academic requirements and to master specific skills, such as bathing and feeding babies, are necessary to your work and may even extend into your personal life. These immensely important aspects of child care, however, are not enough.

Students studying child care must also integrate their *selves* into their work because in no other field is the professional in need of self-integration more than in this most humanistic endeavor. Taking charge of tomorrow's leaders on a daily basis demands human investment, since it supports future human relationships. Just how important are these future connections? Let's look at what other experts have to say.

"The child's self is constructed in the interpersonal relationships that bind her to others, she is known in the experience of connection and is defined by the responsiveness of human engagement" (Gilligan, 1988).

"It is in the context of relationships that the needs and wishes of very young children are met, or not. . . . It is in the context of relationships that infants and toddlers continue to develop expectations about how the world is, how the adults in that world behave, and their own place in the social world" (Pawl, 1990). Mothers who respond to their child's cues with insightfulness (e.g., seeing the problem from the child's perspective) had children who were significantly more likely to have secure attachment (Koren-Karie, Oppenheim, Dolev, & Sher, 2002).

"When there is a sudden breakdown in the relationship between caregiver and child, whether that is natural or due to conflict, the results can profoundly effect momentarily or cumulatively the meanings children give to themselves now and in later experience" (Douville-Watson, 1995).

Jane Healy, in her book *Your Child's Growing Mind,* discusses the importance of warm, loving, verbal interactions between parent or caregiver and child, particularly in the first two years. She indicates that praise, prompt attention, and immediate feedback about objects in the environment lead to better vocabulary and higher scores on later intelligence tests (Healy, 2004). In fact, early (i.e., two years of age) and later (i.e., four years of age) language skills were found to be related to young children's theory of mind. Specifically, those children with larger vocabularies were found to have more advanced false-belief understanding; possibly because the more advanced language skills underpin "the capacity to mark aspects of mind such as perspective, intention, obligation, and degree of certainty . . ." (Watson, Painter, & Bornstein, 2001, p. 454).

How important are these human connections? John Dewey wrote that ". . . every experience lives on in further experiences" (1938, p. 28). Repeated emotional experiences are integrated into children's understandings about themselves, others, and the world they share (Denzin, 1984). In this way, "the experiences and feelings of childhood endure" (Bowman, 1989, p. 450); "they become part of children's biographies, providing the emotional foundation for future interactions and relationships" (Hatch, 1995). If we acknowledge our responsibility as caregivers, we can readily accept that "infants become partners in the give and take of human relationships" (Snow, 1989).

So, what can you learn that will allow you to be available, fresh, interested, involved, and ready to take on this awesome task? Indeed, teachers must learn to take good care of themselves, to not neglect themselves in daily routines, and to use **self-health** techniques. The "master tools" for accomplishing this are the three As: Attention, Approval, and Attunement.

THE THREE As: ATTENTION, APPROVAL, AND ATTUNEMENT AS TOOLS

The three As of child care are the master tools for promoting a positive environment and maintaining a positive emotional connection between the young child and the caregiver. The three As of child care—Attention, Approval, and Attunement—are extremely powerful tools available to any person in just about any situation. They are not only valuable tools; their use is *essential* in the care and education of very young children. The three As are called master tools because they apply to everything we do all day long. Attention, Approval, and Attunement are necessary to function well, have good self-esteem, remain at ease, and interact with other people in a positive and productive manner.

The concepts of Attention, Approval, and Affection are meant to empower the caregiver and help facilitate an attitude change toward yourself, which emphasizes that early childhood educators' feelings have a profound effect on children. The three As are derived directly from the current perspectives on development and care (discussed in Chapters 1 and 2): brain research and ecological systems, sociocultural, and attachment theories. In addition, they are supported by our understanding of the guidelines for developmentally appropriate practice (to be addressed in later chapters; Bredekamp & Copple, 1997). This theoretical knowledge helps a teacher appropriately care for and educate children; when that same caregiver uses this knowledge for personal development, he or she can enjoy benefits as well. These concepts are widely used in areas of psychology and education.

THE ATTACHMENT DEBATE AND THE ROLES OF CAREGIVERS

Discussion of the three As begins with the scientific fact that infants and toddlers require secure attachments, or enduring emotional ties, to their caregivers for normal, healthy development. Further, a large body of research supports positive Attention, Approval, and Attunement between caregivers and children as the foundation for secure attachment.

An ongoing debate in the research literature concerns whether infants exhibit less secure attachment when they experience child care as opposed to being home-reared. This debate cannot be discussed without considering the changing roles of mothers and fathers in the care of infants. As we saw in Chapter 1, one historical view was that *only* the mother could bond with the infant sufficiently to ensure healthy development, and one current perspective suggests that non-familial persons can meet the needs of the infants equally well. Because a great number of infants and toddlers are spending the majority of their day in child care, the question of how much attachment to one consistent person an infant requires in order to develop security and trust is being studied more intensely.

As was introduced in Chapter 2, researchers have identified a secure pattern of attachment and three insecure patterns (Ainsworth, 1967, 1973; Ainsworth, Blehar, Waters, & Wall, 1978; Hesse & Main, 2000; Main & Soloman, 1990).

1. Secure attachment. The infant uses a parent or other family member as a secure base, strongly prefers the parent over a stranger, actively seeks contact with the parent, and is easily comforted by the parent after being absent.

2. Avoidant attachment. The infant is usually not distressed by parental separation and may avoid the parent or prefer a stranger when the parent returns.

3. Resistant attachment. The infant seeks closeness to the parent and resists exploring the environment, usually displays angry behavior after the parent returns, and is difficult to comfort.

4. Disoriented attachment. The infant shows inconsistent attachment and reacts to the parent returning with confused or contradictory behavior (looking away when held or showing a dazed facial expression).

A phenomenon related to attachment is **separation anxiety**, which appears to be a normal developmental experience, since children from every culture exhibit it. Infants from various cultures all over the world have been found to exhibit separation anxiety starting around six months and increasing in intensity until approximately 15 months (Kagan, Kearsley, & Zelazo, 1978). Separation anxiety is exhibited by securely attached infants, as well as different types of insecurely attached infants.

A summary of the research on infant attachment suggests that infants are actively involved in the attachment bond. Drastic changes in family circumstances, such as divorce, death, or job loss, detrimentally affect infant attachment. Babies are normally capable of attaching securely to more than one adult or parent. Contemporary researchers have examined how infants create attachments with caregivers, including fathers (Kazura, 2000), grandparents (Poehlmann, 2003), brothers and sisters (Volling, Herrera, & Poris, 2004), adoptive and foster families (Dyer, 2004; Stams, Juffer, & van IJzendoorn, 2002; Stovall-McClough & Dozier, 2004) and professional early childhood educators (Caldera & Hart, 2004; Howes, 1999; Ritchie & Howes, 2003). Caregiving that is supportive and sensitive to the child's needs using the three As promotes secure attachment, while insensitive or inconsistent care results in insecure attachment. Finally, secure infant attachment and continuity of caregiving is related to later cognitive, emotional, and social competence. The research on adoptive families, for example, illustrates two of these patterns. Infants adopted at younger ages showed higher levels of secure behavior and more coherent attachment strategies (Stovall-McClough & Dozier, 2004) and these positive attachment relationships predicted later socioemotional and cognitive development (Stams, Juffer, & van IJzendoorn, 2002).

From these findings we can draw several important implications for caregiving and parenting and changes in early childhood educators' roles. Research on attachment security of infants with full-time working mothers suggests that most infants of employed mothers are securely attached, and that this relationship is more influential on early social and emotional growth than are the relationships a child has with other caregivers, both inside and outside the home (NICHD Early Child Care Research Network, 1997, 1998a, 1998b, 1999). However, when a child has an insecure relationship to her mother, early childhood educators can establish a secure relationship with the child, providing a buffer against some of the negative developmental outcomes (see Shonkoff & Phillips, 2000, especially Chapter 9). Hence, as more and more mothers of infants enter the workplace, the responsibility for forming secure attachments must be shared with fathers, other family members, and teachers. Everyone must work together to provide secure and consistent attachment and bonding with infants.

Forming reciprocal relationships or partnerships with families will assist in this process. Our responsibilities are twofold: we must not only help children to develop trust and secure attachments with us, but also assist family members to form strong, secure relationships with the infant. As discussed in Chapter 1, employing particular strategies such as a primary caregiving system, family grouping, and continuity of care can ensure that each infant and toddler has as few caregivers as possible, each providing consistency and predictability over time. The second prong of our approach must be to provide family support and education to help family members form and maintain secure attachments with their children. Family education should include the importance of mothers, fathers, and other family members providing direct nurture

Infants and toddlers can form strong, positive attachments to early childhood teachers.

and care of the children so that the infants can experience consistent, loving, and healthy relationships.

Caregiver behaviors that ensure consistent and secure bonding and attachment with infants and toddlers are the three As of child care. Early childhood educators who fully understand the three As, use them effectively with children, and systematically model and teach parents to use them with their children do more than any other current force in society to ensure emotional security for infants and toddlers.

UNDERSTANDING THE THREE As

Attention

"Smile and the whole world smiles with you." We've often been put at ease when greeted by a stranger's smile or felt instant rapport with someone who returns our smile. So much is communicated without words; often the unspoken message conveys exactly how a person is feeling. When we realize that 70 percent of our total communication is nonverbal, it is easy to understand why a smile says so much.

In the simplest way, a smile is a way to attend to yourself and to someone else. When you bring attention to a behavior in another person, you are sending a message about the importance of that behavior. Using the words of Vygotsky, you are helping children to construct an understanding of the meaning behind a smile. For example, the child may construct the notion that people smile when they are happy or see a behavior that they like. In this way, young children begin to associate a smile response with engaging in an appropriate behavior. A neural pathway is then built to remember this association; in this way, what we attend to helps the brain to grow. The opposite is also true. If we attend to negative behaviors displayed by children, then the children may construct an understanding that these behaviors are appropriate ways to interact with others; those neural pathways are strengthened and used to guide future behavior.

Of course, attending is much more complicated than just producing a smile or reacting to a negative behavior. Attention, for early childhood educators, also involves higher mental functions (Bodrova & Leong, 1996) or "cognitive processes acquired through learning and teaching [that] . . . are *deliberate, mediated, internalized* behaviors" (p. 20, emphasis in original). Teachers, then, must learn to engage in focused attention to observe the behavior, skills, and needs of the children in their care. Observing closely, or attending, facilitates your analysis of the child's behaviors and appropriate responses to those behaviors. In other words, attending makes possible the identification of each child's **zone of proximal development (ZPD)**, "the distance between the actual developmental level as determined by independent problem solving and the level of potential development as determined through problem solving under adult guidance or in collaboration with more capable peers" (Vygotsky, 1978, p. 86).

Classifying the ZPD is vital for teachers because it determines where to place educational emphasis. Scaffolding, or assistance from a more-skilled other, facilitates learning at the "higher" end of the zone. In other words, behaviors by the more skilled partner contribute to acquiring skills that were outside of the child's independent level of functioning. Scaffolding behaviors will be addressed more comprehensively in future chapters.

Another component of attending entails recognizing ecological factors from other systems that impact the development and learning of the children (Bronfenbrenner, 1979, 1989). As discussed in Chapter 1, these factors both affect the child and are influenced by the child. Such bidirectional influences must continually be considered by early childhood educators, in order to recognize the active role children play in their own development. For example, teachers must be culturally sensitive and responsive to the way families want to raise their children. Families hold particular beliefs that may or may not be shared by the caregiver; this should affect how you do your work. Altering your routines and behaviors to support family practices assists with more continuous care for very young children (Gonzalez-Mena, 2001).

Approval

Approval from others teaches us to approve of ourselves. The best type of attention is approval. Approval of another person is a clear message that you have respect and positive regard for that person. According to the American Heritage® Dictionary of the English Language (2000) **respect** is all of the following:

- to feel or show differential regard for
- to avoid violation or interference with
- the state of being regarded with honor or esteem
- willingness to show consideration or appreciation

How do early childhood educators translate this multifaceted definition into their daily practice? Swim (2003) suggests that both allowing children time to try or complete tasks and helping them to make choices reflect respect for children because these behaviors demonstrate refraining from interfering with them. In addition, valuing individual children's ways of doing and being shows that they are held in high esteem by the caregiver.

Educational leaders in the municipal infant/toddler and preschool programs of Reggio Emilia, Italy take the understanding of respect to another level. They have declared respect an educational value (Rinaldi, 2001) and devised the concept of the **rights of children**. This concept reflects their image of the child as "rich in resources, strong, and competent. The emphasis is placed on seeing the children as unique individuals with rights rather than simply needs. They have potential, plasticity, openness, the desire to grow, curiosity, a sense of wonder, and the desire to relate to other people and to communicate" (Rinaldi, 1998, p. 114). Teachers use their image of the child to guide their instructional decisions, curricular planning, and interactions with children (see, for example, Edwards, Gandini, & Forman, 1998).

To children, approval says they have done something right, and it helps them feel worthwhile. Approval builds trust and self-confidence, which in turn encourage children to try new things without fear. The most important concept a caregiver must learn is always to approve of the child, even when you disapprove of his or her behavior. For example, it must be made clear to the child that I like who you are, but not what you are doing right now.

Appropriate and consistent approval develops trust in the child. Once a sense of trust is developed, children can readily approve of themselves. According to Erikson's eight stages of man, the general state of trust suggests that one has learned not only to "rely on the sameness and continuity of the other providers, but also that one may trust oneself" (Erikson, 1963).

Trust depends not only on the quantity (e.g., number of interactions), but also on the quality of the caregiver's interactions and relationships with children. Positive approval creates a sense of trust as a result of the sensitive way in which the caregiver takes time to care for the child's individual needs. Adults must convey to the child an honest concern for the child's welfare and a deep conviction that there is meaning in what they are doing. Trust based on consistent, positive caring allows children to grow up with a sense of meaningful belonging and trust.

According to ethological theory, parental responsiveness is adaptive in that it ensures that the basic needs of the infant are met and provides protection from danger. It brings the baby into close contact with the caregiver, who can respond sensitively to a wide range of infant behaviors (Bell & Ainsworth, 1972).

Some caution should be exercised regarding when to give approval. Caregivers who approve of every little behavior and shower children with unconditional approval lose respect with children. Genuine approval for meaningful accomplishments serves to encourage children to try harder and helps them value their own efforts. Make sure the child has made genuine effort or has accomplished something of value and your approval will help children become the best that they can be.

Attunement

Attunement involves being aware of someone, along with her moods, needs, and interests, and responding to all of these. In other words, when you are "in tune," you are providing high quality care and education that meets the individual needs, interests, and abilities of each child.

Attuned caregivers often look natural in their interactions with infants and toddlers. However, being attuned is not instinctual for all persons. Often, our beliefs about child rearing or parenting interfere with providing such care. For example, a strongly held belief by many parents, teachers, and physicians is that responding to the cries of infants too quickly will spoil them. Of course, as we have stated previously, you cannot spoil a young child. All of the research on attachment reviewed in this chapter and the previous chapters discounts this belief. Responding sensitively to a child's communication strategies helps the child to develop trust in his or her caregiver, form strong, secure attachments, and grow socially and emotionally.

Attuned caregivers devote a great deal of time to carefully observing and recording the infants' behaviors. Having this knowledge affords the educator a strong foundation on which to base interactional, instructional, and caregiving strategies. For example, Nicole knows that Tiffany, 27 months, has a very regular routine for eating and sleeping. Today, however, she was not hungry right after playing outdoors and had difficulty relaxing for a nap. Upon closer observation and questioning, Nicole came to understand that Tiffany's throat hurt. Nicole was able to use her knowledge of Tiffany to "tune into" this change of routine and uncover the beginning of an illness.

When caregivers engage in respectful and responsive interpersonal interactions with infants and toddlers, they are attuned in the way researchers use the word. They are in synchrony with the child (Isabella & Belsky, 1991). Reading and responding to the child's cues is crucial to engaging in this "interactional dance." For example, picture caregiver Carlos feeding Judd his lunch. Judd is hungry and eating quickly. Carlos talks about how good the food must be for an empty stomach. He is smiling and laughing between bites. All of a sudden, Judd begins to slow the pace. Carlos reads this behavior and slows down his offering of food and pattern of speech. Judd smiles and turns his head away from Carlos. Carlos pauses and waits for Judd to turn back around. He does turn back and opens his mouth. Carlos provides another bite of vegetables.

Our positive, focused attention toward children's behavior directs our energy and intention, we provide genuine approval for real success and effort, and attunement communicates our feelings of respect, approval, and appreciation of children. When we, as early childhood educators, combine all three of these, children cannot help but

Caregivers are attuned to reactions when a stranger (e.g., parent of another child) enters the room.

respond positively to us, their world, and themselves. That is why the three *As* are the master tools for child development and care.

USING THE THREE As SUCCESSFULLY WITH INFANTS AND TODDLERS

The three *As* of child care are a work in progress. In all likelihood, you use the three *As* already without much thought about them. The three *As* are powerful and rejuvenating. They elicit responses in children that will sustain you in your vocation. When you learn to take care of your own health and lower your stress level along with the three *As*, you assist with the development of positive behaviors in children.

Observe your initial approach to an unknown infant. You get down to her level (floor, blanket, or chair). You are calm, move slowly, make eye contact, enter her space, get even closer to her physically, smile, and gently begin soft speech to engage her. If you believe you have permission from her to stay close, you keep eye contact and begin slowly to inquire what she is doing, such as playing or eating. When she gestures, you follow the gesture with a similar response, this time making a sound that seems to identify her movement and keep pace. This usually elicits a smile or giggle. Once again you smile and make noise. You may try gently touching a shoulder or finger, and before long, you are accepted as an approving addition to the child's space. This slow progression of rapport-building is also the slow progression of the use of the three As. First you give Attention, then Approval, and then Attunement. When this is done consciously, all involved feel worthy.

One of the most positive assurances of worthiness a caregiver can receive on a daily basis is that almighty hug given unconditionally as a gift from the gleeful toddler who sweeps down upon you when you are playing on the floor. This hug, which is often accompanied by a loud and joyful sound, enters your space with such focused positive energy that each of you feels the impact. The result of this positive energy is felt by the two of you, and brings smiles to the faces of all who observe it.

Young children benefit from these important techniques. These tools help shape the child's development toward mastery. Mastery is related to a child's sense of well-being, self-achievement, and eventual self-esteem. Being aware of the master tools of the three As helps encourage children to master their environment. Your outward expression of the three As helps build the child's development of identity. Erikson (1963), in writing about autonomy, discusses the infant's ability to emotionally evaluate his worth as "a series of alternate basic attitudes such as trust vs. mistrust in terms of 'sense of' as in 'sense of health' or 'sense of being unwell.'"

Your ability to create a positive learning environment allows children to feel safe, to gather information, and eventually to trust their senses for information about their world. Remember to see yourself as a sort of recharging station—a physically and emotionally rewarding place where children feel a sense of security. Keep your energy centered and positive, so you can bring that positive energy to the children in your care.

The three As apply not only to the care and education of very young children but also to caregivers themselves. Once teachers take care of their own well-being, the experience generalizes into the care of children. When caregivers take responsibility to care for themselves, they are ready to deal with the needs of children. The fact is, you cannot give what you do not have. The personal resources of the caregiver are vital for successful outcomes with children.

Caregiving is a partnership between the adult and child. No one wants a partnership that is exhausting, draining, and without rewards. No healthy person can make a real commitment to such a relationship. Attention, Approval, and Attunement can become tools to help each child experience the commitment to your partnership. By integrating yourself into your daily activities, you are able to begin to make the children in your care the primary focus of your work. Therefore, you need to take care of yourself so you have the resources to have your day centered on the children.

In summary, the healthiest relationships result in the experience of security and the safety of expressing all of the different emotions. This ability to express emotion without fear promotes a healthy, happy, well-balanced individual who feels competent to handle life's challenges. The best possible connection between caregivers and very young children comes from each person being actively involved in the relationship.

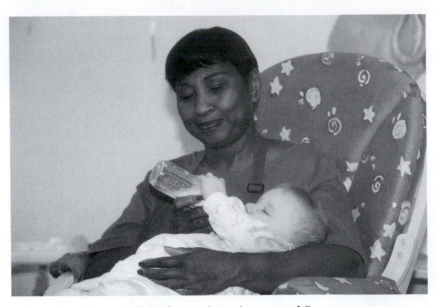

Infants and toddlers who feel safe can relax and rest peacefully.

When the three As are focused on children, they promote appropriate behaviors and enhance a positive learning environment for children. The caregiver structures a safe place in which the young child explores and masters all of his or her growing abilities by solving problems that naturally occur within the environment. A stable, positive environment promotes trust and confidence and allows the growing infant to express all of his or her needs.

When the three As are focused on you as a caregiver, they promote self-health, personal growth, and professional development. These skills help you to be more aware of your impact on children and revitalize you, so that you can sustain a high quality of care throughout the day. Attending to your own well-being promotes trust and ultimately teaches children, by your example, to be self-confident and have trust in themselves. The challenge presented to caregivers centers on their ability to maintain their own sense of well-being while caring for children (Gilligan, 1982; Hochschild, 1989).

■ KEY TERMS

Approval	resistant attachment	separation anxiety
Attention	respect	zone of proximal development (ZPD)
Attunement	rights of children	
avoidant attachment	secure attachment	
disoriented attachment	self-health	

CASE STUDY   Pia

Pia Eduardo was born premature, weighing 2 pounds, 10 ounces. She is now 12 days old and weighs 3 pounds, 4 ounces. She lies on her stomach sleeping in an incubator, where the temperature is mechanically controlled to duplicate the mother's womb. Pia sleeps on a slant board to help her breathe. She has intravenous lines for fluids, and heart and brain monitors are attached to evaluate her life functions continuously.

Anthony, Pia's father, comes to the hospital during his lunch hour and briefly at night because he works overtime to make enough money for Tonya, Pia's mother, to stay most of the time at the hospital with their daughter. Tonya, with the help of the hospital staff, frequently lifts Pia out of the incubator and holds the baby on her chest to provide skin-to-skin contact. Tonya strokes Pia's hands, feet, back, and legs, massaging them gently while she talks softly and slowly to deliberately soothe Pia. She wears no cologne so Pia can smell her natural odor and remains conscious of keeping her breathing in rhythm with Pia's breathing. This procedure of touching the skin has been shown to release brain chemicals that increase physical growth (Schanberg & Field, 1987).

The attention, approval, and attunement that Tonya consciously gives Pia directly affect Pia's life functions, as recorded on the monitors. When Tonya is touching, holding, bonding, soothing, and loving Pia, her heart and brain waves become stronger and more regular, her breathing becomes deeper and calmer, and she generally produces healthier patterns of physiological responses. This procedure of bonding with premature babies and providing conscious attention, approval, and attunement has become standard practice in hospitals, because research shows that infants who receive this bonding grow more quickly and are healthier than babies who do not. In addition, many hospitals now conduct parenting groups to teach parents to give attention, approval, and attunement to infants as a functional tool to promote health and growth.

1. From the case study, what do you think is the most important tool a caregiver can use with a young infant? Why?

2. What is the relationship between physical contact and attachment, as indicated by this case study?

3. How does interactional synchrony apply to this case study?

■ QUESTIONS AND EXPERIENCES FOR REFLECTION

1. Apply all three As to two separate children, and write down their reactions. How did these interactions feel to you? Why?

2. Consider how and why you could apply the three As to yourself and your personal life.

3. Write a scenario using examples of the ways in which the three As might calm children and promote a positive learning environment.

■ CHAPTER REVIEW

1. List, define, describe, and provide a specific example for each of the three As of child care.

2. How are the three As grounded in the theoretical perspectives described in Chapters 1 and 2?

3. What is the difference between giving attention to children and spoiling them?

4. Why is using all of the three As together a powerful tool for motivating children?

5. Why might focusing the three As on yourself help you fight off exhaustion during your day?

6. What is the most important aspect of this chapter for you? Why?

■ REFERENCES

Ainsworth, M. D. S. (1967). *Infancy in Uganda: Infant care and the growth of love.* Baltimore: Johns Hopkins University Press.

Ainsworth, M. D. S. (1973). The development of infant-mother attachment. In B. M. Caldwell & H. N. Ricciuti (Eds.), *Review of child development research: Vol. 3. Child development and social policy.* Chicago: University of Chicago Press.

Ainsworth, M. D. S., Blehar, M., Waters, E., & Wall, S. (1978). *Patterns of attachment.* Hillsdale, NJ: Erlbaum.

Bell, S. M., & Ainsworth, M. D. S. (1972). Infant crying and maternal responsiveness. *Child Development, 43,* 117–119.

Bodrova, E., & Leong, D. (1996). *Tools of the mind: The Vygotskian approach to early childhood education.* Englewood Cliffs, NJ: Prentice Hall.

Bowman, B. (1989). Self-reflection as an element of professionalism. *Teachers College Records, 90*(3), 444–451.

Bredekamp, S., & Copple, C. (Eds.). (1997). *Developmentally appropriate practice in early childhood programs* (Rev. ed.). Washington, DC: National Association for the Education of Young Children.

Bronfenbrenner, U. (1979). *The ecology of human development: Experiments by nature and design.* Cambridge, MA: Harvard University Press.

Bronfenbrenner, U. (1989). Ecological systems theory. In R. Vasta (Ed.), *Annals of child development* (Vol. 6, pp. 187–251). Greenwich, CT: JAI Press.

Caldera, Y. M., & Hart, S. (2004). Exposure to child care, parenting style and attachment security. *Infant & Child Development, 13*(1), 21–33.

Denzin, N. K. (1984). *On understanding emotion.* San Francisco: Jossey Bass.

Dewey, J. (1938). *Experience and education.* New York: Macmillan.

Douville-Watson, L. (1995). *Concerned conscious care: The 3A's in action.* Child care lecture series. Bayville, NY: Instructional Press.

Dyer, F. J. (2004). Termination of parental rights in light of attachment theory: The case of Kaylee. *Psychology, Public Policy, & Law, 10*(1–2), 5–30.

Edwards, C., Gandini, L., & Forman, G. (Eds.). (1998). *The hundred languages of children: The Reggio Emilia approach—Advanced reflections* (2nd ed.). Westport, CT: Ablex.

Erikson, E. H. (1963). The eight stages of man. In *Childhood & society.* New York: W. W. Norton.

Gilligan, C. (1982). *In a different voice: Psychological theory and works development.* Cambridge, MA: Harvard University Press.

Gilligan, C. (1988). Remapping the moral domain: New images of self in relationship. In C. Gilligan, J. Ward, J. Taylor, & B. B. Bardige (Eds.), *Mapping the moral domain* (pp. 3–19). Cambridge, MA: Harvard University Press.

Gonzalez-Mena, J. (2001). *Multicultural issues in child care* (3rd ed.). Mountain View, CA: Mayfield.

Hatch, J. A. (1995). *Qualitative research in early childhood settings.* Stamford, CT: Praeger Publishers.

Healy, J. (2004). *Your child's growing mind: A guide to learning and brain development from birth to adolescence.* (3rd ed.). New York: Broadway Books.

Hesse, E., & Main, M. (2000). Disorganized infant, child, and adult attachment: Collapse in behavior and attachment strategies. *Journal of Psychoanalytic Association, 48*(4).

Hochschild, A. (1989). *The second shift.* New York: Viking Penguin.

Howes, C. (1999). Attachment relationships in the context of multiple caregivers. In J. Cassidy & P. R. Shaver (Eds.), *Handbook of attachment: Theory, research, and clinical applications* (pp. 671–687). New York: Guilford Press.

Isabella, R. A., & Belsky, J. (1991). Interactional synchrony and the origins of infant-mother attachment: A replication study. *Child Development, 62,* 373–384.

Kagan, J., Kearsley, R. B., & Zelazo, P. R. (1978). *Infancy: Its place in human development.* Cambridge, MA: Harvard University Press.

Kazura, K. (2000). Father's qualitative and quantitative involvement: An investigation of attachment, play, and social interactions. *Journal of Men's Studies, 9*(1), 41–57.

Koren-Karie, N., Oppenheim, D., Dolev, S., & Sher, S. (2002). Mothers' insightfulness regarding their infants' internal experience: Relations with maternal sensitivity and infant attachment. *Developmental Psychology, 38,* 534–542.

Main, M., & Soloman, J. (1990). Procedures for identifying infants as disorganized/disoriented during the Ainsworth Strange Situation. In M. Greenberg, D. Cicchetti, & M. Cummings (Eds.), *Attachment in the preschool years: Theory, research, and intervention* (pp. 121–160). Chicago: University of Chicago Press.

NICHD Early Child Care Research Network. (1997). The effects of infant child care on infant-mother attachment security: Results of the NICDH study of early child care. *Child Development, 68,* 860–879.

NICHD Early Child Care Research Network. (1998a). *Chronicity of maternal depressive symptoms, maternal behavior, and child functioning at 36 months: Results from the NICHD study of early child care.* Washington, DC: Author.

NICHD Early Child Care Research Network. (1998b). Relations between family predictors and child outcomes: Are they weaker for children in child care? *Developmental Psychology, 34,* 1119–1128.

NICHD Early Child Care Research Network. (1999). Child care and mother-child interaction in the first three years of life. *Developmental Psychology, 35,* 1399–1413.

Pawl, J. (1990). Infants in day care: Reflections on experience, expectation and relationships. *Zero to Three, 10*(3):1–6.

Pickett, J. P. et al. (Eds.). (2000). American Heritage® Dictionary of the English Language. Boston: Houghton Mifflin.

Poehlmann, J. (2003). An attachment perspective on grandparents raising their very young grandchildren: Implications for intervention and research. *Infant Mental Health Journal, 24*(2), 149–173.

Rinaldi, C. (1998). Projected curriculum constructed through documentation—*Progettazione:* An interview with Lella Gandini. In C. Edwards, L. Gandini, & G. Forman (Eds.), *The hundred languages of children: The Reggio Emilia approach—Advanced reflections* (2nd ed., pp. 113–125). Westport, CT: Ablex.

Rinaldi, C. (2001). Infant-toddler centers and preschools as places of culture. In Project Zero and Reggio Children, *Making learning visible: Children as individual and group learners.* (pp. 38–46). Reggio Emilia, Italy: Reggio Children srl.

Ritchie, S., & Howes, C. (2003). Program practices, caregiver stability, and child-caregiver relationships. *Journal of Applied Developmental Psychology, 24,* 497–516.

Schanberg, S., & Field, T. M. (1987). Sensory deprivation stress and supplemental stimulation in the rat pup and preterm human neonate. *Children Development, 58,* 1431–1447.

Shonkoff, J. P., & Phillips, D. A. (Eds.). (2000). *From neurons to neighborhoods: The science of early childhood development.* Washington, DC: National Academy Press.

Snow, C. (1989). *Infant development.* Englewood Cliffs, NJ: Prentice Hall.

Stams, G.-J. J. M., Juffer, F., & van IJzendoorn, M. H. (2002). Maternal sensitivity, infant attachment, and temperament in early childhood predict adjustment in middle childhood: The case of adopted children and their biologically unrelated parents. *Developmental Psychology, 38,* 806–821.

Stovall-McClough, K. C., & Dozier, M. (2004). Forming attachments in foster care: Infant attachment behaviors during the first two months of placement. *Development & Psychopathology, 16,* 253–271.

Swim, T. J. (2003). Respecting infants and toddlers: Strategies for best practice. *Earlychildhood NEWS, 15*(5), 16–17, 20–23.

Volling, B. L., Herrera, C., & Poris, M. P. (2004). Situational affect and temperament: Implications for sibling caregiving. *Infant and Child Development, 13,* 173–183.

Vygotsky, L. S. (1978). *Mind in society: The development of higher psychological processes* (M. Cole, V. John-Steiner, S. Scribner, E. Souberman, Trans.). Cambridge, MA: Harvard University Press.

Watson, A. C., Painter, K. M., & Bornstein, M. H. (2001). Longitudinal relations between 2-year-olds' language and 4-year-olds' theory of mind. *Journal of Cognition and Development, 2,* 449–457.

■ ADDITIONAL RESOURCES

Douville-Watson, L. (1988a). *Caregiver self-health.* Child care lecture series. Oyster Bay, NY: Lifeskills Institute.

Douville-Watson, L. (1988b).*The 3A's of child care: Attention, approval and affection.* Child care lecture series. Oyster Bay, NY: Lifeskills Institute.

Douville-Watson, L., & Watson, M. (1988c). *Family actualization through research & education: F. A. R. E.,* (3rd ed.). New York: Actualization, Inc.

Nuernberger, P. (1996). *The quest for personal power: Transforming stress into strength.* New York: G. P. Putnam Brothers.

Saarni, C. (1989). Children's understanding and strategic control of emotional expression in social transactions. In C. Saarni and P. L. Harris (Eds.), *Children's understanding of emotion* (pp. 181–208). New York: Cambridge University Press.

■ HELPFUL WEB SITES

Divorce Wizards: Top 10 Tips to Help Your Child. If one parent is disapproving of affection a child expresses toward the other parent, the child will begin to withdraw. **http://www.divorcewizards.com/top10child.html**

Declaration of the Rights of the Child. The 1959 declaration published by the United Nations Office of the High Commissioner for Human Rights. **http://www.unhchr.ch/html/menu2/b/25.htm**

Fernside Online—How to Help a Grieving Child. Volunteer organization; Fernside provides tips in the "Grownups Area." **http://www.fernside.org/grownups/how.html**

ParentCenter. Numerous articles and Ask the Expert sections on development of children from two to eight years old. **http://parentcenter.babycenter.com/topicsaz/**

Parent Passages. Learn about workshops for new or expectant parents. **http://www.parentpassages.com/index.html**

For additional infant and toddler resources, visit our Web site at
http://www.earlychilded.delmar.com

CHAPTER 5

Effective Preparation and Tools for Professional Educators

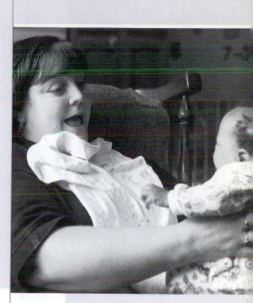

■ OBJECTIVES

After reading this chapter, you should be able to:

- Describe the characteristics necessary to become a competent caregiver.
- Apply ORAOM to your work as a caregiver.
- Explain the various types of knowledge professional educators possess.
- Articulate the relationship between formal education experiences and child outcomes.
- Determine which observational tool is best to use given your needs.

■ CHAPTER OUTLINE

- Introduction
- Characteristics of a Competent Early Childhood Educator
  Early Childhood Educators Are Physically and Mentally Healthy
- Acquiring Knowledge
  About Yourself
  About Children
  About Families
  About Early Child Care and Education

INTRODUCTION

The heart and soul of excellent care and education are people and the tools they use in supporting the development of young children. This chapter provides specific, effective tools that enhance development. The early childhood educator should practice using each of the tools in this chapter within a Developmental Perspective (refer to Chapter 2, Appendix A and Appendix B). The authors subscribe to the idea that careful assessment of infants and toddlers is an essential starting point for professional child care. Recording specific, descriptive observations on an ongoing basis ensures optimal growth and development.

As you learned in Chapter 4, it is essential for caregivers to take good care of themselves in order to provide competent care for young children. Therefore, the first tools we will examine are those related to your professional preparation as a caregiver.

CHARACTERISTICS OF A COMPETENT EARLY CHILDHOOD EDUCATOR

Early Childhood Educators Are Physically and Mentally Healthy

Physical health is necessary to provide the high energy level needed in caregiving. Good health is also necessary to resist the variety of illnesses to which you are exposed. The importance of a healthy staff is reflected in the American Academy of Pediatrics recommendations (1996) that the health record for each employee contains

- evidence of freedom from active tuberculosis and an annual report of a negative tuberculosis Mantoux test.

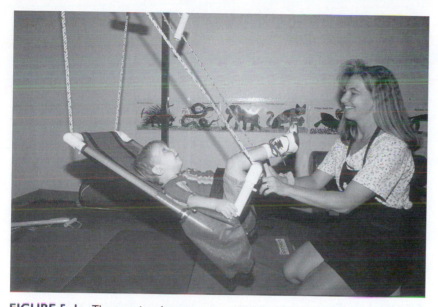

FIGURE 5–1   The caregiver has warm, emotional relationships with children.

- evidence of pre-employment examination or a statement from his or her personal physician indicating a health status permitting the employee to function in his or her assigned role.
- evidence of recovery after specified communicable diseases.
- reports of periodic evaluations.
- evidence of a Hepatitis B vaccine injection.

In your daily relationships, you must provide physical closeness and nurture for an extended time, give emotionally more than you receive, be patient and resolve conflicts caused by someone else, and calm one child right after you have been frustrated with another. Emotionally stable teachers have learned how to handle a variety of emotional demands in their daily experiences and how to encourage greater mental health in others (Figure 5–1).

Early Childhood Educators Have a Positive Self-Image

Your feelings of self-confidence and positive self-worth show that you believe in yourself. This gives you the strength to take risks, solve problems, consider alternatives, and make decisions in situations where there may be no obvious correct answer. Your perceptions, knowledge base, and opinions are all sources of information you can use in evaluating situations and making decisions. Awareness of your expectations and those of children help you remain open-minded. Our decisions are not always accurate or appropriate, because they are based on incomplete information. Admit this, reevaluate the data or gather more information and make a new decision. Doing so

FIGURE 5–2   The caregiver develops skill in working with children and gains satisfaction from interacting with them.

helps you to continue professional growth and enhances your self-image as a competent caregiver.

Early Childhood Educators Are Caring and Respectful

There is pleasure, enjoyment, and satisfaction in providing effective, high-quality care. Although some tasks may be difficult, unpleasant, or repetitious, your accepting behavior and considerate treatment shows that you value meeting the children's needs. They are worthy of your time and effort because they are important people (Figure 5–2). When early childhood educators reflect caring feelings to the children, families, and other staff members, this helps to build good partnerships.

Early Childhood Educators Are Professionals

Caregiving is an essential profession which should receive more respect. You provide a very important service to children, families, and the community. The care you provide directly affects children at critical times in their lives. You have great influence and importance in the child's life and must be rational and objective in your decisions and actions.

Striving to do your best is essential for high-quality caregiving. Read, study, visit, observe, and talk with other early childhood educators. Professional knowledge is not static; it is not possible to finish learning everything you need to know to be an effective caregiver. New information and experiences lead to new insights, understanding, and skills. Openness to learning helps you seek new ideas and take advantage of new opportunities to expand your knowledge and skills.

ACQUIRING KNOWLEDGE

About Yourself

Why do you want to be an early childhood educator? What are your strengths? What are your weaknesses? What are your interests? What are your values? What are your expectations of yourself and others? Are you willing to put forth effort to satisfy yourself and others? How much time and effort do you think is appropriate to put into caregiving? Professional educators value and therefore set aside time for frequent and systematic reflection on their work. What plans do you have to learn about yourself, others, and your program?

About Children

Child development research continues to provide new information about children. The information helps identify each child's individual characteristics and levels of development. Your knowledge of the patterns of physical, emotional, social, and cognitive development influences how you plan for and act with children.

About Families

Each family situation is unique and affects your caregiving. As a caregiver you can expect any kind of family you can imagine: traditional, single parent, grandparent as head of household, gay/lesbian parents, adoptive families with Caucasian parents and Asian children, and diverse cultures. You should continually seek information from and maintain communication with family members. Families have special needs, desires, and expectations of themselves, their children, and you.

About Early Child Care and Education

Developmentally appropriate practice (Bredekamp & Copple, 1997) encompasses emotional interaction, instructional planning, and various types of teaching and learning techniques involving children, families, colleagues, and the community. How do we create experiences that are responsive to the needs of the toddlers? How do we identify which materials are appropriate for the various development levels of infants? Answers to these questions, while not always straightforward, can be found in a number of sources, including licensing laws and accreditation standards. State or county agencies design **licensing regulations** to standardize the care and education of young children in group settings in both home- and center-based programs. These regulations govern such things as teacher-child ratios, space, safety and health requirements, fire codes, and zoning ordinances. Licensing identifies a set of minimum standards that the program meets; it does not guarantee quality of care. However, many states, like Indiana, are working to include important characteristics of quality programming in their licensing regulations. Professional organizations have well-established accreditation programs for family child care programs and center-based care, the National Association for Family Child Care (**NAFCC**) and the National Association for the Education of Young Children (**NAEYC**), respectively. **Accreditation** standards are significantly more stringent than licensing regulations and serve to recognize high-quality programs that meet the physical, social, emotional, and cognitive development of the children and families being served.

Becoming familiar with both licensing regulations and accreditation standards is a must for professional early childhood educators. Doing so will highlight the various roles that infant and toddler teachers engage in on a daily basis. You will need to balance these many roles to provide high quality care and education. Understanding the responsibilities of your roles will help determine your strengths and how to increase knowledge and personal growth.

One way to understand the various responsibilities is to read and discuss with colleagues NAEYC's Code of Ethical Conduct (NAEYC, 2005a). This document, created with significant input from teachers working directly with young children, provides guidance on balancing and resolving any conflicts among your professional responsibilities.

About Program Implementation

There are many successful ways to apply our knowledge of developmentally appropriate practice to nurturing, providing care, and teaching. Knowledge of these can help you adjust and individualize caregiving procedures to meet the specific needs of the environment and the children you serve.

About Partnerships

Early childhood educators cannot work in isolation and provide high-quality care (Bove, 2001; Bredekamp & Copple, 1997). **Partnerships** with families, colleagues, and community agencies are a must. Family members possess knowledge about the child that we often do not have access to, unless we ask. When reciprocal or bidirectional relationships have been established between teachers and families, information flows freely, benefiting everyone involved.

Colleagues are invaluable resources whether you have worked in the early childhood profession five minutes, five months, or five years. The sharing of professional knowledge, skills, and dispositions promotes growth for all parties (see, for example, Buell, Pfister, & Gamel-McCormick, 2002).

Partnerships with community agencies and organizations will add value and resources to your program. The number and type of agencies you form partnerships with will be determined by the characteristics of your community. A great place to start is your public library. Introduce yourself to the children's and adult librarians. They can offer assistance with books, Web sites, magazines, and journals to help you stay on top of the dynamic field of early childhood education. They can also apprise you of state and federal funding sources. Many communities have city- or county-wide consortiums of early childhood educators from public, private, center-based,

Attending conferences renews your enthusiasm as a professional and provides opportunities for meeting other infant/toddler educators.

and family child care settings that can offer services such as mentoring or helping to locate educational opportunities. Moreover, do not forget to participate in your local and state Association for the Education of Young Children. Networking through those organizations can provide additional avenues for partnerships.

About Advocacy

Professionals employ informal advocacy strategies in their daily work with children and families. As mentioned in Chapter 1, each and every time you interact with family members, colleagues, and community members, you are a teacher-leader. Careful consideration must be given to your practices, as others look to you for examples of how to treat infants and toddlers. Engaging in developmentally appropriate practice, for example, demonstrates your beliefs about the capabilities of children and your positive influence on their development and learning. Your dedication to engaging in and sharing professional knowledge and practices makes you an advocate for young children, families, and the early childhood profession.

Formal advocacy involves working with community members, other professional organizations, and even policy makers to improve the lives of children and families and the early childhood profession. Learning to be an effective advocate takes time, dedication, and the acquisition of skills (NAEYC, 2005b; Robinson & Stark, 2005).

PROFESSIONAL PREPARATION OF THE EARLY CHILDHOOD EDUCATOR

Both informal and formal educational opportunities are available to infant and toddler teachers. Informal experiences may be spontaneous or planned. An article in a magazine may stimulate your thinking by providing new information and raising questions. You may take time to do further thinking and discuss your ideas with colleagues, or you may think of the ideas periodically and begin changing your caregiving practices to incorporate what you have learned.

Formal educational opportunities are those that are planned to meet specific goals. You choose experiences to help you gain desired knowledge and skills. The following types of experiences contribute to your learning either by using your experiences with children, through independent study, or a combination of both:

- A mentor or a more-experienced caregiver. Having such a person available gives you opportunities to observe, participate, and discuss techniques. Mentoring is organized, supervised, and evaluated; isolated work does not count.
- Workshops, seminars, or speakers. These may be sponsored by libraries, adult schools, colleges, universities, hospitals, and professional organizations. They usually focus on a single topic or skill.
- short courses provided by local or state associations or agencies
- continuing education courses sponsored by local schools and colleges
- technical school courses and programs in child care
- community college and university courses in early childhood education and/or child development
- Child Development Associate certificate. "The Child Development Associate, or **CDA**, is a person who is able to meet the specific needs of children and who, with parents and other adults, works to nurture children's physical, social, emotional, and intellectual growth in a child development framework. The CDA conducts herself or himself in an ethical manner" (Child Development Associate National Credentialing Program, 1992).
- Early childhood education degrees. Associate, bachelor's, master's, and doctoral degrees can be completed at colleges or universities. Hyson (2003) created guidelines for the educational preparation of teachers based on five core standards and a common set of professional knowledge, skills, and dispositions. Table 5–1 demonstrates the overlap of the CDA and NAEYC core standards. While there is a great deal of similarity of content between the credentials, the expectations of the professional increase with each higher level of education (Hyson, 2003).

IMPACT OF TEACHER EDUCATION ON QUALITY OF CARE AND EDUCATION

Does teacher preparation make a difference to the quality of care and education provided and child outcomes? Evidence is mounting that it does. Teachers who receive training on developmentally appropriate practices use appropriate practices with

TABLE 5–1 OVERLAP OF THE CDA AND NAEYC STANDARDS

CDA COMPETENCY AREAS	NAEYC TEACHER PREPARATION STANDARDS				
	1. PROMOTING CHILD DEVELOPMENT AND LEARNING	2. BUILDING FAMILY AND COMMUNITY RELATIONSHIPS	3. OBSERVING, DOCUMENTING, AND ASSESSING	4. TEACHING AND LEARNING	5. BECOMING A PROFESSIONAL
I. Safe, healthy learning environment	X			X	
II. Advance physical and intellectual competence	X			X	
III. Support social and emotional development; positive guidance	X			X	
IV. Positive and productive relationships with families		X			
V. Well-run, purposeful program			X		
VI. Commitment to professionalism					X

greater frequency than teachers without it (Sherman & Mueller, 1996, as cited in Dunn & Kontos, 1997). In other samples, teachers with the greatest knowledge of developmentally appropriate practice had academic training in early childhood education and/or child development as well as supervised practical experience with young children (Buchanan, Burts, Bidner, White, & Charlesworth, 1998; McMullen, 1999; Snider & Fu, 1990). These results suggest that higher levels of specialized (i.e., early childhood) education influence practices employed with young children.

Do particular practices have a positive effect on child outcomes? Again, investigations have shown the positive impact of teachers' engaging in developmentally appropriate practices. For example, students whose teachers used developmentally appropriate practices had significantly higher social skills scores (Jones & Gullo, 1999) and letter-word identification and applied problem solving (Huffman & Speer, 2000) than those children whose teachers used developmentally inappropriate practices. Moreover, children who experienced preschool programs that were characterized as more active, child-initiated learning experiences (i.e., developmentally appropriate) had more success in their sixth year of school (Marcon, 2002). While these results are for older children, they do indicate that higher levels of education for the caregiver are associated with more appropriate practices with young children, and those more appropriate practices are related to better child outcomes.

Because teachers of infants and toddlers are more likely to have lower levels of education than teachers of older children (Berthelsen, Brownlee, & Boulton-Lewis, 2002) and the early years are critical to brain development (see, for example, Shore, 2003), we can no longer ignore the links between education, developmentally appropriate practice, and child outcomes. While this may seem obvious, learning to be an infant and toddler teacher poses particular challenges not found with other ages. Infants and toddlers have special developmental needs. Here are four reasons to support that claim.

1. As discussed in earlier chapters, this period of growth and development is rapid—noticeable changes occur monthly, weekly, and, in some cases, daily (Swim & Muza, 1999).

2. Physical, social, emotional, and cognitive development are more interrelated for infants than for older children.

3. Infants are more dependent upon a consistent relationship with a caregiver to meet all of their needs.

4. Infants have no effective skills for coping with discomfort and stress, so they are more open to harm (Shonkoff & Phillips, 2000).

Many of these issues were highlighted by beginning teachers as challenges. Recchia & Loizou (2002) found for teachers in their sample that adjusting to the physical and emotional intensity of nurturing very young children, setting limits and guiding the behavior of toddlers, and collaborating with others to ensure continuity of care were particular issues. This line of research, then, highlights the need for infant and toddler caregivers to receive specialized education, mentoring, and ongoing support during the early years of teaching.

OBSERVE, RECORD, ASSESS, ORGANIZE, AND MANAGE (ORAOM)

Before turning to specific tools for each developmental area, the caregiver must learn general skills to Observe, Record, Assess, Organize, and Manage children and the environment. We have given this essential process the acronym **ORAOM** (pronounced "orom").

Observe and Record

Why Observe?

Observations provide important information needed for decision-making and communicating with others. Planning a responsive, developmentally appropriate curriculum requires specific, detailed knowledge about each child in your care. Observation must precede teaching, yet it is an ongoing process. As such, it occurs before, during, and after your experiences with young children. This creates a continuous loop of observing, planning, implementing, observing, and so on (see Chapter 9 for more details).

Observations that include details of your own behavior, the curriculum, and the materials and physical environment can provide particularly important information which is often overlooked. You may have observed that on Tuesday Jessica cried for 10 minutes after being separated from her father. Including the fact that her father and primary caregiver were unable to locate her transitional object, a stuffed elephant, that day would help to explain her sudden, intense reaction to being separated.

In addition, effective communication with families, colleagues, and other professionals requires that you provide thorough reports (written and verbal) of what you observed. Making global or general statements without specific examples can break down communication rather than support it.

Who to Observe?

Each child in the child care home or center needs to be observed. All program plans and implementation start with what the teacher knows about each child and family. Setting aside time each day to observe each child provides you with a wealth of information. Observing how families interact with children and adults helps teachers to plan responsive curriculum. However, because family members participate to varying degrees in a child care program, you might have more information on one or two members rather than all who have significant impact on the child. Do not forget that each caregiver contributes unique ideas and behaviors to the child care setting that others can identify by observing.

What to Observe?

Children's behavior helps us learn about the child. Infants and toddlers often cannot use words to tell about themselves. Each child is unique. Early childhood educators must identify the characteristics and needs of each child, because the child is the focal point of decisions and plans regarding time, space, and curriculum. Each child is continuously changing. This growth and development produces expected and sometimes unexpected changes. Living with someone every day, you may not notice some important, emerging developments. Therefore, it is important to make periodic informal and formal observations (e.g., Developmental Prescriptions and Profiles) and to record them so that the changes in the child can be noted and shared. This information will affect your planning for and interactions with the child.

A caregiver's behavior provides needed information. For example, Ms. Sheila knew that she needed to improve her organization and planning, because every day she would forget some supplies for snack time. She started making a checklist of snack items so she could make sure she had prepared everything. After snack time she noted whether she had all the supplies or whether she should add something else. Her co-teacher provided feedback also. By focusing and recording in this way, Ms. Sheila was able to improve herself. Every early childhood professional is learning and continually developing skills. One caregiver may observe another one in order to learn new strategies or to reinforce those she already uses. Other people's observations can let caregivers know whether their actual practice matches the behavior intended. Continuing evaluation and planning, along with feedback, can help caregivers increase their effectiveness.

Ms. Josephine wanted to involve Monroe more when she shared a book with him. She selected a book she thought he would like and wrote down three questions to ask Monroe that would focus his thinking and questioning on objects from the book. She set up a small cassette tape recorder where she and Monroe would be sitting and invited Monroe over to share the book with him. Later, when Ms. Josephine listened to the tape recording of her time with Monroe, she discovered that she had talked all the time and told everything to Monroe rather than allowing him to talk, share, and question. Observations of interactions provide information about the kind of responses one person has to another person or to material, showing you how you have stimulated or inhibited the desired interaction.

The entire child care setting, including children, equipment, materials, and arrangement of space, should be examined to determine safe and unsafe conditions. The use, misuse, and place of use of equipment and materials, traffic patterns, much-used or little-used space, space where much disruptive behavior occurs, and the separation or merging of quiet and active space should all be evaluated. Make the necessary adjustments after you have evaluated how the setting works in relation to the children's needs.

Why Record?

Making observations without having a method for recording your data is inviting trouble. Infant and toddler teachers may work with between 6 and 12 different children throughout the course of a day and make hundreds of observations. If you do not write down the important ones, you run the risk of incorrectly remembering what you saw or attributing skills or development to the wrong child. Moreover, teachers, like young children, elaborate—add additional information based on previous knowledge

Talking, listening, and *recording* your observations are important caregiver behaviors.

and assumptions—to fill in any gaps (McDevitt & Ormrod, 2004). Thus, we may "see" something that really did not happen but fits with what we already know about the child. These examples should help you to understand the importance of recording what you observed as quickly as you can. The following section provides guidance on methods of observing and recording.

How to Observe and Record

Observations may be spontaneous or planned. You may glance across the room and see Sammy roll over. This the first time you have seen that happen. You record this example in his portfolio and/or home-school journal. Sometimes a staff member will arrange to spend a few minutes specifically observing a child, a teacher, materials, or space. These observations can provide valuable information. Since infants and many toddlers cannot tell us in words what they have learned, we must attend carefully to their behaviors for clues. Writing what you observe gives you and other people access to that information later on.

Descriptions may be brief or very detailed and extensive. In either case, the focus is on reporting the exact behavior or situation in narrative form. You will need to learn the difference between descriptive and interpretative phrasing. **Descriptive phrasing**, the preferred type for reporting observations, involves using words or phrases to describe observable behaviors, behavior that another observer (or reader) could easily verify; **interpretative phrasing**, on the other hand, makes a judgment or evaluation but gives little or no observable data to justify the conclusions (Marion, 2004). An example of interpretative phrasing is "Eva refused to eat her cereal at breakfast." The reader has no way to verify the word "refused" in this description of this meal. Compare that to: "Eva sat in her chair with her eyes squinted, mouth pursed, and her arms crossed. She stated, 'No, oatmeal' and pushed her bowl away from her. I offered her a banana and she smiled and nodded 'yes.' She ate the entire banana and drank her milk." The difference in language is important because evaluative or interpretative phrasing is "emotionally loaded" and often leads to misunderstandings, whereas factual, descriptive statements can rarely be disputed.

There are three main categories of tools that early childhood teachers can use to observe and record the behaviors of young children: narratives (i.e., running and anecdotal records), checklists and rating scales, and authentic documentation. The first two methods are narrative methods because you observe an interesting incident and record essential details to tell a story.

NARRATIVE: RUNNING RECORDS. Running records are long narratives. They tell a story as it unfolds over a significant period of time for a child, a group, or an activity (Marion, 2004). This tool is useful for learning about child development. When you focus your attention on a child for a specific time period, say an hour, you can gather valuable information that might otherwise go unnoticed. Due to time considerations, running records are rarely used spontaneously. Teachers create schedules to routinely observe the development and behavior of every infant and toddler. Running records are closely related to an ethnographic report because they describe a total situation. An *ethnographic report* describes a total situation: the time, place, people, and how the people behave. Description of the total situation lets the specialist know about things that may not be evident in one part of a specific incident. Start with a general question such as "What is going on here?" Spradley (1980) identified nine major dimensions of every social situation.

1. space: the physical place or places
2. actor: the people involved
3. activity: a set of related acts people do
4. object: the physical things that are present
5. act: single actions that people do
6. event: a set of related activities that people carry out
7. time: the sequencing that takes place over time
8. goal: the things people are trying to accomplish
9. feeling: the emotions felt and expressed

Adults unfamiliar with infants and toddlers think that the young child does not do anything. An early education student observed the following during outdoor play in a family child care home one summer afternoon (Table 5–2). She was to focus on one child and write down everything she saw and heard that child do and say. The purpose of this assignment was to identify and categorize the various experiences initiated by a 13-month-old child. The observer was not to interject her own interpretations into the narrative.

TABLE 5–2   RUNNING RECORD WITH OBSERVATIONAL DATA

CONTEXT	OBSERVATIONS (BEHAVIORAL DESCRIPTIONS OF WHAT YOU SEE AND HEAR)	ANALYSIS/INTERPRETATIONS/QUESTIONS
The play yard contained the caregiver Lynn, the observer, and six children ranging from seven months to six years of age.	**2:20** • Lynn puts mat out and stands Leslie up in yard. • Leslie looks around (slowly rocking to keep balance). • Reaches hand to Lynn and baby-talks • Looks at me and reaches for me • Takes two steps, trips and falls on mat, remains sitting on it • Turns around to face me • Cries a little • Reaches for Lynn, then to me • Looks around and watches Jason (four-year-old who is riding trike) • Reaches hand toward Lynn • Watches Jason and sucks middle two fingers on right hand • Looks around • Swings right arm **2:45** • Takes Lynn's fingers and stands • Walks two steps onto grass • Swings right arm and brushes lips with hand to make sound—baby talk • Turns toward Lynn and babbles • Lane arrives. Leslie watches and rubs left eye with left hand. • "Do you remember Leslie?" Lynn asks Lane. • Leslie reaches out arms to Lynn and walks to her. Hugs her • Listens and watches Lynn. Holds onto her for support • Turns around and steps on mulch and lifts foot to see what it is • Watches Lynn tie Jason's shoe • Lynn lifts her in air, then sets her on her knee. • She lies back in Lynn's lap and laughs.	Leslie initiates a variety of interactions with people and materials. She is physically, emotionally, socially, and cognitively involving herself in her world. Teacher planning and facilitating can stimulate and build on Leslie's self-initiated behaviors. Wants to be picked up?

Child's Name: Thomas John   Age: 22 months

Observer's Name: Rachel   Date: October 1

Setting: Block area

WHAT ACTUALLY HAPPENED/WHAT I SAW:

Thomas John was building a tower using the square blocks. Erika toddled into the area and picked up a rectangle block. She held it out to Thomas John. He took it from her hand and placed it on the top of the tower. They both smiled as if to say, "It didn't fall." Thomas John then picked up another rectangle block and placed it on top. The structure wobbled but did not fall. He looked at Erika, smiled and knocked over the structure. They each began to build their own tower. They worked in the same area for 12 more minutes. Occasionally, they would hand blocks to one another and, like before, they did not verbalize.

REFLECTION/INTERPRETATION/QUESTIONS:

Thomas John is new to the class and he has not yet spoken. His parents tell me he tells them all about his day on the ride home. Erika tends to verbalize frequently. She seemed to respect the fact that he was working in silence. I wonder if they will continue to work together and form a friendship.

FIGURE 5–3   Sample anecdotal record.

NARRATIVE: ANECDOTAL RECORDS. An **anecdotal record** is a brief narrative of one event. As the definition implies, you look for or notice one event and then write a short story about it. With spontaneous anecdotal records, something happens that you did not anticipate, but that you want to keep a record of. For example, you have planned to watch Julio's interactions with peers today, but he is sick. You then notice how Thomas John and Erika were sharing the space and materials while in the block area. You record the anecdotal record shown in Figure 5–3.

Checklists and Rating Scales

Checklists and ratings scales are quick, efficient tools for gathering data. They bypass details and merely check or rate development and progress (Marion, 2004). The Developmental Prescriptions discussed earlier and found in Appendix A are a combination of a checklist and a rating scale, so learning more about each will help you to understand how to utilize this important tool.

A **checklist** is a record of behaviors that a child can perform at a given point in time. When you observe a child or group of children, you note whether each child does or does not show that characteristic or behavior. Placing a check beside an item indicates that you observed the child perform that behavior during the observation. Leaving the item blank tells others either that the child cannot execute the behavior or that you did not observe the execution of it at that particular time. Suppose you are

	DAKOTA	TRAVIS	COLBY	RAJI	SARAH	LAKINTA	JOSE
Holds bottle	X		X			X	X
Holds spoon		X	X			X	
Lifts bottle to mouth				X	X		
Lifts spoon to mouth				X	X		

FIGURE 5–4   Sample checklist with data.

Name of Child: _____				Age: _____	
Date of Observation: _____					
	NEVER	**SOMETIMES**	**FREQUENTLY**	**ALWAYS**	
Squeezes toothpaste on brush					
Brushes teeth independently					
Rinses mouth after brushing					
Rinses toothbrush					
Returns toothbrush to proper location					

FIGURE 5–5   Example of a rating scale for brushing teeth.

particularly interested in the children acquiring self-help skills. Thus, you create a checklist to monitor progress in this area. Figure 5–4 shows just part of your checklist for infants.

Rating scales share many characteristics with checklists, but they are a listing of qualities of characteristics or activities (Marion, 2004). For example, instead of just knowing that Raji can lift the spoon to his mouth, you can rate the frequency (i.e., never, seldom, sometimes, often, always) of this behavior or the quality (i.e., all food on spoon placed in mouth, some of food on spoon placed in mouth, none of food on spoon placed in mouth) of it. Figure 5–5 is an example of a rating scale.

Returning to the Developmental Prescriptions in Appendix A, you should now recognize which part of the tool is a checklist and which part is a rating scale. When you note the date of first observation, the tool serves a checklist. When you evaluate the performance level at a later time (i.e., practicing or proficient), you are using the tool as a rating scale.

Authentic Documentation

"Documentation refers to any activity that renders a performance record with sufficient detail to help others understand the behavior recorded. . . . The intent of documentation is to explain, not merely display" (Forman & Fife, 1998, p. 241). This form

Labeling this artwork as "a car" provides evidence of the child's language and representation skills. This artifact can be used as an entry in the child's portfolio.

of assessment involves gathering work samples, taking photographs or videotapes of the children, and organizing the data using methods such as portfolios or documentation panels.

A **portfolio** is a tool for collecting, storing, and documenting what you know about a child and her development and learning (Marion, 2004). All of the information gathered using the methods described previously can be added to the photographs and work samples to create a more complete picture of the child's capabilities. Storing all of the data in one location allows for easy access and reflection. While originally designed for use with older children, portfolios can and should be used with very young children because they serve a number of purposes including but not limited to

1. Show the quality of the children's thinking and work.
2. Document children's development over time (one year or more).
3. Assist when communicating with families and other professionals.
4. Support developmentally appropriate practice by giving teachers "a strong child development foundation on which to build age- and individually appropriate programs" (Marion, 2004, p. 112).

5. Provide a tool for teacher reflection (e.g., expectations, quality of planned experiences).

6. Make available information for evaluating program quality and effectiveness (Helm, Beneke, & Steinheimer, 1998; Marion, 2004).

A **documentation panel** includes visual images and, whenever possible, narratives of dialogue that occurred during the experiences that were documented. The goal of creating documentation panels is to make visible to you, the children, and family members the development and learning that has been occurring in the classroom. As such, documentation panels include not only the objective record of your observations but also your reflections and interpretations of those events (Rinaldi, 2001). As you make visible your reflections and interpretations through the panels, they, too, become part of the data that can be read, reread, and analyzed (Rinaldi, 2001). The sharing of documentation panels with children, families, colleagues, and community members "moves learning from the private to the public realm" (Turner & Krechevsky, 2003, p. 42), something that traditional forms of observing and recording did not accomplish. Like portfolios, this method can be used for children of all ages and ability levels (Cooney & Buchanan, 2001; Edmiaston & Fitzgerald, 2000).

Other records kept on a daily basis serve particular purposes, e.g., communication with families, but often yield little data for use in evaluating development or learning. The daily message center of your classroom, for example, contains a clipboard for each child. On this is a chart of routine care events such as eating, sleeping, toileting, and other. For consistency of care between family life and school, families and teachers have designated locations for recording information. This can often be a useful place for noting supplies that are needed at school (e.g., diapers, dry formula). Figure 5–6 provides an example of a chart that can be found in the daily message center. Use this chart by writing in each time you perform a routine care event (e.g., change a diaper) and details about that event (e.g., record whether the diaper was wet or soiled).

Home-school journals can also be used to record useful information for both families and teachers. The journals are used to record daily or weekly information about key happenings that might be of interest to family members and teachers, like developmental milestones. Teachers write in the journal and then the family members take the journal home to read it. They are strongly encouraged to write back responses or questions, or to explain behaviors or events happening at home. These journals can be a fabulous tool for creating partnerships between teachers and families. Of course, teachers must pay close attention to how events and behaviors are described; descriptive language is a must.

Assess

In her paper "Infant Assessment: Early Intervention," presented at the 1997 annual conference of the National Association for the Education of Young Children, Linda Castellanos stated, "Much controversy has emerged about the assessment of young

Routine Care for _____ on _____.

	HOME EVENTS	SCHOOL EVENTS
Eating		
Sleeping		
Toileting		
Other routine care		
Important information to know		

FIGURE 5–6   Sample routine care events form.

infants. As trained observers, we [caregivers] often suspect, but are not certain of what difficulties our youngest citizens have progressing through the developmental process. Assessment pinpoints developmental difficulties and allows the caregiver to confidently plan a program of treatment. Developmental Profiles and Developmental Prescriptions successfully diagnose current developmental lags and remediate them when possible. One can only speculate the far-reaching impact that this early intervention can have concerning the future endeavors of ones so young" (Castellanos & Douville-Watson, 1997).

In order for teachers to make accurate assessments, they must understand infant and toddler developmental milestones. They must have gathered observational data on the emotional, social, physical, and cognitive aspects of the child. They must know about the effects of materials, equipment, and the arrrangement and management of space on behavior.

Set aside time on a regular basis to share information with colleagues who work with the same children.

Then, they are ready to make an **assessment** or evaluation of the developmental information and capabilities of the children. Care should be taken to act prudently in this age of testing and judging children. You should pay close attention to why you are gathering the data, how you gathered it, and how it will be used.

Early childhood educators are not in the business of testing children (NAEYC, 2003). Rather, developmental assessment is used to determine the child's level of development. It may focus on one area, such as cognition and language, or the whole child, for example, physical, emotional, social, and cognitive/language. Since children are continuously developing in all areas, periodic assessment is useful.

Set aside time to review, reflect on, and analyze the data you have for each child. Compare the child's level of development and behaviors to developmental milestones or expected patterns of development based on chronological age. Because there is a great deal of variation in when children accomplish developmental norms, you should also know the expected age range for a milestone. For example, infants typically produce their first word at 12 months of age; however, this can occur as early as 9 or as late as 16 months and still be considered normal development. Typically, there is a three- to six-month range on either side of the developmental milestone; but this will vary depending on the particular behavior. Knowing this information is vital because it provides you with a context for distinguishing warning signs from red flags. *Warning signs* are those behaviors that, although you and family members should monitor, are not of great concern yet. *Red flags* are those behaviors which deviate both from the developmental milestone and the expected range. When a number of behaviors within a particular area of development are found to be red flags, it is time to invite other professionals, with specialized knowledge in observation, assessment, and early intervention, to join the conversations.

Few caregivers have received the specialized training required to use standardized assessment techniques. If your program wants to carry out specialized assessment, seek out the necessary training first. But, these tools are often not as valuable as your careful, ongoing observations, records, and analysis of observational data from your specific classroom.

Organize

Care and Education Plans

The caregiver organizes care and educational plans on a daily and weekly basis to guide classroom experiences and selection of materials, as well as to promote continuity of development. The child's developmental profile provides information about the child's strengths and about areas where development may occur next. Planning specific experiences in advance for each child helps make sure you are considering the needs and development of the whole child, rather than focusing on one or two areas and forgetting other areas. The results of your developmental assessments should be a strong influence on your planning.

Schedule

The caregiver organizes the schedule. You decide how to use the major blocks of time and how much flexibility you need in that schedule to meet each child's needs. Consistent patterns of events help children learn order in their lives. This develops in them feelings of security and trust, because they know that some parts of their world are predictable. This does not mean that your schedule is bound by the clock. For example, it is 3:00 p.m., most children have awaked from their nap, and it is time for afternoon snack. You would not wake the few sleeping toddlers just to stay on schedule. Your schedule is flexible in that snack comes after nap, whether that is 2:30 for three children, 3:00 for four children, or 3:20 for the last two children. Staggering snacks in this manner incidentally affords caregivers the chance to converse more easily with smaller groups of children. So, in this example, a flexible schedule also supports the children's social development.

Environment and Materials

The caregiver organizes the environment—the room and the play yard—and the materials within it to meet the developmental needs of the children. Good infant and toddler programs need a variety of learning materials every day. Teachers rely on their

Respect each child's individual needs as they occur during the day.

knowledge of the individual children in their care as well as on their background in child development when selecting and arranging some materials and storing away the rest. While each early childhood educator has to decide how and when to change the environment, they should all follow principles of good environments (see Swim, 2004; 2005 and Chapter 8).

Manage

Careful management of time, space, materials, and people is needed to provide meaningful daily experiences for children.

Time

Caregivers manage and coordinate time within the guidelines of the daily schedule and the care and education plans. You give Suzy a five-minute notice before outdoor play time since Suzy takes a long time to put her toys away and start getting ready to go outside. You feed lunch to Jack at 11:00 a.m., because he falls asleep at 11:30. You allow Vanessa to get up after her half-hour sleep, because she usually takes very short naps. You encourage Joshua to stay on his cot, knowing that he usually sleeps two hours. You continue to respect the needs of each individual child.

Space

Caregivers manage space. Before the children arrive, you plan and organize the space in your learning environment. When the children are actively using that space, you will make suggestions, decisions, and adjustments to help each child have positive experiences. Orrin is piling up blocks near the shelf. Shiwanda is trying to reach a block. For Shiwanda to get the block she wants, she will probably bump into Orrin's pile of blocks. You can walk with Shiwanda around to the other side of Orrin, where she can reach the block without getting into Orrin's space. You have helped Shiwanda to experience a new level of learning. By carefully managing the classroom space, you have purposefully involved her in an activity that reflected her goal.

Materials

Caregivers also manage materials. With very young children you make decisions about what kinds of materials are needed, where to store and use them, what is safe or not safe, and how the materials can or cannot be used. Lois asks for a toy and begins pulling toys out of the toy box. She pulls out blocks, dolls, cars, puzzle pieces, fabric scraps, and assorted other toys. She looks back and forth between the inside of the box and the clutter of toys on the floor. She finally walks away to another part of the room, leaving all the toys behind. Too many materials can be confusing, but too few can bore a child. Chapter 8 helps you to consider how to maintain a balance of materials in your environment.

People

Caregivers manage and coordinate people. When two caregivers work with a group of children, they should coordinate their plans and their actions. While the director can provide guidance, the moment-by-moment actions require dialogue and give-and-take between the caregivers.

Teachers coordinate the children's use of time, space, and materials. Willard, a 15-month-old, flings toys. One of the caregivers needs to help him move to a part of the room or outdoors where he can fling toys safely.

SUMMARY: YOUR WORK

Your work with children is different from custodial care. Custodial care is simply the physical maintenance of children. Being an early childhood educator requires a strong grounding in knowledge, skills, and dispositions. Not only should you know what to do in a given situation, have the skills to act in a particular way, but you should value acting in that manner. ORAOM (observing, recording, assessing, organizing, and managing) provides a framework for the work you do.

Working independently and effectively with young children comes after extensive instruction, investigating theories, writing papers, and receiving mentoring. It comes after your positive intentions and caring have transformed into a firm educational base of understanding. You will continue to grow professionally as you see the impact of your behaviors, curriculum, and relationships on the children's development and learning. You work is vital to the lives of very young children, their families, and the community: it is your way of making the world a better place, one child at a time.

■ KEY TERMS

accreditation	documentation panel	partnerships
anecdotal record	home-school journal	portfolio
assessment	interpretative phrasing	rating scale
checklist	licensing regulations	running record
CDA	NAEYC	
descriptive phrasing	NAFCC	
developmentally appropriate practice	ORAOM	

CASE STUDY   Audrey

Eric, a four-and-a-half-month-old, is lying on the floor when he starts to cry. His teacher, Audrey, picks him up. She "eats" his tummy and he laughs. She holds him up in the air and he smiles. She gets his bottle, sits in a chair, and feeds him. Eric gazes at Audrey and smiles between sips.

Grasping her finger, Eric looks around the room. Audrey stands him in her lap, holds his hands to pull him to and fro, and kisses him. He laughs. She holds him while he dances and laughs. He watches Audrey's mouth and responds as she talks to him. He leans on her shoulder and burps as he fingers the afghan on the back of the chair.

The many caregiving responsibilities are accomplished through interactions with the people and environment in the child care setting. Several educational tools have been discussed to help develop the knowledge and strategies needed to become a good observer, recorder, assessor, organizer and manager to support warm, emotional relationships and enhance the physical, cognitive/language, social and emotional development of infants and toddlers.

1. Use the information provided about Eric to assess his social and emotional development.

2. What suggestions would you give to Audrey for organizing the environment to support Eric's social and emotional development? Why?

3. What characteristics about Eric should she consider as she manages her interactions and educational experiences with him?

■ QUESTIONS AND EXPERIENCES FOR REFLECTION

1. Identify your own strengths and weaknesses as a professional. Create a growth plan for yourself. In other words, list two goals you have for professional growth and explain the steps you will take to meet those goals.

2. Observe one infant and one toddler for 30 minutes each. Use narrative running records to describe what you see and hear. Analyze the behaviors of each child.

3. Using the record of Leslie in the play yard (Table 5–2), list her behaviors using the following categories: (a) physical, (b) emotional, (c) social, (d) cognitive and language.

4. Observe two caregivers, each for 10 minutes. Tally a mark in the appropriate category in the chart (shown at right) each time you observe the caregiver assuming that role.

5. List four available community resources and explain how each can be used to add value and resources to your child care program.

	Caregiver 1	Caregiver 2
Observer		
of children		
of self		
Recorder		
routine care events chart		
other observation tools		
Assessor		
of children		
of self		
Organizer		
care and education plans		
schedules		
environment and materials		
Manager		
time		
space		
materials		
people		

■ CHAPTER REVIEW

1. What are important knowledge bases for professional educators to have? Why?

2. How do partnerships with families and community agencies help to promote the development and well-being of very young children?

3. Discuss with someone your understanding of the concept "developmentally appropriate practice." How can you learn more about this concept?

4. How do formal and informal education help early childhood teachers to be more effective in their various roles?

5. Why must teachers observe and record the behavior of infants and toddlers? What observation tools will (or do) you use most often? Why? What are the benefits to you, the children, and families when using these tools?

6. How can you be an advocate of the information presented in this chapter? In other words, how can you teach what you have learned to others?

■ REFERENCES

American Academy of Pediatrics. (1996). *Recommendations for day care centers for infants and children.* Evanston, IL: Author.

Berthelsen, D., Brownlee, J., & Boulton-Lewis, G. (2002). Caregivers' epistemological beliefs in toddler programs. *Early Child Development and Care, 172*(5), 503–516.

Bove, C. (2001). *Inserimento:* A strategy of delicately beginning relationships and communications. In L. Gandini and C. P. Edwards (Eds.), *Bambini: The Italian approach to infant/toddler care* (pp. 109–123). New York: Teachers College Press.

Bredekamp, S., & Copple, C. (Eds.). (1997). *Developmentally appropriate practice in early childhood programs* (Rev. ed.). Washington, DC: National Association for the Education of Young Children.

Buchanan, T. K., Burts, D. C., Bidner, J., White, V. F., & Charlesworth, R. (1998). Predictors of the developmental appropriateness of the beliefs and practices of first, second, and third grade teachers. *Early Childhood Research Quarterly, 13*(3), 459–483.

Buell, M. A., Pfister, I., & Gamel-McCormick, M. (2002). Caring for the caregiver: Early Head Start/family child care partnerships. *Infant Mental Health Journal, 23*(1–2), 213–230.

Castellanos, L., & Douville-Watson. (1997, November). Assessing infants. Paper presented at the annual conference of the National Association for the Education of Young Children, Anaheim, CA.

Child Development Associate National Credentialing Program. (1992). *Child development associate assessment system and competency standards for infant/toddler caregivers in center-based programs.* Washington, DC: Author.

Cooney, M. H., & Buchanan, M. (2001). Documentation: Making assessment visible. *Young Exceptional Children, 4*(3), 10–16.

Dunn, L., & Kontos, S. (1997). Research in review. What have we learned about developmentally appropriate practice? *Young Children, 52*(5), 4–13.

Edmiaston, R. K., & Fitzgerald, L. M. (2000). How Reggio Emilia encourages inclusion. *Educational Leadership, 58*(1), 66–69.

Forman, G., & Fife, B. (1998). Negotiated learning through design, documentation, and discourse. In C. Edwards, L. Gandini, & G. Forman, *The hundred languages of children* (2nd ed., pp. 239–260). Westport, CT: Ablex.

Helm, J. H., Beneke, S., & Steinheimer, K. (1998). *Windows on learning: Documenting young children's work.* New York: Teachers College Press.

Huffman, L. R., & Speer, P. W. (2000). Academic performance among at-risk children: The role of developmentally appropriate practices. *Early Childhood Research Quarterly, 15*(2), 167–184.

Hyson, M. (Ed.). (2003). *Preparing early childhood professionals: NAEYC's standards for programs.* Washington, DC: National Association for the Education of Young Children.

Jones, I., & Gullo, D. F. (1999). Differential social and academic effects of developmentally appropriate practices and beliefs. *Journal of Research in Childhood Edcuation, 14*, 26–35.

Marcon, R. A. (2002, Spring). Moving up the grades: Relationships between preschool model and later school success. *Early Childhood Research and Practice, 4*(1). Retrieved December 12, 2006, from http://ecrp.uiuc.edu/v4n1/marcon.html

Marion, M. (2004). *Using observation in early childhood education.* Upper Saddle River, NJ: Pearson Prentice Hall.

McDevitt, T. M., & Ormrod, J. E. (2004). *Child development: Educating and working with children and adolescents* (2nd ed.). Upper Saddle River, NJ: Pearson Prentice Hall.

McMullen, M. B. (1999). Characteristics of teachers who talk the DAP talk and walk the DAP walk. *Journal of Research in Childhood Education, 13*(2), 216–230.

NAEYC. (2003). Early childhood curriculum, assessment, and program evaluation: Building an effective, accountable system in programs for children birth through age 8. Joint Position Statement of NAEYC and National Association of Early Childhood Specialists in State Departments of Education (NAECS/SDE). Washington, DC: Author.

NAEYC. (2005a). Position statement: Code of ethical conduct and statement of commitment. Washington, DC: Author. Retrieved December 12, 2006, from http://www.naeyc.org/about/positions/pdf/PSETH05.PDF

NAEYC. (2005b). Advocates in action. Building your advocacy capacity. *Young Children, 60*(3), 79.

Recchia, S. L., & Loizou, E. (2002). Becoming an infant caregiver: Three profiles of personal and professional growth. *Journal of Research in Childhood Education, 16*(2), 133–147.

Rinaldi, C. (2001). Documentation and assessment: What is the relationship? In Project Zero and Reggio Children (Eds.), *Making learning visible: Children as individual and small group learners*. Reggio Emilia, Italy: Reggio Children srl.

Robinson, A., & Stark, D. R. (2005). *Advocates in action: Making a difference for young children* (Rev. ed.). Washington, DC: National Association for the Education of Young Children.

Sherman, C. W., & Mueller, D. P. (1996, June). Developmentally appropriate practice and student achievement in inner-city elementary schools. Paper presented at Head Start's Third National Research Conference, Washington, DC.

Shonkoff, J. P., & Phillips, D. A. (Eds.). (2000). *From neurons to neighborhoods: The science of early childhood development*. Washington, DC: National Academy Press.

Shore, R. (2003). *Rethinking the brain: New insights into early development* (Rev. ed.). New York: Families and Work Institute.

Snider, M. H., & Fu, V. R. (1990). The effects of specialized education and job experience on early childhood teachers' knowledge of developmentally appropriate practice. *Early Childhood Research Quarterly, 5*(1), 69–78.

Spradley, J. P. (1980). *Participant observation*. New York: Holt, Rinehart & Winston.

Swim, T. J. (2004). Basic premises of classroom design: The teacher's perspective. *Early Childhood NEWS, 16*(6), 34–42.

Swim, T. J. (2005). Advance reflection on principles of classroom design: Considering the child's perspective. *Early Childhood NEWS, 17*(1), 34–39.

Swim, T. J., & Muza, R. (1999, Spring). Planning curriculum for infants. *Texas Child Care, 22*(4), 2–7.

Turner, T., & Krechevsky, M. (2003). Who are the teachers? Who are the learners? *Educational Leadership, 60*(7), 40–43.

■ ADDITIONAL RESOURCES

Atkins-Burnett, S., & Meisels, S. (2005). *Developmental screening in early childhood: A guide.* (5th ed.). Washington, DC: National Association for the Education of Young Children.

Coopersmith, S. (1967). *The antecedents of self-esteem*. San Francisco: W. H. Freeman.

Copple, C., & Bredekamp, S. (2005). Basics of developmentally appropriate practices: An introduction to teachers of children 3 to 6. Washington, DC: National Association for the Education of Young Children.

Douville-Watson, L. (1993). *3A's of infant development*. Lecture series II. New York: Instructional Press.

Jones, M., & Shelton, M. (2005). Developing your portfolio—Enhancing your learning and showing your stuff: A guide for the early childhood student or professional. Washington, DC: National Association for the Education of Young Children.

■ HELPFUL WEB SITES

American Academy of Pediatrics. Dedicated to the health and well-being of infants, children, adolescents and young adults. http://www.aap.org/

KinderStart—Child Development. KinderStart is an indexed directory and search engine focused on children 0 to 7. Also covers children with emotional needs. http://www.kinderstart.com/childdevelopment

National Network for Child Care (NNCC). Articles and resources provided by Iowa State University. http://www.nncc.org/

ProTeacher! Child Development Research and Resources. Ages and stages—physical, intellectual, and emotional development—during the first year. http://www.proteacher.com

The Talking Page Literacy Organization. A nonprofit association for the improvement of literacy skills in America. http://www.talkingpage.org/

For additional infant and toddler resources, visit our Web site at
http://www.earlychilded.delmar.com

Establishing a Positive Learning Environment

The four chapters in this section integrate the skills, principles, and theories learned in Part I into functional settings for care. Strategies for care include communicating with children, families, and colleagues; accessing community resources for families; preparing positive indoor and outdoor environments; and designing and implementing curricula for infants and toddlers.

This section provides the professional early childhood educator with the tools necessary to assess individual children using Developmental Profiles, establish goals for growth using Developmental Prescriptions, and design and structure specific experiences and activities for each child and the group as a whole. In addition, you will learn positive communication strategies to use when creating partnerships with family members. Only through collaboration with families can we promote the optimal growth and development of very young children.

Infants and toddlers help to develop their own curriculum by engaging energetically in activities that contribute to their growth. Through sensitivity to each child's unique needs, family strengths, cultural traditions, and community resources, a positive learning environment can be established and maintained for each child.

6

Building Relationships with Infants and Toddlers

OBJECTIVES

After reading this chapter, you should be able to:

- Describe reasons for creating a caring community of learners.
- Reflect on your own image of the child.
- Apply strategies for communicating with very young children.
- Understand methods for helping children gain self-regulation skills.

CHAPTER OUTLINE

- Introduction
- Reggio Emilia Approach to Infant-Toddler Education
  History
  Philosophy
  Image of the Child
  Inserimento
- Communicating with Infants and Toddlers
  Label and Express Feelings
  Emotional Regulation
  Foundations for Perspective-taking

- Strategies for Respectfully Guiding Children's Behavior
  Limits
  Consequences
- Case Study: Enrique

INTRODUCTION

As this book emphasizes, children need strong, positive relationships with adults in order to thrive in all areas of development. While these relationships are supported through family grouping, continuity of care, and primary caregiving, these are not enough. The ways in which you interact with very young children need to become a focus of your attention. The first guideline for developmentally appropriate practice, creating a **caring community of learners**, speaks directly to the type of relationships adults need to establish with and among children (Bredekamp & Copple, 1997). In a caring community, each learner is valued and teachers help children learn to respect and acknowledge differences in abilities and to value each person as an individual (Bredekamp & Copple, 1997). Teachers need to select a variety of strategies for helping children acquire the skills for interacting with others, such as emotional management and perspective-taking. How a teacher guides the behavior of the children sends a clear message about what behaviors are socially acceptable: we demonstrate through our interactions how to treat one another.

Conscious caregiving, purposefully focused care of a child, has been a leading premise of this book since its inception. One of the finest child care programs in the world operates in Reggio Emilia, Italy. While that program existed long before this text, they clearly share a common focus on promoting the highest quality care for our youngest citizens.

REGGIO EMILIA APPROACH TO INFANT-TODDLER EDUCATION

History

After World War II, the women of a village in Europe decided to build and run a school for young children. They salvaged and washed bricks from destroyed buildings and used money from the sale of a war tank, trucks, and horses that were left behind by the retreating Germans (Malaguzzi, 1998) to fund the project. They desired "to bring change and create a new, more just world, free from oppression . . ." (Gandini, 2004). This school formed the foundation for the later development of the municipal infant/toddler and preschool programs in Reggio Emilia, Italy (Malaguzzi, 1998). A series of national laws related to women's rights, workers' rights, and children's rights created a context that supported the establishment of nationally funded infant/toddler and preschool programs (see, for example, Gandini, 2004; Ghedini, 2001). While creating nationally funded programs for preschoolers was a challenge, it was less of a battle than they faced with infant/toddler care. The Italian public feared potential damage to children or to the mother-child relationship (Mantovani, 2001). However, with time these attitudes changed and now infant-toddler centers are "viewed as daily-life contexts with the potential to facilitate the growth and development of all children" (Mantovani, 2001, p. 25). As recent as 1997, laws were passed to establish local projects and services that address the needs of all children and youth (0–18 years old; Ghedini, 2001), continuing the view that care and education of very young children is the responsibility of the broader community (New, 1993, 1998).

Philosophy

The programs of Reggio Emilia are built on educational experiences that consist of reflection, practice, and further careful reflection that leads to continual renewal and readjustments (Gandini, 2004). Like the theoretical grounding of this book, many different theorists influenced their philosophy, including but not limited to Dewey, Decroly, Vygotsky, Erikson, Bronfenbrenner, Piaget, and more contemporary people such as Shaffer, Kagan, Morris, Gardner, Von Foerster, and Heinz (Malaguzzi, 1998). Reading and engaging in dialogue about the writings of these educational leaders assisted them in forming their views about the route they wanted to undertake when working with young children.

The educators in Reggio Emilia strive to reflect on and recognize in their practices the following 14 principles (see Gandini, 2004, for an explanation of each principle):

1. The image of the child
2. Children's relationships and interactions within a system
3. The three subjects of education: Children, parents, and teachers
4. The role of parents
5. The role of space: An amiable school
6. The value of relationships and interaction of children in small groups
7. The role of time and the importance of continuity
8. Cooperation and collaboration as the backbone of the system
9. The interdependence of cooperation and organization
10. Teachers and children as partners in learning
11. Flexible planning vs. curriculum (*Progettazione*)
12. The power of documentation
13. The many languages of children
14. Projects

Some of these principles have been discussed in previous chapters (e.g., Chapter 5), some will be addressed later (e.g., Chapters 8 and 9), and some will be addressed in this chapter because they relate to how we build relationships with very young children.

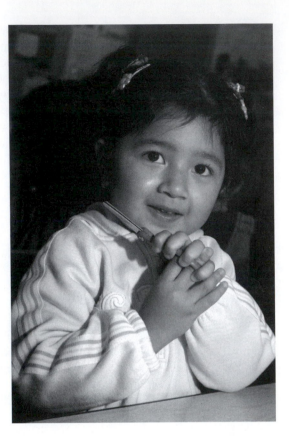

How do you describe the characteristics and capabilities of very young children?

Image of the Child

The educators in Reggio Emilia first and foremost speak about the image they hold of the child and how this affects their interactions, management of the environment, and selection of teaching strategies (Edwards, Gandini, & Forman, 1998; Gandini, 2004; Wurm, 2005).

Take a moment and think about three words or phrases that you would use to describe the characteristics, abilities, or expectations you hold of infants and toddlers. While looking over the list, ask yourself, "What do these words say regarding my beliefs about young children?" Did your list include words such as active, possessing potential, independent, curious, full of desire, competent, capable, problem solvers, communicative, longs for social interactions? The teachers in Reggio believe that all children are unique in their own ways and their job is to recognize and support these differences. More specifically, according to Rinaldi (2001), their "image is of a child who is competent, active, and critical; therefore, a child who may be seen as a challenge and, sometimes, as troublesome" (p. 51). Children need to acquire skills that support their active construction of their own worlds. They must come to understand how they receive as well as produce change in all systems with which they interact (Rinaldi, 2001). This image, then, is a social and political statement about active participation in a democratic society, not just an educational one (Malaguzzi, 1998).

According to Rinaldi (2001), their creation of the image of the child ". . . was developed by the pedagogy that inspires the infant-toddler centers . . ." (p. 50). For educators in Reggio Emilia, there is a constant back-and-forth between theory (i.e., the image) and practice. Knowledge and meaning are never static, but rather generate other meanings (Malaguzzi, 1998). Hence, you should not despair if your **image of the child** is not quite fully developed. Reading, reflecting, reading some more, interacting with children, reflecting, and so on will facilitate this development.

Inserimento

Educators in these programs have deeply respectful ways in which they relate to children and parents. **Inserimento**, which can be roughly translated as "settling in" or "period of transition and adjustment," is used to describe the strategy for building relationships and community among adults and children when the child is first entering an infant-toddler center (Bove, 2001). While this period is individualized for each family, there is a general model to support educators' decision-making: parent interviews and home visits before the child starts at the center; parent-teacher meetings before, during, and after the initial transition process; documentation; large or small group discussions with families; and daily communication between families and teachers (Bove, 2001). The model is an attempt "to meet each family's needs, to sustain parental involvement, and to respond to the parents' requests for emotional support in caring for their young children" (Bove, 2001, p. 112). This process is flexible in order to respond to the cultural variations found in families. Some families transition to school quickly as the need to return to work becomes pressing, while other families may make several visits over a number of weeks to the school before actually leaving the child in the care of the teachers (Figure 6–1). Only careful observation of the family members and the child will indicate the best way to proceed with each family (Bove, 2001; Kaminsky, 2005).

As this model demonstrates, parents are viewed as integral partners in caring and educating the youngest citizens. Helping parents and children become fully participating members of the program community is viewed as vital because this supports the well-being and development of not just the infant or toddler but the entire family. Which of the Reggio Emilia principles discussed previously support the practices of *inserimento*?

COMMUNICATING WITH INFANTS AND TODDLERS

Creating a caring community involves not only learning to read the children's cues but also helping them to learn to read yours (Gonzalez-Mena & Eyer, 2007). Infants and toddlers communicate their needs using a combination of verbal and nonverbal

FIGURE 6–1   Dominique's parents drop in to the university child care center to see him before their next class.

strategies. As we communicate with them, we do the same. The strategies used to facilitate positive and effective communication are an outgrowth of the theories presented earlier as well as the three As. The purpose of your acquiring these strategies is to make possible strong relationships between you and the children and to promote optimal development and learning.

Label and Express Feelings

Caregivers should begin labeling feeling states from the time children are born. A good way to teach feeling states is to verbalize your own feelings and your impressions of the feelings of other people. "I'm feeling rushed today," "Jaime seems sad," and "You really look excited!" are examples of labeling feeling states. Teachers should also model and mirror feeling states. Giving children feedback by **mirroring** (repeating words or mimicking facial expressions) their expressions and modeling feeling states helps to develop self-awareness and sensitivity to other people's feelings.

Feelings are inborn, but emotional reactions are learned. It is important to teach young children to accurately identify their feeling states and express them in healthy ways. It is often easy to determine the emotions of even young infants. For example, young babies often "beam" when happy, have a "tantrum" when frustrated or angry, and "coo and smile" when happy and at ease. Caregivers should label feeling states for nonverbal infants, and as young children develop language, they should be taught to accurately label and express their emotions. One effective tool for helping young children pay attention to and identify feelings is to use a feelings chart such as the one

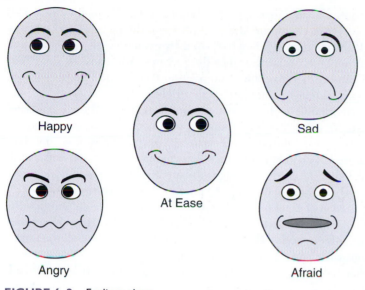

Happy

Sad

At Ease

Angry

Afraid

FIGURE 6–2   Feelings chart.

shown in Figure 6–2. This chart illustrates five primary emotions: At Ease, Happy, Sad, Angry, and Afraid, and can be used to help children accurately label their internal feelings. All human emotions are normal and are therefore healthy; a feeling state is neither bad nor good. The main goal is to help children be consciously aware of their feelings and to express them in ways that are helpful to the child and not harmful to others.

Affective education starts with bringing attention to the child's internal state and labeling the child's feeling. Often the physical meter for children's feeling states are their whole bodies as they respond to different situations, especially the tummy area. The trained observer can easily identify children who are upset by their body language. "The prefrontal cortex receives a strong impulse from the great visceral nerve coming from the stomach area" (MacLean, 1990). This feeling in the gut is the physical link between body intelligence and affect associated with social behavior. Before they are able to discuss or label feelings, children must learn to recognize their at-ease state. This is most recognizable while having fun and feeling happy.

The early childhood educator can help a child to be aware of good feelings when he is in a state of ease after observing the child several times. Ask children how their bodies feel when at ease or while playing and having fun. Often, children will simply smile. State the feeling you sense with nonverbal children and infants. Ask them if their tummies feel good. Then show them the five faces (At Ease, Happy, Sad, Angry, and Afraid). Identify Happy, and point to their stomach area, saying, "Your tummy feels happy! You're happy." If the child indicates agreement, say "Yes, that's right; you feel happy."

Show the children a picture of a happy face and say, "You look like this picture." Children begin to associate this state with the happy face picture over time. Children will then be able to point to the picture and identify this state for themselves.

Give children feedback when they appear to be in a particular feeling state. Tell them that they look At Ease, Happy, or Afraid. Show them the pictures and ask how their tummies feel. If the child says, "I feel bad," quickly respond with "You are good. Tell me how your tummy feels" and show her the pictures. You can also say, "Your body looks like your tummy feels like this," and point to the picture that fits your interpretation of her body language. Then ask, "Is that right?"

As children learn to identify their own body responses, discuss when they started to feel unhappy or afraid. After listening, the early childhood educator can use the specific information about the children's conflicts to address problems. It is important to understand that there are no judgments placed on emotional reactions, because all emotions are normal. When adults do not judge or blame feeling states, children learn to identify and express emotion and develop the potential to be healthy adults.

To facilitate expression of emotions in a positive way, *accept all emotions and the need to express them as normal.* Toddlers are filled with energy, extremely curious, and very busy exploring their world. This often leads to frustration and all the unbridled emotions that go with learning how to handle new experiences. Conflicts arise from not getting what they want immediately. Good caregiving is **child-centered**, meaning that children's needs are valid and important. Children need help to express their feelings in positive ways.

A primary caregiver who knows a child can observe how that child feels in certain situations; she is emotionally available to pick up signals of frustration and alleviate a potential problem by distracting the child, involving him or her in a special project, or giving the child special attention. When you see that children need to release frustration, engage them in a physical activity. Jumping can help to release pent-up emotions. When children have temper tantrums, make sure all furniture and harmful objects are out of the way. Remove undue attention from them until they are through, ask them privately to tell you what they felt if they can verbalize, and then welcome them into the group again. This is the most appropriate way to deal with tantrum behavior.

Emotional Regulation

Teaching infants and toddlers to soothe themselves and manage their emotions, known as **emotional regulation**, may be the single most challenging task a caregiver faces. Infants and toddlers, like all other humans, are unique in the ways in which they express their emotions. As discussed previously, this can be related to their temperament (see Chapter 3), family, community, and culture. Professional early childhood educators honor this individuality when they modify their curriculum to build on each child's preferences and strengths (Hyson, 2004).

Infants rely almost exclusively on other people for their need fulfillment, so they are not developmentally prepared at birth to soothe themselves. They must gradually learn that they can calm and soothe themselves through the feedback given by their caregivers. Professional early childhood educators who sensitively administer the three *A*s and systematically teach children to use the three *A*s for themselves promote and develop **self-soothing**.

You should encourage children's actions and help them to manage emotions as they progress toward set goals. For example, when a child indicates the desire to hold an object and together you have tried several times and finally succeed, the work is validated in a sense of achievement by your attention, approval, and attunement. This builds a feeling of confidence and a willingness to try the next time when the child reaches for the same object. The child may attempt the task on his own, or he may look for your encouragement or help, but eventually he will feel confident enough to succeed without your help.

Verbal praise and appropriate words of encouragement help children of all ages. Timing of when to give approval depends on the needs of the child. The child may start out wanting something, but becomes too tired to finish. If the child is too tired, the primary need must be cared for first (holding the child until he or she goes to sleep). After the primary needs have been met, children will once again bring their attention to other activities.

Early childhood educators can help build strong self-images for the toddlers in their care. As good role models, and by using reinforcing, positive self-talk, they can build language for the child to adopt. **Positive self-talk** is the internalization of messages we hear about ourselves from others. These messages represent how children feel about themselves, and what they are capable of over time. If the messages are positive and encouraging, the child will become confident, but if they are negative, the child feels limited in the ability to succeed. These messages become the belief system of the child and the foundation for self-concept and future success or failure.

Scaffolding, or building sets of ideas and demonstrating how to use them, can be used to promote positive self-talk. Table 6–1 illustrates how scaffolding works when approval sustains the infant's attention. This approval validates children's mastery of

TABLE 6–1   APPROVAL VALIDATES MASTERY

CHILD BEHAVIOR	CAREGIVER RESPONSE	OUTCOME
1. eyes an object	observes child	caregiver attention
2. reaches for object	encourages with words like "You can do it."	approval for mastery attempt; increased child motivation
3. looks at caregiver; tries to grasp objects again	continues to encourage, softly saying "Try again; you can do it!"; models success	approval for mastery attempt; increased child motivation
4. successfully grasps object	compliments effort, makes eye contact, gentle hug	approval and affection for mastery of task
5. smiles and shows excitement—brings object to mouth	says "Nice job! I knew you could do it!" Give three As.	validation of mastery; observable self-approval

their environment. Children internalize the validation they hear and make it their own as you reduce feedback.

Foundations for Perspective-Taking

Successful relationships and social acceptance depend on developing an awareness of other people's perspectives. Children must learn to act without harming themselves, others, or the environment, because internal controls are not innate. Children need to be taught the foundations of **perspective-taking** skills to have successful, positive relationships.

One way of helping children is to explain how their behavior may make others feel. By announcing out loud how others are reacting to a given behavior, you help all of the children involved to begin to understand the others' perspectives. For instance, say Ms. Barbara works in a licensed family child care center. She waits for three-year-old Eroj at the school bus stop with his two-year old sister Inara. She greets Eroj with a smile and hug. His sister is happy to see him too. He has his art projects in both hands, but drops them when he goes to hug Ms. Barbara. His sister grabs the papers and, in the excitement of the moment, she crumples one of them. Eroj becomes angry and begins to yell at his sister, who starts to cry. As the teacher helps him gather up his work, she places Inara on her hip and places her hand firmly on Eroj's shoulder. She says to him, "I'm so sorry you dropped your papers. I can tell that you worked so hard on them (looking at papers he is showing you while walking). You should be proud of them. When we get back, you can show everyone your work and then put them on the wall if you like."

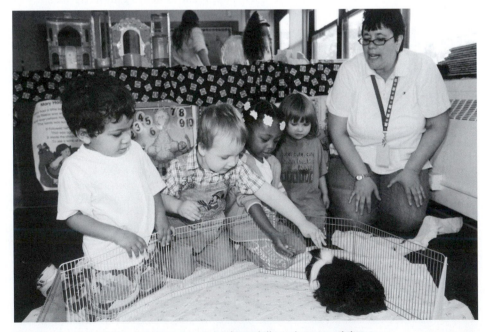

Class pets help toddlers learn perspective-taking skills and responsibility.

To show Inara's perspective, Ms. Barbara continues by saying in Inara's presence, "You know, Eroj, Inara did not mean to crumple your papers. I know she would not do anything to hurt you. I know she misses you when you go to school because several times during the day she stands by the door and says your name. I know she loves you and wants to be with you. I don't think that she meant to crumple your paper. She just got so excited to see you."

This example has a very specific theme. The teacher provided Eroj information he would not have had and dealt with him in a very careful way. She greeted Eroj warmly, validated his feelings of anger and self-worth, soothed his sister by picking her up, and discussed the situation openly and honestly with both children. She expressed positive observations about his relationship with his sister, telling him information he would not have unless she told him. In addition, the teacher was acting as Inara's advocate.

The same theme can be used with very young children. Caregivers can offer similar comfort to children by using statements like "Oh, I know Michael didn't mean to knock down your block pile, Dori; he just lost his balance." The key to successful use of this strategy is to know the child, know the facts of the situation, and communicate the intentions and actions of the people involved.

While very young children may be able to consider another child's perspective with assistance, it is inappropriate to expect them to do so independently. The goal of your behaviors is not to teach them how to take someone's perspective but rather to lay a foundation for it, because acquiring perspective-taking skills is a long, arduous task that lasts from birth through adulthood.

STRATEGIES FOR RESPECTFULLY GUIDING CHILDREN'S BEHAVIOR

Newborns do not arrive in this world knowing how to behave. Yet, they immediately begin to understand the world around them and their role in it. Infants and toddlers work minute by minute to construct their understanding of socially acceptable behaviors. It is your responsibility to help them learn to be socially competent with peers and other adults. The primary avenue adults have to assist very young children with this is to carefully plan the indoor and outdoor learning environments (see Chapter 8) and use positive strategies for guiding their behavior.

Many experts on infant and toddler development avoid discussing discipline out of fear that their comments will be used inappropriately with children. While the current authors understand this, it is essential that teachers use developmentally appropriate guidance strategies to help children learn to follow rules that keep themselves, other people, and property secure and safe (Marion, 2007). Therefore, discipline is an indispensable aspect of helping children develop. The term **discipline** is used here to mean teaching appropriate behavior and setting limits on inappropriate behavior. It *does not* mean punishing children or controlling their behavior.

The first principle of discipline is that adults should not control children's behavior. The most an adult can do for a child is to help the child meet his or her needs and administer consequences for the child's behavior (Douville-Watson, 1997).

One of the most common errors beginning teachers make is to assume responsibility for controlling children's behavior. When you feel responsible for a child's behavior, you set up a no-win situation, wherein you must try to control the child, which is impossible. It is essential to accept the fact that even young children largely control their own behavior, and that you can only control your own behavior. Once you accept the limits of reality regarding your control, you are in a position to learn strategies that can assist young children with becoming motivated, cooperative, and self-regulated.

We have already discussed using the three As to help children learn appropriate behavior and to **self-regulate** those behaviors. When caring for children under 36 months, the approach required is to assess the needs of the children and help fulfill them. It is *never* appropriate to completely remove attention, approval, or attunement from infants, nor is shaking, hitting, or being physically or emotionally "rough" in any way acceptable. Problems usually arise when we have done everything we can think of, and the baby still screams and cries. This is the time to give responsibility to another adult, and take a break from the child to a quiet place where you can relax. Once you have regained your composure, reenter the situation and assess all the baby's needs until you find what the baby requires to become at ease. Check out and observe physical needs such as teething, ear infections, stuffed sinuses, gas, and constipation. When the discomfort continues for more than two hours, call a family member for advice and/or assistance.

Limits

Once children become mobile and enter late infancy and toddlerhood, they must learn to accept "no" about certain behaviors. *However, the number of behaviors they must accept "no" to is much smaller than many adults demand.* The main principle to use in selecting which behaviors children must accept "no" to is to start with only those behaviors that are directly harmful to themselves, other people, or property. For example, hitting another child with a toy and calling another child "stupid" are directly harmful; one is physically harmful and the other is emotionally so.

Limits and rules, while they help children to accept "no" about certain behaviors, are best received if stated positively. Let the children know what to do in as specific language as possible (Marion, 2007). Telling the crawling infant, "No touch" as she is pulling on the lamp to stand is less than helpful. The child will not learn where to pull to reach a standing position, because you have not told her the desired behavior. When you establish rules for children that are phrased in what *not* to do, you are actually increasing attention to the behaviors that you do not want to see. Returning to the example, saying instead "Couches are for pulling up on" and moving the child to the couch will help the child to construct an understanding of safe furniture for pulling on. Limits, then, are for stopping inappropriate behaviors and replacing them with more appropriate behaviors.

While each classroom and early childhood program needs rules or limits, these should be few in number. Infants and toddlers typically lack the cognitive skills to recall more than a few limits (Marion, 2007).

Classroom limits help children and treasured possessions remain safe.

Consequences

Once limits have been defined, discussed, and modeled, **consequences** for each limit need to be established. The most effective consequences for learning appropriate behaviors are natural and logical (Marion, 2007). Natural consequences are those outcomes that occur without teacher intervention. Elisabetta runs through the block area of the classroom, trips over a wooden truck, and falls on the carpet. She is unhurt. Elisabetta has experienced a natural consequence of running in the classroom. Early childhood educators cannot allow all natural consequences to occur because they are too dangerous. Permitting a toddler to fall (i.e., experiencing a natural consequence) because he climbed over the top railing of the climbing structure is not acceptable.

Logical consequences are those outcomes that are related to the limit but would not occur on their own. For example, your rule is for the children to put their toys back on the shelf when they are done. If a child does not put her puzzle back on the shelf after being reminded, she will not be able to choose another activity until the first one is cleaned up.

Establishing "no" helps the young child with becoming an autonomous, self-regulated individual. Unfortunately, this developmental phase is often referred to as the "terrible twos." This important phase of personality and self development is mislabeled as "terrible" by controlling adults who have difficulty accepting children saying "no" to them. It is vital that children be allowed to say "no" to teachers and other adults in order to develop a healthy sense of self. Caregivers who do not accept "no" from a child when he is not harming himself, others, or property do great harm to the child's sense of self-responsibility. Young children must learn to make decisions and establish boundaries with other people. Two additional guidance strategies to use with children who say "no" to practically everything are giving choices and redirection (diverting attention).

Choices

People learn to make wise choices by being able to choose. Caregivers who give children choices that they can handle for their age avoid many confrontations and teach children to choose wisely (Marion, 2007). Yes-no questions are often problematic, as is a statement that commands the child. For example, "Do you want lunch?" is likely to result in "no," as is the statement "You're going to eat your lunch now." A much more effective approach is to give a choice, such as "Do you want a banana or apple slices to go with your grilled cheese sandwich? You choose."

Redirection

Diverting young children's attention to safe and acceptable activities often prevents confrontations. For example, if you take a young child into a setting with many breakable objects, diverting the child's attention to objects and activities in the setting that are not breakable can avoid problems. Your attention and interest most often evokes interest on the child's part, so rather than attending to all the breakable things, pay attention and draw the child into activities that are safe and appropriate. If, instead, a child wants to climb and jump from the shelf, take him outside to jump. Redirecting attention to the appropriate location recognizes children's underlying needs and can help children learn to monitor and regulate their expression of emotions (Hyson, 2004).

As you are guiding the behavior of young children, remember that achieving social competence is a long journey. Do not expect perfection for you or the children. Observe what the children can do on their own and what they can do with assistance (i.e., identify their zones of proximal development). Then, use teaching strategies to scaffold them to the next level of social skill development.

■ KEY TERMS

caring community of learners	image of the child	positive self-talk
child-centered	*inserimento*	self-regulate
consequences	limits	self-soothing
discipline	mirroring	
emotional regulation	perspective-taking	

CASE STUDY   Enrique

"Should I call her mother again?" Enrique, a toddler teacher, asks his co-teacher as Regina struggles to free herself from his gentle hold. Regina has just bit the same peer for the second time today.

"Yes, I think you should. Regina really needs her today." While Regina is 27 months old, this is her first time attending child care.

Ms. Gonzalez arrives about 30 minutes later clearly frazzled and upset, to find Regina working by herself at a table lining up clowns. Enrique and Ms. Gonzalez take a few moments to watch her work. Regina methodically lines the clowns around the perimeter of a piece of construction paper. She seems not to notice the other activities around her. The other children have divided themselves into two groups, working with blocks and pouring water through waterwheels.

Enrique asks Ms. Gonzalez what she was noticing. She replies by asking, "Does she usually play alone?"

"No. She typically works in the same area as other children. This is expected because as children get older, they usually begin to play in small groups. Regina's interactions with the other children sometimes result in her biting them, like today. I am wondering if you can tell me how she interacts with you and your husband at home."

"We usually interact with her. If we ask her a question, she will nod yes or no. She is very quiet and does not seem to have many wants. But, if she does want something, she will point at the object."

"I'm wondering if she is biting because she does not have the language to tell her classmates what she wants. I'm also wondering what I can do to best help her. Can we both take some time to think about Regina and meet early next week to talk further?

"That would be nice. Is it okay if my husband comes also?" inquires Ms. Gonzalez.

"Of course. Let me know what times work best for your schedules. And, thank you so much for coming to get Regina early and taking the time to speak with me. The more we work together the better we can support Regina's needs."

1. How did Enrique's approach serve to value the relationships among Mr. and Ms. Gonzalez, Regina, and himself?

2. Describe what you believe is Enrique's image of the child. What information from the case did you use when drawing this conclusion?

3. What strategies would you suggest Enrique use to support Regina's acquisition of socially accepted behaviors? Why?

■ QUESTIONS AND EXPERIENCES FOR REFLECTION _____

1. Read one of the chapters cited about the Reggio Emilia approach to infant-toddler care and education. Report what you find to your colleagues.

2. Julianne Wurm (2005) asks us to consider other questions about our image of the child. Record your responses to these questions in your journal. Then, compare your responses with a colleague.

- Who is a child?
- What is childhood?
- How do children learn?
- What is the meaning of *to educate*?

- What is the relationship between teaching and learning?
- What is the relationship between theory and practice?
- What is the role of school in society?

3. Observe an adult interacting with a mobile infant or toddler. Collect four anecdotal records on the communication strategies used by the adult and how the child responded to them.

4. Interact with a child that you know well. Try out one new guidance strategy and explain how you felt doing it, how the child responded, and how others around you responded. How might your past interactions with this child have influenced the effectiveness of this strategy?

■ CHAPTER REVIEW

1. Why should infant-toddler teachers focus their attention on creating a caring community of learners?

2. What are some principles of the Reggio Emilia approach to early education? How might knowing these influence your behavior with very young children?

3. What are effective communication strategies to use with children and why?

4. How can you positively guide and support the development of very young children's self-regulation skills?

■ REFERENCES

Bove, C. (2001). Inserimento: A strategy of delicately beginning relationships and communications. In L. Gandini & C. P. Edwards (Eds.), *Bambini: The Italian approach to infant/toddler care* (pp. 109–123). New York: Teachers College Press.

Bredekamp, S., & Copple, C. (Eds.). (1997). *Developmentally appropriate practice in early childhood programs* (Rev. ed.). Washington, DC: National Association for the Education of Young Children.

Douville-Watson, L. (1997). *Concious caregiving.* Bayville, NY: Instructional Press.

Edwards, C., Gandini, L., & Forman, G. (Eds.). (1998). *The hundred languages of children: The Reggio Emilia approach—Advanced reflections* (2nd ed.). Westport, CT: Ablex.

Gandini, L. (2004). Foundations of the Reggio Emilia approach. In J. Hendrick (Ed.), *Next steps toward teaching the Reggio way: Accepting the challenge to change* (2nd ed., pp. 13–26). Upper Saddle River, NJ: Prentice Hall.

Ghedini, P. (2001). Change in Italian national policy for children 0–3 years old and their families: Advocacy and responsibility. In L. Gandini & C. P. Edwards (Eds.), *Bambini: The Italian approach to infant/toddler care* (pp. 38–45). New York: Teachers College Press.

Gonzalez-Mena, J., & Eyer, D. W. (2007). *Infants, toddlers, and caregivers: A curriculum of respectful, responsive care and education* (7th ed.). New York: McGraw-Hill.

Hyson, M. (2004). *The emotional development of young children: Building an emotion-centered curriculum* (2nd ed.). New York: Teachers College Press.

Kaminsky, J. A. (2005). Reflections on *inserimento*, the process of welcoming children and parents into the infant-toddler center: An interview with Lella Gandini. *Innovations in early education: The international Reggio exchange, 12*(2), 1–8.

MacLean, P. D. (1990). *The triune brain in evolution, role in paleacerebral functions.* New York: Plenum Press.

Malaguzzi, L. (1998). History, ideas, and basic philosophy: An interview with Lella Gandini. In C. Edwards, L. Gandini, & G. Forman (Eds.), *The hundred languages of children: The Reggio Emilia approach— Advanced reflections* (2nd ed., pp. 49–97). Westport, CT: Ablex.

Mantovani, S. (2001). Infant-toddler centers in Italy today: Tradition and innovation. In L. Gandini & C. P. Edwards (Eds.), *Bambini: The Italian approach to infant/toddler care* (pp. 23–37). New York: Teachers College Press.

Marion, M. (2007). *Guidance of young children* (7th ed.). Upper Saddle River, NJ: Prentice Hall.

New, R. (1993). Italy. In M. Cochran (Ed.), *International handbook on child policy and programs* (pp. 291–311). Westport, CT: Greenwood Press.

New, R. (1998). Social competence in Italian early childhood education. In D. Sharma, & K. W. Fisher (Eds.), *Socioemotional development across cultures* (New Directions for Child Development No. 81, pp. 87–104). San Francisco: Jossey-Bass.

Rinaldi, C. (2001). Reggio Emilia: The image of the child and the child's environment as a fundamental principle. In L. Gandini & C. P. Edwards (Eds.), *Bambini: The Italian approach to infant/toddler care* (pp. 49–54). New York: Teachers College Press.

Wurm, J. (2005). *Working in the Reggio way: A beginner's guide for American teachers.* St. Paul, MN: Redleaf Press.

◼ ADDITIONAL RESOURCES

Lewin-Behham, A. (2006). *Possible schools: The Reggio approach to urban education.* New York: Teachers College Press.

Noddings, N. (2002). *Educating moral people: A caring alternative to character education.* New York: Teachers College Press.

◼ HELPFUL WEB SITES

KinderStart—Child Development. KinderStart is an indexed directory and search engine focused on children 0 to 7. **http://www.kinderstart.com/childdevelopment**

North American Reggio Emilia Alliance (NAREA). An exchange of ideas about initiatives consistent with the philosophy of Reggio Emilia, along with opportunities for professional development. **http://www .reggioalliance.org**

The Whole Child. ABC's of child care in physical, social, emotional, and cognitive areas. **http://www.pbs .org/wholechild/abc**

For additional infant and toddler resources, visit our Web site at
http://www.earlychilded.delmar.com

7

Supportive Communication with Families and Colleagues

After reading this chapter, you should be able to:

- Develop procedures for informal and formal communication with families.
- Analyze the working relationships and responsibilities of the staff with whom the caregiver is working.
- Analyze your own skills when communicating with family members and colleagues.
- Understand the active listening process and how it differs from mirroring.

■ **CHAPTER OUTLINE**

- Introduction
- Skills for Effective Communication
  Rapport Building
  I Statements versus You Statements
  Active Listening: The "How" in Communication
  Mirroring

INTRODUCTION

Caregivers and family members* have a common goal: to provide high-quality experiences for children. When children are being cared for by someone other than an immediate family member, all persons involved must join in partnership to achieve this goal. The fifth guideline for developmentally appropriate practice as outlined by NAEYC is "Establishing reciprocal relationships with families" (Bredekamp & Copple, 1997). Recognizing the complexity of this guideline is necessary for beginning teachers. Oversimplifying and regarding the objective as just parent education, on the one hand, or total parent control, on the other, minimizes the role of the teacher in joining with parents to provide the best care and education for their very young children. The primary components of this guideline are highlighted here.

- Reciprocal relationships require mutual respect, cooperation, shared responsibility, and negotiation of conflicts to achieve shared goals.

---

*In this chapter, the terms *family, families, family member,* and *family members* will be used interchangeably to refer to people who interact with and impact the learning and development of infants and toddlers in their home settings. This term should be understood to include mother(s), father(s), legal guardians, grandparent(s), siblings, aunt(s), uncle(s), etc. The term *parent* or *parents* is used to refer specifically to a mother and/or father.

- Frequent two-way communication must be established and maintained between early childhood teachers and families.
- Families are welcomed into the program and invited to participate in decisions about their children's care and education as well as program decisions.
- Family members' choices and goals are responded to with sensitivity and respect, without abdicating professional responsibility.
- Teachers and families share their knowledge of the child, including assessment information, to maximize everyone's decision-making abilities.
- Families are linked with community resources based on identified priorities and concerns.
- Professionals having educational responsibility for a child should, with family participation, share information (Bredekamp & Copple, 1997).

Our experiences with pre-service teachers and beginning educators demonstrate that building relationships with families can provoke fear. "I'm comfortable with children, not adults" is a common statement. Thus, this chapter is devoted to assisting you in considering this topic more in depth and developing the skills to be successful.

Effective communication between caregivers and families and among the early childhood program staff is a must. Communication is a two-way process. It requires both active listening and effective expression of thoughts and feelings.

The attitudes caregivers and families have toward each other are reflected through their communication process. The nonverbal, emotional messages that are sent in the questions asked and the statements made will either help or hinder successful communication. We must also give attention to cultural diversity; families differ in how they communicate (Christian, 2006).

In order to be an effective caregiver, it is necessary to communicate well with children, families, staff, other professionals, and community members. This chapter teaches you important communication skills such as rapport building, "I statements," active listening, and mirroring. These skills will assist you in effectively communicating with other people in a sensitive and accepting style. Practicing these skills will help you listen to and understand others and be able to express yourself so that other people will understand and accept what you say.

SKILLS FOR EFFECTIVE COMMUNICATION

In Chapter 4 we discussed the three *As* of child care and how they affect communication between caregiver and child.

Figure 7–1 shows the general communication process. A *sender* (A) sends a message verbally and nonverbally to a *receiver* (B), who interprets the message and gives the sender feedback as to what the message means to the receiver.

Rapport Building

Rapport is an agreement between two people that establishes a sense of harmony. This harmonious agreement with infants and toddlers has been discussed in previous

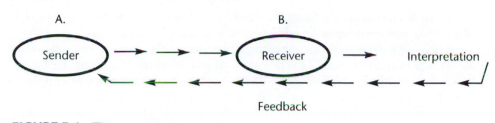

FIGURE 7–1   The communication process.

chapters as interactional synchrony. When you learn to build rapport with an adult, just as you've done with an infant or toddler, you must follow the person's lead while you carefully observe his or her movements. Think of this as learning to dance well with another person. Rapport building involves two components: calibrating and pacing. **Calibrating** means carefully observing the specific steps and **pacing** means carefully moving in harmonious synchrony. There are three specific sets of behaviors that must be calibrated and paced for you to build rapport and dance well with another person.

1. Posture. Align yourself in a complementary physical posture with the adult. If he is sitting, sit also. Change your posture to "dance" with the person face to face.
2. Nonverbal communication. Listen carefully to the tone of voice, tempo of speech, and the intensity of the physical and emotional undertones of the gestures. What is the adult trying to tell you? Do the nonverbal communication strategies match the verbal ones?
3. Representational systems. This set of behaviors is hardest to learn to calibrate and pace because it includes all ways that the adult represents his or her beliefs, perceptions, and understanding of the world. Representational systems are culturally based, so it is imperative that you spend considerable time learning how culture influences communication for the families with whom you are working.

   You should observe calibrating and pacing with the families in your classroom. Ask yourself questions such as "How does the adult let the child lead?" "How is the adult sensitive to the three sets of behaviors?" and "How does the adult pace the child?" Once you have practiced observing the calibrating and pacing that others use, try them in your own relationships with adults and children. You'll find out quickly that it is well worth the effort; you can establish rapport effectively when you become proficient at using this strategy.

I Statements versus You Statements

We also communicate to other people from the perspective of expressing our own thoughts and feelings through **I statements**, or giving advice or judgments about the other person by making **you statements**.

I statements usually start with the word *I* and express responsibility for our own perceptions without judging the other person. For example, "I am angry" is an I statement because it expresses a feeling without blaming another person. You statements are often disrespectful and tell the other person how he or she is thinking, feeling, or behaving. You statements often start with the word *you* and offer advice or an opinion about the other person. For example, "You make me angry" is a you statement because it offers an opinion about the other person (he or she is doing or saying something wrong) and it makes the other person responsible for the speaker's feeling (anger).

When you want the other person to feel accepted and understood, make I statements rather than you statements. I statements are respectful and take responsibility for the speaker's thoughts, feelings, and behaviors. You statements, on the other hand, offer opinions, advice, and judgments about the other person and often close off further communication.

We can also make *disguised* I and you statements. Active listening responses, which are discussed below, are an example of disguised I statements. When we give feedback to a sender that clearly takes responsibility for our own perceptions and map of the world, we are making I statements. For example, if a person sends the message, "I can't stand Mary, she is always complaining," a good active listening response might be, "It sounds like Mary's complaining is making you feel angry." Notice that, although neither *I* nor *you* were used, the feedback takes responsibility for the receiver's perception by using the words "It sounds (to me) like . . ." without blaming or criticizing the sender. Active listening and I statements keep communication open by giving nonjudgmental feedback, which allows the sender to confirm that the message was understood ("That's right, I really get angry with her") or correct the message ("Well, I don't really get angry, just a little annoyed").

Disguised you statements sometimes sound like I statements and may even start with the word *I*, but they always end up judging or giving advice to the sender. For example, "I'm angry because you did that" is a disguised you statement because, even though it starts with *I*, it blames and judges the other person.

Caregivers need to practice daily using I statements with children, family members, and colleagues. Once you master making I statements and giving active listening feedback, other people will respond by feeling open, relaxed, and understood in their interactions with you. Caregivers who communicate using you statements cause other people to feel disrespected, uncomfortable, and unwilling to continue interactions with the person.

Active Listening: The "How" in Communication

Most common communication errors can be avoided by applying a technique called **active listening**. This technique, which was developed primarily by psychologist Carl Rogers, has been put into very practical form for teachers and families in the training program called Family Actualization through Research and Education, or F. A. R. E. (Douville-Watson, 1993). The most important skill in active listening is very simply to "feed back" the deeper feeling message (not the words) of the sender in the words of the receiver. This simple definition of active listening requires further explanation because, although it may sound simple, it takes practice to learn to give deeper feedback effectively.

Active listening differs from most common types of communication in the kind of feedback given to the sender. The type of feedback most commonly given is a *reaction* to the words in the message. When we give reactionary feedback, we most often close off the communication process because we become emotionally involved in the words of the message. Common reactionary feedback messages are "You shouldn't say that!" "I don't agree with you!" "You're wrong!" and "I don't want to hear that kind of talk!"

Active listening, on the other hand, involves objectively listening, in a nondefensive way, for the deeper message of the sender and then giving *reiterating* feedback. Rather than reacting to the words of the sender, the active listener interprets the entire message of the sender and gives it back to the sender.

Active listening feedback allows the sender to affirm, reject, or clarify his message. By continuing to feed back the total message of the sender, the receiver can help the sender clarify the problem and, in most cases, arrive at his or her own solution.

An active listener also looks at body language. The look on a person's face, the position of the body, and what the person does with his or her hands and arms can help you to understand the full message on the deepest level. Nonverbal behavior, as well as words, feelings, and attitudes, combine to transmit the complete, deep message.

Although active listening may sound simple enough to learn, it requires practice because most of us have learned to give reactionary feedback, particularly to children. With practice, however, caregivers will find the rewards of active listening worth the effort it takes to master the technique.

Here are some ways to test how well you are communicating with others.

1. Listen to the way you now respond to people. If you catch yourself reacting to the words of messages instead of the deeper meaning, you are "just talking." An active listener listens for the whole, deep message, including the words, feelings, attitudes, and behaviors.

2. An active listener never judges, criticizes, or blames another. Listen for deeper feelings, because feelings can never be wrong! Since the active listener looks for the deeper message, most feedback starts with words such as "It sounds like . . . ," "You seem to feel . . . ," "I hear you saying . . . ," and other phrases that reflect the sender's feelings.

3. An active listener never responds to a message with advice or personal feelings. The idea of communication is to completely understand what the other person thinks and feels. This skill may be more difficult for caregivers to learn in their relationships with children in their charge because adults have so much more experience than children and it is hard to accept the fact that children can arrive at their own solutions to problems. Adults tend to want to teach and advise children before they have completely understood the whole message that children are trying to communicate. Doing so, however, would contradict the image of the child as capable and competent. These behaviors would actually reflect an image of the child as incapable of problem solving about important matters. Which image do you hold? Which image do you want to display to families and colleagues? Reflecting on your behaviors in

light of the image you hold will assist you with keeping your theory (i.e., image) and your practice consistent. One of the causes of the well-known generation gap is that children learn that adults don't understand them and don't "know where they're at." Even young children will furnish good solutions to problems if adults have the patience to hear them out and give back the meaning of the messages they hear and experience without teaching or advising.

4. An active listener only adds information to a message when the other person directly asks for it and after that person has completely expressed the entire message. You will know you have received the entire message when you hear real feelings and concern about what to do. At this point, feedback such as "Have you thought about what you can do?" or "How would you solve this?" will give the child a chance to ask for advice or begin problem solving on his or her own.

Mirroring

A simple but very effective technique for establishing rapport and making sure your messages are understandable and that you understand theirs, is **mirroring** (Hendrix, 1993). Mirroring simply means repeating exactly what is said without adding or interpreting any of the speaker's words. When you communicate with staff, families, or children, it can be very helpful to ask the person to repeat exactly what you say before he or she responds. When the other person mirrors you before responding, and you mirror him or her before responding, a sense of trust and understanding quickly develops that is very hard to obtain any other way. By mirroring each other, mutual respect and understanding is quickly developed. Mirroring is especially effective when communicating with others from cultural and/or language backgrounds different from your own.

Try mirroring with your family or friends first so you get the idea of how it works. The only words you are allowed to change in mirroring are personal pronouns, so if the other person says "I am happy," your mirroring response is "You are happy." One final rule in mirroring is that each speaker uses I statements rather than you statements, as discussed previously. By using I statements when speaking and mirroring each other before you respond, you can prevent many conflicts and misunderstanding.

COMMUNICATING WITH FAMILIES

Using Active Listening with Families

Active listening helps caregivers understand families as they express their concerns and raise questions about parenting. Family members are often isolated from other support systems and need the caregiver to listen to them and help them come up with solutions (Figure 7–2). Active listening and mirroring helps overcome language and cultural barriers as well (Lally, 1992).

FIGURE 7–2 Parents and caregivers need to communicate to ensure the best care for the child.

Family members may want the caregiver to agree with them or reassure them, to confirm or reject ideas, and to respond to pressures from family and friends. For example, Mabel rushed in one morning with her son and said, "I called my mother last night and told her I went back to work this week and she had a fit. She said it was too soon and that right now my place was at home." Listen to Mabel's words, her tone of voice; read her nonverbal cues, her facial expressions and degree of tenseness. She may be telling you that she is feeling frustrated and guilty, or she may be stating her mother's view while feeling fairly comfortable with her own choice of going back to work. You must listen to the whole story (words, tone, cues) to interpret accurately what Mabel is telling you.

Families express their desires for their children. One parent might say, "I want Velma to be happy. It bothers me to see her cry when I leave." A mother, Arlene, may tell you, "I want Pearl to get used to babies because my baby is due next month." Listen to what the parent is saying about the child and about his or her own needs.

Actively listen to family members so that you will fully understand what care they expect you to provide. Some family members have very definite ideas and will tell you about them. Others do not say anything until they disagree with something, and then they may express frustration or be angry with you. If this happens, give feedback that takes into account the family members' emotions, as well as the words they say to you.

Families tell you much information about their children and themselves. Details about what the child does at home are needed by the caregiver each morning (Figure 7–3). Listen carefully and record the information as soon as possible.

FIGURE 7–3   Parent and caregiver assist the child in making the transition between home and the early childhood program.

Gathering Information

Families have a wealth of information about their children. For continuity between home and school, teachers need to know how the family typically responds to the child's needs. Many states require that licensed infant/toddler programs have families complete and regularly update questionnaires that ask about child characteristics, habits, and preferences as well as family routines, goals, and expectations for the child. For example, knowing that Oliver has difficulty relaxing for nap if he does not have his favorite blankie and his back patted will help the early childhood educator to meet his body's needs for sleep.

While questionnaires are effective means for gathering information, going beyond the minimal requirements will help you to form effective partnerships, meeting the guidelines for developmentally appropriate practice. Talking informally during drop-off and pick-up about the child's experiences at home and school help all of the caregivers to have updated information that will shape their reactions to the child's behavior. When face-to-face interactions are not possible, home-school journals, mentioned in Chapter 5, are valuable tools for sharing and gathering information. This two-way communication strategy involves family members writing a few notes about the child's day(s) when at home and then the caregiver responds with information about the child's experience while at the early childhood program. Of course, it is overoptimistic to think that caregivers and families will write in the journal every day. Yet those who do develop a strong sense of partnership (Gandini, 2001).

Sharing Information

Families need information about the daily experiences their child has in your care. Many tools are available (see Chapter 5) to help organize and record important things the child has done and share them with family members. Special experiences, such as the child's excitement about a visiting rabbit, may go into the written record or the caregiver may tell a family member.

The child's rate and pattern of development should be shared with family members. Refer to the child's Developmental Profile (see Appendix B) to focus on recent developments and identify developmental tasks the child may soon be mastering.

Share ideas for stimulating the child's development, emphasizing the difference between facilitating and pushing the child. Families are often very interested in written directions for age-appropriate activities and homemade toys (see Chapters 10–16; Herr & Swim, 2002).

Share information relating to concerns about the child. Mabel may be interested in information relating to the effect of child care on her two-month-old child. Phyllis may be ready for information about separation anxiety. Arlene may need information to help her understand that Pearl's sharing Mommy with the new baby involves much more than practice in getting used to babies. Changing sleeping and eating patterns and toilet learning are other areas families frequently raise questions about with caregivers.

Families need information about the child care program. Before the child is admitted, the program director shares with them program goals, policies, and a description of the daily program and the practical use of Developmental Prescriptions. Many programs will include a developmental screening of the child as part of the initial evaluation of the incoming child. This will help guide caregivers as they make their decisions about program implementation. Many situations occur that family members need to clarify and discuss with caregivers. For example, Sal wants his 23-month-old daughter Gabriele to stop using her fingers when she eats. The caregivers can help Sal by sharing development information with him, assuring him that eating with fingers is perfectly normal at this age and use of utensils will come later when fine motor control is further developed.

Feelings

Caregiving involves feelings and emotions. Family members want to know that you are concerned about their child and about them. In a variety of ways, let families know that you like and respect their child. Families look for caregivers who accept and like their child and who provide emotional security.

Share the excitement of the child's new developments with family members. The first time you see children pulling themselves up on the table leg, teetering two steps, holding utensils, riding a tricycle, turning book pages, hugging a friend, asking to go to the toilet, or catching a ball, you should be excited and pleased with their accomplishments. When you share these experiences with families, let them know how excited you are. Yet much caution must be exerted in this type of communication. Many family members, especially mothers, feel guilty about needing or even wanting to return to work. They may feel that they are missing the most important moments of their children's lives. Sharing "firsts" with them would only serve to reinforce these feelings. An alternative approach would be to alert families for behaviors to look for at home without explicating stating that you saw the behavior first. While some readers might interpret this as lying by omission, the news should be reframed so that you help family members to see and share an important event for their child.

Uncovering Families' Expectations

All families have expectations for their children; some will be explicitly stated, while others may not be fully articulated (Christian, 2006). Engage families in ongoing conversations to uncover these expectations and support them in achieving their goals. Not all families will have realistic or developmentally appropriate expectations for their child. Some families, especially first-time parents, set goals that are too high, while other families set their expectations too low. Either case can lead to poor child outcomes. It is your responsibility as a professional early childhood educator to work with them to realign their expectations. The communication skills discussed earlier are very important in these situations. You want to establish rapport, use active listening and I statements, and mirror their words. When asked your opinion, you can be ready to guide them toward more developmentally appropriate expectations. This approach reflects the guidelines for establishing reciprocal relationships with families, especially that parents' choices and goals are responded to with sensitivity and respect without abdicating professional responsibility (Bredekamp & Copple, 1997).

Sharing Expectations

After uncovering the families' expectations, share your goals and expectations of the child care program with them. Your casual statements may take on more meaning than written goal statements. One caregiver described a situation when she encouraged a child's independence: "We want to help children become as independent as they can, so when Louella resisted my helping her take off her bib, I let her try to take it off by herself. She got stuck once, and I helped her lift one arm out, and then she could do the rest by herself. Her big smile and chatter showed me how pleased she was."

Next, expect to devote considerable time to negotiating the goals that you will work toward together as partners. Negotiating means working until a common ground is found. This should be a win-win situation, not a hostile takeover of the families' goals in favor of your own or vice versa (see, for example, Gonzalez-Mena, 2001).

Families are interested in what you expect of yourself as a caregiver. What kinds of things do you do? How committed are you? How friendly are you? Do you think you are more important than they are? Do you extend and supplement the roles of families or do you expect to supplant them? You communicate these expectations through your words, attitudes, mannerisms, and interactions with children and family members.

What do you expect of the children in your care? A child care program utilizing a developmental perspective emphasizes the development of the whole child and of individuality among children. Assure families that development does not follow a rigid schedule and is not identical among children. Adults often compare their child's development with another child's and gloat or fret at what they see. Caregivers who show that they believe children behave differently within a broad range of normal activity communicate to families that adults can challenge children without putting harmful pressure on them.

Caregivers expect many things of family members. Some expectations you may express; others you should keep to yourself. You might expect them to

- love and like their child.
- want to hear about special occurrences in their child's day.
- want to learn more about their developing child.
- be observant of the child's health or illness.
- be willing to share information about the child with the caregiver.
- use respect as a basis for forming relationships.

Some families will not meet your expectations. Because caregiving occurs in the family as well as in the child care program, you will need to resolve your differences with those important in the child's life. In some cases, you may need to change your expectations of family members. We speak of accepting children as they are, so we need to take the same attitude toward families. They come to the child care program because they need care for their child outside the home. While they often need and want additional information about parenting and a sense of community, they usually are not looking for situations that place additional demands and expectations on them as parents (Mantovani, 2001). Creating systems to serve families and build a stronger community is an important advocacy function that early childhood programs can easily provide (Galardini & Giovannini, 2001). Information to help family members grow can be offered but not forced upon them. You may increase your awareness of the unique situation each family faces simply by actively listening to them without judgments.

Partnering with Families

Family members should have an active relationship with their caregivers. This partnership exists in order to facilitate the learning and well-being of children.

In Decision-Making

Some programs involve family members in decision-making. Many not-for-profit child care centers have policy boards that include family representatives. These boards may make recommendations and decisions about center policy. Sometimes family members even serve on boards that make administrative decisions about hiring and firing staff and selecting curricula. However, few family child care homes and for-profit child care centers involve families in decision-making about policy, staff, or curricula.

Families of infants and toddlers must be involved in some decisions relating to their child's care. The family or pediatrician selects the infant's milk or formula; the caregiver does not make that decision. Families and caregivers must share information about the child's eating and sleeping schedules. The length of time from afternoon pick-up to mealtime and to bedtime varies among families. Since late afternoon naps or snacks may improve or disrupt evening family time, early childhood educators should set aside time to discuss what schedule is best for the child and family. Toilet learning must be coordinated between families and caregivers. Both parties share information about the appropriateness of timing, the failures and successes of the child, and the decision to discontinue or continue toilet learning. If a family member insists that toilet learning start or continue when you think the child is not ready, share with that person information about the necessary development of the child before learning can occur. Tell him, for example, about actions children take when they are showing an interest in or a readiness for toilet learning. Communicate also the harmful effects on children of consistent failures and too much pressure. When the child is ready for toilet learning, the procedures at home and in child care must be the same so that the child does not become confused. Reassure the family members that you do not mind changing their child's diapers. Emphasize that this is another time for you to spend relating positively one on one.

About Children

Most adult family members of infants and toddlers in child care are employed. Therefore, family involvement during the child care day is often limited to arrival and pick-up time. They can help the child take off a coat or unpack supplies when leaving the child in the morning, and can share with the caregiver information about the child's night, health, or special experiences. At pick-up time the caregiver initiates conversations about the child's experiences and projects during the day, while the family member helps the infant or toddler make the transition back to home life by hugging the child or helping to put on outdoor clothes. Sharing written notes and photographs taken of work that occurred during the day is always a good way to start conversations.

Family Assessment and Education

Within the past few years, there has been a growing need to quantify the skills and characteristics necessary to be a competent parent. Social and governmental interest in family values, increased laws regarding family responsibilities, and the need for better family education have necessitated identification, definition, and assessment of the skills that make up competent parenting. In response to these needs, instruments to measure parent competence have been designed, most of which are checklists and survey tools.

National Parenting Scale

A set of scales called the **National Parenting Scales** (NPS), Experimental Edition (Watson, 1996) assesses parents[†] in the essential skills included in Table 7–1 in addition to personality characteristics, environmental resources, and interactional dynamics between parents and children.

[†] In Table 7–1, *parent* was the term used by the original author. For our purposes, we need to continue to think of the term inclusively to mean family member, parent, or legal guardian (see previous footnote).

TABLE 7–1   PARENT COMPETENCY GOALS AND FUNCTIONAL AREAS

I.   Establish and maintain a safe, healthy living environment.
   1. Safe: Parent provides a safe environment to prevent injuries.
   2. Healthy: Parent promotes good health and nutrition and provides an environment that contributes to the prevention of illness.
   3. Learning environment: Parent uses spatial relationships, materials, and routines as resources for constructing an interesting, secure, and enjoyable environment that encourages play and exploration.

II. Advance physical and intellectual competence.
   4. Physical: Parent provides a variety of equipment, activities, and opportunities to promote the physical development of children.
   5. Cognitive: Parent provides activities and opportunities that encourage curiosity, exploration, problem solving, and responsibilities appropriate to the developmental levels and learning styles of children.
   6. Communication: Parent actively communicates with children and provides opportunities and support for children to understand, acquire, and use verbal and nonverbal means of communicating thoughts and feelings.
   7. Creative: Parent provides opportunities that stimulate children to play with sound, rhythm, language, materials, space, and ideas used in individual ways to express creative skills and abilities.

III. Support social and emotional development and provide positive guidance.
   8. Self: Parent provides physical and emotional security and helps each child to know, accept, and take pride in himself or herself and develop a sense of independence and self-esteem.
   9. Social: Parent helps each child feel accepted in groups, helps children learn to communicate and get along with others, and encourages feelings of empathy and mutual respect among children and adults.
   10. Guidance: Parent provides a supportive environment in which children can learn and practice acceptable behaviors as individuals and in groups.

IV. Maintain positive and productive relationships within the family and community.
   11. Relationships: Parent maintains open, friendly, honest, and cooperative interactions with each family member, encourages involvement, and supports relationships with all family members and members of the community.

V.   Ensure a well-run, purposeful home, responsive to individual needs.
   12. Management: The parent is a manager who uses all available resources to ensure effective home operation. Competence in organizing, planning, and cooperating with others is demonstrated.

VI. Commit to constructive family values.
   13. Family values: Parent makes decisions based on knowledge of sound childhood principles and practices, and sets limits and values that are in the best interest of each child as a regular priority.

A general requirement of excellent child care involves a team approach among families, the child care program, and community resources. Initial research found that a group of 80 parents entering children in child care who took the NPS worked more closely with early childhood educators and program goals than did parents not taking NPS (Watson, 1997). When combined with Developmental Profiles and Prescriptions for children, assessment of adult family members' strengths and weaknesses appears to result in a cooperative team approach consistent with child care program goals.

Four scales were developed for each of three developmental levels based on the ages of the children in care.

Scale I. Parenting Skills Scales: An objective multiple-choice scale measuring the essential skills in the 6 Goals and 13 Functional Areas listed in Table 7–1.

Scale II. Family Values Scale: A projective assessment measuring social and moral judgment and values applied to conflict situations with children.

Scale III. Home Environment Study: A structured study of the home environment from the perspective of children for developmentally appropriate care.

Scale IV. Parent/Child Observation and Interview: A structured observation and interview of parents with children that evaluates interaction and communication dynamics.

Quantitative results from all four scales are combined to establish a Parent Profile and a Parent Prescription detailing individual parent/guardian strengths and weaknesses and providing procedures and resources to improve caregiving skills.

Because the NPS are available in both self-administered and professional versions and provide developmental levels from birth to 18 years, they can be used easily by the caregiver or child care program to help family members understand their strengths and weaknesses and to ensure that developmentally appropriate activities and practices are continued in the home setting. Since families can take the scales home to complete, the scales are not threatening, as they might be in a test situation.

Results from initial research using the NPS reveal four **parenting styles**: Controlling, Detached, Selfless, and Healthy (Watson, 1996; see Chapter 3 for descriptions of each style). Knowing the strengths and weaknesses of the families in your group can help you communicate effectively and plan ways to extend the care program into the home to enhance the development of each child. Many families need assistance with choosing and creating safe, developmentally appropriate, and growth-producing environments for their children. They need to understand the ongoing responsibilities that caregivers have for children, what constitutes a highly qualified teacher, and how to evaluate a caregiver's level of education. In this way, they can become effective advocates for their children. However, advocacy should not be limited to local concerns. Informing families of national issues concerning child care that will affect their children and community, as well as who to write to at local, regional, and national levels to lobby for solutions, will empower them and can benefit everyone involved in early childhood education.

When families need information, it should be delivered by someone they trust and whose competence and experience will meaningfully affect the decisions they make. This type of education should also reflect how adults learn. Making resources available that they can read, listen to, and view will help them to construct their ideas about rearing young children. As part of this education, they may also need a designated time and place to discuss ongoing concerns, such as balancing work and family commitments, with other families with similarly aged children.

The child care facility, regardless of the type of setting, can fill all these needs. All the measures are suggested with the goal of building strong partnerships between families and caregivers so that optimal child growth and learning results.

Family-Caregiver Conferences

When a primary caregiving system is used in conjunction with regular conferences, the teacher is able to be a well-informed advocate for each child in her care. Having specific knowledge about a child that can be shared with family members strengthens relationships between teachers and families (Huber, 2003).

It is important that **family-caregiver conferences** have structure and occur at least twice per year. Preparing and sharing in advance an agenda and checklist, being a good listener, and keeping confidences are some of the important factors to consider (Orstein & Chapman, 1988). Consideration of differences in education, language, and culture is also important (Bauette & Peterson, 1993).

Busy families often have difficulty scheduling formal conferences. To make the most efficient use of time, plan the conference thoroughly. Identify the major purpose of the conference. If a family member requests a meeting, ask what concerns need to be discussed so you can prepare for the conference. If the teacher requests the conference, tell the family member why, so she has time to think about it before the conference begins. Gather background information to discuss the topic. Caregiver records of observations, both formal and informal, may be helpful. Outside sources such as articles, books, pamphlets, tapes, and videos may provide information for the caregiver and can be shared with the family members. You may also need information on community agencies or organizations in your region.

Providing an agenda, checklist, and feedback sheet at least three days in advance helps everyone involved in the meeting be prepared. This will give them time to look over what you want to accomplish and to understand what their role in the conference will be. A sample agenda for a teacher-initiated conference might resemble the following:

1. Welcome
2. How do you see ____ (Rodney) ____ developing at home?
3. Do you have any questions or concerns about his development?
4. Review checklist sent home to discuss what behaviors and skills have been noticed at school.
5. What developmental and learning goals should we set for ____ (Rodney) ____ ?
   a. Discuss: Families' goals
   b. Discuss: Teachers' goals
   c. Create list of our goals together.
6. Brainstorm: How can we work on these goals together?

Do you have any feedback to share about the program or our (family-teacher and teacher-child) relationships?

Step 4 serves the purpose of interpreting each child's progress to family members from a developmental approach to help family members understand and appreciate developmentally appropriate early childhood programs (NAEYC, 2005).

"Good two-way communication is essential to a positive family-caregiver relationship. Both parties should feel free to bring up concerns, problems or issues as well as joys and accomplishments. Each should feel that your perspective is being understood and valued" (Davis & Keyser, 1997). To support such a feeling, family-initiated conferences should have an agenda as well. The following points might be included:

1. Welcome and thank you for calling this meeting.
2. What are your concerns? (*Then, be sure to listen actively.*)
3. Respond with information or observations if it is appropriate and helpful to the discussion.
4. How can we deal with these concerns?
5. Create a plan of action together.
6. Set a follow-up meeting to monitor progress.

While having the conference, it is vital that you minimize power differences between you and family members. One way to do so is to arrange the physical environment so that all adults are sitting next to one another with no barriers. Placing chairs in a circle with no desk or table in between you accomplishes this. Physical comfort should also be considered. Early childhood educators are accustomed to sitting in child-size chairs on a regular basis. However, family members rarely are. Providing adult-size chairs can help everyone feel more at ease. Having water, coffee, or juice and a box of tissues nearby may also add to everyone's comfort.

Home Visits

Home visits are a regular part of Head Start programs, but few other child care programs make them. Home visits can be valuable opportunities for the family and the caregiver to learn more about each other. The teacher can see how the family members and child relate to each other in their own home. Home visits must be planned carefully to respect the family's time and space.

1. Identify and discuss with the family members the purpose for the visit: to get acquainted? to gather information? to work with the parents, child, or both?
2. Negotiate a time that is convenient for all family members and yourself. It can often be helpful to have a couple of dates in mind when you call to schedule the home visit.
3. Gather background information the visit requires. Do you need to take along any forms to be filled out? Will you be sharing your program goals? If so, do you have a flyer or pamphlet or will you just tell them? Are there specific problems or concerns you want to discuss? Do you have written documentation of the child's behavior to share, such as daily reports or notes, or resource and referral information?
4. Conduct the home visit as you would a family-teacher conference. For example, ask questions to elicit information from family members, work together to create solutions for any issues of concern, and ask for feedback.

Effective Tools for Current Issues in Early Child Care and Development

The master tools for infant and toddler caregiving are positive attention, approval, and attunement. Life energy is the force behind all human needs. Providing attention is directing our life force outward or inward, so that whatever we pay attention to grows. To commit our energy to the needs of young children, we must first give positive attention, affection, and be "in tune" with ourselves. Conscious care requires that we recognize the stress we create in ourselves, and learn how to create calm within, before we can direct our positive attention, and approval, toward the children in our care. First-time parents tend to direct all their attention toward their child and thus create stress, fatigue, and exhaustion for themselves. The child care specialist should model and instruct first-time parents in the conscious care of themselves, as well as their children.

Child care specialists need emotional intelligence, and the tools to communicate with parents and children in ways that teach them emotional intelligence. There are five domains or skills involved in becoming emotionally intelligent. The caregiver can develop tasks and activities that promote interactional synchrony between everyone involved, to teach parents and children the skills involved in being emotionally healthy. Current research in brain development clearly indicates that the consistency of our reactions to children actually program neural pathways to determine how children respond. Good or bad, happy or sad, feeling at ease or feeling "dis-eased"—your attitude imparts permanent changes to the nervous systems of the children in your care.

The bond between father and child is just as important for healthy child development as is the mother-child bond. In fact, recent research indicates that fathers can bond with infants just as well as mothers can. The child care specialist must actively encourage fathers to be involved in the child care program, by using communication tools such as mirroring, "I" messages, and active listening. Communicating with all family members is essential for a child care program that aims to enhance children's growth in all four developmental areas: physical, emotional, social, and cognitive.

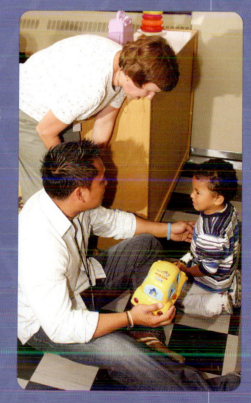

No less important are the relationships you build with other adults. Family members and colleagues should be partners, not competitors, in meeting the needs of young children. Families know important information about the children that you could never know. For example, you are typically not present in the homes before bedtime to determine the routine for sleeping. Asking questions about such events and explaining that your goals is to be as consistent as possible to facilitate the child feel secure is one way to build a reciprocal relationship. Moreover, inquiring about how the morning was at home before coming to your classroom may help you to transition the child or explain difficult behaviors.

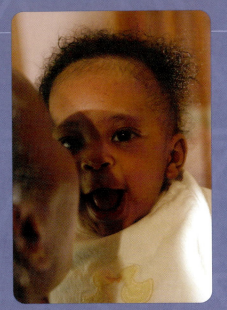

Very young children are social, almost from birth. They learn how to interact with peers by generalizing knowledge gained through their relationships with adults. Even when they have strong, positive relationships with adults, acquiring skills for interacting with peers takes a long time and significant amounts of adult support. Adults are obligated to use positive guidance strategies to help children attain these skills. Setting a few, positively-worded limits, explaining consequences, providing choices, and redirection are all part of this approach. Children want to be independent and adults want them to be also. These strategies also assist young children with gaining self-regulation skills, so they can make good decisions while interacting with peers or when working alone.

Establishing healthy relationships with children is a primary concern in child care, especially for infants and toddlers. Development is impacted significantly by the quality of relationships between each caregiver and child, so it is important the early childhood education programs be designed to support such relationships. Utilizing a primary caregiving system, planning for continuity of care, and organizing classrooms for family grouping are strategies for building positive relationships. These strategies help children to form strong, lasting bonds with a caregiver; they help children learn what it means to engage in reciprocal, responsive relationships. In other words, they help children learn to trust. Often times, these relationships mimic those the child experiences within her own family. However, sometimes these relationships provide another, new way of interacting.

C hild care specialists also need to enhance all areas of development for the children in their care. Designing curricular experiences to enhance development in several areas can be used throughout a daily schedule. For infants and toddlers, the curriculum can be divided into two main components: routine care times and planned learning experiences. Both of these times are learning times. Naming and labeling during diapering, feeding, and when exploring outdoors, for example, are effective strategies to use with young children because they encourage the development of cognitive structures and promote the development of receptive language. Early childhood educators should frequently observe and record the behavior of the children in their care. Gathering data and establishing developmental prescriptions are necessary for planning experiences. Teachers then use those data to carefully design curriculum that enhances the development of each child in their care.

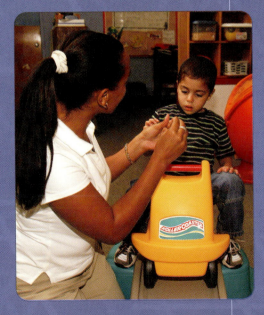

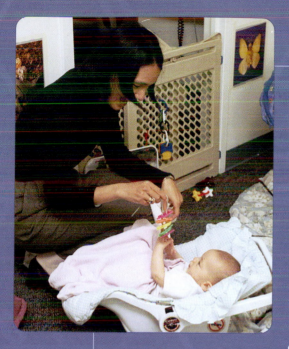

Developmental delays are areas of current concern in the field of early childhood education, especially for infants and toddlers because the earlier interventions occur, the better outcomes children typically have. Child care specialists are often the first person to become aware of learning or developmental delays. Knowing and being able to recognize the signs of developmental problems and making referrals to other professionals for further evaluation are fundamental responsibilities of the professional. In addition, adapting your strategies to the individual needs of the child facilitates development. For example, with children who exhibit language delays or speech problems, the tool of baby signing is very effective for decreasing frustration, helping them to communicate and interact with peers, and increasing their cognitive skills.

The field of child care has become more complex and more professional within the past few years, so it is important to understand the characteristics of a good child care specialist. A caregiver must acquire formal education in child development, early childhood education, and professionalism as well as skills such as observing and communicating before working with infants and toddlers. Professional preparation is necessary today because caregivers must be experts at ORAOM—the ability to Observe, Record, Assess, Organize, and Manage a care program for infants and toddlers. Although sensitivity, caring, and love are still the most important qualities of a caregiver of young children, formal training and preparation is also necessary to deal with the intricacies of child development in our complex world.

When you make a home visit, you are a guest in the family's home. You are there to listen and learn. When you have finished talking about the issues, thank them for their interest, time, and hospitality, and then leave.

FAMILY SITUATIONS REQUIRING ADDITIONAL SUPPORT

This section discusses four types of families that may need additional support from early childhood educators: grandparents as parents, families who have children who are at risk for later difficulties, families where abuse or neglect is present, and teenage parents. For all of these families, it is imperative that you utilize the positive communication skills discussed earlier.

Grandparents as Parents

Statistics indicate grandparents are taking care of children more than ever before. According to Children's Defense Fund, more than 1.4 million children lived with grandparents with a parent absent from the household during 1995 (Weill & Jablonski, 1997). This is a 66 percent increase since 1989.

You should extend a special invitation to grandparents who are now facing the challenge of raising grandchildren as primary caregivers, since this family situation is sometimes not obvious. Some grandparents are frustrated and some are isolated. Often they try to balance the demands of working full time and acting in the role of primary caregiver. All these factors add to grandparents' increased stress. They need encouragement, support, and a place to confide in someone.

Families with At-Risk Children

As discussed in Chapter 2, children can be *at risk* for a number of reasons, including genetic or chromosomal disorders and environmental influences. Significant contributors to being at risk are living in a poverty-stricken home, having one or more caregivers who have low levels of education, experiencing malnutrition or being undernourished, and lacking positive environmental stimulation (for reviews, see Duncan & Brooks-Gunn, 1997; Shonkoff & Phillips, 2000). Many families, especially single-parent households, struggle financially to meet the basic needs of their infants and toddlers, so they may focus their attention on survival rather than on strategies for promoting optimal development and learning. Families who are poverty-stricken care deeply for their children. They may work two or three jobs to provide shelter, food, and clothing, and even these may not be completely adequate.

Supporting families in these situations involves not only listening actively but also having contact information for community resources readily available. Including community resources regularly as part of your communication with families (such as in a section of your newsletter) is relatively simple for you but can have a significant impact. Knowing when and where to receive free immunizations, for example, can be key to

Early childhood educators are often the child's first line of defense for preventing and identifying abuse and neglect.

promoting the physical well-being of infants and toddlers. In addition, providing strategies for interacting with the child during the car or bus ride home can facilitate the development of language and cognition skills and are free of cost (Herr & Swim, 2002).

Families Experiencing Child Abuse or Neglect

Child abuse and neglect, while often closely linked in discussions, are two distinct constructs. Abuse is an action that causes harm to another and comes in three forms: physical, sexual, and emotional/psychological; neglect is failing to provide for the basic needs or affection of a child or not adequately supervising children's activities (McDevitt & Ormrod, 2004). Abuse and neglect can and do occur in families of any racial and ethnic background, socioeconomic status, and community. Early childhood educators are often the child's first line of defense for preventing and identifying abuse and neglect (see information on NAEYC under Helpful Web Sites at the end of this chapter).

Continually communicating about and modeling strategies for implementing the three As can foster family members' thinking about capabilities and appropriate expectations for children from birth to age three. Oftentimes, children are abused because family members do not know what is reasonable to expect of children (English, 1998).

For example, not knowing that it is unreasonable to expect a toddler to sit quietly in a restaurant and not interrupt the after-dinner conversation can result in stress and anger for the adult and abuse for the child.

Identifying children who are being abused or neglected is part of your professional and ethical responsibilities. Use your observation skills to inspect the child's body during routine care times to notice physical or sexual abuse. For example, while diapering, look at the child's arms, body, and legs. Any suspicious marking should cause you to politely and discreetly inquire of family members as to how the marks occurred. Immediately after your conversation, write down in the child's file exactly what you asked and what was told to you. The use of descriptive language (see Chapter 5) cannot be overemphasized in this situation. Interpretative language will make the record of little use to other professionals who may need to investigate the case. Reread your entry and reflect on the conversation. Ask yourself, Does this seem like a reasonable event to have happened to a child of this age and mobility? If your answer is yes, then do nothing. However, if your answer is no, you need to involve other professionals.

Each early childhood program should have a stated policy on how to handle suspected cases of child abuse. In some programs the director or staff social worker must be informed of the situation and be the one to report the incident to the appropriate community agency. This policy is often set in place to protect the teacher-family relationship. However, it is not that staff member's job to decide whether or not the incident needs reporting. If you, the teacher, believe that an incident should be reported, then it must be reported to protect you and your colleagues from being accused of neglect (i.e., failure to report a crime).

Deciding whether or not to report an incident can be emotionally difficult. The ethical dilemma stems from the fact that you are responsible for safeguarding the health and well-being of the children and maintaining relationships with families (NAEYC, 2005). To ease your mind, the determination of whether intentional abuse has occurred has nothing to do with your obligation under the law to report it. Your responsibility is to report your suspicions. Therefore, you are not to launch a full investigation to verify or disprove your suspicions; this is the responsibility of the community agency. If you report an incident in good faith, you are not legally liable if it is not substantiated by other professionals.

Supporting families who are experiencing abuse or neglect is essential for them to acquire more positive ways of interacting and meeting each others' needs. Reporting child abuse to the appropriate community agency can be the first intervention step. Contrary to popular belief, these agencies do all they can to assist parents in making good parenting choices. Linking families to other community resources, such as support groups or agencies that can provide education, is a way to facilitate the acquisition of positive parenting strategies.

Teenage Parents

According to Martin, Hamilton, Sutton, Ventura, Menacker, & Munson (2005), the teenage birth rate in 2003 was 41.6 births per 1,000 women aged 15–19. These figures represent a three percent decrease from the 2002 rate and a 33 percent decrease from the 1991 rate. While the occurrence of U.S. teenage pregnancy is still the highest among developed countries, this rate represents a record low birth rate for U.S. teens (Annie E. Casey Foundation, 2005; Martin et al., 2005).

The consequences of teenage parenting can be severe for both the teens and the infants. Teenage mothers are more likely to experience poverty and receive public assistance, while teen fathers are more likely to engage in delinquent behaviors such as alcohol abuse or drug dealing (Planned Parenthood Federation of America, 2005). Both teen mothers and teen fathers complete fewer years of schooling than their childless peers (Planned Parenthood Federation of America, 2005). In 2002, only 10 percent of teen mothers aged 15–17 had graduated from high school. After giving birth, it is estimated that only 33 percent of teen mothers will eventually graduate from high school, and only 1.5 percent will receive a college degree by the time they reach 30 years of age (Annie E. Casey Foundation, 2004).

The stress of limited financial resources coupled with a lack of life experiences can impact a teen parent's ability to interact with his or her infant or toddler. As any family member knows, raising children can be trying and very difficult even under the best of circumstances. Possessing sound coping mechanisms and the ability to make informed decisions is vital. These skills develop over time with life experiences and emotional maturity. Thus, parenting can be very challenging for teen parents, especially those who do not have family support. Add to this the necessity to set aside childhood dreams and aspirations and place a baby's needs before their own, and it is no wonder that a large majority of teenage parents have emotional conflicts that decrease their ability to provide good parenting.

The role of the early childhood educator cannot be underestimated in these situations. Teenage parents (both mothers and fathers) need you to support their positive parenting abilities and acknowledge their efforts, successes, and challenges. This requires you to set aside additional time to empathize, actively listen, and mirror the teen parent. Additionally, providing contact information for community services (e.g., parenting courses, financial management, and social service agencies) as part of your regular communication with families can be invaluable for both the teen parents and their infants and toddlers.

Teenage parents need good information, support, and role models that teach, through example, the daily competent care of infants and toddlers. This modeling should include the conscious application of attention, approval, and attunement in addition to the mechanics of care. A competent child care professional will help the teenage parents to develop by appropriately extending positive attention, approval, and attunement to them. Teenage parents are not yet adults and need to be accepted, not judged or labeled, for who they are as individuals.

COMMUNICATING WITH COLLEAGUES

When a child care program has more than one staff member, effective communication among staff is essential. Arranging to meet with staff members regularly enhances communication. Although family child care providers often work alone in their own homes, they can contact licensing staff and other family child care providers for support. Group family child care arrangements employ at least two people who work with a larger group of children in the home. Child care centers usually have a staff that includes a director and one or more caregivers. The size of enrollment determines the number and kind of additional staff; these may be caregivers, cooks, custodians, bus drivers, early childhood educators, social workers, and health personnel. No matter if the staff is two or 22, regular, uninterrupted time to communicate, solve problems, and make decisions is necessary.

Listening to Colleagues

Each caregiver needs to be a listener. Staff can exchange information and discuss program issues in a reasonable way only if all are active listeners. How you listen to one another reflects how you respect one another.

Collaborating with Colleagues

Share Information and Areas of Expertise

Your educational and professional experiences give you information, insights, and perspectives that will help others understand issues and deal with problems. Each person has special talents and unique insights to share with colleagues, children, and families. Nobody appreciates know-it-alls, but we all benefit from people who are willing to share ideas that can be discussed, accepted, modified, or rejected.

Share Your Feelings and Actively Listen While Expressing Your Excitement and Joy about Working with Your Colleagues

As a part of a team, you all benefit from sharing pleasurable experiences. Tactfully express frustrations, disappointments, and anger. Keeping those feelings bottled up can harm all of you. Determine what is distressing you and discuss the issue. By staying within your active listening guidelines you can focus on how staff activities are affecting program goals. You will be more likely to clear up misunderstandings and misperceptions if you focus your discussion on issues rather than on personalities.

Share Feedback

Both informal and formal observations provide you with feedback to share with your colleagues. Noting how other caregivers behave with people and materials in various settings, schedules, and routines can help the entire staff evaluate the current program and make necessary adjustments. Feedback can highlight caregiver actions that are helpful and effective, but you should use tact when commenting on a situation in which you believe your colleagues might act differently. Focus on what is best for the children and what changes can improve the situation, not on what a caregiver did wrong. Actions are more often *inappropriate* than wrong. Since all caregivers are developing their skills, comments that make colleagues feel incompetent are not helpful, while focusing on appropriate alternative actions is productive.

Share Responsibilities

Your colleagues will notice whether you are willing to carry your load. Not all of your responsibilities are explicit in your job description. Martha is responsible for getting snacks ready, but today she is rocking Natalie, who after crying and fussing has finally settled down but does not seem quite ready to be put down to play. If another caregiver volunteers to set up snacks, Natalie will not become distressed again and so will not disturb the other children.

Supporting Colleagues

Caregiving is physically and emotionally draining. Remember and put into practice the three As of caregiving presented in Chapter 4 to help yourself and your colleagues cope with stress. For example, assisting a colleague when extra help is needed reduces stress. You can provide positive emotional support by listening, using honest compliments, giving credit, and reassuring colleagues about ideas or actions of theirs that you think are appropriate. Knowing that you are working together rather than against each other is in itself powerful emotional support.

Making Decisions

Early childhood educators need information to make intelligent staff decisions. Meet with other staff members regularly. Study issues and learn to identify relevant factors so that you will be able to discuss subjects intelligently and make wise decisions. Raise questions with colleagues; listen, think, and take an active part in making decisions related to delivering professional care and education for very young children.

Supportive relationships are necessary among caregivers who work together in a child care program.

■ KEY TERMS

active listening	I statements	parenting styles
calibrating	mirroring	rapport
family-caregiver conferences	National Parenting Scales (NPS)	you statements
home visits	pacing	

CASE STUDY   Sheila

Amanda Hasha is a nine-month-old girl who has been in child care for the past three months. Sheila, her primary caregiver, has noticed that Amanda is not gaining weight, looks tired but does not sleep well, and cries often. Sheila met with the director and other caregivers to share her concerns and actively listened as they all confirmed her observations and suggested a family conference. Sheila then set up a conference with Mrs. Hasha to discuss Amanda's problems.

Sheila starts the conference by describing her observations using I statements. She informs Mrs. Hasha that the other caregivers have observed the same behaviors and tells her the steps that have been taken to comfort Amanda. Sheila then asks Mrs. Hasha what she sees at home, and is actively listening to her.

Mrs. Hasha: "I've had a lot of problems lately that I'm sure have affected Amanda. Her father had an accident and has been in the hospital, so I go to see him every chance I can."

Sheila: "My! It sounds like you have been under a lot of stress and worry lately."

Mrs. Hasha: "I just don't know what to do. No one else is around to help, so I sometimes have Amanda's sister watch her even though she's only eight."

Sheila: "So, you've had no help except for your older daughter. It sounds overwhelming."

Mrs. Hasha: "Yes, it certainly is! I wish I knew how to get the kids cared for so I could be at the hospital more often."

Sheila: "It sounds like you really need help with the children so you can help your husband more."

Mrs. Hasha: "That's right. Do you have any idea who might help me?"

Sheila: "I know there are many sources for help in the community. Have you thought to ask at the hospital, your church, or at school?"

Mrs. Hasha: "That's a very good idea. Our church has a volunteer program, so I'm going to ask our minister."

Sheila: "I'll also ask around at some of the programs the county offers. I'm sure help is available for this kind of situation."

Mrs. Hasha: "Thank you so much. I know that Amanda will be better if she has an adult to care for her when I can't be there."

Within a week, Mrs. Hasha has volunteers from her church helping to care for the children. Amanda's disposition has changed from stressed and insecure to calm and happy. Through the use of a family conference, active listening, I statements, and mirroring, Sheila was able to help Mrs. Hasha share her problems and arrive at solutions to improve Amanda's health and development.

1. Discuss what communication tools Sheila used and their effectiveness in producing outcomes.

2. How did Sheila use her colleagues to support and enhance her work with Amanda's family?

3. Imagine that Sheila used the following you statements in her conversation with Mrs. Hasha: "You leave Amanda with your eight-year-old daughter. Do you know how dangerous that is?" How might the outcome of the conversation been affected? Why?

■ RESOURCES FOR PARENTS AND STAFF

Governmental Agencies
Administration for Children, Youth and Families
P.O. Box 1182
Washington, DC 20013
(202) 651-3514

Bureau of Community Health Services
Office of Maternal and Child Health
Public Health Service
U.S. Dept. of Health and Human Services
5600 Fishers Lane
Rockville, MD 20857
(301) 443-2170

Centers for Disease Control
1600 Clifton Road, NE
Atlanta, GA 30333
(404) 639-3311

Children's Bureau
Office of Human Development Services
Administration for Children, Youth and Families
U.S. Dept. of Health and Human Services
Washington, DC 20201

Early Head Start National Resource Center
   @ ZERO TO THREE
2000 M Street, NW, Suite 200
Washington, DC 20036
(202) 638-1144, Fax (202) 638-0851
http://www.ehsnrc.org/

Food and Nutrition Services
U.S. Dept. of Agriculture
301 Park Center Drive
Alexandria, VA 22302
(202) 645-5518

Head Start Bureau
Office of Human Development Services
Administration for Children, Youth and Families
U.S. Dept. of Health and Human Services
Washington, DC 20201

National AIDS Hotline
(800) 342-2437

National Caries Program
National Institute of Dental Research
9000 Rockville Pike
Bethesda, MD 20892
(301) 496-3571

Additional Agencies
State departments of health
County health departments
State and regional poison control centers
State and county cooperative
   extension services

Professional
American Academy of Dermatology
930 North Meacham Road
Schaumburg, IL 60173-6016
(647) 330-0230

American Academy of Pediatrics
141 Northwest Point Boulevard
P.O. Box 927
Elk Grove, IL 60009
(800) 433-9016
http://www.aap.org/

American Dental Association
211 East Chicago Avenue
Chicago, IL 60611
(312) 440-2500

American Optometric Association
243 North Lindbergh Boulevard
St. Louis, MO 63141
(314) 991-4100

Health and Safety
American Automobile Association
(check local listings)
http://www.aaa.com/

American Red Cross
(check local listings)
http://www.redcross.org/

Childhood Lead Poisoning
(888) 232-6789

Johnson and Johnson Consumer Products
    Information Center
199 Grandview Road
Skillman, NJ 08558
(800) 526-3967

Metropolitan Life
Health & Welfare Division
One Madison Avenue
New York, NY 10010
(212) 578-2211

National Center for Clinical Infant Programs,
    Zero to Three
2000 14th Street, North #380
Arlington, VA 22201
(800) 411-1222

Parents' Health Report
Child Health Care Newsletter
2 Taylor Drive
Glen Cove, NY 11542
E-mail: energynurse1@yahoo.com

U.S. Consumer Product Safety Commission
Office of Information and Public Affairs
Washington, DC 20207
(800) 638-2772

■ QUESTIONS AND EXPERIENCES FOR REFLECTION

1. Actively listen to a dialogue between a family member and the caregiver when a child arrives in the morning. Write down the statements and then categorize them in the chart below.

	Family Member	Caregiver
Information		
Questions		
Affirmation		
Other		

2. Conduct one simulated family-caregiver conference initiated by the caregiver and another initiated by a family member.

3. Interview a teacher in an Early Head Start or a Head Start program about a home visit they have completed. Determine this teacher's purposes and procedures for the visit.

4. Role-play a child care center staff meeting about the problems of sharing play yard space.

5. Identify the responsibilities of a caregiver in a setting with which you are familiar. Categorize the activities according to whether the caregiver attends to them independently or in cooperation with other staff members, using a chart like the following.

Task	Accomplishes Independently	Needs Cooperation of Other Staff

6. Describe two situations in which caregivers interact with each other. Identify the interpersonal skills needed.

Situation	Skills Needed: Caregiver 1	Skills Needed: Caregiver 2

7. List your perceived strengths in interpersonal relationships with families and staff. List areas where you need to set growth goals.

■ CHAPTER REVIEW

1. What are effective communication skills and why?

2. Why is effective communication with families important?

3. Why is effective communication with colleagues important?

4. Write an agenda for a family-teacher conference initiated by you to discuss a child's toilet learning.

5. How can you contribute to effective, positive staff relationships?

■ REFERENCES

Annie E. Casey Foundation. (2004). *Kids Count 2004*. Baltimore, MD: Author. Retrieved December 14, 2006, from http://www.aecf.org/kidscount/databook/pdfs_e/kc2004_e.pdf

Annie E. Casey Foundation. (2005). *KIDS COUNT indicator brief: Reducing the teen birth rate*. Baltimore, MD: Author. Retrieved December 14, 2006, from http://www.aecf.org/kidscount/sld/auxiliary/briefs/teenbirthrateupdated.pdf

Bauette, G., & Peterson, E. (1993). Beginning to create a multicultural classroom. *Dimensions of Early Childhood, 21*(2), 11–12.

Bredekamp, S., & Copple, C. (Eds.). (1997). *Developmentally appropriate practice in early childhood programs* (Rev. ed.). Washington, DC: National Association for the Education of Young Children.

Christian, L. G. (2006, January). Understanding families: Applying family systems theory to early childhood practice. *Beyond the Journal: Young Children on the Web*. Retrieved December 14, 2006, from http://www.journal.naeyc.org/btj/200601/ChristianBTJ.pdf

Davis, L., & Keyser, J. (1997). *Becoming the parent you want to be*. New York: Broadway Books.

Douville-Watson, L. (1993). *Family actualization through research and education: F. A. R. E.* (3rd ed.). New York: Actualization.

Duncan, G. J., & Brooks-Gunn, J. (1997). *Consequences of growing up poor*. New York: Russell Sage Foundation.

English, (1998). The extent and consequences of child maltreatment. Protecting Children from Abuse and Neglect [Issue]. *The Future of Children, 8*(1), 39–53.

Galardini, A., & Giovannini, D. (2001). Pistoia: Creating a dynamic, open system to serve children, families, and community. In L. Gandini & C. P. Edwards (Eds.), *Bambini: The Italian approach to infant/toddler care* (pp. 89–105). New York: Teachers College Press.

Gandini, L. (2001). Reggio Emilia: Experiencing life in an infant-toddler center, An interview with Cristina Bondavalli. In L. Gandini & C. P. Edwards (Eds.) *Bambini: The Italian approach to infant/toddler care* (pp. 55–66). New York: Teachers College Press.

Gonzalez-Mena, J. (2001). *Multicultural issues in child care* (3rd ed.). Mountain View, CA: Mayfield.

Hendrix, H. (1993). *Getting the love you want*. New York: Institute for Relationship Therapy.

Herr, J., & Swim, T. (2002). *Creative resources for infants and toddlers* (2nd ed.). Clifton Park, NY: Thomson Delmar Learning.

Huber, L. K. (2003). Knowing children and building relationships with families: A strategy for improving conferences. *Early Childhood Education Journal, 31*(1), 75–77.

Lally, J. R. (Ed.). (1992). *Language development & communication: A guide, infant/toddler caregiving series*. San Francisco: Far West Lab.

Mantovani, S. (2001). Infant-toddler centers in Italy today: Tradition and innovation. In L. Gandini & C. P. Edwards (Eds.), *Bambini: The Italian approach to infant/toddler care* (pp. 23–37). New York: Teachers College Press.

Martin, J. A., Hamilton, B. E., Sutton, P. D., Ventura, S. J., Menacker, F., & Munson, M. L. (2005). Births: Final data for 2003. *National Vital Statistics Reports, 54*(2). Hyattsville, MD: National Center for Health Statistics.

McDevitt, T. M., & Ormrod, J. E. (2004). *Child development: Educating and working with children and adolescents.* Upper Saddle River, NJ: Pearson Merrill Prentice Hall.

National Association for the Education of Young Children (NAYC). (2005). Position statement: Code of ethical conduct and statement of commitment. Washington, DC: Author. Retrieved December 14, 2006, from http://www .naeyc.org/about/positions/pdf/PSETH05.PDF

Orstein, A. C., & Chapman, J. K. (1988). The parent-teacher conference. *PTA Today, 14*(1), 8–10.

Planned Parenthood Federation of America (2005). Pregnancy & childbearing among U.S. teens. Washington DC: Author. Retrieved December 14, 2006, from http://www.plannedparenthood.org/files/PPFA/fact-teen-pregnancy.pdf

Shonkoff, J. P., & Phillips, D. A. (Eds.). (2000). *From neurons to neighborhoods: The science of early childhood development.* Washington, DC: National Academy Press.

Watson, M. A. (1996). *The national parenting scales: Experimental edition.* Bayville, NY: Instructional Press.

Watson, M. A. (1997, November). *Giving & receiving family support through using the National Parenting Scales.* Paper presented at the annual conference of the National Association for the Education of the Young Child, Anaheim, CA.

Weill, J. D., & Jablonski, M. (Eds.). (1997). *Children's Defense Fund: The state of America's children: 1997 yearbook.* Washington, DC: Children's Defense Fund.

ADDITIONAL RESOURCES

Gordon, T. (1976). *Parent effectiveness training: P. E. T.* New York: Peter H. Wyden.

Greater Minneapolis Day Care Association. (1983). *Child health guidelines.* Minneapolis: Author.

Hewlett, B. S. (1992). *Father-child relations.* New York: Adline DeGruyter.

Lally, R. J. (1995). The impact of child care policies and practices on infant/toddler identity formation. *Young Children, 51*(1), 58–67.

Lamb, M. E. (1987). *The father's role: Cross cultural perspectives.* Hillsdale, NJ: Erlbaum.

Owen, M. T., & Cox, M. J. (1988). Maternal employment and the transition to parenthood. In A. E. Gottfried & A. W. Gottfried (Eds.), *Maternal employment and children's development: Longitudinal research* (pp. 85–119). New York: Plenum Press.

Rogers, C. (1961). *On becoming a person.* Boston: Houghton Mifflin.

Saul, R. (1999). Teen pregnancy: Progress meets politics. *The Guttmacher Report on Public Policy, 2*(3), 6–9.

HELPFUL WEB SITES

Annie E. Casey Foundation. Provides useful statistics on children and teens in the United States as well as brief reports that could easily be shared with colleagues. **http://www.aecf.org**

Choosing Child Care—A Checklist for Parents. Steps in choosing child care. **http://www.childcare.org/families/choosing-provider.htm**

Head Start Information & Publication Center. Download Early Head Start tip sheets for colleagues or parents on up-to-date topics and issues regarding child care and parenting. **http://www.headstartinfo.org/infocenter/ehs_tipsheet/index.htm**

National Association for the Education of Young Children (NAEYC). All early childhood educators should be a member of this professional organization. Publishes *Beyond the Journal,* which adds online content to the *Young Children* print journal. Downloadable brochure and discussion guide entitled *Building CIRCLES, breaking CYCLES, Preventing child abuse and neglect: The early childhood educator's role.* http://www.naeyc.org

Planned Parenthood. Information on adoption, healthcare, parenting, pregnancy, and STDs. http://www .plannedparenthood.org

Search Institute. This nonprofit promoting child health lists Developmental Assets™, which are important for raising healthy, well-adjusted infants. http://www.search-institute.org/

Women's Bureau. Compilation of work and child care issues for women. http://www.dol.gov/wb/

For additional infant and toddler resources, visit our Web site at http://www.earlychilded.delmar.com

The Indoor and Outdoor Environment

■ OBJECTIVES

After reading this chapter, you should be able to:

- Identify components of high-quality and developmentally appropriate indoor and outdoor learning environments from the teacher's perspective.
- Identify components of high-quality and developmentally appropriate indoor and outdoor learning environments from the child's perspective.
- Understand criteria for selecting materials.
- Evaluate policies and procedures for protecting the health and safety of very young children.

■ CHAPTER OUTLINE

- Introduction to Principles of Environmental Design
- The Teacher's Perspective
  Learning Centers
  Use of Space
  Calm, Safe Learning Environment
  Basic Needs

- The Child's Perspective
  Transparency
  Flexibility
  Relationships
  Identity
  Movement
  Documentation
  Senses
  Representation
  Independence
  Discovery
  Ongoing Reflection on the Physical Environment
- Selecting Equipment and Materials
  Age-appropriate Materials
  Homemade Materials
- Protecting the Children's Health and Safety
  Emergency Procedures
  Immunization Schedule
  Signs and Symptoms of Possible Severe Illness
  First Aid
  Universal Precautions
  Injuries
  Outdoor Safety
- Case Study: Ena

INTRODUCTION TO PRINCIPLES OF ENVIRONMENTAL DESIGN

"...the issue is not having space but how it is used"
V. Vecchi, quoted in Gandini, 1998, p. 165

Reflecting on the role of space is imperative, as has been demonstrated as a principle of the schools in Reggio Emilia, Italy (Chapter 6). The classroom environment is considered the "third teacher" (e.g., Edwards, Gandini, & Forman, 1998), a concept that acknowledges the role of adults in carefully preparing and selecting materials for indoor and outdoor learning environments. In other words, the environment is planned to provide guidance to the children and adults about appropriate behavior.

Consider for a moment how your behavior is influenced differently by being in a place of worship, a library, a shopping mall, or a family dining restaurant. All of these environments reflect messages of appropriate behavior. For example, a library may have special sections designated for quiet reading, small groups to gather and enjoy stories, computer work, and playing with puppets. The way space and materials are arranged provides clues for appropriate behavior. The adults responsible for managing the space seldom have to remind others of their expectations; the environment does it for them. Similar to the designer of the library environment, a teacher's careful classroom environment planning will help children meet expectations for the use of the space and promote optimal development and learning.

We must design learning environments so that they facilitate the optimal care and education of young children. "The drive to protect our children is profound and easily can lead to cleansing their lives of challenge and depth. Early childhood is a time when children begin to live in the world and hopefully learn to love the world. They can't do this when fenced off from the messy richness of life to live in a world of fluorescent lights and plastic toys, two-dimensional glowing screens, and narrow teaching instruction" (Greenman, 2005, p. 7). Think about what the classroom environment you help create says about your educational values, your beliefs about the capabilities of young children, and the role of families. The focus of this chapter is on answering *how do teachers create meaningful learning environments that facilitate optimal development for the children?*

THE TEACHER'S PERSPECTIVE

Many teachers prepare their indoor and outdoor areas for learning, but do they prepare them to promote optimal learning?* When making educational decisions such as the arrangement and selection of materials, you should begin by reflecting on the age of children in your classroom; their needs, interests, and abilities; your program's philosophy; licensing and accreditation standards; and guidelines for developmentally appropriate practice (to be discussed more in Chapter 9). Each of these factors helps you to shape the various areas in which the children will grow and learn.

Learning Centers

Learning centers organize the space and materials and encourage specific types of behaviors in one location. For infants and toddlers you can organize learning centers in several ways. A popular approach for toddlers involves dividing the indoor and outdoor space into use areas. A quiet zone or private space, a construction center, a wet center, a project area, a reading and listening center, or a dramatic play center can be created by using tables, short shelves, transparent dividers, and flooring to indicate an

---

*This section was originally published in a slightly different form as T. J. Swim, "Basic premises of classroom design: The teacher's perspective," *Early Childhood NEWS*, 16(6), (2004), 34–42. Article commissioned by Jonti-Craft. Copyright © 2004 by Excelligence Learning Corporation. Reprinted by permission.

A library center with developmentally appropriate materials can foster a love of reading.

area inside. For infants, these areas may be less well defined. For example, a manipulation area will allow for exploring toys with the hands, while a more open space becomes a gross motor area. The rest of the room might be subdivided into areas for specific types of routine care times such as diapering or napping. The outdoor space should also be divided into learning centers. Any experience done inside can be done outside; teachers should not overlook the importance of the outdoor learning environment (DeBord, Hestenes, Moore, Cosco, & McGinnis, 2002; Stephenson, 2002). Painting, riding trikes, climbing and jumping, sand and water play, growing vegetables or flowers in a garden, dramatic play, and storytelling are all centers that should be outside (DeBord et al., 2002; Torquati & Barber, 2005). Sutterby and Frost (2002) also suggest the use of outdoor cooking experiences for promoting healthy eating. Given the importance of learning centers for promoting development, it is assumed that your child care setting will be flexibly organized into them.

When planning your learning environment, base the number and type of learning centers on the size of the space and the age of the children. In general, to maximize choice and minimize conflict over possessions, a rule of thumb to follow for toddlers and older children is to provide one-third more work spaces than the number of children in your classroom. To illustrate, if you have 12 older toddlers in your group, you will need at least $(12 \times \frac{1}{3}) + 12$ or 16 spaces for working. This might mean including two or three spaces at the sensory table, two at the easel, two or three at the art center, three or four in blocks/construction, three or four in dramatic play, two in the listening/library area, and two private spots. The same rule of thumb can apply to outdoor space, but having more play spaces available maximizes the amount of time children are moving and exercising and thus remaining physically fit and healthy (Sutterby & Frost, 2002).

Real Objects versus Open-Ended Materials

Children need a balance of novel and familiar materials to attract and maintain their attention (see the next section for a more in-depth discussion). When children are engaged with materials and ideas, they have less opportunity to create mischief or misbehave, thus enabling teachers to change their supervision from guidance of behavior to guidance of learning. Developmentally, throughout the early childhood period, young children are learning to use objects as tools for representing their thoughts and theories about how the world works. Therefore, providing a balance of real and open-ended materials promotes cognitive development. Making available real objects such as child-size shovels for digging in the garden, Navajo pottery for

Open-ended materials can provide extensive opportunity for play and representation of ideas.

storing paintbrushes, or child-size glass tumblers for drinks during meals (for older toddlers) serves two further purposes: (1) it demonstrates trust in the children's ability to care for objects and (2) it connects home and school environments. Real objects, when provided in response to the children's expressed interests, can also facilitate thinking about a particular topic or concept.

Open-ended materials, on the other hand, can be used by the children to expand their understanding of concepts and demonstrate creative uses of materials. Open-ended materials include collected items such as fabric, cardboard, plastics, pebbles, shells, pinecones or egg cartons, as well as commercially produced objects such as wooden blocks, animal and people figurines, or connecting manipulatives. Open-ended materials can spark, support, and enhance learning and development in any learning environment. Neatly arranging them in baskets or clear containers and displaying them on a shelf at the children's height will make them easily accessible to the children whether they are working indoors or outdoors. Of course, some open-ended materials might pose a choke hazard for infants and toddlers, so never leave the child unattended during the experience.

Independence versus Dependence

A primary goal for adults is that children become independent, self-regulated learners. In order for this to occur, teachers must carefully plan the physical environment with this in mind. As mentioned above, providing easily accessible open-ended materials promotes cognitive development. This practice also promotes social and emotional development, since the children can independently select the materials they need for their work and can more easily help with cleanup before they leave the learning area. Moreover, modifying the bathroom so that all necessary hand-washing supplies can be reached fosters the children's independence. Outside faucets that have an attachment allowing children to serve themselves encourage the toddlers to get water whenever they need it for their work.

Use of Space

An important question to begin your work is "How do I want the children to use this space?" Teachers create environments to promote learning in all areas of development as well as in particular content areas, such as mathematics or social studies. Therefore, a thorough understanding of child development and learning theories will guide you in planning how to use your classroom space.

Messy versus Dry

Designing space for daily opportunities to explore messy materials is a must. In fact, Bredekamp and Copple (1997) suggest that toddlers should have daily experiences with sand and water because of their educational value. Messy experiences are particularly significant for young children because they build cognitive structures or schemas (i.e., tightly organized sets of ideas about specific objects or situations) through sensorimotor and hands-on, minds-on experiences. Some typical messy

Messy experiences for young children build cognitive structures through sensorimotor and hands-on, minds-on experiences.

centers include water and/or sensory tables, painting easels, and art. Water play, for example, provides opportunities for learning about quantity, building vocabulary, and negotiating the sharing of materials.

What does a teacher need to consider when managing messy experiences in a classroom setting? First, setting up messy experiences in an area with vinyl or linoleum flooring allows for ease of cleanup when spills occur. Second, placing these experiences near a water source can aid in cleaning up and refilling containers or even adding a new element to an experience. For example, if a sensory table is filled with dry sand, children can transfer water from the source using pitchers, thus transforming the properties of the sand. Third, placing a hand broom and dustpan nearby prompts children to keep the area clean.

If you do not have an area with flooring that allows for easy cleanup, you will need to be creative in order to provide such valuable learning experiences. Placing newspaper, towels, or a shower curtain under a sensory table or easel can resolve this issue. Another way to address this challenge is to plan daily experiences with messy materials outside.

Noisy versus Quiet

Some classroom experiences are noisier than others. Cooperating and negotiating requires children to interact with one another. Although sometimes interactions can become heated, a caregiver's goal should be to enable such interactions so that the children gain necessary perspective-taking and problem-solving skills, not to stop the interactions or prevent them in the first place. To manage the environment and facilitate learning, teachers can place noisy areas close together. Noisy centers include blocks and construction, dramatic play, music and movement, and project work space. Placing these centers adjacent to one another serves two purposes. First, the higher noise levels will be located in a particular section of the room. This allows children to concentrate better in the quiet areas, with fewer distractions close by. Second, placing areas that require more supervision and support together permits the teacher to engage in these interactions (e.g., assisting children with problem solving) without having to travel between different parts of the room.

Quiet centers consist of the library, listening centers, and private spaces. For your mental health and that of the children you must provide both indoor and outdoor areas for children to be alone. These private spaces allow the children to regroup and gather their thoughts before rejoining others. A note of caution is needed here. You should never send a child to the quiet or private areas as a consequence for misbehavior. Children should freely choose these areas to help them relax. If you use the areas for punishment or the children perceive them as such, they will not serve their purpose of helping children to relax and regroup.

Play in some other centers, such as with manipulatives or science/discovery, fluctuates between quiet and noisy, depending on the type of materials provided and the children's levels of engagement. These areas can be used to transition between the noisy and quiet centers.

When deciding where to place learning centers, teachers also need to consider the needs of the different types of centers. To illustrate, the music and movement center needs an electrical outlet for a tape or CD player, shelves for musical instruments, baskets for scarves or strips of fabric, mirrors for observing motions, and space for creative movement and dance. Teachers often have limited resources and need to maximize the use of the equipment and materials that they do have. Locating the music and movement center near the dramatic play area is one way to do this: these two centers can share materials such as a mirror or basket of fabric.

Calm, Safe Learning Environment

Another question that you will encounter in your work is "How can I create a calm, safe environment that provides stimulating learning experiences for the children?" In this section, we will focus attention on the last part of this question: "stimulating learning experiences."

Novel versus Familiar

Teachers and children deserve to be surrounded by beautiful objects and materials that are displayed in an aesthetically pleasing fashion. Some of these objects should be part of the environment on a regular basis, while others can be included occasionally to spark interest. For example, hanging a framed print of Monet's sunflowers on the wall near the easel will create a beautiful environment for toddler children. Surprising the children with a display of Pueblo Indian pottery one day will create a different motivation to use the easel.

Learning spaces should be varied so that children have the opportunity to explore different perspectives. To illustrate, having the ability to change one's physical location by climbing up the stairs to a loft or playscape and looking down on a teacher provides a child with a new view of the world. Another way that teachers can vary the space and provoke thinking is by providing a new display or object to explore and discuss. A ground covering with two or more variations can naturally demonstrate hard versus soft and warm versus cold. Sitting an infant on soft, lush grass on a hot summer day will feel cool to the touch, thus providing him an opportunity to experience his environment in a different way.

Another way to conceptualize the familiar is to create spaces that parallel those found in home environments. For example, placing a couch, rocking chair, and end table with a lamp in the entryway mimics a living room in a home. A cozy nook like this not only adds warmth and comfort to the learning environment but also helps to create a sense of security at school: a home away from home. Having a hanging swing, the kind families might have on their front porch, gives the adults and children a place to snuggle and relax on a warm springtime afternoon.

Pathways versus Boundaries

As you are planning your layout, you need to consider how you will define your learning centers. Having visible boundaries for learning centers provides children with a clear message about the use of materials in a particular area. Use a variety of dividers, such as short shelving units, bookcases, transparent fabrics, and sheets of decorated acrylic. Flower beds, raised gardens, or cobbled pathways make great dividers for outdoor learning centers. Transparency, or the ability to see between centers, both allows teachers to supervise and facilitates children's play, because they can make connections between materials in different centers in each environment. Even though materials are organized into learning centers, we should be flexible in allowing the children to move materials that they need from one center to another. When planning the boundaries for a learning center, you must carefully consider how much space to devote to that area. As described above, the noisier areas often require more space than quieter areas. This is due to the fact that these areas tend to elicit more associative and cooperative play, requiring two or more children at a time.

A teacher also needs to consider how to utilize open space. Because we need gathering spaces for toddlers that can easily accommodate most of the children and caregivers in the room at one time, we often set aside this space for that one purpose. Then, when no one is using the space, children may convert it to a place for "rough and tumble" play. Using the gathering space for movement and gross motor activities as well may be logical, given the space needs of a particular center.

Pathways into and out of the room as well as between centers need to be carefully considered. When children arrive for the day, they should be able to complete a gradual transition from home to school. Having to walk to the opposite side of the classroom to store their belongings in their cubbies can be stressful, especially if they must pass by noisy centers. When considering movement between centers, remember that walking through one center to get to another can cause children to become distracted. Do you want the children to walk through a center such as the block/construction area to get to the music center? It would quickly become evident from the children's behavior that such an arrangement does not work well.

Basic Needs

As you are considering the educational needs of the children, you must also dedicate space for meeting the children's basic needs for eating, toileting, resting, and playing. The question here is: "How do I plan the environment to meet the basic needs of the children?"

Eating versus Toileting

Some infant and toddler classrooms separate the changing table and food preparation counter with a small sink. This practice may seem to be an efficient use of counter space, but it could jeopardize both the early childhood educators' and the children's

Teachers must plan the environment and adopt practices to protect their own and the children's health.

health. For hygienic purposes, then, it is imperative that the eating and toileting areas be separated. Although this is relatively simple in a preschool classroom, it may be more difficult in an infant and toddler classroom, because the typical restroom just does not have enough space for toilets, sinks, and a changing table. Since infant and toddler teachers must both continually supervise the children and also spend a significant amount of time diapering, changing tables are often placed in the classroom. Where should a changing table be located? Placing it next to a water source assists with good hand-washing practices. You should also position it away from a wall, so that your back is not to the rest of the children when you are changing a diaper.

The food area can require a number of small appliances such as a mini-refrigerator or microwave (per licensing regulations); therefore, cabinet space near electrical outlets is very important. For toddlers and older children, space for eating can be shared with other areas of the classroom. For example, the tables that are used for art can be cleaned and sanitized when it is snack or meal time. Infant teachers must address other issues when planning the environment. Depending upon your state regulations, you may or may not need a separate high chair for each infant. Finding storage space for mealtime equipment must be given careful consideration.

Sleep and Comfort versus Play

Children and adults need locations to store special items and belongings from home. This not only reaffirms the importance of both environments but it also teaches respect for one's own and others' belongings. Switching between environments can be stressful for people of all ages, so plan for comfortable places for children to make the transition from home to school, snuggle, relax, and enjoy reunions with family members. Couches and rocking chairs located in a variety of classroom areas provide an excellent avenue for this.

All children need time throughout the day to rest and rejuvenate. Teachers should create a calm, relaxing environment during nap or rest time. Closing blinds on the windows, plugging in a night light, playing soft instrumental music, and providing comfort items for each child (e.g., blankets, favorite stuffed animals) might assist with shifting from play to sleep. You should also organize the environment to address the needs of children who require less sleep during the day, by creating baskets with books, paper and pencils, and other quiet toys that can be used by a child lying on a cot or sitting at a table.

At times children may prefer to nap outdoors after exerting themselves during activities and play. A shady and easily supervised space made soft with quilts or blankets should be readily available for resting.

We have now considered the learning environment from the teacher's perspective, but it is time to consider the child's perspective. While presenting the material in this manner may create paradoxes (seemingly contradictory messages), keep in mind that these are different sides of the same coin. In other words, consider and prepare to articulate the common focus of each perspective.

THE CHILD'S PERSPECTIVE

First and foremost, the educational space has to guarantee the well being of each child and of the group of children.[†] Children have the right to educational environments that facilitate their social, emotional, moral, physical, linguistic, and cognitive development; they also have the right to environments that are free of excessive stress, noise, and physical and psychological harm (Malaguzzi, 1998). The following section explains 10 principles that are important to consider when creating your educational environment from the child's perspective. You may notice that these principles are not restricted to a particular learning center, but rather apply across educational spaces.

Consider each of the general principles in relationship to the specific children in your care. The environment must reflect and be responsive to the unique developmental characteristics of children of specific ages as well as the individual children within that age group (Bredekamp & Copple, 1997). Although the general principles are relevant to all environments for young children, they may manifest themselves differently for the various age groups. One or two principles may be more relevant for a particular age group or setting. To briefly illustrate, continuity of care between home and school environments is vital for the appropriate care of infants (see, for example, Bergen, Reid, & Torelli, 2001; Bove, 2000; Essa, Favre, Thweatt, & Waugh, 1999). Thus, plenty of space needs to be devoted to areas where family members and teachers can comfortably communicate and ease each infant's transition. Less space may be required for this purpose with preschoolers.

Before providing detailed explanations of each principle, a general overview of each will be provided, highlighting questions that a child might want to ask:

Transparency—Can I see my friends, teachers, and family members from almost any place in the room? Is there a place I can have some time alone? Can I quickly find the materials I want to use?

Flexibility—Can I find areas that support my interests in the classroom?

Relationships—Can I build relationships with other people in my classroom?

Identity—Am I an important person in this environment?

Movement—Can I move my body freely?

Documentation—Do the important adults in my life communicate about me frequently?

Senses—Is the environment warm and welcoming and a place that I want to spend 4–10 hours of my day?

Representation—Can I tell you in multiple ways about my understanding of and theories about the world?

Independence—Can I do things myself?

Discovery—Can I find interesting things to examine closely and learn about?

---

† This section was originally published in a slightly different form as T. J. Swim, "Advance reflection on principles of classroom design: Considering the child's perspective," *Early Childhood NEWS, 17*(1), (2005), 34–39. Article commissioned by Jonti-Craft. Copyright © 2005 by Excellence Learning Corporation. Reprinted by permission.

Transparency

Can I see my friends, teachers, and family members from almost any place in the room? To support connections and relationships, children need to be able to see materials and one another. From the adult's viewpoint, transparency adds to the ease of supervision. You should be able to see from one side of the room to the other. This should not remove all privacy, however. Children and adults need secluded spaces to be alone and gather their thoughts (Marion, 2007). To achieve this principle, you can use translucent fabrics, shelves with the backing removed, or sheets of decorated acrylic to divide areas (Curtis & Carter, 2003).

A second concern a child might have is, "Can I quickly find the materials I want to use?" Another aspect of transparency considers the amount and the presentation of materials in the environment. In general, you want the room to be as uncluttered as possible. You should regularly analyze your environment to identify unused toys or materials and then locate places to store those items to minimize clutter (Cutler, 2000).

For those items that are being used regularly, carefully observe the quantity of material being used by the children; have you provided too many objects or not enough? You should strive to provide a sufficient amount of material. The definition of *sufficient* is guided by your professional interpretation; realize that it differs for each group of children. The aim is to provide materials to spark older toddlers' interests, yet not totally satisfy them; thus provoking them to use their emerging skills of

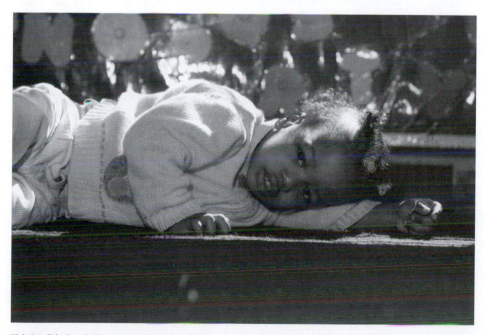

"Hiding" behind the transparent barrier.

imagining, pretending, and transforming objects for use. The phrase "less is more" is key to this principle. Try to display the materials and supplies in baskets or clear containers on shelves that are low and open, because displaying materials in this manner permits children to see what is available and to select and clean up materials independently (Isbell & Exelby, 2001; Marion, 2007; Topal & Gandini, 1999).

Flexibility

Can I find areas that support my interests in the classroom? The environment should change in response to individual children and each group of children living in it (Bredekamp & Copple, 1997). To illustrate, an infant-toddler teacher modified her classroom as the children got older and she noticed particular interests. For example, to support and further enhance the children's interests in building, she designed her room with two separate construction areas. This seemed to work well for this group because they could spread out to work in the distinct spaces. As one of the children's projects grew, she altered another area of the classroom to support their representation of a city surrounded by train tracks. For a short period of time, this teacher had three classroom areas devoted to construction! She flexed her environment to best meet the needs of the children.

To many teachers' dismay, child care programs often lack adequate space for all that the children and teachers want to do. Combining or rotating learning centers is one way to maximize learning opportunities without overloading the setting (Isbell & Exelby, 2001). For example, a toddler teacher in a church-based program had to combine the writing and art center, while her colleague decided to carefully select materials to merge science exploration and reading/library into one center. In contrast, another of their colleagues provided space in the outdoor environment for daily experiences at the sensory table and easel and to better utilize classroom space.

Related to that idea of combining centers is the notion of providing open-ended materials that can be used in many areas of the classroom (Curtis & Carter, 2003). Encouraging the children to borrow or move materials between the learning centers is another way to demonstrate the flexibility of the environment. Hence, another question a child might wonder is, "Can I move the materials and supplies around the room to do my work?"

Relationships

Can I build relationships with other people in my classroom? The environment needs to support and facilitate the development of strong, enduring relationships among children, families, and staff members (Honig, 2002; Galardini & Giovannini, 2001; New, 1998). As discussed in previous chapters, continuity of care should be a priority to support optimal social and emotional development. Space needs to be allocated and arranged so that adults and children have soft, warm areas for gathering, snuggling, communicating, or just being together. This space also serves to create an "at home" feeling, which is important because it helps high-quality child care programs avoid an institutional feel.

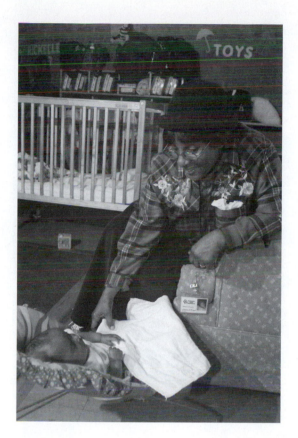

Space needs to be allocated so that adults and children have soft, warm areas for gathering, snuggling, or just being together.

To illustrate this principle, consider the infant teacher who reorganized the entry to his classroom to include two rocking chairs and a small table. This provided space for him to speak with families at the beginning of the day, gathering information about family events and sharing anecdotes from the previous day. He also noticed that some families would linger in this area to say their goodbyes. Moreover, he used the same chairs to read to and snuggle with individual children before naptime.

Identity

Am I an important person in this environment? Your learning space should provide traces of those who live in it. Providing special spots for belongings is also a must, because it tells children that items of value from home are welcomed and respected in the classroom. Photographs of children working and playing, as well as family members and staff members both at work and at home should be displayed in prominent locations around the classroom. Panels documenting the work of the children and teachers provide clear explanation and evidence of the persons living and learning in the space (Turner & Krechevsky, 2003; Brown-DuPaul, Keyes, & Segatti, 2001; Forman & Fyfe, 1998). Such documentation also communicates that the children and

Mirrors also provide valuable information that contributes to the development of children's identity.

their work are important to understand and adds to their sense of self (Project Zero & Reggio Children, 2001; Malaguzzi, 1998).

Do not restrict yourself to displaying traces of the children, families, and staff on classroom walls. No space should be considered marginal (Gandini, 1998). Using the door of the playground shed, a shelf in the entryway, bathroom walls or stall doors to display photographs or works of art, for example, demonstrates to children the importance of that space and can provide additional information to help them build their identities (see Wien, Coates, Keating, & Bigelow, 2005). For example, a toddler teacher created a hand-washing chart using photographs of the children engaged in the various steps of the process. This chart not only provided the necessary information required to be posted by the state regulatory agency, but also assisted the children with independently completing this self-help task. An additional idea is to strategically place mirrors around the classroom so that children notice their work or actions from another perspective (Smith, 1998).

Movement

Can I move my body freely? The environment needs to provide plenty of opportunities for children to move around and explore their bodies in space. Rather than trying to suppress children's bodies and their energy, teachers should find ways to include them in the learning process (Curtis & Carter, 2003). Large areas can be devoted to small climbers, obstacle courses, dancing, or acting out stories. The materials in this section of the classroom should be easily transportable so that they can be moved when the space is needed for other purposes, such as a classroom gathering (Isbell & Exelby, 2001).

High-quality spaces for infants and toddlers minimize, or eliminate entirely, equipment that confines children. A playpen, for example, not only physically limits a child but creates a barrier that socially and emotionally isolates the child from others. Holding a child offers more safety and security than the most expensive playpen. In addition, wheeled walkers do not enhance upright mobility development of infants; they can actually promote the acquisition of bad habits such as walking on tiptoes. Before using equipment that confines children (indoors or out), check with your state and local licensing regulations.

Creating multilevel spaces inside and outside provides additional ways for the children to explore their bodies in space. Playscapes, platforms, and lofts, for example, provide not only a quiet space for reading or writing but also offer a different viewpoint of the room and the objects within it (Curtis & Carter, 2003). When standing in a loft, many toddlers are larger than their caregivers for the first time, thus filling them with a new sensation: power!

Another aspect of this principle involves the ability to easily move from one area to another. Learning areas should be well defined but have clear traffic paths between them. These paths afford the children spaces to deeply engage in their work with minimal interruptions from those seeking new experiences (Marion, 2007).

Documentation

Do the important adults in my life communicate about me frequently? Some classroom space should be dedicated to communicating and record keeping, because reciprocal relationships are built on open, ongoing communication among the adults in the children's lives (Bredekamp & Copple, 1997). Adults require comfortable places to read and send messages, record observations, and store or display documentation about each child, such as portfolios or panels. Returning to the example provided in the "Relationship" section above, the teacher also used his entryway as a place for providing written communication with families. Beside one chair, he placed a basket that held the home-school journals (see Chapter 5). In addition, he had a bookshelf where all of the children's portfolios were stored. The table provided space for him to spread out artifacts collected over the week and make decisions about what to add to the portfolio.

Senses

Is the environment warm and welcoming and a place that I want to spend 4–10 hours of my day? The environment should be pleasing to the senses. There needs to be a balance of hard and soft, rough and smooth, novel and familiar, simple and complex, and quiet and noisy (Bergen, Reid, & Torelli, 2001). Neutral or natural tones are preferable for both furniture and walls. Young children bring plenty of color to the environment; their natural beauty should be a focal point rather than having it competing with "loud background noise."

The senses principle also includes the use of natural light. As often as possible, rely on natural sunlight to supply lighting for the classroom, since it is less harsh on the senses for you and the children. However, when this is not possible, you can provide additional incandescent lighting in the form of lamps. Place them on shelves, end tables, or on the floor to create smaller areas for work and gatherings. Avoid relying on overhead, fluorescent lighting, which tends to be less warm and welcoming.

To provide complexity and aesthetic pleasure, you can include paintings, sculptures, or photographs in the environment (Curtis & Carter, 2003). Pillows, potted plants, and fabrics can also be used to soften the environment and lower the height of the ceiling. Moreover, scented potpourri, oils, or plug-ins (kept out of the reach of the children, of course) can be used to provide a pleasant aroma.

You also need to provide opportunities for infants and toddlers to explore and learn using their senses. You can't be afraid to get dirty or to let the children get dirty. For example, imagine that an older infant is crawling outside on a small mound of dirt. She repeatedly pats the dry dirt flat. If you pour a bit of water in one area to see how she responds, she is likely to squish the mud between her fingers and giggle in delight. Adding water may make the child dirtier, but enhances the experience for her.

Representation

Can I tell you in multiple ways about my understanding of and theories about the world? Children need multiple opportunities to express their current understanding of the world. Representation of ideas can occur through painting, drawing, dramatic play, music, writing, sculpting, or any of the other "hundred languages" (New, 2003; Edwards, Gandini, & Forman, 1998). The environment, then, needs to provide space and open-ended materials for these purposes.

Independence

Can I do things myself? Children desire independence. This is a natural and healthy aspect of social-emotional development. A developmentally appropriate environment supports young children in making decisions, doing things alone, solving problems, and regulating their own behavior (Marion, 2007; Bredekamp & Copple, 1997). Use care in selecting where to place materials, supplies, and learning areas, since this is one way to foster independence. As mentioned previously, displaying materials and supplies in baskets or clear containers on low shelves allows children to select and clean up materials, with assistance from others (Isbell & Exelby, 2001; Marion, 2007).

Careful placement of learning centers adds to this sense of independence. One toddler teacher placed her easel on the tile floor closest to the sink. Not only was

A developmentally appropriate environment supports young children in making decisions and in doing things alone.

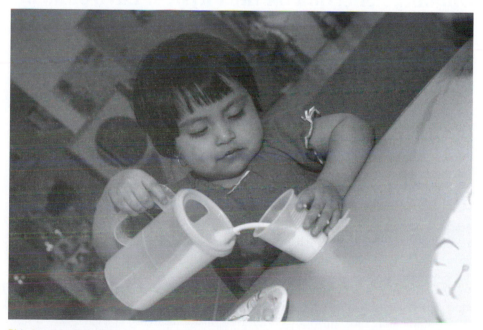

Plan for independence.

this more convenient for her, but it also encouraged the children to take responsibility for cleaning up spills or splatters. In the beginning of the year, she discussed with children where paper towels and sponges were kept, while assisting them in cleaning up the paint. In no time at all, many of the children were cleaning up after themselves, oftentimes without even notifying her.

Discovery

Can I find interesting things to examine closely and learn about? As mentioned in the "Senses" section, the environment needs to provide a balance of novel and familiar materials, permitting new discoveries that keep the learners engaged. Providing unique things to explore, examine, and learn about does not have to be expensive. Arranging familiar materials in a new location or display is one technique for renewing interest. Another method is to use treasures or items from nature. Rocks, feathers, flowers, tree branches, and things that sparkle or shine are all worthy of investigation (Curtis & Carter, 2003). In addition, providing recycled or found materials in aesthetically pleasing arrangements or containers provokes children to think about them in new ways (Topal & Gandini, 1999). The intention is to help the children with "finding the extraordinary in the ordinary" (L. Gandini, personal communication, January 26, 2001). Of course, remember to carefully examine each item or material provided to ensure that it is safe for the infants and toddlers.

Ongoing Reflection on the Physical Environment

We hope we have made it clear that an environment should never be considered "finished" or "complete." You should frequently (i.e., at least once a month) consider the primary question of this chapter, "How do teachers create meaningful learning environments that facilitate optimal development for the children?" Regularly review all the ways that the physical environment impacts the children's development and learning and vice versa, because the answer is constantly evolving. Teachers must continually assess and respond to the changing developmental needs and interests of young children.

SELECTING EQUIPMENT AND MATERIALS

Early childhood educators must carefully select the equipment and materials they make available to the children, based on the children's needs and abilities (Table 8–1). For example, with young infants you should have a high chair available for feeding; infants who can sit unassisted skillfully can sit on a low chair at a table. Materials include nesting toys, balls, books, rattles, paper, paint, clay, sand, glue, tricycles, water, boxes, tires, and other items that children use indoors or outdoors.

The following table provides a brief list of materials to use in a child care setting depending on the children's needs (Table 8–2). Kate, for example, may need a toy that

TABLE 8–1   BASIC EQUIPMENT FOR INFANTS AND TODDLERS

CHILD CARE CENTER CLASSROOM	CHILD CARE HOME
Indoor	
Eating	
high chairs	low chairs and tables
	booster seats for kitchen and dining room chairs
low chairs and tables	kitchen and dining room table
Sleeping	
rocking chair	rocking chair
cribs	cribs
cots	family beds and sofa covered with the child's sheet and blanket for naps
Toileting	
changing table	changing table or counter space in the bathroom for changing
sink and handwashing supplies	
free-standing potties	diapers, hand washing and storing supplies
supply storage	
toilet seat adapter	toilet seat adapter
steps (if needed at sink)	steps (if needed at sink)
Storage	
coat rack	coat rack near door
cubbies	especially designated shelves in the family room, living room, and/or bedroom where books and toys are kept for the child care children
shelves: toys, books	
Record Keeping	
bulletin boards	corked wall and refrigerator door space to exhibit art treasures
record-keeping table, counter	table, counter, drawer
Outdoor	
Climbing Structures	
wood, tile, rubber tires, steps, tied ropes	rubber tires, steps, tied ropes
Containers	
sand table or box	large plastic trays, pools for sand and water
water table or pool	

TABLE 8–2   TYPES OF EQUIPMENT AND MATERIALS

SOFT	HARD
cloth puppets	blocks
cloth and soft plastic dolls	hard plastic dolls
dress-up clothes	cars, trucks
fur	plastic curtains
pillows	sand
mats	paper
rugs	cardboard
cloth curtains	books
water	posters
clay	plastic, wood mobile
paint	wood
cloth wall hangings	linoleum
glue	baseball
ribbon	plastic bottles
cushions	catalogs
cloth mobile	magazines
rubber balls	buttons
sponge balls	metal cans
cloth scraps	sandpaper
foam scraps	
yarn	

OPEN-ENDED	CLOSED/REAL OBJECTS
puppet	puzzle
doll	zipper
water	button/buttonhole
sand	snaps
clay	stacking rings
blocks	wind-up doll
	wind-up mobile

SIMPLE	COMPLEX
one-piece puzzle	four-piece puzzle
doll	doll clothes
clay	clothes fasteners

INTRUSION	SECLUSION
bike	large box to hide in
balls	

HIGH MOBILITY	LOW MOBILITY
bike	water
toy cars, trucks	slide
stroller, buggy	books
balls	blocks
	clay
	painting
	sand

puts her into contact with others, such as a beach ball. Another time she may need a soft, cuddly toy that encourages seclusion, such as a teddy bear.

When selecting materials from catalogs, know that the age classifications provided will not accurately fit each child. This brings up the crucial distinction between age and individual appropriateness. Caregivers must determine when an item is appropriate for a particular child. Materials may have merit for some children but not others, or for some experiences and not others.

Classical music is a great educational resource because you can select some slow and some fast music. For example, for children 18 to 21 months a great contact activity is to form a circle with classical music playing in the background. Dance with all of the children or use "The Flight of the Bumble Bee" (Rimsky-Korsaskov) to pretend everyone is a bumblebee buzzing around the room. However, playing this music right before nap time would not serve to assist children with relaxing and transitioning to sleep.

Materials and equipment must be selected with special care because very young children put everything they touch to a hard test: they bite, pinch, hit, fling, bang, pound, and tear at whatever they can. In their exploration, they focus on actions and do not think in terms of cause and effect, so far as use is concerned. Therefore, caregivers must take care to provide only materials and equipment that can safely withstand use by multiple children.

Age-Appropriate Materials

Selection of appropriate equipment and materials involves the caregiver's knowledge of the program goals, the children's needs and interests, the time and space for use, and the budget. With program goals emphasizing holistic development, a variety of items facilitating physical, emotional, social, and cognitive development are needed. Use Table 8–3 to help you visualize which items match a particular category. Some materials attract interest at particular ages. The age groupings in the guide are approximations; an 11-month-old and a 13-month-old may use the same item. The guide will help you see which items a wide age range can use and which ones only a limited age range can use. Each age group needs a variety of items.

Since infants and toddlers interact with their environment through their senses, they need items that stimulate the senses. Remember that children of different ages make use of their senses in different ways. In the first few months of life, infants see many things and need items that stimulate their interest in seeing. They do not have much control of their hands and fingers, so touching is limited to bumping, banging, and finally grasping. A limited number and kind of items are needed to stimulate touching. However, two-year-olds actively use all their senses, so they need a wider range of items to stimulate each of their senses.

Some equipment and materials can be used in only one way; others have flexible uses (refer to the discussion of open-ended materials versus real objects in previous sections). Children and caregivers can adjust and adapt open-ended materials in a variety of ways to facilitate development. Single-use materials are in themselves neither good nor bad, but may be costly.

When initially purchasing equipment for all child care settings, consider buying a **choke tube** (Figure 8–1), because many states require its use. Toy pieces are dropped

TABLE 8–3 GUIDE FOR ANALYZING EQUIPMENT OR MATERIALS

ANALYSIS	ITEMS
Facilitated development	Telephone (example)
physical	
emotional	
social	X
cognitive	X
Age group	
0–6 months	
6–12 months	
12–18 months	X
18–24 months	X
24–30 months	X
30–36 months	X
Senses appealed to	
seeing	
hearing	X
touching	X
tasting	
smelling	
Number of uses	
single	X
flexible	
Safety factors	
nontoxic	X
sturdy	X
no sharp edges	X
Construction	
MATERIAL	
fabric	
paper	
cardboard	
rubber	
plastic	
wood	X
metal	
QUALITY	
fair	
good	
excellent	X
DURABILITY	
fair	
good	
excellent	X
Cost—$	
commercial	$15.00
homemade	
Comments:	

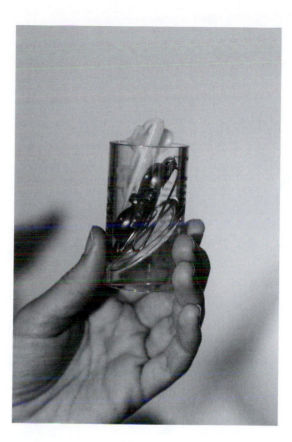

FIGURE 8–1 Many states require a choke tube in all child care settings.

through an opening in the device; if the pieces go through the tube they are considered a swallowable hazard and are discarded. Only toys with pieces larger than the opening are presented to the child.

It is important to analyze how materials and equipment are constructed. What they are made of and how they are put together will determine their durability when used by the children. This in turn will determine whether the item can serve the purposes for which it is intended in the program. Poorly constructed items that fall apart are frustrating, often unsafe for children, and costly.

All child care programs must consider costs. To determine whether an item is cost effective, analyze the following factors for each item:

- the importance for program goal attainment
- the areas of development facilitated
- the durability of construction
- the number of ways it can be used
- the number of children who can use it
- the ages of children who can use it

A $45 wooden truck that is well constructed may be used for years and years by hundreds of children. In contrast, five $9 plastic trucks will probably be damaged and have to be thrown away within a year or so. Thus, for the same amount of money, the wooden truck would be more cost effective.

The cost of equipment and materials can become astronomical. Therefore, most programs must decide which commercially made items they can purchase and which items they can make themselves. Some maintain that only commercially made equipment and materials have the quality young children require. No child care program can afford to purchase all items, so quality must be built into their home-made items or the program must get along without some items.

Homemade Materials

Homemade items should meet high standards for construction, durability, and safety. Some things we make can be more individualized than commercially prepared items can, which stimulates the interest and development of children in the program. For example, a cardboard-mounted color photograph of each child in your room or home is an individual homemade item.

Diligent scrounging of free and inexpensive materials from parents, friends, and community businesses and industries can greatly reduce the cost of homemade items. One group that has developed a very creative and beneficial support system to help child care programs locate and use scrounged materials is the Maryland Committee for Children. In Baltimore, Maryland, it operates reSTORE, a recycling

The refrigerator door becomes a bulletin board in a family child care home.

center for discarded or excess industrial materials that can be used by child care providers and parents to provide learning activities for children at a fraction of the usual cost.

Some books and articles are available that specify appropriate homemade materials. Burtt and Kalkstein (1981), Herr and Swim (2002), and Zeller and McFarland (1981) are but a few resources that will help you to match homemade materials, ages, and skill development levels. In addition, Part III of this text includes ideas for homemade materials.

PROTECTING THE CHILDREN'S HEALTH AND SAFETY

All early childhood education programs must have clearly defined policies and procedures for protecting the children's health and safety. The child care program should be a model for families to duplicate. These policies should be well thought out and designed from the viewpoint of the child and with prevention as the underlying tenet for health and safety.

Policies will need to be determined on such issues as:

- respectful care and treatment of children, families, and staff
- confidentiality of children's records
- detection and prevention of child abuse
- emergency care and training for staff
- communicable diseases
- keeping medical records and files for children and staff up to date performance evaluations for staff

A policy similar to the Back To Sleep Campaign should be in place to protect the safety of infants. This national campaign involves placing babies on their backs to sleep, refraining from smoking around them, laying them on flat, firm mattresses, washing all bedding before using it, removing all articles (including pillows) from cribs, and arranging regular health checkups.

Emergency Procedures

Each program should have policies and procedures in place and practice them regularly to insure that the needs of the children can be immediately and effectively met in the event of natural disasters that are common to the area (e.g., hurricane, tornado) as well as fire. Emergency numbers, evacuation routes, and established meeting places should be up to date and posted in a convenience place for staff to see.

Materials or supplies needed during an emergency, such as fire extinguishers, need to be organized in a convenient location and tested periodically to ensure they are in proper working condition.

Fire drills should be performed, timed, and recorded on a monthly basis. In fact, many state licensing regulations require this. Talk with the children about times when all of you might need to get out of the building quickly; be careful, however, not to scare them. Discuss how the sirens or signals might be loud and hurt their ears. When practicing a fire drill, warn the children in advance to minimize feelings of fright. If you have non-walkers, select one crib that can fit through doorways, put heavy-duty wheels on it, and put a special symbol on it. In case of fire or during a drill, put the non-walking children in this special crib and wheel the crib outside. If you have toddlers, hold hands, talk calmly, and walk the toddlers as quickly as possible out of the building to the designated spot.

Immunization Schedule

All children must be immunized before attending a child care program in a center or home. Center policies should reflect the requirements set forth by the appropriate state licensing agency. However, the immunization schedule in Table 8–4, from the American Academy of Pediatrics, provides a general guide of immunizations for very young children.

Signs and Symptoms of Possible Severe Illness

Each center or family home program that provides care to young children must have policies and procedures in place to recognize and respond to illnesses and communicable diseases. Severe illness may be indicated by the following signs and symptoms:

- temperature
- change in typical behavior (e.g., uncontrolled crying)
- unusual lack of movement
- uncontrolled crying
- coughing
- different breathing or wheezing
- uncontrolled diarrhea
- vomiting
- rash
- sores in the mouth
- red conjunctivitis
- head lice

Children who exhibit any of the above symptoms or who demonstrate unusual behavior in relation to any of the above symptoms should be removed to a predetermined place of isolation, where they should be supervised until a parent takes them home. For additional information, contact The American Red Cross, National Headquarters, Health and Safety, 2025 E Street NW, Washington, DC 20006.

Another publication available for health and safety is the *Child Care Health Handbook* published by the King County Department of Public Health in Washington (see "Additional Resources"). You can also contact your local Health Department, or a local registered nurse or pediatrician, who will be happy to help you with additional library source information.

TABLE 8–4   RECOMMENDED IMMUNIZATION SCHEDULE

DEPARTMENT OF HEALTH AND HUMAN SERVICES • CENTERS FOR DISEASE CONTROL AND PREVENTION

Recommended Childhood and Adolescent Immunization Schedule UNITED STATES • 2006

Vaccine ▼ Age ▶	Birth	1 month	2 months	4 months	6 months	12 months	15 months	18 months	24 months	4–6 years	11–12 years	13–14 years	15 years	16–18 years
Hepatitis B[1]	HepB	HepB		HepB[1]		HepB					HepB Series			
Diphtheria, Tetanus, Pertussis[2]			DTaP	DTaP	DTaP		DTaP			DTaP	Tdap	Tdap		
Haemophilus influenzae type b[3]			Hib	Hib	Hib[3]	Hib								
Inactivated Poliovirus			IPV	IPV		IPV				IPV				
Measles, Mumps, Rubella[4]						MMR				MMR		MMR		
Varicella[5]						Varicella					Varicella			
Meningococcal[6]											MCV4	MCV4		MCV4
									MPSV4					MCV4
Pneumococcal[7]			PCV	PCV	PCV	PCV			PCV		PPV			
Influenza[8]					Influenza (Yearly)					Influenza (Yearly)				
Hepatitis A[9]									HepA Series					

Legend: Range of recommended ages · Catch-up immunization · 11–12 year old assessment

This schedule indicates the recommended ages for routine administration of currently licensed childhood vaccines, as of December 1, 2005, for children through age 18 years. Any dose not administered at the recommended age should be administered at any subsequent visit when indicated and feasible. ▇ Indicates age groups that warrant special effort to administer those vaccines not previously administered. Additional vaccines may be licensed and recommended during the year. Licensed combination vaccines may be used whenever any components of the combination are indicated and other components of the vaccine are not contraindicated and if approved by the Food and Drug Administration for that dose of the series. Providers should consult the respective ACIP statement for detailed recommendations. Clinically significant adverse events that follow immunization should be reported to the Vaccine Adverse Event Reporting System (VAERS). Guidance about how to obtain and complete a VAERS form is available at www.vaers.hhs.gov or by telephone, 800-822-7967.

1. Hepatitis B vaccine (HepB). *AT BIRTH:* All newborns should receive monovalent HepB soon after birth and before hospital discharge. Infants born to mothers who are HBsAg-positive should receive HepB and 0.5 mL of hepatitis B immune globulin (HBIG) within 12 hours of birth. Infants born to mothers whose HBsAg status is unknown should receive HepB within 12 hours of birth. The mother should have blood drawn as soon as possible to determine her HBsAg status; if HBsAg-positive, the infant should receive HBIG as soon as possible (no later than age 1 week). For infants born to HBsAg-negative mothers, the birth dose can be delayed in rare circumstances but only if a physician's order to withhold the vaccine and a copy of the mother's original HBsAg-negative laboratory report are documented in the infant's medical record. *FOLLOWING THE BIRTHDOSE:* The HepB series should be completed with either monovalent HepB or a combination vaccine containing HepB. The second dose should be administered at age 1–2 months. The final dose should be administered at age ≥24 weeks. It is permissible to administer 4 doses of HepB (e.g., when combination vaccines are given after the birth dose); however, if monovalent HepB is used, a dose at age 4 months is not needed. Infants born to HBsAg-positive mothers should be tested for HBsAg and antibody to HBsAg after completion of the HepB series, at age 9–18 months (generally at the next well-child visit after completion of the vaccine series).

2. Diphtheria and tetanus toxoids and acellular pertussis vaccine (DTaP). The fourth dose of DTaP may be administered as early as age 12 months, provided 6 months have elapsed since the third dose and the child is unlikely to return at age 15–18 months. The final dose in the series should be given at age ≥4 years.
Tetanus and diphtheria toxoids and acellular pertussis vaccine (Tdap – adolescent preparation) is recommended at age 11–12 years for those who have completed the recommended childhood DTP/DTaP vaccination series and have not received a Td booster dose. Adolescents 13–18 years who missed the 11–12-year Td/Tdap booster dose should also receive a single dose of Tdap if they have completed the recommended childhood DTP/DTaP vaccination series. Subsequent tetanus and diphtheria toxoids (Td) are recommended every 10 years.

3. *Haemophilus influenzae* type b conjugate vaccine (Hib). Three Hib conjugate vaccines are licensed for infant use. If PRP-OMP (PedvaxHIB® or ComVax® [Merck]) is administered at ages 2 and 4 months, a dose at age 6 months is not required. DTaP/Hib combination products should not be used for primary immunization in infants at ages 2, 4 or 6 months but can be used as boosters after any Hib vaccine. The final dose in the series should be administered at age ≥12 months.

4. Measles, mumps, and rubella vaccine (MMR). The second dose of MMR is recommended routinely at age 4–6 years but may be administered during any visit, provided at least 4 weeks have elapsed since the first dose and both doses are administered beginning at or after age 12 months. Those who have not previously received the second dose should complete the schedule by age 11–12 years.

5. Varicella vaccine. Varicella vaccine is recommended at any visit at or after age 12 months for susceptible children (i.e., those who lack a reliable history of chickenpox). Susceptible persons aged ≥13 years should receive 2 doses administered at least 4 weeks apart.

6. Meningococcal vaccine (MCV4). Meningococcal conjugate vaccine (MCV4) should be given to all children at the 11–12 year old visit as well as to unvaccinated adolescents at high school entry (15 years of age). Other adolescents who wish to decrease their risk for meningococcal disease may also be vaccinated. All college freshmen living in dormitories should also be vaccinated, preferably with MCV4, although meningococcal polysaccharide vaccine (MPSV4) is an acceptable alternative. Vaccination against invasive meningococcal disease is recommended for children and adolescents aged ≥2 years with terminal complement deficiencies or anatomic or functional asplenia and certain other high risk groups (see *MMWR* 2005;54 [RR-7]:1-21); use MPSV4 for children aged 2–10 years and MCV4 for older children, although MPSV4 is an acceptable alternative.

7. Pneumococcal vaccine. The heptavalent pneumococcal conjugate vaccine (PCV) is recommended for all children aged 2–23 months and for certain children aged 24–59 months. The final dose in the series should be given at age ≥12 months. Pneumococcal polysaccharide vaccine (PPV) is recommended in addition to PCV for certain high-risk groups. See *MMWR* 2000; 49(RR-9):1-35.

8. Influenza vaccine. Influenza vaccine is recommended annually for children aged ≥6 months with certain risk factors (including, but not limited to, asthma, cardiac disease, sickle cell disease, human immunodeficiency virus [HIV], diabetes, and conditions that can compromise respiratory function or handling of respiratory secretions or that can increase the risk for aspiration), healthcare workers, and other persons (including household members) in close contact with persons in groups at high risk (see *MMWR* 2005;54[RR-8]:1-55). In addition, healthy children aged 6–23 months and close contacts of healthy children aged 0–5 months are recommended to receive influenza vaccine because children in this age group are at substantially increased risk for influenza-related hospitalizations. For healthy persons aged 5–49 years, the intranasally administered, live, attenuated influenza vaccine (LAIV) is an acceptable alternative to the intramuscular trivalent inactivated influenza vaccine (TIV). See *MMWR* 2005;54(RR-8):1-55. Children receiving TIV should be administered a dosage appropriate for their age (0.25 mL if aged 6–35 months or 0.5 mL if aged ≥3 years). Children aged ≤8 years who are receiving influenza vaccine for the first time should receive 2 doses (separated by at least 4 weeks for TIV and at least 6 weeks for LAIV).

9. Hepatitis A vaccine (HepA). HepA is recommended for all children at 1 year of age (i.e., 12–23 months). The 2 doses in the series should be administered at least 6 months apart. States, counties, and communities with existing HepA vaccination programs for children 2–18 years of age are encouraged to maintain these programs. In these areas, new efforts focused on routine vaccination of 1-year-old children should enhance, not replace, ongoing programs directed at a broader population of children. HepA is also recommended for certain high risk groups (see *MMWR* 1999; 48[RR-12]:1-37).

The Childhood and Adolescent Immunization Schedule is approved by:
Advisory Committee on Immunization Practices www.cdc.gov/nip/acip • American Academy of Pediatrics www.aap.org • American Academy of Family Physicians www.aafp.org

First Aid

First aid refers to treatment administered for injuries and illnesses that are not considered life threatening. While states vary in their laws, the authors believe that all staff members (including cooks and cleaning staff) be trained in first aid, universal precautions, and cardiopulmonary resuscitation (CPR). Thus, first aid procedures should be based on principles that are familiar to everyone involved in the care setting. Take the following steps in the event of an emergency:

1. Summon emergency medical assistance (call 911 in most areas) for any injury or illness that requires more than simple first aid.
2. Stay calm and in control of the situation.
3. Always remain with the child. If necessary, send another adult or child for help.
4. Keep the child still until the extent of injuries or illness can be determined. If in doubt, have the child stay in the same position and await emergency medical help.
5. Quickly evaluate the child's condition, paying special attention to an open airway, breathing, and circulation.
6. Carefully plan and administer appropriate emergency care. Improper treatment can lead to other injuries.
7. Do not give any medications unless they are prescribed to save a life in certain life-threatening conditions.
8. Do not offer diagnosis or medical advice. Refer the child's parents to health professionals.
9. Always inform the child's parents of the injury and first aid care that has been administered.
10. Record all the facts concerning the accident and treatment administered; file in the child's permanent folder.

As stated above, all early childhood educators should be educated in first aid and keep their certification up to date. Most states grant legal protection to individuals who administer emergency care unless their actions are judged grossly negligent or harmful. This protection is commonly known as the Good Samaritan Law. Many states require a signed Emergency Care Permission form from the parent.

First aid kits should be open, visible, and easily accessible to teachers, but out of the reach of children. Kits should be available in all indoor classrooms and outdoor environments. If the playground is large, you should consider having two kits so they are more easily reached. The contents of first aid kits should reflect your particular state's licensing regulations, but might include:

- adhesive tape
- bandages of assorted sizes
- blanket
- cotton balls
- flashlight
- gauze pads, sterile, 2" × 2"s, 4" × 4"s

- hot water bottle
- instant ice pack or plastic bags
- needle, sewing
- roller gauze, 1- and 2-inch widths
- latex gloves
- safety pins
- scissors, blunt tipped
- soap, preferably liquid
- spirits of ammonia
- splints
- thermometers
- tongue blades
- towels, large and small
- tweezers
- vaseline
- first aid book

Universal Precautions

Universal precautions must be understood and used by every person in the care setting who is around body fluids. Medical gloves must be worn every time bodily fluids are present, such as when changing diapers and wiping up spills. Universal precautions are a set of procedures to prevent coming into contact with bodily fluids.

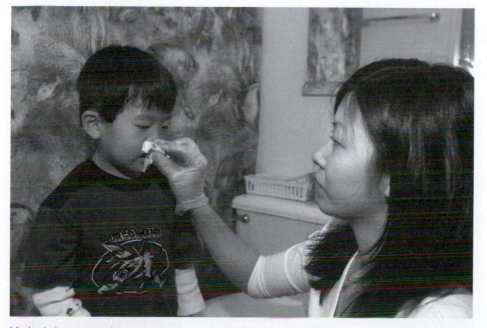

Medical gloves must be worn every time bodily fluids are present.

It is the responsibility of each caregiver to receive the training and updates necessary to be aware of current policies.

Blood contaminants such as hepatitis B pose a real health threat. Blood fluid (watery discharge from lacerations and cuts) poses a risk of the greatest concern. In addition, hepatitis B can survive in a dried state in the environment for at least a week or even longer. Other fluids, such as saliva contaminated with blood, may contain the live virus. Procedures for handling spills of bodily fluids—urine, feces, blood, saliva, nasal discharge, eye discharge, and tissue discharges—*after putting on the medical gloves*, are as follows:

1. For spills of vomit, urine, and feces: The floors, wall, bathrooms, tabletops, toys, kitchen countertops, and diaper-changing tables should be cleaned and disinfected.
2. For spills of blood or blood-containing bodily fluids, as well as injury and tissue discharges: The area should be cleaned and disinfected.
3. Persons involved in cleaning contaminated surfaces are to avoid exposure of open skin sores or mucous membranes to blood or blood-containing bodily fluids by using gloves to protect hands. Illnesses may be spread in varying ways, such as coughing, sneezing, direct skin-to-skin contact, or touching an object or surface with germs on it. Infectious germs may be contained in human waste (urine, feces and body fluids, saliva, nasal discharge, tissue and injury discharges, eye discharges, and blood). Because many infected people carry communicable diseases without symptoms, and many are contagious before they experience symptoms, staff need to protect themselves and the children they serve by routinely carrying out sanitation and disinfection procedures that prevent every potential illness-spreading condition.

   Education of staff regarding cleaning procedures can reduce the occurrence of illness in the entire group of children. Use a solution of 1/4 cup liquid chlorine bleach to one gallon tap water when cleaning contaminated surfaces.
4. Mops should be cleaned, rinsed in sanitizing solution, wrung as dry as possible, and hung to dry.
5. Blood-contaminated material and diapers should be disposed of in a plastic bag with a secure tie, and labeled with a tag.
6. Sanitize, disinfect, and maintain toys and all equipment. Ensure that frequently used rooms and items are disinfected regularly. Rooms with non-diapered children should be cleaned weekly. Thermometers, pacifiers, and the like should be disinfected between uses. Individual children's items and travel items for personal hygiene should be sent home with parents to be cleaned weekly, or after each use if more than one child uses a crib. Crib mattresses should be cleaned at least weekly. Each child should have his or her own bed, not to be shared with other children. Regular cleaning of the entire facility should be done weekly.

Hand-washing instructions (see Chapter 9) involve modeling and assisting children in adjusting water temperature and pressure, cleaning palms and backs of hands and wrists, using liquid soap properly, cleaning nails and between fingers, drying hands properly, and disposing of paper towels.

Human Immunodeficiency Virus (HIV) Infection

This infection attacks and destroys white blood cells making the person more susceptible to illnesses. Acquired Immune Deficiency Syndrome (AIDS) is the final stage of the **HIV infection**. "On the basis of available data, there is no reason to believe H. I. V.-infected adults will transmit H. I. V. in the course of their normal child duties" (American Academy of Pediatrics, 1996). HIV cannot be transmitted as long as there are no open sores or other blood sources existing. HIV-positive adults may care for children. However, the HIV caregiver is at great risk due to the highly contagious environment that child care settings represent.

Parents of HIV-infected children should be alerted to exposure to such agents as measles and chicken pox. Their pediatrician will probably inject them with an immune booster such as immunoglobulin. Universal precautions are used in every incident of spilled blood or possible blood exposure.

If an HIV-infected child leaves the center due to exposure, the decision to return will be made by the child's pediatrician or nurse practitioner, the parents, and the director of the center. This is also a procedure for a known HIV-infected caregiver. Laws from federal, state, and local authorities are designed to protect families, and confidentiality is a legal right. All information, medical records, and personal information is set aside and kept confidential. No one shall have access to this information unless the parents give written releases. Only staff who have a need to know will be informed. They also must sign a disclosure form that is kept in the child's record.

Injuries

Aronson (1983) analyzed insurance claims for injuries in child care. She found that the following were associated with the most frequent or more severe injuries: motor vehicles, climbers, slides, hand toys, blocks, other playground equipment, doors, indoor floor surfaces, swings, pebbles or rocks, and pencils. Aronson recommended the following:[†]

1. Unsafe climbers, slides, and other playground equipment should be modified or eliminated. The American Academy of Pediatrics, American Public Health Association, and the National Resource Center for Health and Safety in Child Care (2002) suggests these modifications to make safer playgrounds: place climbing structures closer to the ground (i.e., one foot per year of age for intended users); mount them over 6–12 inches of uncompressed, shock-absorbing material such as pea gravel, tree bark, or shredded tires; have

---

[†] Courtesy of Susan Aronson, PhD, Associate Clinical Professor Pediatrics and of Community and Preventive Medicine.

Only sterilized sand should be used in sandboxes for children.

enough space (33–75 square feet of space for each child using the playground at any one time, depending on the child's age) to place all equipment far enough away from other structures and child traffic patterns to prevent collisions; cover sharp edges and exposed bolts; and teach children to play safely.

2. Hazardous activities require closer adult supervision than activities with a lower injury rating.

3. Architectural features such as doors and indoor floor surfaces require special attention. Doors should have beveled edges and mechanisms which prevent slamming or rapid closure. Full-length-view vision panels will help assure that small children are seen before the door is opened. Floor surfaces and edges which might cause tripping should be modified. Long, open spaces should be interrupted to discourage running in areas where running is dangerous.

4. Children must always travel in safety-approved restraints in cars, vans, and buses and follow all other safety rules.

5. Training and resources to change hazardous conditions should be made available to all staff. Injury reports should be routinely examined by trained personnel to identify and correct trouble spots. A systematic study of injury in child care centers and in home child care is needed to assist adults in making provision for the safe care of children (1983, pp. 19–20).

Outdoor Safety

Guidelines for playground safety are also set by the Consumer Product Safety Commission (2003). According to the April 2001 publication of the CPSC, 63 percent of

TABLE 8–5   INJURIES ASSOCIATED WITH PUBLIC PLAYGROUND EQUIPMENT, AGE OF VICTIM BY TYPE OF EQUIPMENT

AGE OF VICTIM (YEARS)	TYPE OF EQUIPMENT						
	TOTAL	CLIMBERS	SWINGS	SLIDES	SEE-SAWS	MERRY-GO-ROUNDS	OTHER
Total	100%[a,b]	100%	100%	100%	100%	100%	100%
	(100%)[c]	(53%)	(19%)	(17%)	(3%)	(1%)	(7%)
<2	3%	0%	2%	11%	4%	63%	0%
	(100%)	(0%)	(10%)	(64%)	(4%)	(21%)	(0%)
2–4	24%	21%	8%	40%	0%	25%	58%
	(100%)	(45%)	(6%)	(29%)	(0%)	(1%)	(19%)
5–9	55%	65%	53%	42%	66%	12%	29%
	(100%)	(60%)	(18%)	(13%)	(4%)	(<1%)	(4%)
10–12	15%	12%	30%	7%	31%	0%	13%
	(100%)	(41%)	(38%)	(8%)	(7%)	(0%)	(7%)
13–14	3%	3%	8%	0%	0%	0%	0%
	(100%)	(48%)	(52%)	(0%)	(0%)	(0%)	(0%)

[a]Detail may not add to total due to independent rounding.

[b]Upper percents sum vertically.

[c]Lower percents sum horizontally.

Source: National Electronic Injury Surveillance System (NEISS), 11/1/98–10/31/99, U.S. Consumer Product Safety Commission/EPHA (2001).

children under two years of age who are injured by playground equipment were on a merry-go-round (Table 8–5). Consideration should be given to eliminating their installation or increasing supervision, including not allowing children under two to use the merry-go-round unaccompanied. Rules allowing use only with adult accompaniment should become a standard of care.

Injuries related to playground equipment that required a hospital visit are reflected in Table 8–6, which is taken from CPSC publication number 325, National Program for Playground Safety. Additional information can be obtained from CPSC Publication number 35.

Safety standards for all child care facilities should meet or exceed these standards. Careful selection of equipment and planning is necessary.

The Massachusetts Department of Public Health has developed a Site Safety Checklist and a Playground Safety Checklist that can be used or adapted for assessing and providing safe and healthy indoor and outdoor environments for infants and toddlers (see Appendix A).

TABLE 8–6   PLAYGROUND EQUIPMENT INJURIES TREATED IN U.S. HOSPITAL EMERGENCY ROOMS, AGES
OF VICTIMS BY LOCATION OF INCIDENT

AGE OF VICTIM (YEARS)	LOCATION OF INCIDENT					
	TOTAL	HOME	PUBLIC PARK	SCHOOL	COMMUNITY DAY CARE	OTHER
Total	100%	100%	100%	100%	100%	100%
<2	3%	5%	8%	0%	2%	<1%
2–4	27%	34%	23%	9%	54%	56%
5–9	56%	59%	55%	66%	42%	30%
10–12	12%	1%	12%	20%	2%	13%
13–14	2%	1%	2%	5%	0%	0%

Source: National Electronic Injury Surveillance System (NEISS), 11/1/98–10/31/99, U.S. Consumer Product Safety Commission/EPHA.

■ KEY TERMS

choke tube	identity	representation
discovery	learning centers	senses
documentation	movement	transparency
flexibility	relationships	universal precautions
HIV infection		

CASE STUDY   Ena

Ena Robson, who was seven-and-a-half months old, had an unusual first day in the group family child care center. One of the helpers got sick in the middle of the day and another provider was called on to take her place. The first provider had been ready to begin an assessment of Ena, but her replacement was not told of this, so she did not conduct one.

Ena was small, frail, and odd-looking. Her skull was box-shaped, her eyes were set far apart, and her mouth seemed to be in an unusual position when you looked straight at her. She had only a wisp of hair, she was mostly inactive, and her eyes appeared to be slow in reacting to visual changes. On her first day Ena was dressed in a tattered but clean outfit with strawberry patches and a hat.

Since the regular provider was sick again the next day, the director took care of Ena and noted her odd appearance after checking her medical records. She performed a developmental assessment with the following results.

Physical, cognitive, and language skills were at the four-month level. Her social and emotional skills were at the six-month level. Since there was a significant delay in three areas (two months with a seven-and-a-half-month-old), the director decided to make referrals for further evaluation to a pediatrician, language, therapist, and psychologist to follow up.

A parent conference was arranged with Ena's mother to obtain permission in writing for the referrals. Mrs. Robson arrived with Ena's grandmother, who was a trained nurse's aide, early in the morning for the conference. The director had reviewed the medical and family records in advance and found no unusual medical or family history. Della, Ena's mother, was tall but appeared to have been sick because she needed help walking, had deep circles under her eyes, and had a rather gray color to her skin. Della explained that Ena had experienced many fevers off and on but that she was well at present. The director began asking questions from an interview form, and after a short time Della became visibly stressed. Her voice changed, her arms and hands waved when she spoke, and she refused to answer questions about the pregnancy and Ena's birth. When the director rephrased the question to ask if Ena was a full-term baby, Mrs. Robson became agitated and Ena's grandmother answered in a calm voice that it would probably be best if they stopped the conference but that she would like to set up an evening appointment. A home visit was scheduled for that evening in Ena's home, and her grandmother said she would speak to Della in the meantime.

The apartment where Della and Ena lived was small and sparsely furnished. The grandmother and a registered nurse were administering an intravenous injection to Mrs. Robson when the director arrived. When Mrs. Robson saw the director, she began to cry, and Ena's grandmother sadly explained that both Della and Ena had AIDS. The director maintained a professional demeanor and actively listened to the grandmother as she discussed her sadness, anger, and disappointment. It was obvious that both Della and her mother were very fearful that the director would not allow Ena to stay in the child care setting. The director learned that Della's disease was progressing rapidly in spite of medications, and that Ena would start on medication the next day. Both Della and her mother asked the director to please keep Ena.

The director assured them that they would keep Ena in the child care center as long as she was not running a fever or showing other disease complications. She assured the family that all of her staff used universal precaution techniques, and they were all aware that blood was the only transmitter of the disease. She reassured the family that her staff would hold, feed, and play with Ena in both the indoor and outdoor environments. They discussed the importance of administering the medication on a regular basis at the same time of day. As long as Ena was without disease symptoms, the director assured them that Ena was welcome to attend the center. Both Della and her mother were relieved to hear that the staff would keep the illness confidential, since that was permitted by law.

Ena was cared for in both indoor and outdoor environments at the child care center, just like the other children. The staff provided her with more rest and activities to enhance her physical, cognitive, and language skill areas, and Ena showed improvement in her growth and development.

1. Discuss your feelings about working with a child like Ena, who has AIDS. How do you feel you would handle such a responsibility?

2. What tools did the director use to deal with this situation? List them.

3. What information should the caregivers use when selecting equipment or materials for Ena?

4. What other steps or help might the director have provided to this family?

■ QUESTIONS AND EXPERIENCES FOR REFLECTION

1. Use the Guide for Analyzing Equipment and Materials, Table 8–3, to analyze five pieces of equipment and five materials used indoors, along with five pieces of equipment and five materials used outdoors in your child care setting.

2. Observe two children playing with materials. Write down the actions of each child as he or she manipulates the objects. Are the objects age appropriate?

3. Observe and sketch the basic layout of an infant-toddler classroom, including all attached spaces that are used throughout the day, such as a child bathroom or covered patio area. Also, indicate on your sketch the location of electrical outlets, partitions, and other permanent structures or furniture that cannot be moved (e.g., a classroom sink with surrounding cabinets), as well as the type of floor covering. After leaving the classroom, evaluate the layout from both the teacher's and the children's perspectives.

4. How are the teacher's and child's perspectives in agreement about planning learning environments? Discuss your responses with a colleague.

5. Draw a diagram of the playground arrangement. Identify activity areas. List equipment and materials in each area. Evaluate their appropriateness.

6. Interview a caregiver at a child care program in which age groups share the outdoor space. Describe how that program facilitates playground use and ensures safety.

7. Research grants available for equipment for both indoor and outdoor use.

8. "Go shopping" and "buy" all the fine motor equipment and materials a group of 24-month-olds will need (use supply catalogs from companies such as Child Craft and Community Playthings) and give yourself a realistic budget to work with.

■ CHAPTER REVIEW

1. How can caregivers determine whether a piece of equipment or material is useful in the program?

2. When planning classroom environments, why do we need to balance opposites such as real objects versus open-ended materials, noisy versus quiet, and novel versus familiar?

3. Compare the teacher's perspective and the child's perspective on environmental design. How are they alike and how are they different?

4. List four safety factors caregivers must consider in selecting toys and equipment for infants and toddlers.

5. Describe how a toy or piece of equipment may be safe for one child and unsafe for another child.

6. Explain how universal precautions serve to protect everyone's safety, but especially the caregivers.

■ REFERENCES

American Academy of Pediatrics, American Public Health Association, and National Resource Center for Health and Safety in Child Care. (2002). *Caring for our children: National health and safety performance standards: Guidelines for out-of-home child care programs (2nd ed.).* Elk Grove Village, IL: American Academy of Pediatrics and Washington, DC: American Public Health Association. Also available at http://nrc.uchsc.edu.

Aronson, S. S. (1983). Injuries in child care. *Young Children, 38*(6), 19–20.

Bergen, D., Reid, R., & Torelli, L. (2001). *Educating and caring for very young children: The infant/toddler curriculum.* New York: Teachers College Press.

Bove, C. (2000). *Inserimento:* A strategy for delicately beginning relationships and communication. In L. Gandini & C. P. Edwards (Eds.), *Bambini: The Italian approach to infant/toddler care.* New York: Teachers College Press.

Bredekamp, S., & Copple, C. (Eds.). (1997). *Developmentally appropriate practice in early childhood programs* (Rev. ed.). Washington, DC: National Association for the Education of Young Children.

Brown-DuPaul, J., Keyes, T., & Segatti, L. (2001, Summer). Using documentation panels to communicate with families. *Childhood Education,* 209–213.

Burtt, K. G., & Kalkstein, K. (1981). *Smart toys.* New York: Harper & Row.

Consumer Product Safety Commission. (2001). Publication 35: *Playground equipment injury.*

Consumer Product Safety Commission. (2003). Publication 325: *Playground safety.* Available at http://www.cpsc.gov/CPSCPUB/PUBS/325.pdf

Curtis, D., & Carter, M. (2003). *Designs for living and learning: Transforming early childhood environments.* St. Paul, MN: Redleaf Press.

Cutler, K. (2000). Organizing the curriculum storage in a preschool/child care environment. *Young Children, 55*(3), 88–92.

DeBord, K., Hestenes, L. L., Moore, R. C., Cosco, N., & McGinnis, J. R. (2002). Paying attention to the outdoor environment is as important as preparing the indoor environment. *Young Children, 57*(3), 32–34.

Edwards, C., Gandini, L., & Forman, G. (Eds.). (1998). *The hundred languages of children: The Reggio Emilia approach—Advanced reflections* (2nd ed.). Westport, CT: Ablex Publishing.

Essa, E., Favre, K., Thweatt, G. & Waugh, S. (1999). Continuity of care for infants and toddlers. *Early Child Development and Care, 148,* 11–19.

Forman, G., & Fyfe, B. (1998). Negotiated learning through design, documentation, and discourse. In C. Edwards, L. Gandini, & G. Forman (Eds.), *The hundred languages of children: The Reggio Emilia approach—Advanced reflections* (2nd ed.). Westport, CT: Ablex Publishing.

Galardini, A., & Giovannini, D. (2001). Pistoia: Creating a dynamic, open system to serve children, families, and community. In L. Gandini & C. P. Edwards (Eds.), *Bambini: The Italian approach to infant/toddler care.* (pp. 89-105) New York: Teachers College Press.

Gandini, L. (1998). Educational and caring spaces. In C. Edwards, L. Gandini, & G. Forman, *The hundred languages of children: The Reggio Emilia approach—Advanced reflections* (2nd ed.). Westport, CT: Ablex Publishing.

Greenman, J. (2005, May). Places for childhood in the 21st century: A conceptual framework. *Beyond the Journal: Young Children on the Web.* Retrieved January 9, 2007, from http://www.journal.naeyc.org/btj/200505/01Greenman.pdf

Herr, J., & Swim, T. J. (2002). *Creative resources for infants and toddlers* (2nd ed.). Clifton Park, NY: Delmar Learning.

Honig, A. S. (2002). *Secure relationships: Nurturing infant/toddler attachment in early care settings.* Washington, DC: National Association for the Education of Young Children.

Isbell, R., & Exelby, B. (2001). *Early learning environments that work.* Beltsville, MD: Gryphon House.

Malaguzzi, L. (1998). History, ideas, and basic philosophy: An interview with Lella Gandini. In C. Edwards, L. Gandini, & G. Forman (Eds.), *The hundred languages of children: The Reggio Emilia approach—Advanced reflections* (2nd ed.). Westport, CT: Ablex Publishing.

Marion, M. (2007). *Guidance of young children* (7th ed.). Upper Saddle River, NJ: Prentice Hall.

New, R. (1998). Theory and praxis in Reggio Emilia: They know what they are doing, and why. In C. Edwards, L. Gandini, & G. Forman (Eds.), *The hundred languages of children: The Reggio Emilia approach—Advanced reflections* (2nd ed.). Westport, CT: Ablex Publishing.

New, R. (2003). Reggio Emilia: New ways to think about schooling. *Educational Leadership, 60*(7), 34–38.

Project Zero and Reggio Children (2001). *Making learning visible: Children as individual and group learners.* Reggio Emilia, Italy: Reggio Children srl.

Smith, C. (1998). Children with "special rights" in the preprimary schools and the infant-toddler centers of Reggio Emilia. In C. Edwards, L. Gandini, & G. Forman (Eds.), *The hundred languages of children: The Reggio Emilia approach—Advanced reflections* (2nd ed.). Westport, CT: Ablex Publishing.

Swim, T. J. (2003). Respecting infants and toddlers: Strategies for best practice. *Early Childhood NEWS, 15*(3), 16–23.

Swim, T. J. (2004). Theories of child development: Building blocks of developmentally appropriate practices. *Early Childhood NEWS, 16(2),* 36–45.

Stephenson, A. (2002). Opening up the outdoors: Exploring the relationship between the indoor and outdoor environment of a centre. *European Early Childhood Education Research Journal, 10*(1), 29–38.

Sutterby, J. A., & Frost, J. L. (2002). Making playgrounds fit for children and children fit for playgrounds. *Young Children, 57*(3), 36–41.

Topal, C. W., & Gandini, L. (1999). *Beautiful stuff: Learning with found materials.* Worcester, MA: Davis.

Torquati, J., & Barber, J. (2005). Dancing with trees: Infants and toddlers in the garden. *Young Children, 60*(3), 40–46.

Turner, T., & Krechevsky, M. (2003). Who are the teachers? Who are the learners? *Educational Leadership, 60*(7), 40–43.

Wien, C. A., Coates, A., Keating, B., & Bigelow, B. C. (2005, May). Designing the environment to build connection to place. *Beyond the Journal: Young Children on the Web.* Retrieved January 9, 2007, from http://www.journal.naeyc.org/btj/200505/05Wien.pdf

Zeller, J. M., & McFarland, S. L. (1981). Selecting appropriate materials for very young children. *Day Care and Early Education,* 8(4), 7–13.

■ ADDITIONAL RESOURCES

Colker, L. J. (2005). *The cooking book: Fostering young children's learning and delight.* Washington, DC: National Association for the Education of Young Children.

Greenman, J. (2005, May). Print and online resources on environments that support exploring, learning, and living. *Beyond the Journal: Young Children on the Web.* Retrieved January 9, 2007, from http://www.journal.naeyc.org/btj/200505/06Resources.pdf

Johnson, J. E., Christie, J. F., & Wardle, F. (2005). *Play, development, and early education.* Boston: Pearson.

King County Department of Public Health. (2001). *Child Care Health Handbook.* Seattle: Author. Order form available at http://www.metrokc.gov/health/childcare/education.htm#handbook

Sanders, S. W. (2002). *Active for life: Developmentally appropriate movement programs for young children.* Washington, DC: National Association for the Education of Young Children.

Van Hoorn, J., Nourot, P. M., Scales, B., & Alward, K. R. (2003). *Play at the center of the curriculum* (3rd ed.). Upper Saddle River, NJ: Prentice Hall.

■ HELPFUL WEB SITES

Jonti-Craft. Company that provides high-quality equipment and materials for infants and toddlers. For a free catalog, call 800-543-4149 or access at http://www.jonti-craft.com

National Foundation for Infectious Diseases. Fact Sheets. http://nfid.org/factsheets/

National Network for Child Care. Articles and resources on children's health and safety and other topics. http://www.nncc.org/

Outdoor and Yard Safety. Arizona Child Care Resource and Referral Center. http://arizonachildcare.org/childproof/outdoorsfty.html

Sudden Infant Death Syndrome Network. A world of information and support. http://sids-network.org/

For additional infant and toddler resources, visit our Web site at
http://www.earlychilded.delmar.com

9

Designing the Curriculum

INFANT-TODDLER CURRICULUM

We have already discussed how teachers actively construct the physical and social environments for infants and toddlers. Now, we will turn our attention to the intentional design of the intellectual environment. **Curriculum** is everything that you do with a child or that a child experiences through her interactions with the environment from the time she enters the classroom until the time she leaves it (Greenman & Stonehouse, 1996). While this definition may seem simplistic, it is rather complicated because it causes you to consider all of your actions and reactions throughout the day.

You should plan curriculum based on what you know about each child's development; that is, what the child can do now independently and what he can do with assistance. Your teaching or caregiving strategies should scaffold or challenge the child to move toward the next level.

Infants and toddlers participate actively in selecting their curriculum and initiating their activities. When Jessie babbles sentence-like sounds and then pauses, Ms. Howard looks over at her, smiles, and answers, "Jessie, you sound happy today. That is a pretty red ring in your hand." Jessie is playing with a large, colored plastic ring that Ms. Howard has set near her. Jessie determines what she will do with the ring and what she will say. Her sounds stimulate Ms. Howard, who makes a conscious choice to respond, reinforcing the child's competence as a communicator (Figure 9–1). Daily experiences provide an integrated curriculum for children actively involved with themselves and the world around them. All are parts of the curriculum.

In Figure 9–1, Mrs. Howard (caregiver) offers choices to the child. Then, Jessie (the child) chooses—makes a decision to play with the toy the way she wants to, is self-stimulated, and looks to the caregiver and vocalizes sounds. In response to Jessie's behaviors, Mrs. Howard is stimulated and motivated to respond.

Since infant and toddler curriculum involves the whole child, the child should have experiences that enhance his or her physical, emotional, social, and cognitive/language development. The caregiver is responsible for planning and facilitating this holistic curriculum.

Each child is a distinct being, differing from others in some ways, yet sharing many of the same basic needs. *There is no single curriculum for all infants*. Caregivers have a special responsibility to design each child's curriculum by observing, thinking, and planning. We must compile many different skills and information, using a developmental perspective as a framework and analyzing observational data as the method.

In order to meet the individual needs of infants and toddlers, early childhood educators need to continually gather observational data, analyze it, and use it when selecting materials and planning curricular experiences (see Chapter 5). Thus, careful, ongoing observation on the part of the adults (e.g., caregivers and family members) facilitates child contributions to the curriculum; it is responsive to the needs, abilities, and interests of each child. Daily curriculum should be designed with a purpose in mind. In other words, you should be scaffolding skill development in all areas with the goal of addressing development of the whole child.

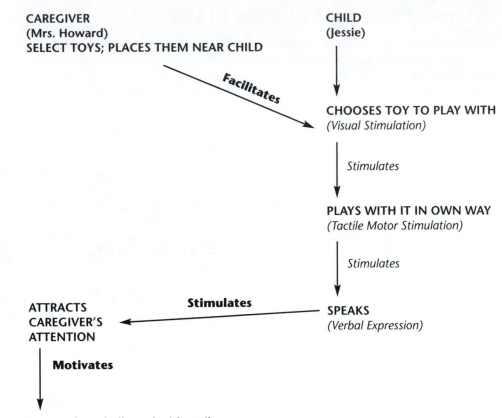

CAREGIVER
(Mrs. Howard)
SELECT TOYS; PLACES THEM NEAR CHILD

CHILD
(Jessie)

Facilitates

CHOOSES TOY TO PLAY WITH
(Visual Stimulation)

Stimulates

PLAYS WITH IT IN OWN WAY
(Tactile Motor Stimulation)

Stimulates

ATTRACTS
CAREGIVER'S
ATTENTION

Stimulates

SPEAKS
(Verbal Expression)

Motivates

Responds verbally and with smile

FIGURE 9–1   An example of an interaction among caregiver, child, and material that individualizes the curriculum.

INFLUENCES ON THE CURRICULUM

Society, the setting, the child, and the caregiver all influence the infant and toddler curriculum. Each of these influences on the child is discussed in detail in the following sections.

Influences of Society

Society

As discussed in earlier chapters, aspects of society beyond the family influence the functioning of that family. For example, as you learned in Chapter 6, citizens in Italy have made high-quality child care a priority by voting into law policies for funding such programs. The democratic process allowed the voices of families to be heard. However, this law was not viewed as beneficial only to children and families but rather to society as a whole. "The broad intention is to promote, within a new social welfare system, a relationship between citizens and institutions that allows for shared responsibility among local public and private institutions, nonprofit organizations, and families. . ." (Ghedini, 2001, p. 45).

In the United States, child care is seen as the responsibility of each individual family. The two exceptions to this trend are for very low-income families who cannot afford to pay for child care and work at the same time and for some corporate workers. Families with low incomes must rely on early childhood education programs to provide quality care at extremely reduced costs. Unfortunately, families often get what they pay for: the ratings of quality in both home- and center-based programs vary significantly based on costs (see, for example, Kontos, Howes, Shinn, & Galinsky, 1995).

Some larger corporations and institutions are beginning to recognize the need for the organization to help workers manage family- and work-life issues. One way in which they have assisted families with this balance is to provide on-site child care centers. Banks, manufacturers, the federal government, school districts, colleges, and hospitals lure new employees with this unique perk. Families particularly like having child care on site, because they can visit their children during their breaks or can be paged when their child is attempting or accomplishing a new task such as a first step or toilet learning. While the decision to offer corporate child care is up to each individual company or institution, a recent president of the United States supported such efforts when he said, "The private sector needs to make an increasing effort to support partnerships between themselves and their employees. Child care is a national concern. . . . The welfare of tomorrow's business depends on the services offered to today's children" (Clinton, 1997).

Parents

Parents place children in child care outside their own homes for a variety of reasons. The majority of families do so because the adults work. Since parents' primary goal is to make sure their children are safe in a stable situation they can trust, they are concerned about the physical environment and how it is used.

Parents may share their expectations with caregivers. One aspect of curriculum is to help parents meet their needs as they relate to child-rearing and child care. Cultural differences will be evident during your meetings with them. Different parents have different ideas about child-rearing and parenting techniques. The following questions can stimulate varying responses from parents:

- Should a mother breast-feed or bottle-feed?
- How frequently should a parent hold and cuddle the infant?
- Should adults respond immediately to the crying infant?
- When and how should family members talk, sing, and play with the infant?
- What are appropriate mothering (grandmothering) behaviors?
- What are appropriate fathering (grandfathering) behaviors?

Parents also look to teachers to reinforce and extend their own child-rearing practices. They usually convey to the early childhood educator their expectations for their children and their attitudes concerning parenting roles and children's behaviors.

Family members view themselves in various ways. Some family members expect to be *perfect* parents. The realities of parenting often cause them to feel guilty when they fall short of perfection or when they turn the child over to the caregiver. Their frustrations may affect their attitudes about themselves and their interactions with their children and caregivers. Sometimes jealousies develop. Early childhood educators can help these parents establish more realistic expectations.

Some family members seem very casual. They move in a very off-hand way from one parenting task to the next with seemingly little thought of goals or consequences. Some of these family members seem to place their children into child care with the attitude, "Do what you want to with them; just keep them out of my hair." The caregiver may need to emphasize the worth of the child and tell the family how important it is for them to value the child. Between these two extremes are family members who want to engage in positive parenting behaviors and who look to caregivers to assist them and their children.

Family members will express positive and negative expectations about what the caregiver should do verbally and nonverbally, in direct and indirect ways. They expect caregivers to help their children learn their values and to reinforce behaviors the family approves of. Families expect caregivers to be professionally competent. They place their trust in the caregiver to provide safe, healthy, reliable, affectionate, concerned, and intellectually engaging care and education for their children. Family members have their own ways of judging caregiver competence. Some judgment is intuitive, based on listening to and watching the caregiver with their child, while some judgment is based on what they think is responsible caregiver behavior.

Influences from Cultural Expectations

Families feel pressure from their friends and relatives about their own child-rearing activities. They receive comments, praise, suggestions, scolding, and ridicule on a variety of topics. Sometimes they hear conflicting comments on the same topic, such as the following:

- The parent should stay home with the newborn and very young infant vs. It is acceptable for the parent of a child of any age to work outside the home.
- The parents are wasting their time when talking to and playing with a young baby vs. The parents should talk to and play with the infant.
- The infant should start solid foods at four months of age vs. The infant should start solid food at a later age.

Parents must reconcile their attitudes and expectations with those of people around them. This is a long and laborious task that often results in inconsistent beliefs and practices. It may seem that parents are wishy-washy or flip-flopping about what they do versus what they want you to do. When you understand the various pressures on families and use active listening, you can help them to resolve these parenting conflicts. Like families, each caregiver brings unique cultural experiences and expectations to the caregiving role. Be aware of how these are similar to or different from those of the families and other staff in order to plan and provide a curriculum acceptable to all.

Each infant is a unique being who deserves positive support to remain unlimited and reach his or her full potential.

Cultural Diversity

Caregivers must be sensitive to **cultural diversity**, the cultural differences in the children and families with whom you have contact. If you are embarrassed about discussing differences or prejudices, you might actually help and encourage children to form biases. You could, through omission, perpetuate oppressive beliefs and behavior (Jones & Derman-Sparks, 1992).

Child care settings offer many opportunities to experience cultural diversity. In order not to limit young children's beliefs and perceptions, plan activities and experiences that directly include multiculturalism (Turkovich & Mueller, 1989).

Every culture has somewhat different customs, mores, beliefs, and attitudes toward child care. While the style and form may vary from one culture to the next, all cultures have healthy child care practices. An example of different forms is the use of unleavened bread to provide nourishment. In the Mexican culture corn flour is made into tortillas, in Sweden and Norway people eat a flat wheat bread, and in China and India, rice is used. An example of different styles are the bright, contrasting colors of some cultures and the more subdued colors of other cultures. Each style is important and valuable to the people who practice it.

Prejudging the style and forms of a culture is called having **bias**. To successfully integrate style and form into a curriculum, early childhood educators must be aware of and examine their bias for certain styles and forms. These biases may not be obvious until they are carefully examined, and only then can they be changed.

When working with young children, it is important to be able to relate to each of them without bias or prejudice. Each infant or toddler is a unique being who develops in the same way and deserves the same positive support to remain unlimited and reach his or her full potential.

Some cultures do not talk to young children as much as other cultures. Some do not smile at them or expect a response. Some carry their babies on their backs; other cultures carry them over their hearts. Father involvement is different from one culture to another, as is the way family members interact with each other. Families also differ on how they define independence for their child. Brainstorming and other problem-solving techniques, along with active listening, will help to address any misunderstandings that may occur. Moreover, valuing these differences and working to understand child-rearing practices within every culture is important for becoming a competent early childhood educator. Acceptance of these differences and the ability to perceive healthy child care practices within every culture is important for infant and toddler teachers.

It is crucial that the child care program honor individual families' sociocultural milieus. Pacific Oaks College, in Southern California, has done exemplary work in their Anti-Bias Curriculum. Merril Palmer Institute Child Development Lab in Detroit, Bank Street College in New York, and Thomson Delmar Learning in Clifton Park, New York, have also developed materials that focus on cultural diversity. Other materials available for young children and adults include:

Anti Bias Curriculum: Tools for Empowering Young Children (1989), by Louise Derman-Sparks and the A. B. C. Task Force. Washington DC: National Association for the Education of Young Children.

What if All the Kids Are White? Anti-bias Multicultural Education with Young Children and Families (2006), by Louise Derman-Sparks and Patricia Ramsey. New York: Teachers College Press.

Creative Resources for the Anti-bias Classroom (1999), by Nadia Saderman Hall. Clifton Park, NY: Thomson Delmar Learning.

Roots and Wings: Affirming Culture in Early Childhood Programs (1991), by Stacey York. St. Paul, MN: Redleaf Press.

Teaching/Learning Anti-racism (1997), by Louise Derman-Sparks and Carol Brunson Phillips. New York: Teachers College Press.

Different and Wonderful: Raising Black Children in a Race-Conscious Society (1992), by Darlene Powell Hopson and Derek S. Hopson. Washington DC: Fireside.

Everyday Acts Against Racism: Raising a Child in a Multicultural World (a collection) (1996), by Marian Reddy (Ed.). Seattle: Seal Press.

Beyond the Whiteness of Whiteness: A White Mother of Black Sons (1996), by Jane Lazarre. Durham, NC: Duke University Press.

Child care programs represent stepping stones to the formal education system and need to create partnerships with families for progressive change. Some school systems have added into their curriculum programs with great promise for bridging the cultural gap that results from teacher biases. Early childhood educators need to work with the local school districts to ensure that anti-bias techniques and tools are consistent in the transition from child care to formal schooling. For example, the national **Seeking Educational Equity and Diversity (SEED)** Project on Inclusive Curriculum prepares teachers to lead year-long seminars in their schools reflecting on local practices. The project helps teachers welcome and respond to all children in a class and deal with student sensitivity to complex identity matters, such as race and gender.

Andre King, director of the Easter Seals California Child Development Center Network, discussed providing culturally consistent care (2001). "The 'Anti-Bias' movement asks us to acknowledge that each of us is biased toward what we have always known, and to be open to looking at other ways of doing things that might be equally valid. We are asked to consider people who are different from us and ideas that are different from ours, and find ways of living together, to tolerate each other."

In her discussion of cultural empowerment she presented six guidelines:

1. Culture is learned. Children learn rules both directly by being taught ("hold your fork in your left hand and your knife in your right") and through observation. It can be a mistake to assume a person's culture from [his or her] appearance.

2. Culture is characteristic of groups. Cultural rules come from the group and are passed from generation to generation; they are not invented by the individual. Do not mistake individual differences for cultural differences. We share some characteristics with our cultural group, but we are also defined by our individual identities.

3. Culture is a set of rules for behavior. Cultural rules influence people to act similarly, in ways that help them understand each other. For instance, how we greet each other and address each other is influenced by our cultural backgrounds. Culture is not the behavior, but the rules that shape the behavior.

4. Individual members of a culture are embedded to different degrees within their culture. Because culture is learned, people learn it to different degrees. Family emphasis, individual preferences, and other factors influence how deeply embedded one is in one's culture.

5. Cultures borrow and share rules. Every culture has a consistent core set of rules, but they are not necessarily unique. Two cultures may share rules about some things, but have very different rules about other things. This gets very confusing for a person operating within two cultures that have some similarities and some differences.

6. Members of culture groups may be proficient at cultural behavior but unable to describe the rules. Because acculturation happens gradually, as a natural process, a person may not even be aware of the consistent rules that govern

his/her behavior. Just as a four-year-old who speaks very well may not know the technical rules of the language, people who are culturally competent may not know that they are behaving according to a set of cultural rules. They have simply absorbed the rules by living with them.

Influences from the Care Setting

Family Child Care Home

Influences of the setting on your curriculum are varied. Physical location, financial limitations, family work schedules, and other factors influence the schedule, environment, and curriculum in family child care homes. Establishing a positive learning environment is essential to quality care no matter which resources and limitations you find in your particular setting. Establishing a consistent, warm, friendly environment where large doses of the three As (Attention, Approval, and Attunement) are administered is the way to create the most powerful positive influence in any physical setting.

Family child care homes provide a homelike situation for the infant or toddler. During the transition for a child to a new caregiver and a new situation, the caregiver should quickly establish a setting that is familiar to the child: crib, rooms, and routines of playing, eating, and sleeping. A warm one-on-one relationship between the teacher and the child provides security in this new setting.

Child Care Center

Some child care centers care for infants six weeks of age and older, and a few centers are even equipped to care for newborns. The very young infant must receive special care. One caregiver in each shift needs to be responsible for the same infant each day. The caregiver should adjust routines to the infant's body rhythm rather than trying to make the infant eat and sleep according to the center's schedule. The early childhood educator will need to work closely with family members to understand the infant's behavior and changing schedule of eating and sleeping. Consistently recording and sharing information with the family is necessary to meet infant needs and involve the family in their child's daily experiences.

Time

The number and age of children in a group will affect the amount of time the caregiver has to give each child. The needs of the other children also affect how the time is allocated. Schedules in the child care home or center should be adjusted to meet the children's needs and the family members' employment schedules. For instance, if the father works the 7 a.m. to 3 p.m. shift, special planning may be required for the infant who awakens from a nap at 2:45 p.m. to be ready when he arrives. Through the use of attunement, the quality of interaction can remain high, even when time for interactions is limited.

Educational Philosophy of Program and Teachers

The **philosophy** of the program needs to be clearly articulated to teachers and families. Educational decisions should be evaluated in light of the program's philosophy. However, philosophy statements are often broad statements, leaving much room for interpretation. This is where your personal philosophy, or *image of the child*, comes into play. You must consider your beliefs and how they apply to daily interactions with children, family members, and colleagues. The authors have spent considerable time pondering the educational philosophies that serve as the basis for this book. They are as follows:

1. All people are viewed developmentally. From the moment of birth to the time of death every person is constantly growing in many ways. Focusing on the positive changes resulting from growth helps maintain a positive learning environment.
   a. Each infant and toddler is progressing through specific sequences or stages of development at his or her own rate.
   b. Parenting styles differ: some are new parents, some are experienced, some anxious, some relaxed, some informed, some nonchalant, and some eager.
   c. Each family member adds to his or her knowledge and skills. Each caregiver has his or her own level of competence too. Caregivers have knowledge obtained from talking, reading, and studying, as well as individual experiences with children and families. Their views and expectations of themselves as people and caregivers all contribute to their increasing competence as caregivers.
2. Development and growth occur through active interaction with one's environment and can be observed through the four major Developmental Areas. Each person
   a. is an active learner with rights and responsibilities.
   b. constructs knowledge through active interactions with people and materials.
   c. adapts previous experiences to current situations.
   d. builds on the knowledge and skills learned from previous experiences.
   e. initiates interactions with other people.
   f. initiates interactions with materials in the environment.
   g. uses multiple modes of representation to express understanding about the world.

Influences from the Child

Every child has an internal need to grow, develop, and learn. During the first years of life children's energies are directed toward those purposes both consciously and unconsciously. Though children cannot tell you this, observers can see that both random and purposeful behaviors help children.

The children look, touch, taste, listen, smell, reach, bite, push, kick, smile, and take any other action they can in order to actively involve themselves with the world.

FIGURE 9–2   The caregiver facilitates each child's development by making the child feel secure.

The fact that children are sometimes unsuccessful in what they try to do does not stop them from attempting new tasks. Sometimes they may turn away and begin a different task, but they will keep seeking something to do.

Infants learn from the responses they get to their actions. When the caregiver consistently answers cries of distress immediately, infants begin to build up feelings of security (Figure 9–2). Gradually these responses will help infants learn to exert control over their world. If caregivers let infants cry for long periods before going to them, the infants remain distressed longer, possibly causing them to have difficulty developing a sense of security and trust. Remember that the more immediately and completely needs are fulfilled, the more securely and happily children will develop. You can't love or fulfill an infant or toddler too much. Add large measures of the three As to this principle, and the result will be happy and secure children.

Joey, age seven months, is crying a lot. After checking to see if he is wet, tired, hungry, too hot, or too cold, Paulette picks him up and holds him close. She walks with him slowly around the room, rocking him gently in her arms. Joey soon calms down. We can see how Paulette's actions influenced Joey. A child can influence her caregiver in many ways as well. Eden, 30 months, has started to hide and make faces during her bowel movements. Mrs. Frank has noticed and recorded it in Eden's daily log. Mrs. Frank soon begins to introduce Eden to toilet learning as a result of Eden's influence.

As you will learn in your day-to-day work with children, influence runs in many directions. The family can influence your behavior just as society can, and all come into play within the walls of your program.

ROUTINE CARE TIMES

Infants and toddlers have needs that must be met. Some needs, such as eating and eliminating, occur frequently throughout the day. Infant and toddler teachers often think that all they do is feed, rock, and diaper children. Our traditional notion of teaching seems—and is—inappropriate for very young children (Swim & Muza, 1999). That is why our definition of curriculum presented earlier is so important. You must come to understand that everything you do facilitates development and learning. As discussed in previous chapters, using the three *As*, attention, approval, and attunement, while meeting the basic needs of infants and toddlers promotes optimal development and learning. The following provide examples of ways to organize and plan the **routine care times** of the curriculum. First, however, we need to discuss daily schedules.

Flexible Schedule

The schedule you create for the day should reflect each individual child's physical schedule. Thus, your schedule depends on the infant or toddler you are caring for. The goal is not to coordinate the children's physical schedules but rather to have a flexible plan for meeting the needs of the children. During the first months the infant is in the process of setting a personal, internal schedule. Some infants do this easily; others seem to have more difficulty. So when a child is first entering your care, ask family members what the infant or toddler does at home. Write this down to serve as a guideline. Next, observe the child to see whether he or she follows the home schedule or develops a different schedule.

The daily schedule must be individualized in infant and toddler care. It focuses on the basic activities: sleeping, feeding, and playing. Andrea arrives at 7:45 a.m.; Kevin is ready for a bottle and nap at 8:00 a.m.; Myron is alert and will play until about 9:00 a.m., when he takes a bottle and a nap; and Audrey is alert and will play all morning and take a nap immediately after lunch. As caregiver, noting these preferences will provide you with guidelines for your time.

Children's schedules and preferences for routines change over time. Each month infants sleep less. This affects when they eat and when they are alert. As infants change their sleeping schedules, they will adjust to allow more time for exploration and engagement with materials. Toddlers will also differ in how much time they spend asleep and awake. Morning and afternoon naps do not fit into a rigid schedule from 8:30 to 9:45 or from 12:00 to 2:00, respectively. You can identify blocks of time for specific types of activities but should keep in mind that no schedule can fit all children.

Arrival Time

During this special time the primary caregiver greets the parent and child and receives the infant or toddler. This is the time for the caregiver to listen to the family member tell about the child's night and about any joys, problems, or concerns. They should write down important details on the message board, for example, "exposed to measles last night."

Arrival time is also a time to help the infant or toddler make the transition from home to school. The caregiver's relationships with the child should provide a calming, comfortable, accepting situation so that the child will feel secure. Touching, holding, and talking with the child for a few minutes helps the child re-establish relations with the caregiver. When the child is settled, the caregiver may move on to whatever activity the child is ready to do.

Sleeping

Most of a newborn's time is spent sleeping, although the time awake gradually lengthens. If you are responsible for several infants or toddlers, plan your time carefully so you are available to help each child fall asleep by providing quiet time, holding, talking, singing, rubbing, and rocking. Make available open-ended materials for the other children who are awake so they will be productively occupied. You control many factors that determine how well a child will sleep, so consider how you separate the sleeping and playing areas of your classroom. Have you blocked sunlight during the afternoon? Do you play calming background music? Each child has preferences that you must learn in order to build your curriculum. Some infants like to be rocked to sleep; some enjoy backrubs. Some prefer to snuggle with a favorite blanket or stuffed animal. Ask family members how they put their child to sleep at home so that you can coordinate your routines at school.

Even though they are the same age, Yolanda takes a morning and afternoon nap, while Simonyi takes only an afternoon nap.

Each child should have a separate crib for sleeping. If children share a crib on different days (e.g., Emily attends Monday and Friday and Samantha attends Tuesday, Wednesday, and Thursday), always remove sheets and personal belongings and disinfect the crib between children. Some infants and toddlers have difficulty relaxing and falling asleep. Schumann (1982) has described relaxation techniques she has used with children as young as 18 months old. After creating an environment conducive to sleep, she uses the following procedures. A quiet, steady voice along with stroking facilitates relaxation even when the child may not understand all the words being used.

Use a quiet even voice to help the children relax each part of their bodies. Repeatedly (six to eight times) state that the body part is "heavy." For some children it may help to stroke firmly with two hands over the body part to be relaxed. Begin with the toes and work up the body in the following fashion: toes, feet, legs, back (or abdomen, depending on position), fingers, hands, arms, shoulders, neck, eyes, lips, and chin. After relaxing each body part, check it to see how successful each child has been. Tenseness is indicated by a raised bulging or rigid muscles or by movement of a muscle or body part. Using firm hands, strive for being able to move the body part yourself at the joint without the child's helping or keeping the area stiff. Give POSITIVE reinforcement for the way you want the body part to be. Explain to the children to let the feet stay "heavy" while you are checking that part. As you move from talking about one body part to the next, keep your voice a continuous monotone rather than pausing. After doing two or three body parts, repeat the idea that the previous ones are still "heavy" also.

For example, "Your toes are heavy. Your toes are heavy. Your toes are heavy. Your toes are heavy." (Check for relaxation, insert positive reinforcement) "Your feet are heavy. Your feet are relaxed. Your feet are heavy. Your feet are heavy." (Check for relaxation, insert positive reinforcement) "Your toes are heavy. Your feet are heavy. Your legs are heavy." By the time each child is told his eyes are heavy, it is likely that he will either already have them closed or be willing to close them at your request. . . . If a child still seems fairly alert at the end of the toe-to-head release sequence, try repeating the sequence but eliminating touch and checking of the body for relaxation. Some children might require or seek more body contact than others (pp. 17–18).

Waking

Some infants and toddlers wake up alert and happy. Others awaken groggy and crying. You can help ease the infant or toddler into wakefulness. Some you can pick up and cuddle. Talk quietly to them, and move them around so they see things in the room that may be interesting. Usually infants and toddlers need to have their diapers changed or need to go to the bathroom when they wake up. Some infants will be hungry and need a bottle at this time.

Record the child's sleeping time. Family members need to know how long and at what time their child slept, and the caregiver needs to know when each infant or

To help very young children learn that cribs are for sleeping, remove them as soon as they wake.

toddler can be expected to sleep. Each infant or toddler in your home or room may have a different nap time.

Eating

The very young infant may eat every two to four hours. They should eat when they are hungry. This is called **demand feeding**. Demand feeding involves more flexibility for the caregiver and is one of the first steps to building a bond between that person and the children in his or her care. It is also the first step toward the child internalizing a sense of trust and security. Ask family members how often the baby eats at home. Infants will tell you when they are hungry by fussing and crying. Learn their individual schedules and their physical and oral signals, so you can feed them before they have to cry. Record the time of feedings and the amount of milk or formula the baby drank.

Hold the infant when you are giving a bottle. This curricular time is to meet the nutritional needs of the child. All food offered to the children should be nutritious. State licensing regulations often provide plenty of information on how to address the children's nutritional needs. (See the "Additional Resources" and "Helpful Web Sites" sections at the end of this chapter more on nutrition.) But eating is also a curricular time for nurturing physical, emotional, social, cognitive, and language development. There are great advantages to consciously caring for the child. Holding, feeding, relating, maintaining eye contact, and ultimately building a secure foundation for the child are only possible through this type of care.

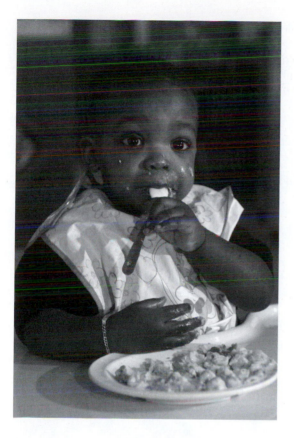

As children get older, they begin to exert independence while eating.

As children get older, they begin to exert independence while eating. They no longer want you to hold the bottle for them or feed them with a spoon. This is normal behavior and should be supported as much as possible. During this time, however, parents and caregivers often worry that the child is not getting enough to eat. You may find that a child in this situation wants to eat more often; providing additional opportunities to eat can ensure that the child's need for food is being met. Children may also want to exert their independence by skipping a meal or snack occasionally. Encourage community involvement by having the child stay in the area where the other children are eating, or allowing the child to sit on your lap.

All eating must be supervised, as the chance of choking is high for very young children who are learning to eat solid foods. Food for older infants should be cut into pieces no larger than a quarter of an inch. Older toddlers can have one-half-inch pieces. But the best way to supervise is to eat with the older infants and toddlers. Sit at the table and engage them in conversation.

Diapering and Toileting

Most infants and toddlers cannot communicate that they need a curricular experience involving a diaper change. You must be vigilant about checking. Often they need their diapers changed or to sit on the toilet after eating. The toddler who is engaged in toilet learning may also need special attention after nap and during play. Children who have learned to use the toilet may need to be reminded when they typically need to go to the bathroom (for example, after a nap).

Attending to this routine care time requires planning. Doing so will allow you to talk and sing and engage in positive experiences while you are providing for this basic need (see Herr & Swim, 2002, for example). Make this a pleasant time for both of you. The steps in the diapering process (Aronson, 2002; Swim, 1998) are as follows:

1. Gather all of the supplies (e.g., latex gloves, diaper wipes, clean diaper, and change of clothes) you will need and place them in the changing area within reach.
2. Put on latex gloves. Remove the infant's clothes or pull them up to the chest level. Remove the soiled diaper and place it on the edge of the area out of the reach of the infant.
3. *Keep one hand on the infant at all times.*
4. Wipe off bowel movement with a diaper wipe or toilet tissue, going from front to back. Put this wipe on the soiled diaper. Continue until the child's bottom is clean.
5. Take off your gloves and wrap the soiled disposable diaper and wipes inside of them. Do this, for example, by holding the diaper in your right hand and using your left hand to pull the glove over and around the diaper. Then, put the diaper into your left hand and pull the glove over them again.

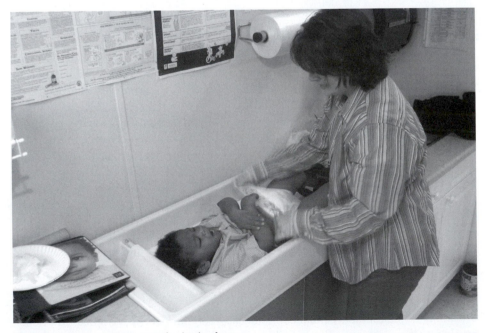

Make diapering a pleasant time for both of you

6. Throw away a soiled disposable diaper immediately in a foot-activated, covered, plastic-bag-lined container. Put a soiled cloth diaper in a plastic bag, which will be closed with a twisty when you are finished. If the diaper is of cloth, throw away the soiled wipes separately in the trash container.

7. Wash your hands with a diaper wipe. If at any time from this point forward you notice bodily fluid, *put gloves on*.

8. Put a clean diaper on the child, fitting it snugly around the child's legs and waist. Dress the infant again or put on new clothes, as necessary.

9. Wash the child's hands in running water and carry the child to the next activity.

10. Return to the changing area to clean it. Use a twisty to tie the plastic bag closed for a cloth diaper, if applicable. Spray the changing area with disinfectant. Wash your hands thoroughly with soap and running water before you do anything else.

11. Record the time and consistency of bowel movements. You and the child's family members need this information to determine patterns of normalcy and to look for causes of irregularities.

Toilet learning should begin when the toddler is ready. Toddlers will indicate when they are ready to begin this process. Their diapers may be dry for a few hours; they may tell you they have urinated or had a bowel movement after they have; they may watch other children use the big toilet—a motivation available when you have children who are already toilet-trained (Figure 9–3).

FIGURE 9–3 Children who have already learned to use the toilet can help motivate younger children.

Discuss the timing with the toddler's parents. Both the home and the child care program need to begin at the same time and use the same procedures. Frequent, regular dialogue between parents and caregivers is needed to determine whether to continue toilet-learning or to stop and begin again a few months later.

It is often difficult for families to resist cultural pressures for early toilet learning even when they know the toddler is not ready and is unsuccessful in attempts. The caregiver can help family members understand the needs and development of their toddler.

The toddler needs two major functions for toilet learning—biofeedback and muscular control. Toddlers learn to recognize the feelings their bodies have before they urinate or have a bowel movement. They can use this biofeedback to decide what to do. At first they seem to just observe the feelings and afterward label what has happened.

When they decide to go into the bathroom *before* elimination, they need to use muscular control until they are safely on the toilet. Timing and control must be coordinated. At first toddlers may have some control but not enough to last as long as it takes to get into the bathroom, get clothes out of the way, and get seated or standing. Through trial and error, feedback and adjustments, toddlers learn what their bodies are doing and what they can control and plan.

When the child starts toilet learning, use training pants at home and at the child care program. Do *not* put diapers on the toddler during nap time. Outer clothes must be loose or easily removed to facilitate self-help.

Take the toddler to the bathroom and instruct how to pull down necessary clothes and how to get seated on the adapter seat or potty chair. For the boy who can reach while standing, determine where he should stand and where he should direct his penis. Put on your gloves before proceeding. Wait until the child goes to the toilet, or wait a few minutes. Teach how to get toilet paper and how to wipe from front to back. Then let the child try to do it alone. Check to see if assistance is needed in cleaning the child's bottom. Assist in getting clothes back up. Assist in washing the child's hands with soap and water.

Wipe off the toilet seat and spray with disinfectant if there is urine or feces on the seat or sides. *Remove gloves and wash your hands thoroughly before doing anything else.*

Occasionally during play time ask children whether they need to go to the bathroom. Ask them to go after lunch and before nap time. As soon as they get up from their naps, have them go to the bathroom.

Toilet learning should be a positive developmental experience and take a very short time. Problems in learning to use the toilet most often arise when adults do not notice the child's lack of readiness. They pressure the child through weeks of unsuccessful experiences, during which they blame the child for the failure rather than blaming themselves for wrong timing. Help family members and colleagues understand that timing for toilet learning is individual, as is learning to walk. There is no *right* age by which all children should be using the toilet independently. However, girls often can between 30 and 36 months of age and boys by 36–42 months (Carr, 1993).

Hand Washing

Frequent hand washing is a vital routine for caregivers and children to establish, since failure to do it is directly related to the occurrence of illness. Hand-washing procedures should be thorough: A quick rinse with clear water does not remove microorganisms.

The caregiver must wash hands before

- working with children at the beginning of the day.
- handling bottles, food, or feeding utensils.
- assisting child with face and handwashing.
- assisting child with brushing teeth.
- changing a diaper (after rubber gloves are removed).

The caregiver must wash hands after

- feeding.
- cleaning up.
- diapering (remove medical gloves first).
- assisting with toileting (remove gloves first).
- wiping or assisting with a runny nose (remove gloves first).
- working with wet, sticky, dirty items (remove gloves first).

The child must wash hands before

- handling food and food utensils.
- brushing teeth.

The child must wash hands after

- eating.
- diapering or toileting.
- playing with wet, sticky, and/or dirty items (e.g., sand, mud).

Proper procedures for hand washing include wetting the whole hand with warm water, applying soap, and rubbing the whole hand—palm, back, between fingers, and around fingernails. Rinse with clean water, rubbing the skin to help remove the microorganisms and soap. Dry hands on a disposable paper towel that has no colored dyes in it. Throw away the towel so others do not have to handle it. You can also use small washcloths as towels, with each child using his own once and then putting it in the laundry basket.

Toddlers who can stand on a stepstool at the sink can be assisted in washing their own hands. You can turn on the water, push the soap dispenser, verbally encourage them to rub their hands together, turn off the water for them, and if necessary hand them a towel.

Toothbrushing

Help toddlers step up on the stepstool at the sink if they need assistance. Turn on the faucet so a small stream of water is running. Wash your hands. Assist in the child's

Help children to establish healthy habits early.

hand washing. Then, allow the toddler to wet her own toothbrush. Shut off the water. Put a small amount of toothpaste on the toothbrush and then encourage the toddler to brush all of her teeth (not just the front ones).

Fill a small paper or plastic cup half full with water. Encourage the toddlers to rinse their mouths well. Give them more water if needed. Turn on the faucet and allow the toddlers to rinse their own toothbrushes and rinse out their cups. Have the children wipe off their mouths with a tissue. Return the toothbrush and plastic cup to their proper place or throw away the paper cup.

End of the Day

At the end of each child's day, collect your thoughts and decide what to share with family members. To help you remember, or to gather information for other caregivers who work with the child, review the notes in the child's portfolio or on the report sheet. This sharing time includes the family members in the child's day and provides a transition for the child from the school to home.

PLANNED LEARNING EXPERIENCES

In between sleeping and eating, infants and toddlers have **alert times** when they are very alert and attracted to the world around them. This is the time when the caregiver does special activities with them (see Part III for suggestions). The infant or toddler

Plan time throughout the day to interact one on one with each infant or toddler.

discovers him- or herself, plays, and talks and interacts with you and others. Children have fun when in an alert state, as they actively involve themselves in the world.

Determine the times when the infants and toddlers in your care are alert. Decide which times each individual child will spend alone with appropriate materials you have selected and which times you will spend together one on one or in a small group. Each infant or toddler needs some time during each day to play with his or her primary caregiver. This play time is in addition to the time you spend changing diapers, feeding the child, and helping the child get to sleep.

As you play with the infant or toddler, you will discover how long that child remains interested. Stop before the child gets tired. The child is just learning how to interact with others and needs rest times and unpressured times in between highly attentive times. With an infant you might play a reaching-grasping game for a couple of minutes, a visual focusing activity for about a minute, and a standing-bouncing-singing game for a minute. Watch the infant's reactions to determine when to extend the activity to two minutes, five minutes, and so on. Alternate interactive times with times playing alone. Infants will stay awake and alert longer if they have some times of stimulation and interaction.

Toddlers spend increasing amounts of time in play. There should be opportunities for self-directed play as well as challenge and interaction with the caregiver. Toddlers also need quiet, uninterrupted time during their day. Constant activity is emotionally and physically wearing on them.

NAEYC's guidelines for creating appropriate curriculum support our understanding of how to create learning experiences. They include:

1. providing experiences for all areas of development: physical, cognitive, social, emotional, and language
2. including a broad range of content across disciplines that is intellectually engaging and meaningful to the children
3. building on what the children already know and are able to do to foster the acquisition of new concepts and skills
4. integrating content across subject matter or developmental areas
5. promoting the development of knowledge and understanding, processes and skills, as well as a disposition toward learning
6. creating curriculum that has intellectual integrity
7. supporting home cultures and languages while developing a shared culture of the learning community
8. setting goals that are realistic and attainable for each child (Bredekamp & Copple, 1997)

The following sections discuss the specifics of how to create curriculum for infants and toddlers.

Daily Plans

For infants and young toddlers, you should plan experiences daily for each child. Assess the four areas of development for children using the Developmental Prescriptions (Appendix A). Next, copy the Developmental Profile form in Appendix B. Use the sample profile to plot a profile for each child in your care. Finally, analyze your data and determine the skills that the child can do independently and with assistance. Translate these skills into **daily plans**.

After implementing some **planned experiences**, you can use the data observed and recorded to plan new experiences for the next day. You can see how curriculum planning becomes a circular process that builds on itself (see Table 9–1).

When planning experiences you should not only consider the children's developmental needs and abilities but also their interests. If you want an infant to practice finding hidden objects, for example, hide a rattle that the child likes. Curricular experiences should balance practicing or reinforcing skills with introducing new ones. Introducing too many new experiences can overstimulate the infant or make him overtired. Carefully read the child's nonverbal communication to know when to stop the experience.

This child might be thinking, "I pushed them together. Now do they come apart?"

TABLE 9–1   SAMPLE SECTION OF A WEEKLY PLAN FOR AN INDIVIDUAL CHILD

EXAMPLE:

CHILD'S NAME: **WEEK:**

AREA OF DEVELOPMENT[a]	MATERIALS	CAREGIVER STRATEGIES AND COMMENTS
Physical: Vision R: Visual tracking	Red ribbon bow	Hold bow where infant can focus. Slowly move bow to side, to front, to other side. Observe eyes holding focus. Stop. Talk to infant, and repeat moving bow.
N: Changing focus	Red and blue ribbon bow	Hold red bow where infant can focus. Lift up blue bow and hold a few inches to side of red bow. Observe eyes changing focus. Continue changing positions with both bows.

[a]Behavior: R = reinforced, N = new

Weekly Plans

For older toddlers, you can plan experiences by the week, but you must modify the **weekly plans** throughout the week to respond to the children's needs. Planning for the entire week affords you the ability to carefully plan the learning environment (see Chapter 8) and make available appropriate materials, equipment, and supplies. Materials are a vital part of the curriculum. The infants and toddlers learn by interacting with materials; the construction of knowledge comes from holding, tasting, shaking, hitting, throwing, taking apart, and listening to objects. Select open-ended materials such as wooden unit blocks, clay, and sand, because they provide a variety of experiences and can be used by each child to meet his or her needs and ideas (Curtis & Carter, 2003).

Learning Centers

As discussed in Chapter 8, learning centers organize the room and materials and encourage specific use of a particular space. Select materials for each learning center by matching them with the needs, interests, and abilities of the children. Do so carefully, because a poor selection of materials can actually impede the children's development. Materials that are too easy can be boring, and those that are too difficult can be frustrating. Using currently popular materials or those labeled "educational" may or may not be appropriate or effective for promoting development for your group of toddlers or a particular toddler. On the other hand, selecting developmentally appropriate materials for each child can facilitate growth and skill advancement (see Part 3).

For example, you notice that José seems to attend carefully to the wind chime outdoors. You want to promote his reaching and grabbing of objects, so you secure a wind chime in the manipulative area just within his reach. In Elizabeth's case, however, you want her to practice transferring objects from hand to hand, so you put out attractive clear blocks with interesting materials inside. You anticipate that when she picks one up to examine it, the material inside will shift locations, encouraging her to switch hands for a better view.

Projects

Once you know the children's interests and abilities, it is time to plan a week's worth of engaging curriculum. Instead of selecting themes, you should identify *moments* that can be developed into an ongoing project. Many **projects** have no clear beginning; they emerge (with much teacher observation and reflection) slowly over time from the documentation (see Chapter 5) that the teacher has collected or her experiences interacting with the children. Small moments encountered by one or two children can become projects in their own ways (May, Kantor, & Sanderson, 2004). Following our approach about the daily plans, weekly plans should be individualized for each child.

You can outline experiences and questions to support the project or line of thinking and integrate the areas of development. In the infant-toddler centers of Reggio Emilia, teachers have constructed a particular approach to curricular planning referred to as *progettazione* or flexible planning (Rinaldi, 1998). Teachers there plan open-ended experiences to facilitate the co-construction of knowledge for children and themselves.

To plan engaging and challenging experiences, create curriculum based on your prior observations of each individual child.

They view the teacher's role as that of a resource who does not simply satisfy needs or answer questions, but instead helps children discover their own answers and, more importantly, helps them learn to ask good questions (Rinaldi, 1998). Therefore, this ". . . is a dynamic process based on communication that generates documentation and is regenerated by documentation" (Gandini & Goldhaber, 2001, p. 128).

As discussed earlier, a key principle of the educational approach used in Reggio Emilia, Italy, involves the many languages of children. Children are provided with multiple opportunities and avenues for expressing their understanding of the world. Thus, children use their "one hundred languages" to tell adults and peers what they know. Some avenues for expression include but are not limited to sculpting with clay or wire, painting, building with found materials, sketching, acting out stories, and dancing with scarves. These types of curricular experiences serve to cultivate and elaborate on the image of the child as a competent, capable, active learner who is constantly creating and re-creating theories about the world.

SAMPLE PROJECT.   The following is a project about wheeled vehicles that was created for a group of older toddlers. Joan and Derek displayed interest when the wheels fell off a vehicle in the block area. They immediately noticed that the car didn't move as easily without the wheels and after about five minutes of "hard" pushing, left it lying on the edge of the carpet.

Picking up on the children's frustration about the car, Sue decided to provoke the children's thinking about wheels further. She placed a full-size car tire (that had been cleaned) in the center of the room and waited to see what the children would do. Derek ran right to it and began to climb on it. Sue stood back and watched as other children began to join in the excitement. After about seven minutes, she sat on the floor near the children and asked questions such as "What is this?" "What is this for?" "How does it help a car move?" "Can a wheel help you move?" "What helps you move?" and recorded their answers. Later that day when the children were napping, she took a few moments to review her notes. She began to *web* what the children knew about the movement of wheels and people (Figure 9–4).

Sue decided to build on the children's interest in the wheels and planned the curricular experiences for the following week. To "kick off" the project, she planned to take the children on a walking field trip in their neighborhood to look for wheels. She mapped out the route to take so they would pass by the used car dealership and the playground with the tire swings. She prepared a clipboard (e.g., a piece of cardboard

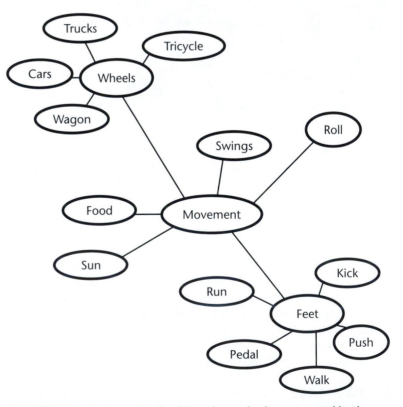

FIGURE 9–4 An example of webbing about wheels, constructed by the teacher after conversing with the children.

cut to 9" × 12" with unlined paper held on by a binder clip) with a pencil for each child to sketch what he or she saw. Later in the week, they were going to work with clay to represent wheels and possibly cars. She would put books about transportation in the reading/listening center and in the art center for when they worked with paint or clay. She planned to add wheels to the block area that fit on the unit blocks so children could construct their own cars.

Of course, Sue and her co-teacher, Joni, will document these classroom events using their digital video camera (which takes still photographs as well), running records of conversations, and work samples. These data will be reviewed daily during naptime and on Friday before planning experiences for the next week.

As mentioned in the previous chapter, the educators in Reggio Emilia speak of the importance of finding the "extraordinary in the ordinary" (L. Gandini, personal communication, January 26, 2001). In other words, early childhood educators should balance novel and familiar objects in the environment. Exploring flashlights on a dreary, rainy day meaningfully engages the children in investigating light, dark, and shadows. Wurm (2005) explains that there are four types of overlapping projects that teachers and children in Reggio engage in on a regular basis. The four types of projects are intentional, daily life, self-managed, and environmental projects. The ones most important to infants and toddlers are daily life and environmental, which can both lead into intentional projects. Daily life projects are those events which occur repeatedly, or on an ongoing basis for very young children. Learning to eat and dress independently and to separate from family members, for example, are daily life projects. May, Kantor, and Sanderson (2004) provide additional examples of daily life projects about object permanence and identity development.

Environmental projects are inherently built into the classroom as part of the learning environment (Wurm, 2005). In other words, these projects emerge directly from the space and materials in which the children live and work. Children investigate methods of construction and principles of physical sciences (e.g., balance, force) due to the availability of different types of blocks (e.g., large, hollow, unit blocks or cardboard bricks). Returning to our example above, the children noticed the importance of wheels to make a vehicle move while pushing cars around on the carpet. When the teachers provided provocations to extend the children's thinking, they moved the work in the direction of an intentional project. Intentional projects result from the teachers' careful observation of and attention to the children's daily life and environmental projects and the teachers' planning and designing of flexible learning experiences (Wurm, 2005).

Good infant-toddler curriculum, then, should provide children with continuity from home to school and from day to day or even week to week. Children need time and support to construct and co-construct their knowledge of the world (see, for example, Cross & Swim, 2006).

Feedback

Feedback is a critical part of the curriculum cycle. You should solicit feedback from family members, colleagues, your own reflections, and the children themselves. Analyzing the documentation of the children's involvement, for example, ensures that the children have a balanced curriculum in the formal, planned times with you. Putting these data together with those collected during routine care times should provide evidence of a holistic, nurturing curriculum for each child in your care. If you find that any child is not receiving well-thought-out care, determine what changes are needed and make them to improve the quality of care and education provided for each child.

■ KEY TERMS

alert times

bias

cultural diversity

curriculum

daily plans

demand feeding

philosophy

planned experiences

progettazione

projects

routine care times

Seeking Educational Equity and Diversity (SEED)

toilet learning

weekly plans

CASE STUDY   Merissa

Merissa Golabar was born three weeks prematurely, with a low birth weight of four pounds, six ounces. The split in her lower lip at birth alerted the doctors to check her mouth carefully. Upon examination, it was apparent that the area immediately behind the top gum (called the hard palate) and the area farther back (the soft palate) were split. This condition, called *cleft palate*, creates an unnatural airway through the roof of the mouth to the floor of the nose. As a result, Merissa needs to breathe harder to pull air into her lungs, although the condition is not life threatening. As she grows older, the condition will not be as noticeable.

The immediate concern was whether Merissa would be able to suck for breast-feeding. A nurse gently pinched Merissa's lips while she taught her mother how to help Merissa breast-feed. However, Merissa was not able to suck and became extremely frustrated, as did her mother. To ensure proper nutrition and maintain her electrolyte balance, Merissa was placed in an incubator and an intravenous line was started.

After two days, it was time for Merissa's mother to go home, but Merissa needed to stay in the hospital. Mrs. Golabar had attempted almost hourly to help

Merissa breast-feed without success and felt depressed and inadequate. Hospital staff counseled her and helped her understand that her feelings were normal and partly physically based. Often, approximately three days after delivery, some mothers experience a decrease in hormones called postpartum depression, which can last a few days. Given the problem with her daughter, it was understandable that Mrs. Golabar was very upset.

The next morning, the parents met with a plastic surgeon, who explained that Merissa's lips could be repaired later that day. The couple held and rocked their baby until time for surgery and were extremely relieved to find that the surgery was a complete success. They were told that Merissa would need several additional surgeries on her palate as she grew, but her condition could be corrected through medical and behavioral interventions. Since Mrs. Golabar had to return to work shortly, the family was referred to a local group family child care center, where staff were trained in feeding programs and cleft palate.

Mr. and Mrs. Golabar were very relieved the next week to speak with Mrs. Brown, the director of At Ease Family Child Care, to find that she and her staff would design an individualized curriculum to fill Merissa's special needs. To begin, they would assess her needs in the four major areas of development on a regular basis using Developmental Profiles and Prescriptions. Then, data analysis would be completed to determine the steps necessary to enhance Merissa's growth and development. They planned to select materials and experiences support and enhance her development daily. Ongoing daily evaluation of her growth and response to the experiences would be conducted to give staff and family members feedback so they could adjust methods, materials, and/or experiences as necessary.

In addition to the individualized curriculum, specific objectives were designed for Merissa's special feeding, vocalization, and language development. The director explained how feedings would be accomplished slowly, with an up-and-down rhythm and motion at first to aid sucking and swallowing. As Merissa started more solid foods and underwent further surgeries, staff would task-analyze the steps, methods, and materials necessary to help her eat well, form clear vocalizations, and work with Mr. and Mrs. Golabar to help Merissa develop at her optimal rate. The Golabars left At Ease Child Care with optimism that they would not have believed possible just a few days before.

1. What were the major factors that allowed the Golabar family to resolve the problem and be optimistic about Merissa?

2. What must be accomplished before an individualized curriculum can be developed for any child? Why?

3. Discuss the emotional factors everyone in this case study—caregivers, family members, and child—bring to the situation.

QUESTIONS AND EXPERIENCES FOR REFLECTION

1. Interview a teacher in a family child care program. Inquire how she responds to cultural diversity. For example, how does she use the home language of the children? How does she modify curriculum to respond to the cultural beliefs of families?

2. Diaper a child and reflect on your behavior. How well did you follow the guidelines as presented in the chapter? How did you interact with the child to promote security and development?

3. Observe a child in a child care center and record your observations using the Developmental Prescriptions (Appendix A). Transfer your data to the Developmental Profile (Appendix B). Create two daily plans in response to this data.

4. Observe toddlers on a playground. Use a narrative method for recording your observations (Appendix A). Think about the children's interests and create a flexible plan for a project.

CHAPTER REVIEW

1. Write a statement for a new caregiver that explains why flexibility in schedules is important in an infant and toddler program.

2. Write a brief newsletter article for a child care center explaining their approach to cultural diversity.

3. List three routine care times. Explain how each event can be used to promote the development of the child.

	Routine	Development
1.		
2.		
3.		

4. List three reasons for creating daily plans for infants and young toddlers.

5. How can a project be used to involve a child physically?

emotionally?

socially?

cognitively?

■ REFERENCES

Aronson, S. S. (Ed.), compiled with P. M. Spahr. (2002). *Healthy young children: A manual for programs.* Washington, DC: National Association for the Education of Young Children.

Bredekamp, S., & Copple, C. (Eds.). (1997). *Developmentally appropriate practice in early childhood programs* (Rev. ed.). Washington, DC: National Association for the Education of Young Children.

Carr, L. (1993). Toilet training toddlers. Selden, NY: Lecture Series to Suffolk County "Mommy & Me Parent Trainers."

Cataldo, C. Z. (1983). *Infants and toddlers programs: A guide to very early childhood education.* Reading, MA: Addison-Wesley.

Clinton, W. J. (1997). National Child Care Forum [Television broadcast]. Washington, DC: National Broadcasting Corporation.

Cross, D. J., & Swim, T. J. (2006). A scholarly partnership for examining the pragmatics of Reggio-inspired practice in an early childhood classroom: Provocations, documentation, and time. *ScholarlyPartnerships.EDU, 1*(1), 47–68.

Curtis, D., & Carter, M. (2003). *Designs for living and learning: Transforming early childhood environments.* St. Paul, MN: Redleaf Press.

Gandini, L., & Goldhaber, J. (2001). Two reflections about documentation. In L. Gandini & C. P. Edwards (Eds.), *Bambini: The Italian approach to infant/toddler care* (pp. 124–145). New York: Teachers College Press.

Ghedini, P. (2001). Change in Italian national policy for children 0–3 years old and their families: Advocacy and responsibility. In L. Gandini & C. P. Edwards (Eds.) *Bambini: The Italian approach to infant/toddler care* (pp. 38–45). New York: Teachers College Press.

Greenman, J., & Stonehouse, A. (1996). *Prime times: A handbook for excellence in infant and toddler programs.* St. Paul, MN: Redleaf Press.

Herr, J., & Swim, T. (2002). *Creative Resources for Infants and Toddlers* (2nd ed.). Clifton Park, NY: Thomson Delmar Learning.

Jones, E., & Derman-Sparks, L. (1992). Meeting the challenge of diversity. *Young Children, 47*(2), 12–17.

King, A. (2001, November). Providing culturally consistent care for infants and toddlers—strategies from the Program for Infant/Toddler Caregivers. Paper presented at the National Association for the Education of Young Children Annual Conference, Anaheim, CA.

Kontos, S., Howes, C., Shinn, M., & Galinsky, E. (1995). *Quality in family child care and relative care.* New York: Teachers College Press.

May, N., Kantor, R., & Sanderson, M. (2004). There it is! Exploring the permanence of objects and the power of self with infants and toddlers. In J. Hendrick (Ed.), *Next steps towards teaching the Reggio way: Accepting the challenge to change* (2nd ed., pp. 164–174). Upper Saddle River, NJ: Pearson Merrill Prentice Hall.

Rinaldi, C. (1998). Projected curriculum constructed through documentation—*Progettazione:* An interview with Lella Gandini. In C. Edwards, L. Gandini, & G. Forman (Eds.), *The hundred languages of children: The Reggio Emilia approach—Advanced reflections* (2nd ed., pp. 113–125). Westport, CT: Ablex.

Schumann, M. J. (1982). Children in daycare: Settling them for sleep. *Day Care and Early Education, 9*(4), 14–18.

Swim, T. J. (1998). Proper procedures: Preventing the spread of disease in infant and toddler classrooms. *Early Childhood News, 10,* 45–47.

Swim, T. J., & Muza, R. (1999, Spring). Planning curriculum for infants. *Texas Child Care, 22*(4), 2–7.

Turkovich, M., & Mueller, P. (1989). The multicultural factor: A curriculum multiplier. *Social Studies and the Young Learner, 1*(4), 9–12.

Wurm, J. (2005). *Working in the Reggio way: A beginner's guide for American teachers.* St. Paul, MN: Redleaf Press.

ADDITIONAL RESOURCES

Howard, G. R. (2006). *We can't teach what we don't know: White teachers, multiracial schools* (2nd ed.). New York: Teachers College Press.

Marotz, L. R., Cross, M. Z., & Rush, J. M. (2006). *Health, safety and nutrition for the young child.* Clifton Park, New York: Thomson Delmar Learning.

Ramsey, P. G. (2004). *Teaching and learning in a diverse world* (3rd ed.). New York: Teachers College Press.

Topal, C. W., & Gandini, L. (1999). *Beautiful Stuff! Learning with found materials.* Worcester, MA: Davis Publications.

HELPFUL WEB SITES

Healthy Meals Resource System. Resources on child menu planning and food safety for caregivers. http://healthymeals.nal.usda.gov/

NAEYC – Beyond the Journal. Provides recent resources concerning, health and safety, nutrition, and fitness. http://journal.naeyc.org/bij/200403/, http://journal.naeyc.org/btj/200605/

National Network for Child Care. Links to articles and resources on child care evaluation and assessment. http://www.nncc.org/

Rethinking Schools. Resources on equity and social justice for teachers. http://www.rethinkingschools.org/

Teaching for Change. Resources on equity and social justice (pre-K to college) for adults and children. http://teachingforchange.org/

For additional infant and toddler resources, visit our Web site at http://www.earlychilded.delmar.com

Matching Caregiver Strategies, Materials, and Activities to the Child's Development

The chapters in Part 3 describe how the caregiver works with infants and toddlers at specific age ranges. Each chapter refers to the developmental profiles and characteristics of children in a specific age range, lists materials, and presents examples of caregiver strategies that can be used with individual children. Recall that this text applies a developmental perspective to the work of early childhood educators who care for and teach infants and toddlers. Thus, careful observation and analysis of each child's pattern of development serves as a foundation for caring for a child.

As discussed earlier, the *sequence* of development presented is common to all infants and toddlers. The *age* at which behaviors occur or the *rate* of development may differ. Since two 11-month-olds may be at different levels of development, concentrate on each child as an individual. Accept the uniqueness of each child, and compare each one only to his or her developmental progression. Look at their individual records to see where they are making appropriate progress, gradually developing new, more complex skills and behaviors, or where they seem to be stuck at one level.

10

The Child from Birth to Four Months of Age

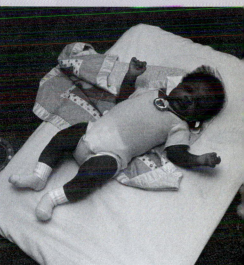

■ OBJECTIVES

After reading this chapter, you should be able to:

- Identify and record sequences of change in the physical, emotional, social, and cognitive/language development of infants from birth to four months of age.
- Select materials appropriate to a particular infant's developmental level.
- Devise caregiving and teaching strategies for an infant appropriate to his or her age level.

■ CHAPTER OUTLINE

- Materials
  Types of Materials
  Examples of Homemade Materials
- Caregiver Strategies to Enhance Development
  Developmental Profile
  Physical Development
  Emotional Development
  Social Development
  Cognitive and Language Development
- Case Study: Carol

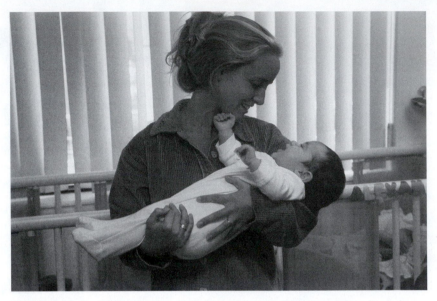

FIGURE 10–1   The caregiver anticipates and provides for the newborn's needs.

Antonia's Story

Antonia, two-and-a-half-months old, has just arrived at the child care home. She sits in her infant seat, which is on the floor by the sofa. Antonia's fists are closed and her arms and legs make jerky movements. As each of the other children arrive, they smile and "talk" to her, with the caregiver watching close by. Antonia looks at each child, and after a few minutes she starts to whimper, then cry. Bill, the caregiver, picks her up and says, "Are you getting sleepy? Do you want a nap?" Bill takes Antonia into the bedroom and puts her in her crib, where she promptly falls asleep (Figure 10–1).

MATERIALS

Materials used with infants of this age must be both challenging and safe. Every object infants can grasp and lift will go into their mouths. *Before* you allow an infant to touch a toy, determine whether it is safe. Each toy should meet *all* the following criteria:

1. It is too big to swallow (use a choke tube to measure objects; see Chapter 8).
2. It has no sharp points or edges to cut the skin or eyes.
3. It can be cleaned.
4. It has no movable parts that can pinch.
5. Painted surfaces have nontoxic paint.
6. It is sturdy enough to withstand biting, banging, and throwing.

To be challenging for the young infant, each material should do the following:

1. It should catch the infant's attention so the infant will want to interact with it in some way, such as reaching, pushing, grasping, tasting, or turning, and being able to practice these movements over and over again.

2. It should be movable enough to allow the infant to successfully manipulate the object and respond to it with arms, legs, hands, eyes, ears, or mouth.
3. It should be usable at several levels of complexity, so that the infant can use it with progressively more skill.

Look for toys and materials that the infant can use in several different ways. These provide greater opportunities for the infant to practice and develop new skills. Change the toys often so they seem new and interesting.

Types of Materials

Small toys to grasp   Mirrors
Mobiles   Sound toys
Rattles   Pictures, designs
Yarn or texture balls   Crib gym

Examples of Homemade Materials

Materials may be homemade or commercially made. Following are suggestions for making some of your own materials.

CRIB GYM

Tie a sturdy cotton rope between two sides of the crib. Tie on three different objects (these can be changed regularly) so they hang just at the end of the infant's reach. Poke a small hole in the bottom of a small colored plastic margarine tub; thread and knot it on one rope. It will swing when the infant hits it. CAUTION: The crib gym should be removed from the crib as soon as a child grabs the items and tries to pull herself up.

RATTLES

Film canister (plastic or metal): Put in one teaspoon uncooked cereal. Replace the cap and tape it on with colored tape.

Plastic measuring spoons: Tie together on a circle of strong yarn.

YARN BALLS

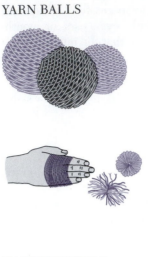

Roll up balls of washable yarn. Tuck the loose end inside. Make the balls different sizes and different colors.

Wrap yarn around the palm of your hand until you have a thick mitt. Carefully slide it off your hand and tie a short piece of yarn tightly around the middle of the "mitt." Cut the ends apart. Pull the loose ends around to shape a pom-pom.

FABRIC TWIRLS

Cut out the center of a lid from a margarine tub. Cut carefully, leaving a clean, smooth edge. Use the remaining rim ring. Sew on three strips of printed washable fabric 3 inches long by 2 inches wide. Hang from the crib gym or put on the infant's wrist.

DESIGNS

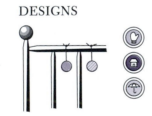

Cut faces, wallpaper, pictures, and contrasting colored fabric to fit inside the lids of margarine or yogurt tubs. Glue one piece in each lid. Hang some from the sides of the crib or give several to the infant to play with.

CAREGIVER STRATEGIES TO ENHANCE DEVELOPMENT

Developmental Profile

Perhaps the single most difficult task of caregiving is assessing the developmental strengths and weaknesses of children. References, scales, and a step-by-step format, such as the Prescriptions in Appendix A, give only general guidelines to milestones and expectations. The caregiver still must make estimates based on observations of behavior, past experience, cultural mores, and comparisons with other children. Further, judgments of what is considered *average*, *normal*, or *appropriate* differ depending on the age of the child. For example, a three-month-old who is two months below age level in a skill may have a significant deficit, whereas a 30-month-old who is two months below expectations is probably within normal limits.

Because of the difficulties inherent in assessing what is expected of young children, some authorities advise caregivers not to assess children at all! Avoiding assessment is not only impossible but also results in care and education without any clear goals. The best approach, then, is to formally observe children often and make frequent adjustments in activities according to their progress in development, while honoring the uniqueness of each child.

Have a look at the Developmental Profile for 10-week-old Antonia in Figure 10–2, and be careful not to view it as a test result or diagnosis. Developmental Profiles are pictures of skill *estimates* and *trends* and should be used to help direct activities in major areas of skill development.

Antonia is a healthy and normal 10-week-old who was observed over a five-day period using the Child Behaviors in each of the four major areas from the Developmental Prescriptions, birth to four months. The Profile shows that her skills fall within expected ranges, with her lowest skill estimate being eight weeks and the highest estimates being 14 weeks.

In area I, the physical area, Antonia exhibits 100 percent of the reflexes, successfully demonstrates 75 percent of muscle control behaviors, and functions as expected in eating, sleeping, and elimination. She is estimated to be a little above age in muscle control (12 weeks) because her muscle control is more like that of a three-month-old than of a two-and-a-half-month-old.

Within the emotional area (II), Antonia exhibits 100 percent of "types of feelings" and 75 percent of "control of feelings" (she doesn't increase sounds with conversations yet). Displaying all types of feelings is more like a 14-week-old, and not increasing sounds with conversation is more like an eight-week-old.

Within the social area (III), Antonia has a little difficulty with attachment to her caregiver, but is very aware of herself and others for her age. Because she has a little trouble with attachment, Antonia is estimated to be a little below expectations in that area (8 weeks), but is above expectancy in awareness of self and others (11 and 12 weeks).

Antonia demonstrates skills in the cognitive and language area (IV) that are expected for her age. She functions in "sensory levels 1 and 2" and "permanence" as expected for her age of 10 weeks.

One strategy Antonia's caregiver can utilize in interacting with her is to take cues from the baby's movements and imitate her simple behaviors. Adults naturally do this with facial expressions but seldom with shoulders, arms, hands, or fingers. For example, when the baby flares her fingers, do the same with your own fingers. Then watch the baby carefully for evidence of even the crudest attempt to make the movement again. Encourage her effort to join the imitation game verbally and nonverbally. Even though she may not understand your actual words, she will certainly get your message—that you are pleased to see her mastering the world around her (Acredolo & Goodwin, 2000). Attunement is important in infant development. The child should set the pace and the caregiver should match it, paying close attention to the child's nonverbal cues to ensure that you are not expecting the child to do something he is not ready to do.

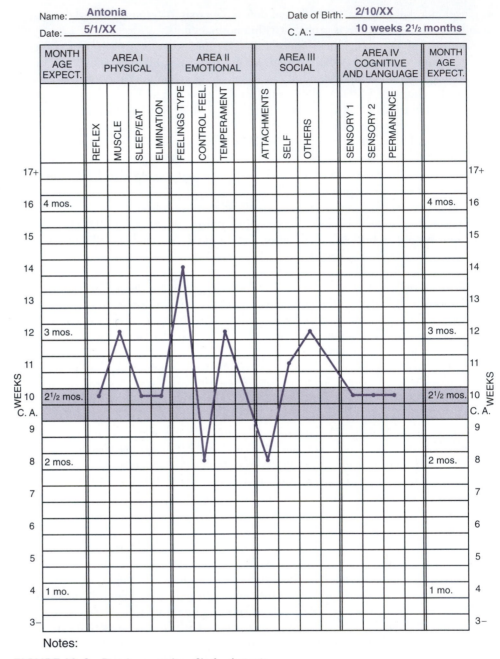

FIGURE 10–2 Developmental profile for Antonia.

Using the Developmental Profile and the materials and caregiver strategies listed below, early childhood educators should focus on those tasks and activities that are less developed, while maintaining activities in all other skills. In this way, the caregiver encourages balanced development in all areas important to an infant's growth.

Physical Development

Infants from birth to four months of age show a very rapid rate of physical development, which varies widely from infant to infant. One baby may turn from stomach to back early and another may reach for objects early and turn over late. Starting at birth with reflexive movements, infants rapidly gain an increasing level of **muscular control** over much of their bodies. In general, development moves from the simple to the more complex movements.

The control begins with their heads and necks and continues to their shoulders, backs, waists, and legs. For example, they first lift their heads up before they have the muscular control to sit, and they sit before they can use their legs for standing.

Muscular control also develops from mid-body out to the hands and feet. Gradually infants are able to control to some degree their arm and leg movements, before they develop control of their hands, and to control their hands before they can grasp or pick up things with their fingers.

Infants also increase their ability to notice differences and experience their world through seeing, hearing, touching, smelling, and tasting (Figure 10–3). While these perceptual senses are listed in the Prescription in Appendix A as part of the Physical area, they also influence cognitive development (see Chapter 3).

Movements

Newborns' movements are reflexive; they occur without the infants' control or direction. Through growth and learning infants begin to control their movements.

FIGURE 10–3   When an infant brings an object to his mouth, he is exploring the world around him.

In the first few months infants learn to perform many movements well but they have not yet coordinated them. Bruner (1968) observed, recorded, and analyzed infant behavior. He found that infants learn to control their sucking in the first month of life and that sucking is used for relieving distress, holding attention, and exploration as well as for feeding. Infants may require being held more than older children, which is why it is important to hold a baby while feeding instead of simply propping up a bottle.

Reflexive hand and arm movements develop into a grasping-groping action, which can be independent of vision. Within the first four months "this slow reaching has the mouth as its inevitable terminus. There is an invariant sequence: activation, reach, capture, retrieval to the mouth, and mouthing" (Bruner, 1968, p. 38). In the next year these hand and arm movements will become directed voluntary activity, which may be visually controlled.

Stability

The newborn's head moves reflexively from side to side. When upright, the neck cannot yet support the head. Within the first month infants can lift their heads when lying on their stomachs. By the third month they are using their arms to push against the floor or bed to raise their heads and chests.

During these first three months infants are also busy with their legs. The legs have been kicking and pushing in the air and against anything within range. Infants roll and kick their legs from side to side. Their upper and lower back muscles are developing so that one day when they kick and roll to one side, they keep going right onto their backs or their stomachs. The baby has rolled over!

Many caregiving strategies at this time involve providing appropriate space so infants can move as they want to. Of course, the caregiver does not tell the infants to arch their backs, kick their legs, or wave their arms wildly. Infants do this naturally. The caregiver facilitates infant movement by making sure their clothes do not limit movement, by providing a circle of safety, and by offering the infant materials and toys that are safe and appropriate.

Sleep

Most newborns sleep between 14 and 17 hours a day. There will be times when they are actually awake, though their eyes are closed, and they will respond to stimulation. Newborns are relatively light sleepers, and deep sleep periods are only about 20 minutes long. The longest sleep period is usually four or five hours.

Marisol is sleeping for three to four hour stretches, befitting her age. She wakes at 11:30 a.m. from her morning nap each day. Bernice has recorded Marisol's sleep patterns and begins her caregiving for Marisol at 11:15 by preparing a bottle of formula and cleaning/arranging the changing table with her supplies. Bernice wants to be prepared so that the time to meet the infant's routine care needs is efficient and allows plenty of time for talking and singing. When Marisol stirs, Bernice greets her verbally but does not pick her up, to give her time to fully wake up. Due to Bernice's timing strategy, the process of changing and feeding proceeds without a hitch and she is able to engage meaningfully with her.

Infants' living patterns usually take on regularity in the first months of life. The infant who establishes a regular, though slowly changing, schedule for eating and sleeping creates a predictable world into which the caregiver can easily fit. Infants whose feeding and sleeping times remain erratic create stress for themselves and their caregivers. Gradually gaining stability in the sleep-wake cycle is not only important for growth and physical development but also social development (Feldman, 2006). Infants who are more consistent in their sleep-wake cycles were associated with greater mother-infant synchrony at three months of age. When analyzed separately, high-risk premature infants displayed disorganized biological rhythms, lower thresholds for demonstrating negative emotions, and lower levels of mother-infant synchrony (Feldman, 2006). With increases in infants born prematurely, teachers and parents must find ways to assist the infants with organizing their sleep-wake patterns.

Suggestions for Implementing Curriculum

Physical development can be encouraged by providing opportunities for physical activity, changing the baby's position, and motivating movement without instilling "pressure to perform" (Eisenberg, Murkoff, & Hathaway, 1989).

The caregiver can employ several strategies to enhance the infant's muscular control.

1. Place infants in positions where they can practice developing muscular control. For example, when you lay them on their stomachs, they can keep trying to lift their heads, shoulders, and trunks. Never place infants on their stomachs to sleep.
2. Until infants can roll over, sit up, and stand by themselves, they will need to be moved into those different positions several times each day during their waking hours.
3. Interact with the infant in order to stimulate her. Grasp the infant's hands and slowly lift the child upright. Hold your hands in different places so the infant will look around and reach for you. Gently snap your fingers behind, beside, and in front of the infant and watch the child turn her head to locate the sound.
4. Use toys and materials to play with the infant; offer some for the infant to use independently.

Place objects within the vision and reach of the infant. Select toys the infant can grasp. First there is a gross, grabbing movement. Later the infant is able to use a more refined finger-thumb or pincer grasp.

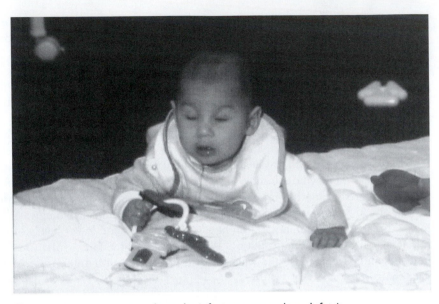

The caregiver moves a toy where the infant can see and reach for it.

SUGGESTIONS FOR IMPLEMENTING CURRICULUM—PHYSICAL DEVELOPMENT

CHILD BEHAVIOR	MATERIALS	EXAMPLES OF CAREGIVER STRATEGIES
Reflex		
Grasp reflex (hand closes)	finger, rattle	Lift infant's body slightly. Place object in palm of infant's hand.
Startle reflex	mirror, mobile	Touch, hold infant to calm him.
Tonic neck reflex (head facing one side or other, not facing up)	toys, designs	Place objects at side of crib, not above middle of crib.
Muscular Control (develops from head to feet)		
HEAD AND NECK		
Turns head	stuffed toy	Place infant on back or stomach. Place toy to one side.
Holds head upright with support		Support infant's head when holding infant upright.
Lifts head slightly when on stomach		Place infant on stomach.
Holds head to sides and middle		Place infant on stomach.
Holds up head when on back and on stomach		Place infant on stomach or back.
Holds head without support		Set and hold infant upright.

CHILD BEHAVIOR	MATERIALS	EXAMPLES OF CAREGIVER STRATEGIES
TRUNK		
Holds up chest		Place infant on stomach.
Sits with support; may attempt to raise self; may fuss if left lying down with little chance to sit up		Place infant in sitting position. Support head and back with arm or pillow. Lengthen sitting time as infant is able.
Holds up chest and shoulders		Place infant on stomach.
LEG		
Rolls from stomach to back		Place infant on flat surface where infant cannot roll off.
Muscular Control		
(develops from mid-body to limbs)		
ARM		
Moves randomly	toys	Place objects within reach of infant.
Reaches	bright toys that make noise	Place objects slightly beyond reach of infant; give to infant when child reaches for it.
HAND		
Opens and closes	toys with handles that fit in fist	Place handle in fist; help infant close fist around object.
Keeps hands open		
Plays with hands	colorful plastic bracelet	Place colorful, safe objects that attract infant's attention on infant's hands, fingers.
Uses hand to grasp object, whole hand and fingers against thumb	toys with bumps to hold on to	Place object within reach of infant.
Thumb and forefinger	toys that can be grasped with one hand	Place object within reach of infant.
Holds and moves object	toys that can be pushed, pulled, or lifted with hands; toys that make noise	Place toy on flat surface free from obstructions.
EYE-HAND COORDINATION		
Moves arm toward object; may miss it	toy, bottle	Place within reach of infant.
Reaches hand to object; may grab or miss it	toy, bottle	Place within reach of infant.

SIGHT. The teacher can use several strategies to enhance the infant's seeing.

1. Place the infant or objects at the correct distance so the infant can focus to see people or objects. The newborn focuses at about 8 to 14 inches. When infants are about four months old, they can adjust focal distance as adults do. The caregiver can place materials that attract the infant's attention at the proper focusing distance.
2. Select eye-catching materials. Contrasts seem to interest infants: designs, patterns, shapes, colors. Faces also attract their attention.

SUGGESTIONS FOR IMPLEMENTING CURRICULUM—SIGHT DEVELOPMENT

CHILD BEHAVIOR	MATERIALS	EXAMPLES OF CAREGIVER STRATEGIES
Seeing		
Focuses two inches from eyes	mirror, mobile, toys, pictures, designs (e.g., patterns, faces)	Place object eight inches from infant's face.
Follows with eyes	mobile, toys, hand	Move object slowly after infant focuses on object.
Sees objects beyond eight inches	people, pictures, toys	Attract attention by shape, color, movement.
Looks from object to object	toys, mobile, designs, pictures	Provide two or more objects of interest to infant.
Looks around; stops to focus on object that has caught attention, then looks at something else; continual visual searching		Provide eye-catching items in room: faces, patterned designs, contrasting colors in objects, and pictures.

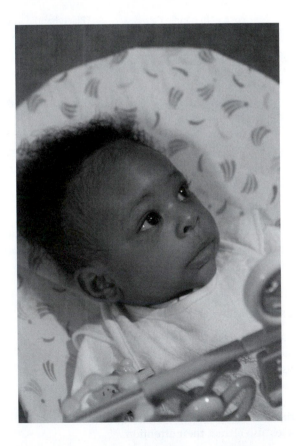

The caregiver talks and listens to the infant.

SLEEP. The caregiver can use several strategies to enhance the infant's sleep. Antici-pate when the infant probably will take a nap. Plan a very calming time and activities for the infant just before nap time so the infant can get in the mood to sleep. Sitting with the infant in a rocking chair and humming a lullaby often proves very effective.

SUGGESTIONS FOR IMPLEMENTING CURRICULUM—SLEEP DEVELOPMENT

CHILD BEHAVIOR	MATERIALS	EXAMPLES OF CAREGIVER STRATEGIES
Sleeping		
Sleeps much of the day and night	flat, firm mattress	Provide restful environment and moderate temperature, free from sudden loud noises.
Takes a long morning nap and a long afternoon nap		Adjust routines to fit infant's changing sleep schedule.
May have irregular sleep habits		Shorten or lengthen activities with infant to assist in establishing some pattern for sleeping.

EATING. The caregiver can use several strategies to enhance the infant's eating. Parents and pediatricians determine what and how much infants are fed during their first four months. The caregiver is responsible for making eating a happy, successful time for the infant. Organize your time so you can hold each infant when bottle-feeding. Eye focusing, eye-hand coordination, as well as emotional bonding, language, and communication all occur while holding the infant for feeding.

SUGGESTIONS FOR IMPLEMENTING CURRICULUM—EATING DEVELOPMENT

CHILD BEHAVIOR	MATERIALS	EXAMPLES OF CAREGIVER STRATEGIES
Eating		
Takes bottle on demand	formula and bottle	Determine formula with parent. Determine schedule with parent. Hold infant when bottle-feeding. Tilt bottle so milk fills the nipple to prevent infant's swallowing excess air. Burp the infant. Put infant straw in bottle.

ELIMINATION. The caregiver can use several strategies for **elimination** of waste. Two important caregiver responsibilities are to change the infant's diaper frequently and to record the time and any abnormalities of bowel movements. Eating schedules affect the time infants have bowel movements. As they establish eating schedules, some infants develop predictable elimination patterns. Cleanliness is critical for the infant and the caregiver.

The infant's bowel movements reflect the child's health. Ask the parent what color, texture, and frequency are normal for the infant. Record the frequency daily. Record any differences in color and texture and inform the parent.

SUGGESTIONS FOR IMPLEMENTING CURRICULUM—ELIMINATION DEVELOPMENT

CHILD BEHAVIOR	MATERIALS	EXAMPLES OF CAREGIVER STRATEGIES
Elimination		
Begins to establish predictable eating and elimination schedules	diapers, cleansing supplies	See Chapter 9 for diapering guidelines.
Establishes regular time for bowel movement		Record time of bowel movement. Note changes in times of bowel movements.
May have diarrhea or constipation (either problem calls for attention)		Record type of bowel movement. Record changes in type of bowel movement. Discuss with parent. If diarrhea, notify parent immediately. Do not wait until the end of the day; the baby can dehydrate rapidly and may need medical care.

Emotional Development

During the first months of life infants develop their basic feelings of security. There seems to be little "catch-up" time for emotional security. If the infant does not develop these feelings of security now, it is difficult to develop them as adequately later. Along with the parents, the caregiver plays a key role in providing the kinds of relationships and experiences that enable the infant to develop this basic security.

Feelings of security and trust develop out of relations with others, not by infants on their own. Infants develop these feelings from the way other people treat them. Parents and the primary caregiver are probably the most influential people in the lives of young infants in child care. Therefore, the caregiver is very directly responsible and involved in helping the infant feel secure.

Two caregiver behaviors of special importance are responding immediately to the infant's distress signals and responding unfailingly to the infant's signals of stress, need, or pleasure.

Temperament, or the infant's basic style of behavior, gradually emerges in the first four months. Some styles are easily recognized, whereas others may be more difficult to observe.

The activity level of infants is obvious. They may kick and wriggle and squirm a great deal or they may lie quietly while either asleep or awake. Highly active infants may kick their covers off consistently and get tangled in their clothes. Their bodies get plenty of activity. They may need to be checked frequently to be sure they can move freely. A blanket may be more of a bother than it is worth, since it seldom covers the infant. Infant suits or long smocks and socks may keep the active infant just as warm. Very quiet infants may seem easy to care for. They seldom kick off their covers or need their clothes adjusted. They may, however, need to be picked up and moved around to stimulate their physical movement.

Differing levels of **sensory threshold** are apparent in young infants. One infant will awaken when a light is turned on or a person steps into the room. Another infant will sleep in a brightly lit room with the CD player on. When several children are in one room, special adjustments must be made for the sleeping infant who reacts negatively to light and sound.

Infants characteristically use differing levels of energy when responding to stimuli. One infant will cry loudly whenever she cries. Another infant will whimper and fuss and occasionally cry more loudly when very distressed. The caregiver, when responding to the infant's cries, will need to learn cues other than loudness to determine the type and severity of stress. The caregiver may need to check infants who fuss and cry quietly to make sure their needs are being met. While the link between temperament and attachment security is still empirically debated, Marshall & Fox (2005) found that infants who showed high levels of negative affect in response to stimulation at 4 months were more likely to be classified with an insecure attachment at 14 months than were infants who scored low on affective reactivity.

The caregiver can use several strategies to enhance the infant's emotional development. Whereas physical development can be enhanced by moving the infant, toys, and oneself around, emotional development demands more than manipulation, it requires consistent interactions. When relating to the infant, the three As—Attention, Approval, and Attunement—play a most crucial part in the daily emotional development of the child (Figure 10–4). The following strategies

FIGURE 10–4   Gentle touching and cuddling comforts the infant.

will help the caregiver to be conscious of the three As while performing tasks such as diapering and feeding:

- Use your relationship with the child.
- Focus your attention on the child's needs.
- Engage the child—make eye-to-eye contact.
- Move slowly and with intention.
- Make meaningful physical contact.
- Actively listen to his or her whole body message.
- Reflect vocal expressions and sounds back to him or her.
- Try to sense how the child is feeling—is the child excited, happy, frustrated?
- Try to judge the amount of stimulation the child prefers.
- Try to get in rhythm with the child. Let him or her lead you vocally.
- Talk and sing, hum and smile.
- Place the child where he or she can observe room activity.
- Involve the child in activity.
- When leaving the infant, tell him or her where you'll be in the room if he or she needs you.

SUGGESTIONS FOR IMPLEMENTING CURRICULUM—EMOTIONAL DEVELOPMENT

CHILD BEHAVIOR	MATERIALS	EXAMPLES OF CAREGIVER STRATEGIES
Types of Emotions-Feelings		
Shows excitement	attention-catching objects	Use voice and facial expression to mirror excitement.
Shows stress	calming touch, talk, music, singing, ruing	Determine cause. Change situation to reduce stress, e.g., change diaper, change position, talk to infant (child may be bored).
Shows enjoyment	Interesting, challenging toys, objects	Provide pleasant experiences, e.g., give infant a bath, snuggle, converse, smile.
Shows anger or frustration		Determine cause. Remove or reduce cause. Divert infant's attention, e.g., turn infant around to look at something else.
Shows fear		Hold, comfort infant. Remove fear-producing object or change situation, e.g., hold infant startled by sudden loud noise.
Protests		Determine what infant is protesting about. Eliminate activity or do it a different way, e.g., change how you wash infant's face. If behavior continues, ask another caregiver to take child for you.
Control of Emotions-Feelings (seems to occur automatically)		
Decreases crying	activities, toys that catch infant's attention and that infant likes	Involve infant in an activity.

CHILD BEHAVIOR	MATERIALS	EXAMPLES OF CAREGIVER STRATEGIES
Increases sounds (talking)		Initiate "conversations" and respond to infant's talking.
Reflects feelings in sounds		Respond to the feelings expressed, e.g., comfort (by talking) a whining child, change situation.
Comforted by holding		Consistently hold, caress, cuddle, and comfort when infant needs it.
Temperament		
Observe the nine behavior categories (see Table 3–1 in Chapter 3)		List adjustments you need to make to result in better "goodness of fit."

Social Development

The caregiver must become emotionally involved with infants in order to provide for their social needs. According to **attachment theory**, just as infants develop a unique attachment to their mothers, they can develop an additional attachment to their primary caregivers in child care settings. Thus, many of the caregiver strategies previously discussed for building emotional relationships between infants and teachers involve frequent use of looking and touching, which serve a dual function of supporting attachment.

Attachment theory and research have identified phases in the development of attachment. Ainsworth (1982) identified infants' social behaviors during the first few months of life that relate to developing attachment.

Phase 1: Undiscriminating Social Responsiveness (first two to three months)

- orienting behaviors: visual fixation, visual tracking, listening, rooting, postural adjustment when held
- sucking and grasping to gain or maintain contact
- signaling behaviors: smiling, crying, and other vocalizations to bring caregiver into proximity or contact

Infants from birth to four months are egocentric; they have only their point of view. They use their senses to begin to develop a global concept of self. They need to see, hear, smell, touch, and taste for themselves. People and objects are familiar insofar as they interact with the infant's sense experiences. For infants at this level people and objects do not exist as separate objects.

Herr & Swim (2002) suggests that the most important plaything for infants is a responsive caregiver. The caregiver can use several strategies to enhance the social development of infants of this age. The caregiver can respond quickly to the infant's needs and can initiate interactions by looking, holding, stroking, talking, playing, carrying, and rocking the infant. While interacting, teachers should remember to use positive communication skills such as active listening and mirroring. In fact, the positive outcomes for mirroring have been established through research. High-affect-mirroring mothers were associated with infants (2- to 3-month olds) who ranked high on prosocial behavior and social expectancy—responded more frequently with smiles, vocalizations, and gazes (Legerstee & Varghese, 2001).

CHILD BEHAVIOR	MATERIALS	EXAMPLES OF CAREGIVER STRATEGIES
Attachment		
Shows special closeness to parent; differentiates response to parent—voice, touch, presence, absence		Accept that the infant will respond differently to you than to parent. Closely observe the parent-infant interaction and then model some of the caregiving behaviors, sounds, and other characteristics of the parent.
Develops familiarity with one primary caregiver (significant other)		Same caregiver provides most of infant's care, although other caregivers may share responsibility occasionally.
Needs security		Provide consistent care of infant: feed; comfort; change diapers and clothes; talk, sing, and play with infant; rock and hold; put to bed; pick up when awake; respond to infant's special needs, likes, and dislikes. Touch, hold, caress, and cuddle the infant.
Self		
Becomes aware of hands	bright clothes, materials for hands, feet; bare feet sometimes	Provide clothes that allow freedom of movement. Occasionally put bright colors or dots on hands and feet to attract infant's attention.
Smiles spontaneously, sometimes immediately at birth		
Smiles at self in mirror	mirror	Smile with infant.
Others		
Establishes eye contact with another person		Hold infant so the caregiver is in infant's range of vision. Engage infant in eye contact.
Recognizes voice of parent		
Smiles at people (social smile)		Hold infant. Smile, talk with infant.
Watches people		Place infant where you can be seen moving about. Carry infant around to see others.
Talks (coos) to people		Respond and initiate talking, singing with infant.
Shows longer attentiveness when involved with people		Spend time during infant's alert times interacting with infant.
Recognizes parent visually		
Recognizes individual people		Provide daily care, interactions with a few persons other than parent.
Behaves differently with parent than with others		Accept different responses.
Interacts with people		Initiate interactions, respond; place or carry infant where infant can meet people.
Laughs		Play with infant, laugh with infant, respond to infant's laugh.
Differentiates self from parent		
Initiates talking to others		Answer infant's talk.
Plays with toys	toys that attract and challenge infant	Provide toys; change toys to renew interest.

Cognitive and Language Development

Cognitive Development

Early childhood educators provide for the care *and* education of very young children. What we do matters immensely to the developing child, especially when considering brain development. Neuropsychologist Jane Healy discusses brain development of an infant in her book *Your Child's Growing Mind* (2004).

> Amazingly, although the number of cells actually decreases, brain weight can double during the first year of life. As neurons respond to stimuli seen, heard, felt or tasted, they fire off messages that build new physical connections to neighboring cells, linking them into efficient relay systems. . . . During the first six months after birth, they become extremely active as sensory messages bombard the infant brain, which must learn to receive them and then pass them from one area to another. . . . Synaptic connections are strengthened by repeated use; if they fail to connect, they die off. . . . Every response to sights, sounds, feelings, smells, and tastes make more connections. (pp. 17–20)

This means that caregivers take every opportunity to teach, knowing that to increase an infant's stimulation is to increase ultimate human intelligence.

Piaget's theory of **cognitive development** categorizes the first four months of life as a part of the sensorimotor stage. Infants get information in this stage through their senses and motor activity. Infants use all their senses. With experience they refine their capacities for seeing, hearing, smelling, tasting, and touching. Moving themselves, moving others, and handling objects become coordinated with their senses. For example, when hearing a sound, infants turn their heads in the direction of the sound.

> Sensorimotor intelligence is primarily focused on action, not on classification and organization . . . the knowledge that young infants have of objects is in terms of the sensorimotor impressions the objects leave on them and the sensory and motor adjustments the objects require. For young infants objects do not have an existence independent of their reactions to them. (Anisfeld, 1984, p. 15)

The **sensorimotor stage** has been divided into six substages; the first two are evident in the first four months. In each stage the infant develops new behaviors.

In Stage 1 the newborn's behavior is reflexive. Infants quickly start to change their behavior from passive reactions to active searching. Each of the senses operates independently.

During Stage 2 infants begin to coordinate their senses. They begin to develop hand-mouth coordination, eye coordination, and eye-ear coordination. One behavior can stimulate another; for example, a reflexively waving arm may attract the infant's attention so that the child visually focuses on his own hand.

Newborns spend a great deal of time looking at the human face and demonstrate preferences for looking at faces which are upright with a straight head (Farroni, Menon, & Johnson, 2006). Infants also show a preference for looking at female faces (Ramsey, Langlois, & Marti, 2005). While the authors believe that their results have implications for how infants learn about males and females, teachers should make a habit of supporting fathers' interactions with their newborns, infants, and toddlers as these are equally important to the mental health (e.g., socio-emotional development) of very young children (see, for example, Collins, Mascia, Kendall, Golden, Schock, & Parlakian, 2003; Susman-Stillman, Appleyard, & Siebenbruner, 2003).

The caregiver uses several strategies to enhance cognitive development. Selecting items for and arranging an attention-catching environment stimulates the infant to respond in any way possible at his or her particular stage. Repeating and reinforcing the infant's behaviors pleases and stimulates the infant.

SUGGESTIONS FOR IMPLEMENTING CURRICULUM—COGNITIVE DEVELOPMENT

CHILD BEHAVIOR	MATERIALS	EXAMPLES OF CAREGIVER STRATEGIES
Piaget's Stages of Sensorimotor Development		
STAGE 1 (*Reflex*)		
Carries out reflexive actions— sucking, eye movements, hand and body movements		Provide nonrestricting clothes, uncluttered crib, which allow freedom of movement.
Moves from passive to active search	visually attractive crib, walls next to crib, objects; occasional music, singing, talking, chimes	Provide environment that commands attention during infant's period of alertness.
STAGE 2 (*Differentiation*)		
Makes small, gradual changes that come from repetition		Provide change for infant; carry infant around, hold infant, place infant in crib. Observe, discuss, record changes.
Coordinates behaviors, e.g., a sound stimulates looking	face and voice, musical toy, musical mobile, rattle	Turn on musical toy; place where infant can see it.
Puts hand, object in mouth and sucks on it	objects infant can grasp and are safe to go in mouth	Place objects in hand or within reach. Infants attempt to put *everything* in their mouths. Make sure they get only safe objects.
Moves hand, object to where it is visible	objects which infant can grasp and lift	Provide clothes that allow freedom of movement. Place objects in hand or within reach.
Produces a pleasurable motor activity and repeats activity		Provide time, space for repetition.
Piaget's Concept of Object Permanence[a]		
SENSORIMOTOR STAGES 1 AND 2		
Follows moving objects with eyes until object disappears; looks where object has disappeared; loses interest and turns away; does not search for it	toys and objects that attract visual attention	Place object in range of infant's vision. Allow time for infant to focus on object. Move object slowly back and forth within child's field of vision. Move object where infant cannot see it, e.g., roll ball behind infant.

[a]Object permanence means knowing that an object or person exists even when out of sight or touch.

Language Development

Language is a tool used to communicate with oneself and with others. Crying is one way infants communicate with others. Even newborns cry in different ways, depending on whether they are startled or uncomfortable.

"Prelinguistic vocalizations contribute to the infant's developing ability to speak. In the first eight weeks vocalizations are of two kinds: One category consists of vegetative sounds and includes burping, swallowing, spitting up, and the like. The other category consists of discomfort sounds and includes reflexive crying and fussing" (Anisfeld, 1984, p. 221). Infants produce sounds as they use their mouths and throats. These sounds are the infants' "talk." At first they seem unaware of their sounds, and then gradually they begin to repeat their own sounds. Infants talk to themselves for the pleasure of making the sounds and hearing themselves talk.

Infants use several kinds of sounds as part of their language. They produce sounds as they eat and as they play with their tongues and mouths. They use their throats, saliva, tongues, mouths, and lips to produce gurgling, squealing, smacking, and spitting noises. Gradually they produce repetitive, vowel-like sounds that can be classified as **cooing**. A second stage of vocalization occurs between nine and 20 weeks. "It is characterized by cooing and laughter; sustained laughter occurs at 16 weeks" (Anisfeld, 1984, p. 222).

When infants hear someone talk to them, it stimulates them to talk (see the parental selection hypothesis in Locke, 2006). This dialogue is very important. Effective dialogue can occur when the caregiver looks at the infant while alternately listening to and answering the child's talk. The one-to-one dialogue is what stimulates the infant to engage in more positive vocalizing at later ages (Henning, Striano, & Lieven, 2005). Talking that is not directed to the infant personally is not as effective a stimulator. Adults conversing with each other in the presence of the child, or playing a radio or television broadcast, do not involve the child in language dialogue.

SUGGESTIONS FOR IMPLEMENTING CURRICULUM. The caregiver can use several strategies to enhance the infant's language development.

1. Talk: Say words, sentences, and nursery rhymes; read stories aloud and show the baby pictures of different faces and designs.
2. Sing: Hum; sing words set to your own music, nursery rhymes, lullabies, and songs; play African drums or recorded bagpipe music.
3. Listen and respond: Infants will make sounds by themselves for a few months. This talk will decrease if the infants do not have someone to listen to them and to "answer" them.
4. Initiate conversation: Almost every encounter with an infant is an opportunity for conversation. Routine physical care like feeding, changing diapers, and rocking all present the necessary one-on-one situations where you and the infant are interacting. It is not necessary or helpful to talk all the time or to be quiet all the time. The infant needs times for language and conversation and times for quiet.

SUGGESTIONS FOR IMPLEMENTING CURRICULUM—LANGUAGE DEVELOPMENT

CHILD BEHAVIOR	MATERIALS	EXAMPLES OF CAREGIVER STRATEGIES
Physical Components Involved in Language Communication		
Back of throat		Observe and record infant's use of sound.
Nose		
Mouth cavity		Record repetitions, changes, and new sounds.
Front of mouth		Record mood of infant when infant is making longer repetitions of sounds.
Tongue		
Lips		
Saliva		
Actions Involved in Language Communication		
Changes air flow: through nose through mouth		
Uses tongue to manipulate air flow, saliva		
Plays with tongue: twists, turns, sticks it out, sucks on it		
Uses saliva in various places and changes sounds: gurgle in back of throat, bubbling in center of mouth, hissing, spitting with partially closed lips and tongue		
Initiating-Responding		
	rattle, objects that make sounds or noises, music box, music, talking, singing	Talk, sing to infant while feeding, changing diapers and clothes, holding, carrying around, rocking. Carry on normal conversation with infant—talking, listening, silence.
Initiates making sounds		"Answer" infant with sounds or words.
Responds vocally to another person		Hold infant: look at infant eye to eye; make sounds, talk, sing to infant; listen to infant's response; talk, sing again; listen, and so on.
Makes sound, repeats sound, continues practicing sound a few minutes and lengthening to longer blocks of time		Talk with infant, show interest, look at infant.
Imitates sounds already known		Repeat sound infant has just made; listen to infant make sound; repeat it again; and so on.
Experiments with sounds		

CHILD BEHAVIOR	MATERIALS	EXAMPLES OF CAREGIVER STRATEGIES
Crying		
Cries apparently automatically, in distress and frustration		Rue with the infant. Respond to infant's crying immediately and consistently.
Cries differently to express hunger, discomfort, anger		Attend to the need infant expressed by crying.
Cries to gain attention		Find out what infant wants.
Cries less as vocalizing increases		
Cooing		
Repetitive vowel-like sounds		Imitate, respond, and talk to infant.
Adds pitch		

■ KEY TERMS

attachment theory	elimination	sensorimotor stage
cognitive development	muscular control	sensory threshold
cooing		

CASE STUDY   Carol

Kierston is the youngest of eight children and her closest sibling is 17 years her senior. Both of her parents are first-generation immigrants. Her mother is over 45 years old, and during her pregnancy Kierston's father, who was 15 years older than her mother, suddenly died of a heart attack. Kierston was delivered by cesarean. Since her birth, her mother has cared for her only occasionally, while her siblings, aunts, and uncles provide most of her care. The grief of the family is obvious to anyone observing them. The well-meaning but numerous caregivers provide a very inconsistent parenting style for Kierston. The variety of different faces and personalities who care for Kierston may help explain her inconsistent strengths and weaknesses on the Developmental Profile.

The child care center is aiming to compensate for the lack of consistency in Kierston's environment by assigning one primary caregiver, Carol, to her. Carol will establish a very consistent daily routine around her needs and plans to handle and speak to her gently in order to enhance her sense of trust and security. Home visitations at regularly scheduled times will also benefit Kierston because the home visitor will discuss consistent rules and schedules with her various family members.

1. What effect do you think a depressed family has on the development of a four-month-old? Support your thoughts with references.

2. How will Carol implement the three As with Kierston?

3. What should be Carol's next steps if Kierston's development does *not* improve after her home life becomes more consistent?

■ QUESTIONS AND EXPERIENCES FOR REFLECTION

1. Observe one infant under four months of age. Record the infant's behavior in two five-minute sequences. Transfer the descriptions to the Developmental Profile.

2. Select toys from catalogs and newspaper ads that are said to be appropriate for an infant under four months of age. Read the toy description. Do these toys match the level of development for the infant you observed (for the first question)? Why or why not?

3. Select one category of the Developmental Profiles (for example, physical development). Observe a caregiver and classify the strategies the caregiver used from that category (for example, physical support: holds hand behind infant's head and neck).

4. List five strategies that you competently use with infants from birth to four months.

5. List strategies you need to develop and list ways you intend to develop them.

■ CHAPTER REVIEW

1. In each area state a purpose for using the Developmental Profiles with infants from birth to four months of age.

Area	Purpose
a. Physical	
b. Emotional	
c. Social	
d. Cognitive and Language	

2. Describe how you get information about the infant's developmental levels.

3. List three toys or materials that can be used with infants from birth to four months of age. List the area(s) of development that each can enhance.

Toy/Material	Area(s) of Development
a.	
b.	
c.	

4. State two reasons why it is helpful to the infant to have the caregiver talk to him or her.

■ REFERENCES

Acredolo, L. P., & Goodwyn, S. (2000). *Baby minds: Brain-building games your baby will love.* New York: Bantam Books.

Ainsworth, M. D. (1982). The development of infant-mother attachment. In J. Belsky (Ed.), *In the beginning: Readings on infancy.* New York: Columbia University Press.

Anisfeld, M. (1984). *Language development from birth to three.* Hillsdale, NJ: Lawrence Erlbaum Associates.

Bruner, J. S. (1968). *Processes of cognitive growth: Infancy.* Worcester, MA: Clark University Press.

Collins, R., Mascia, J., Kendall, R., Golden, O., Schock, L., & Parlakian, R. (2003). Promoting mental health in child care settings: Caring for the whole child. *Zero to Three, 23*(4), 39–45.

Eisenberg, A., Murkoff, H. E., & Hathaway, S. E. (1989). *What to expect the first year.* New York: Workman Publishing.

Farroni, T., Menon, E., & Johnson, M. H. (2006). Factors influencing newborns' preferences for faces with eye contact. *Journal of Experimental Child Psychology, 95*(4), 298–308.

Feldman, R. (2006). From biological rhythms to social rhythms: Physiological precursors of mother-infant synchrony. *Developmental Psychology, 42*(1), 175–188.

Healy, J. (2004). *Your child's growing mind: A guide to learning and brain development from birth to adolescence.* (3rd ed.). New York: Broadway Books.

Henning, A., Striano, T., & Lieven, E. V. M. (2005). Maternal speech to infants at 1 and 3 months of age. *Infant Behavior & Development, 28*(4), 519–536.

Herr, J., & Swim, T. J. (2002). *Creative resources for infants and toddlers* (2nd ed.). Clifton Park, NY: Thomson Delmar Learning.

Legerstee, M., & Varghese, J. (2001). The role of maternal affect mirroring on social expectancies in three-month-old infants. *Child Development, 72*(5), 1301–1313.

Locke, J. L. (2006). Parental selection of vocal behavior: Crying, cooing, babbling, and the evolution of language. *Human Nature, 17*(2), 155–168.

Marshall, P. J., & Fox, N. A. (2005). Relations between behavioral reactivity at 4 months and attachment classification at 14 months in a selected sample. *Infant Behavior & Development, 28*(4), 492–502.

Ramsey, J. L., Langlois, J. H., & Marti, N. C. (2005). Infant categorization of faces: Ladies first. *Developmental Review, 25*(2), 212–246.

Susman-Stillman, A., Appleyard, K., & Siebenbruner, J. (2003). For better or worse: An ecological perspective on parents' relationships and parent-infant interaction. *Zero to Three, 23*(3), 4–12.

■ HELPFUL WEB SITES _____

AfitTot.com. A child development capabilities timeline for the first six months. http://topcondition.com/temp/Afittot/development.htm

Beyond the Journal Archive. "Helping Babies Play," two pages of ideas for engaging infants (birth—18 months) in play, is available at http://www.journal.naeyc.org/btj/200305/HelpingBabies_Sawyers.pdf

National Child Care Information Center. Links to publications and Web sites about quality care for children. http://www.nccic.org/

The NICHD Study of Early Child Care and Youth Development. National Institute of Child Health and Human Development publication. http://www.nichd.nih.gov/publications/

Toy Industry Association. Publications for parents about toy safety are available. http://www.toy-tia.org/

For additional infant and toddler resources, visit our Web site at http://www.earlychilded.delmar.com

11

The Child from Four to Eight Months of Age

■ OBJECTIVES

After reading this chapter, you should be able to:

- Identify and record sequences of change in the physical, emotional, social, cognitive, and language development of infants from four to eight months of age.
- Select materials appropriate to the development of infants at that age level.
- Devise strategies appropriate to infants of that age level.

■ CHAPTER OUTLINE

Theresa's Story

Theresa, six months old, is lying on her stomach on the floor, kicking her legs and waving her arms. She looks at a toy radio and drools. She fingers the toy radio, chews, and drools some more. She "sings" with the music. Ellie, the caregiver, winds up the toy radio. Theresa kicks her feet and smiles. She watches the radio and kicks her feet. Ellie smiles at Theresa and Theresa smiles back. She kicks her feet rapidly. While Theresa looks at Wayne, another infant, Ellie speaks to her. Theresa tries to lift herself by pushing on the floor with her arms. She turns herself around, still on her tummy. She kicks her feet and keeps trying to lift herself up onto her knees to a crawling position. She presses her feet against furniture. During this time she has turned about 180 degrees.

MATERIALS AND ACTIVITIES

Materials for this age group must be safe for the infants to mouth and hit and bang on themselves. These infants have developed some manual skills, but their limited control of their arm and hand muscles causes them to be rather rough on their toys and themselves. Attention-catching toys stimulate the interest of these infants and lengthen their playtime.

Types of Materials

foam toys

small toys and objects to grasp

soft balls

sound toys

toys safe to throw

toys safe to bang and hit

low material and equipment to climb
    on and over

mirror

teething toys

Examples of Homemade Materials

BLOCKS

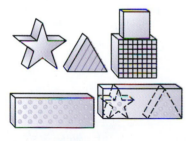

Cut foam rubber into squares, circles, rectangles, triangles, and other shapes. Cover the foam with printed fabric sewn to fit the shapes. Large shapes can be stacked as blocks.

Cut 1-inch-thick sponges into shapes. Make sure the finished pieces are a good size to handle but too big to swallow.

Cover foam ball with washable pattern fabric.

CRIB GYM

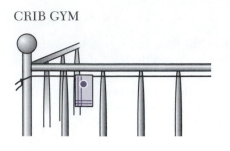

Tie a colorful 3-inch-wide strip of fabric in between the slats. Make individual cloth toys that will move when the infant pulls the ties. CAUTION: The crib gym should be removed from the crib as soon as a child grabs the items and tries to pull herself up.

RATTLES

Empty and wash childproof clear plastic medicine bottles. Put in uncooked cereal— one teaspoon white, one teaspoon red (dyed in food coloring). Use sturdy glue to fasten cap tightly.

MUSIC, SOUND TOYS

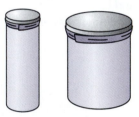

Use empty cardboard cans with lids (e.g., from oatmeal). Put jingle bells or loose items like blocks inside. Glue the lid on securely and tape around the edges. When the infant pushes and rolls it, the bells or blocks will make a noise.

FOIL PIE PANS

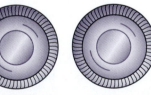

Place disposable pie pans near the infant to use for a mirror, for grasping, and for banging. Check frequently. If a sharp edge or tear develops, discard.

BEANBAG

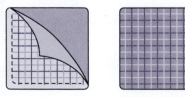

Sew together along three sides two double layers of 3-inch-square colorful terry cloth. Turn right side out. Fill the pouch half full with aquarium rocks that have been boiled to sanitize them. Sew the fourth side shut.

BRACELET

Sew a 4-inch length of elastic together to make a circle. Sew on several yarn pom-poms. Place on wrist or ankle for infant to watch while waving arms and kicking feet.

SOCK DOLL

Use a child's sock. Make eyes, nose, and mouth with permanent nontoxic marker or sew features with embroidery thread. Sew on short yarn hair. Stuff with foam or nylon scraps. Sew closed at bottom (top of sock). Caution: Make sure the "hair" is secured and cannot be pulled out.

CAREGIVER STRATEGIES TO ENHANCE DEVELOPMENT

Developmental Profile

Please refer to the Developmental Profile in Figure 11–1 for Theresa Y., a healthy infant with a chronological age (C. A.) of six months. Theresa was observed over a two-week period and estimates were made of her skill development in the Child Behaviors from the Prescriptions in Appendix A. The profile indicates her lowest development area as teeth (five months) and her highest as attachment and visual-motor control (eight months).

Specifically, Theresa can perform behaviors in Area I (Physical) under Muscular Control that are indicative of an eight-month-old, such as sitting unsupported for short times and pulling herself to a standing position. Because two upper teeth and two lower teeth are not through her gums yet, she is estimated at the five-month rather than the six-month level in that area. Theresa was estimated to be a little above C. A. (seven months) in temperament in Area II (Emotional) because she has a very good attention span and persistence for her age. Regarding Area III (Social), Theresa is estimated at the eight-month level because she differentiates well between people and exhibits strong attachments to people she cares about. In Area IV (Cognitive/Language) she was estimated to be at C. A., except that Theresa misses special toys, which suggests a little higher level of object permanence (seven months). Theresa's language development is as expected.

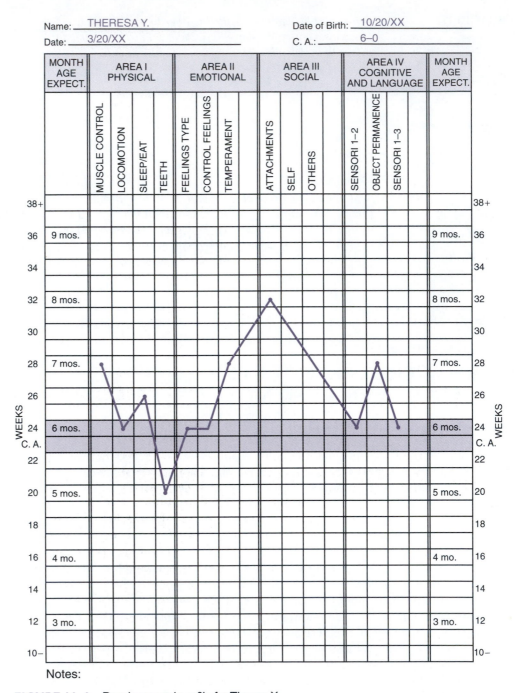

FIGURE 11–1 Developmental profile for Theresa Y.

To summarize, Theresa is a healthy six-month-old who exhibits average to above average skills in all areas, with the exception of teeth. The caregiver should design activities for all developmental areas and focus specific tasks on teething, for example, a teething ring and other chewable things when her teeth begin to erupt. In this way, Theresa is assured of a balanced developmental program.

Physical Development

Infants are highly motivated to master physical skills and explore their environments (McDevitt & Ormrod, 2007) and as a result they develop rapidly during this four-month period. They are awake and alert longer. Their movements are becoming more coordinated: They can sit when propped or in a high chair, and are developing the ability to sit alone. They can roll over and may creep. They can grasp objects intentionally and move and bang them purposefully.

The head, neck, arm, chest, and back muscles are used to maintain a sitting position. These are developing from the pushing and pulling and kicking and rolling the infant does. Even when the infant can sit when propped or sit alone, these muscles tire easily, so care must be taken to allow the infant to change positions.

By the middle of the first year infants can stand on their legs. The muscles in their heads, necks, arms, chests, backs, and legs are all functioning but are not yet coordinated. With the aid of people and furniture infants can stay standing and begin to take steps. Their ankle, foot, and toe muscles develop strength and coordination with the rest of their bodies (Figure 11–2).

FIGURE 11–2 The caregiver smiles, talks, and encourages the infant's movements.

Locomotion

While infants are developing some stability in relation to the force of gravity (sitting, standing), they are also attempting to move their bodies forward through space (**locomotion**).

Between the fourth and fifth months, the infant will roll from stomach to back, and by the sixth month most can roll from back to stomach. Creeping is the first loco-motor movement, starting around the sixth month (refer to Physical Development in the Developmental Prescriptions in Appendix A). Regan is lying on her stomach, reaching for a toy. She twists her body, pulls with her arms, and pushes with her legs. Slowly she moves forward to the toy. To accomplish this major task Regan used her head, neck, back, arm, and leg muscles to move and to lift the top part of her body up and down without tipping over. She may even get up on her hands and knees and rock. Infants can be encouraged to move at this stage by placing toys just out of reach.

By the seventh month she may actually be able to crawl about on her hands and knees and may pull herself to a standing position. By the eighth month she may put one foot in front of the other when held in a standing position.

Manipulation

Manipulation involves reaching, grasping, and releasing. In the first year infants move from reflexive to voluntarily controlled manipulation. During the first six months arm movement develops from erratic waving to carefully controlled reaching. Infants use shoulder, elbow, wrist, and hand movements to coordinate with what they see in order to reach purposefully and successfully grasp an object. Control of reaching must accompany the task of grasping.

Newborns grasp reflexively. For the next few months their hands will close on anything that touches them. They will grasp objects with either hand. Gradually infants begin to open their hands and use the whole hand to "palm" a toy. Around the end of the fourth month, the child will be able to move toys from one hand to the other. By the end of the first year, an infant will be able to use thumb and forefinger to assist in grasping objects (see the "Hand" section in the Developmental Prescriptions).

Eating

Many pediatricians recommend that infants begin solid foods at about six months of age. Mouthing and swallowing solid foods involves a coordination of muscles different from those used for sucking. Begin solid foods when family members request it. Use the same kind of spoon they use so the infants do not have to adjust to different sizes and shapes of spoons while they learn to retrieve food from a spoon and swallow the food without spitting it out or choking.

Feeding time presents an opportunity to socialize; the infant may be distracted from eating to coo and gurgle with his caregiver between eating spurts. This social exchange is very important to later social development.

By the sixth month, the infant may insist on holding the bottle or may try drinking from a cup, even without being ready to give up the bottle. By the seventh month, even though it is too early to use a spoon, the infant will want to feed himself or herself and will show resistance to being fed. It's time to let the child try it! At this time **finger foods** are developmentally appropriate. The experience of eating with fingers is an important one.

Teething

Infants usually begin **teething** at this age. Infants react differently to teething. Sometimes an emerging tooth causes an infant to be very fussy and irritable, while other times a new tooth just seems to appear with no change in the infant's behavior. Teething infants often like to bite on something. They use teething rings as well as anything else they can put into their mouths. If an infant seems to be hurting, a cold teething ring or crushed ice in a clean cloth provides coldness as well as hardness for the child's gums. Since teething infants may drool profusely, they may need to wear bibs all day, changed frequently to keep their clothes dry.

SUGGESTIONS FOR IMPLEMENTING CURRICULUM—PHYSICAL DEVELOPMENT

CHILD BEHAVIOR	MATERIALS	EXAMPLES OF CAREGIVER STRATEGIES
Muscular Control		
HEAD AND NECK		
Holds head up independently		Allow infant to lift head. Keep hand near to provide support.
Holds head in midline position	mobiles, crib gyms	Put some objects above center of crib.
Holds head up when on back, stomach, and sitting		Place infant where child can safely look around.
TRUNK		
Holds up chest, shoulders; arches back, hips		Provide clothes that allow freedom for pushing up, kicking, and wriggling. Check area for safety.
Sits with support; may attempt to raise self; may fuss if left lying down with little chance to sit up		Provide pillows and firm items to prop infant against. Hold infant in sitting position.
Leans back and forth	toys within reach	Keep area around infant free of sharp objects. Infant topples over easily.
Sits in a chair	chair with back	Use chair strap for safety. Let infant sit in chair, but for a short time, since the infant's muscles tire quickly.
Sits unsupported for short time	safe, flat sitting space	Place in safe area where infant can sit and play or watch. Infant will tire soon and will lie down.
Pushes self to sitting position	flat sitting space	Provide uncluttered space where infant can roll around and push with arms and legs to sit up alone.

(Continued)

CHILD BEHAVIOR	MATERIALS	EXAMPLES OF CAREGIVER STRATEGIES
LEG		
Lifts legs when on back and stomach		Provide clothes that allow free kicking.
Rolls from stomach to back		Place where infant can move freely and safely. Keep crib sides up. Keep hand on infant while changing diapers.
Straightens legs when standing		Hold infant in standing position for short periods. Hold infant's sides firmly when child bounces.
Stamps feet when standing		Firmly hold infant upright and provide flat surface for infant to push and move feet against.
Rolls from back to stomach		Place where infant can move freely and safely. Keep crib sides up. Keep hand on infant while changing diapers.
Raises to hands and knees		Place on flat, firm surface.
Stands with support		Hold infant's sides or hands while infant is standing on flat surface.
Pulls self to standing position		Hold infant's hands and allow infant to use his or her own muscles to pull self up. Check furniture and shelving to make sure neither will tip over when infant pulls on them to stand up.
LOCOMOTION		
Kicks against surface to move	floor space, sturdy furniture	Provide area where there is safe resistance, e.g., carpeting that helps traction, bare feet on vinyl, furniture to push against.
Rocks on hands and knees	blanket on floor	Provide clear, safe area where infant can safely raise self up and rock, then lurch forward and fall on face. Praise infant for success in getting to hands and knees.
Creeps on stomach	blanket on floor	Provide clear safe area where infant can creep. Place a toy slightly out of reach to motivate creeping. Encourage and praise creeping.
Uses legs to pull, push self when sitting	floor space	Sit a short distance from infant. Call child's name. Encourage infant to come to you. Show excitement and give praise.
ARM		
Visually directs reaching, hitting	crib toys, movable toys	Provide toys that infant can reach and hit. Provide large toys infant can accurately hit against.
Throws objects	soft, light toys and objects	Select toys that are light and will not go far and hit other children. Place infant in an area where child can safely throw objects.

CHILD BEHAVIOR	MATERIALS	EXAMPLES OF CAREGIVER STRATEGIES
HAND		
Grasps objects with whole hand and fingers against thumb	clutch ball	Provide toys that allow infant to wrap hand around some part. Flat surfaces slip out of grasp.
Uses thumb and forefinger	small toys of any shape	Make sure toys are too big to be swallowed. Infant will pick up anything and mouth it.
Picks up object with one hand; passes it to the other hand	small toys of any shape	Place toys around infant so child will use both hands. Ask for toy from one hand. Give toy to each hand.
Uses objects in both hands	banging toys	Play banging game with blocks, bells, balls.
Grasps and releases objects	toys that fit in one hand or have handles	Play game, "Put it here." You put toy in a pile. Infant picks up and puts down a toy in the same place.
Drops objects	unbreakable toys and objects, pail	Provide space for dropping. Play game, "Drop it." Stand up and drop toy into pail. Infant stands against chair and drops toys into pail.
Seeing		
Focuses on objects near and far	designs, pictures, wall space	Regularly change pictures, floor-to-ceiling projects, and bulletin boards to stimulate vision.
Distinguishes color, distance; depth perception	colorful objects	Provide colorful items. Put materials within reach so infant can succeed. Respect infant's resistance to moving where child does not feel safe.
Distinguishes visually attractive objects	faces, designs, shapes, color in room's materials and space	Note preferences for faces, designs, shapes. Make frequent changes.
Has visual preferences	favorite faces, pictures, objects	Observe infant's reactions to pictures, objects. Provide access to favorites by displaying them again later.
Hearing		
Listens to others' voices		Place near other infants and caregivers. Direct your talking to the infant.
Looks around to locate sound	sound toys, cans, bells	Play game: shake can beside infant. Wait for child to turn around and find you shaking the can. Shake bells beside you. Wait for infant to locate the ringing bells. Talk and sing with the infant.
Sleeping		
Takes a long morning nap and a long afternoon nap		Adjust routines to fit infant's changing sleep schedule.

(Continued)

CHILD BEHAVIOR	MATERIALS	EXAMPLES OF CAREGIVER STRATEGIES
Eating		
At six months, begins solid foods		
Eats baby food (new tongue and swallowing technique)	mashed foods, baby spoon, heated dish, plastic-lined bib, washcloth	Clean up infant and self for feeding time. Check with the family about desired food. Feed patiently while infant learns to eat from a spoon. Talk calmly. Praise infant's accomplishments. Clean up.
drinks from cup tongue and swallowing	new cup with special cover to control flow of milk, juice	Hold cup for infant. Tilt up and back to give infant time to swallow before next drink. Allow infant to help hold cup.
eats at "mealtimes" with solid foods, milk, juice	food grinder	Provide milk or juice in cup and solid foods at regular mealtimes to fit into the infant's sleep and play schedule.
feeds self finger foods	bite-size food	Clean up infant, self, and eating area. Provide food and time to eat it. Minimize distractions. Talk with infant, encourage infant, label food and actions. Clean up.
Teeth		
First teeth emerge: two middle lower, two middle upper	hard teething rings: firm, safe objects to bite, cold objects to bite	Provide objects safe for infant to bite on hard.

Emotional Development

Infants at this age now express a wider range of emotions. Pleasure, happiness, fear, and frustration are displayed in a variety of sounds, such as gurgles, coos, wails, and cries, along with physical movements like kicking rapidly, waving arms, bouncing, rocking oneself, and smiling.

Fear

Many infants experience what is called **stranger anxiety** in the latter half of the first year and well into the second year of life (McDevitt & Ormrod, 2007). People whom the infant doesn't know or does know but does not often see may find that the infant fears them. The infant may cry, cringe, hide, or move away. This very normal infant behavior occurs at a time when the infant is beginning to construct the idea of self as separate from others. It is important that "strangers" not feel something is wrong with them. A substitute teacher may experience this infant withdrawal because the infant has established familiarity and attachment to the primary caregiver, whereas he is different and unknown.

It is also during this period that the infant may demonstrate anxiety at being separated from his mother or other primary caregiver. The infant may become nervous or distraught if the caregiver is too far away or out of sight. Take every opportunity to tell the child that you will leave and will return. Introduce the other early childhood educator and explain that this person will take good care of him until you return. It is important to tell the infant when you have returned.

Temperament

As discussed previously, infants have different temperaments or characteristic ways of approaching their surroundings. You will need to know where a child falls in each of the nine behavioral categories (activity level, regularity, response to new situations, adaptability, sensory threshold, positive or negative mood, response intensity, distractibility, and persistence; for descriptions, see Chapter 3) so that you can adjust to the child's approach to the world and help the infant cope with daily situations. As discussed previously, the important issue surrounding temperament is the teacher's ability to create a *goodness of fit* between the child and her environment (Marion, 2007). When family members provided responsive care despite infants' negative reactions, children were more willing and eager and less angry in interactions as they became toddlers (Kochanska, Aksan, & Carlson, 2005). It is logical to deduce that similar outcomes would result when teachers provide responsive care.

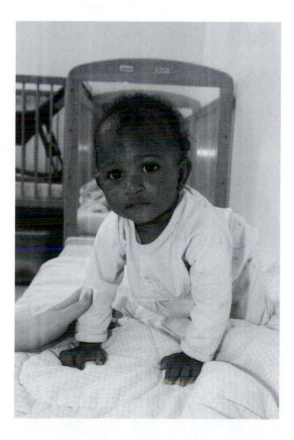

Special attention must be provided to children who hesitate to try new experiences.

For example, the **high active** infant may kick and wriggle and jerk, and therefore tip over when sitting propped up more often than the **low active** infant. High active infants need sitting times too, even though they need more caregiver assistance. On the other hand, low active children are easy to leave in a sitting position longer than may be good for their muscles because they may not fuss and move enough to tip over. These children need to be moved from sitting to lying on their stomachs, to holding, to sitting. The teacher must attend and be attuned as well as use her understanding of each child's temperament in order to create appropriate learning experiences.

SUGGESTIONS FOR IMPLEMENTING CURRICULUM—EMOTIONAL DEVELOPMENT

CHILD BEHAVIOR	MATERIALS	EXAMPLES OF CAREGIVER STRATEGIES
Types of Emotional Feelings		
Shows pleasure in watching others		Place infant where child can see others playing.
Shows pleasure in repetitive play	favorite toys	Provide favorite toys. Share pleasure in repetitive actions, e.g., clapping hands.
Shows depression		Discuss possible causes with family. Provide consistent loving, touching, holding, and playing whenever possible.
Shows fear of strangers		Introduce new people carefully. Do not let strangers hover closely. Give the infant time to become accustomed to the stranger at a distance. Use ruing.
Shows fear of falling down		When infant is standing and falling, keep area safe. Comfort when needed and then encourage infant and praise infant's standing.
Shows frustration with stimulation overload		Provide quiet space and time for the infant. Constant visual and auditory stimulation is nerve-racking. Comfort, hold, and talk softly to frustrated infant.
Shows happiness, delight, joy; humor expressed with laughs, giggles, grins		Share laughing, giggling. Play funny games, e.g., "Touch your nose; hold your finger by your head and slowly move it to touch the infant's nose while you say excitedly, "I'm going to touch your nose."
Shows rage		Allow infant to kick legs, flail arms, scream, and cry for a short time. Determine the cause of the rage. Reduce or eliminate the cause if possible. Use touching, rocking, soothing talk to help the infant calm down.
		Verbally affirm and acknowledge the infant's anger and distress. Remain calm and present soothing support.
Control of Emotions-Feelings		
Sometimes stops crying when talked to, sung to		Talk calmly, soothingly to crying infant. Use ruing.

Social Development

Infants are now developing definite and strong attachments to family members and primary caregivers. The primary caregiver's presence, consistent care, and emotional involvement with the infant all reinforce the attachment.

Infants are engaged in several new social experiences. Their developing physical skills of manipulating objects and moving themselves around contribute to the cognitive development of constructing a concept of self and not-self. During this time, from four to eight months of age, many infants interact more frequently with other children and adults. Their interest and mobility contribute to their initiating and responding to interactions with others.

Ainsworth (1982) identified several social behaviors during this age range.

Phase 2: Discriminating Social Responsiveness
(at six months or older)
> Discriminates between familiar and unfamiliar persons.
> Responds differently to them.
> Differential smiling, vocalization, crying.

Phase 3: Actively Seeking Proximity and Contact
(around seven months)
> Signals intended to evoke response from mother or attachment figure.
> Locomotion facilitates proximity seeking.
> Voluntary movements of hands and arms.
> Following, approaching, clinging—active contact behaviors.

Caregivers help children who can sit upright to explore materials and interact with each other.

SUGGESTIONS FOR IMPLEMENTING CURRICULUM—SOCIAL DEVELOPMENT

CHILD BEHAVIOR	MATERIALS	EXAMPLES OF CAREGIVER STRATEGIES
Attachment		
Shows strong attachment to family members		Reinforce attachment to family members.
Differentiates response to family members		
Shows familiarity with one specific caregiver		Assign a specific, primary caregiver to a specific infant. One caregiver can be a primary person (significant other) to four or fewer infants. Primary caregiver assumes responsibility for emotional involvement with the infant while providing care for the whole child.
Shows intense pleasure and frustration with person to whom attached		Accept and share pleasure; calm, soothe, stroke, and sing during infant's frustrated periods.
Self		
Recognizes self in mirror	foil, metal, or plastic shatterproof mirrors	Provide hand mirror for the infant to see self. Provide full-size mirror for infant to see self and others.
		Dots on bare feet and hands extend the infant's interest in his or her body.
Seeks independence in actions		Allow infant to accomplish tasks by self when possible, e.g., creeping to toy, pulling self up.
Plays self-designed games		Allow infant to play his or her own game. Do not distract infant or make infant change and play your game.
Others		
Observes others		Place the infant where child can observe others' activities.
Imitates others		Play games with the infant. Imitate each other, e.g., open mouth wide, stick out tongue.
Recognizes children		Allow infant to touch and "talk to" other children. Stay close so each is safe from pinching or hitting.
Plays with people		Let older children and other adults play games with the infant involving looking, hearing, and touching.
Seeks family's and caregiver's attention by movement, sounds, smiles, and cries		Respond immediately and consistently to happy, sad, or angry pleas for attention.
Follows adults		Arrange the room so the infant can see you from any place in the room.
Resists pressures from others regarding feeding and eating		Encourage but do not force the infant to eat. Adjust the time to stop and start according to the infant's rhythm.
Acts shy with some strangers		Hold and provide security to the infant when meeting a stranger. Allow the infant time to hear and see the stranger before the stranger touches the infant or even gets too close.

Cognitive and Language Development

Cognitive Development

Infants in Piaget's sensorimotor stage 3 are constructing the beginnings of the concept of objects separate from themselves. When an object an infant is watching disappears, she will visually search for it, but not manually. When an object she is holding disappears, she will search manually for it. Infants' senses still strongly control their actions; when the object is found, they will usually celebrate by mouthing it. As Dr. Healy said in her book *Your Child's Growing Mind*,

> Each child must build individual networks for thinking; this development comes from within, using outside stimuli as materials for growth. Most babies give explicit clues about what kind of input is needed and let you know when it is overpowering or not interesting anymore. . . . Human brains come equipped with the "need to know"; our job is to give them love, acceptance, and the raw material of appropriate stimulation at each level of development. Your own common sense augmented by current knowledge is the best guide (Healy, 2004, p. 50).

A ball poses particular challenges, cognitive as well as physical, for a newly mobile child.

SUGGESTIONS FOR IMPLEMENTING CURRICULUM—COGNITIVE DEVELOPMENT

CHILD BEHAVIOR	MATERIALS	EXAMPLES OF CAREGIVER STRATEGIES
Piaget's Substages of Sensorimotor Development		
SUBSTAGE 3 (Reproduction)		
Produces a motor activity, catches interest, and intentionally repeats the activity over and over	objects that attract attention: contrasting colors, changes in sounds, variety of textures, designs	Watch movements the infant repeats. Waving arm may hit the crib gym; the infant may wave arm more to hit the crib gym again. Watch which movements the infant repeats. Provide materials that facilitate, e.g., new items on the crib gym.
Repeats interesting action		The infant may pound fists on legs. Watch to see that child's actions are safe.
Develops hand-eye coordination further; looks for object, reaches for it, and accurately touches it	toys	Place blocks, dolls, balls, other toys near the infant where child can reach them.
Imitates behavior that is seen or heard	toy, food, body	Initiate action; wait for infant to imitate it; repeat action, e.g., smile, open mouth.
Piaget's Concept of Object Permanence		
SUBSTAGE 4 (Coordination)		
Visually follows object	toys, bottle, or objects that attract visual attention	Show infant a toy. Play with it a minute and then hide the toy. Bring it out and play with it again. (You will not *teach* the infant to look for the toy. Enjoy playing with the infant and toy.)
Searches visually for short time when object disappears		
Does not search manually		
Sees part of object; looks for whole object when object disappears	familiar toy, bottle, rattle, teething ring, ball, doll	Cover up part of object with a blanket or paper. Infant will pull object out or push off blanket, i.e., play peekaboo.

Language Development

The crying, cooing, and babbling of the infant help develop the physical mechanisms that produce speech (Figure 11–3). Developmentally, the cooing period is followed by an extended period of **babbling**. Babbling continues the diversification of sounds begun in cooing yet with the addition of consonants (e.g., *g, t, k, b, r*). According to Anisfeld (1984), the main difference between the two is in function: cooing has the function of expressing feelings of comfort whereas babbling is primarily playing with sounds.

Infants seem to produce sounds first and then discover them to reproduce over and over again. They experiment with these sounds and begin to make changes in

FIGURE 11–3   The caregiver talks and listens to the infant's new sounds.

them. The difference may consist of the same sound made from a different part of the mouth. For instance, when infants play with a voiced sound and the tongue and saliva at the back of their mouths, they produce a gurgle. With the same sound, tongue, and saliva at the front of the mouth, they produce a hissing or spitting sound. Infants listen to themselves and seem to enjoy their vocal play.

Babbling is playing with speech sounds. It is spontaneously produced rather than planned. While babbling, infants use and learn to control their physical speech mechanisms. They babble different speech sounds and combine them into two- and three-syllable sounds. They control air flow to produce wordlike sounds and change the intensity, volume, pitch, and rhythm of their babbling sound play.

Babbling does not occur in social isolation. Infants listen to the sounds around them. When you repeat the sound infants have just made, they may imitate your sound. Contingent (i.e., attuned), maternal behavior was found to facilitate more frequent, complex, and phonologically advanced vocal behavior by infants six to ten months in age (Goldstein, King, & West, 2003). Vocal stimulation that is relevant to the infant's behaviors and vocalizations seems to increase their babbling and, therefore, their control over their language. This stimulation also helps infants begin the two-way communication process of talking-listening-talking. They are finding that when they talk, you will listen; infants make you talk to them. Cooing and babbling sounds are used to provide pleasure as well as to convey feelings. Conversations include pitch and volume added to strings of sounds that seem like syllables or words. Infants imitate and initiate private and social talking.

Researchers have discovered that by six months, infants can distinguish **lexical words** or words that have a concrete or abstract connection to objects or events (e.g., nouns, verbs, and adverbs) from **grammatical words** or function words that have little meaning on their own yet affect the meaning of other words (e.g., articles, prepositions, or conjunctions; Shi & Werker, 2001). Moreover, infants demonstrate a distinct preference for lexical words (Shi & Werker, 2001, 2003) which may be related to the acoustic and phonological salience of these words (2003). In response to this developmental preference, teachers should label and describe objects and events in the environment using rich language. For example, when an infant is lying on her back looking at a sun catcher, you could say, "You are looking at the shimmering sun catcher. It sparkles in the sunlight."

SUGGESTIONS FOR IMPLEMENTING CURRICULUM—LANGUAGE DEVELOPMENT

CHILD BEHAVIOR	MATERIALS	EXAMPLES OF CAREGIVER STRATEGIES
Coos for many minutes		Respond with talk.
Babbles syllable-like sounds		Respond with talk.
Responds to talking by cooing, babbling, and smiling		Talk directly to infant.
Imitates sounds		Make sounds, talk, sing to infant.
Initiates sounds		Listen and respond.
Makes vowel sounds		
Looks for person speaking		Place yourself so that the infant can see you when you converse together.
Looks when name is called		Call the infant by name and talk with child.
Makes consonant sounds		
Babbles conversation with others		Respond with talking.
Reflects happiness, unhappiness in sounds made		Let your voice reflect response to mood.
Babbles two- and three-syllable sounds		Respond with talking.
Uses intensity, volume, pitch, rhythm		Use normal speaking patterns and tones when talking to the infant.

■ KEY TERMS

babbling	lexical words	stranger anxiety
finger foods	locomotion	teething
grammatical words	low active	
high active	manipulation	

CASE STUDY   **Theresa**

Theresa's parents both work at home. Her mother works late evenings and her father works early mornings. Theresa's mother is breast-feeding her on demand except for one day a week, when both parents are out of the house. During that day, she gets thawed, previously frozen breast milk from a bottle.

Both parents care for Theresa. They both manage to take breaks at the same time to give quality time to "Terry Bear," as she is affectionately called. Sometimes they all take walks together, taking turns carrying the baby. She enjoys the movement and facing her parents in her infant backpack, but she is also curious about the sights and sounds around her.

Theresa recently started going to child care and is learning to adjust and make the transition. One thing

that helps is her satin blanket, which she enjoys chewing on when resting. The level of stimulation and support Theresa's parents provide is extraordinary. She is above average in most of her developmental areas. However, her teething development is somewhat weak, which points out the wide fluctuations in development of infants and toddlers.

1. Why is Theresa allowed to keep her blanket and chew on it?

2. What would happen to Theresa if you took away her blanket? Why do you think that would happen?

3. How old should a child be before he or she no longer needs "attachments" to favorite things?

■ QUESTIONS AND EXPERIENCES FOR REFLECTION

1. Listen to the talk of one infant between four and eight months of age. Write down the sounds you hear (they may be strings of vowels or syllables, e.g., *aaaa* or *babababa*).

2. Observe a caregiver talking to an infant of this age. Write down what the caregiver says and how the infant responds, both vocally and behaviorally.

3. Observe one infant from four to eight months of age. Record the infant's behavior in two five-minute sequences, using narrative description. Transfer the descriptions to the Developmental Profile.

4. Examine the written records of one infant from four to eight months of age. List the Wednesday nap times for eight weeks. Identify any changes in nap times.

5. Observe one infant who is creeping. Write a description of the infant's physical movements.

6. List five strategies to use with an infant from four to eight months of age.

7. List strategies you need to develop and list ways you intend to develop them.

■ CHAPTER REVIEW

1. When an infant can roll from stomach to back and from back to stomach, what additional caregiver strategies are needed? Explain three.

2. Deborah, a five-month-old, is sitting up against a pillow on the floor. She is looking at the toy she has just thrown out of her reach. She leans forward, tips over, and cries. Describe

what you would do next. Explain why you would do it.

3. List three caregiver strategies that facilitate the emotional development of the infant between four and eight months.

4. Describe the development in eye-hand coordination of an infant between four and eight months old.

■ REFERENCES

Ainsworth, M. D. (1982). The development of infant-mother attachment. In J. Belsky (Ed.), *In the beginning: Readings on infancy*. New York: Columbia University Press.

Anisfeld, M. (1984). *Language development from birth to three*. Hillsdale, NJ: Lawrence Erlbaum Associates.

Douville-Watson, L., & Watson, M. (1995). *Improving learning development with games*. Glen Cove, NY: Instructional Press.

Goldstein, M. H., King, A. P., & West, M. J. (2003, June). Social interaction shapes babbling: Testing parallels between birdsong and speech [Electronic version]. *Proceedings of the National Academy of Sciences, USA, 100*(13), 8030–8035.

Healy, J. (2004). *Your child's growing mind: A guide to learning and brain development from birth to adolescence*. (3rd ed.). New York: Broadway Books.

Kochanska, G., Aksan, N., & Carlson, J. (2005). Temperament, relationships, and young children's receptive cooperation with their parents. *Developmental Psychology, 41*(4), 648–660.

Marion, M. (2007). *Guidance of young children* (7th ed.). Upper Saddle River, NJ: Prentice Hall.

McDevitt, T. M., & Ormrod, J. E. (2007). *Child development: Educating and working with children and adolescents* (3rd ed.). Upper Saddle River, NJ: Pearson Prentice Hall.

Shi, R., & Werker, J. F. (2001). Six-month-old infants' preferences for lexical words. *Psychological Science, 12*(1), 70–75.

Shi, R., & Werker, J. F. (2003). The basis of preference for lexical words in 6-month-old infants. *Developmental Science, 6*(5), 484–488.

■ ADDITIONAL RESOURCES

Lally, J. R., Ledon Torres, Y., & Phelps, P. C. (1993, December). Caring for infants and toddlers in groups: Necessary considerations for emotional, social, and cognitive development. Based on a plenary presentation conducted at ZERO TO THREE's Eighth Biennial National Training Institute, Washington, D.C. Retrieved December 28, 2006, from http://www.zerotothree.org/caring.html

■ HELPFUL WEB SITES

Beyond the Journal Archive. "Helping Babies Play," two pages of ideas for engaging infants (birth–18 months) in play, is available at **http://www.journal.naeyc.org/btj/200305/HelpingBabies_Sawyers.pdf**

GeoParent. Experts answer questions on health, including eating and nutrition, such as when to start solid foods. **http://geoparent.com/directory/Experts/Health/Eating_and_Nutrition/**

Early Head Start National Resource Center. Information for teachers and parents about programs and resources. **http://ehsnrc.org**

KidsHealth. The parents' section has articles including "Teething Tots" with facts on teething and tips for baby teeth hygiene. **http://kidshealth.org/parent/general/**

Your Baby's Development. Articles on social and emotional development, including Developmental Milestones: Socialization. **http://www.babycenter.com/baby/babydevelopment**

For additional infant and toddler resources, visit our Web site at
http://www.earlychilded.delmar.com

12

The Child from Eight to Twelve Months of Age

Leroy's Story

Leroy, eight months old, is sitting on the floor with several toys in front of him that Miss Virginia, the caregiver, has just placed there. He picks up a pink toy elephant, lifts it up and down with his right hand and says, "Ahh. Ah, Ah, Yah, Ahya." He picks up lock blocks, saying, "Eee, Ahh, Ahh." He throws down the blocks and then picks up blocks and twirls one in his left hand. He puts down the blocks and crawls away to another part of the room and sits up to watch a child run cars. He crawls to Miss Virginia, who pulls him up to his knees. He stares at her and says, "Ayy." He crawls to the toys, sits back, and then pulls to the train. He pulls up on his knees to the toys and pats the ball. He starts to stand up and goes back to his knees. He pushes the train and it goes forward; his eyes get big. Miss Virginia pulls him up. Leroy stands and goes up on his toes as he holds her hands. Miss Virginia picks him up and holds him in her lap a minute.

MATERIALS AND ACTIVITIES

Infants in this age range are mobile and will encounter an expanded world. All objects within reach must be safe to taste and touch and move. These infants need space as they continue to develop control of gross motor movements, such as crawling, standing, pulling, and throwing objects. Materials to manipulate must be small enough to grasp with the palm and fingers or with thumbs and forefingers, but not small enough for them to swallow. Attention-catching materials stimulate infants to select and use those materials (Figure 12–1).

Types of Materials

very low materials to climb over
sturdy furniture to pull self up
    next to and walk around
balls to clutch
stacking objects
nesting objects
pail and small objects
    to drop into it

stroking, textured objects
sound toys
mirrors
crayons
puppets
pictures
one-piece puzzle

Examples of Homemade Materials

CLUTCH BALL

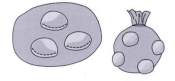

Cut a circle of colorful, washable fabric. Put polyester filling on one part of the fabric and sew around it, creating a lump. Repeat, making a second lump. Baste around the edge of the circle and pull the circle almost closed. Stuff in polyester filling to pad the ball. Sew through the fabric and wind thread around the gathered end, creating a tuft of fabric.

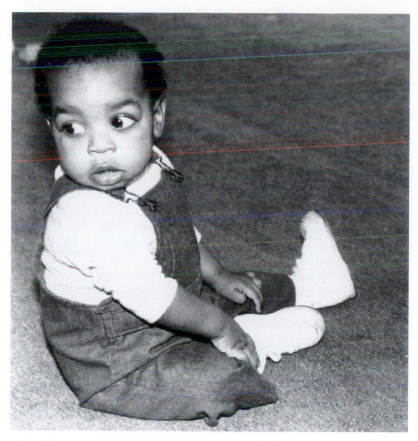

FIGURE 12–1   Sounds and objects attract the infant's attention.

NESTING TOYS

Select three containers of different sizes, such as plastic margarine tubs or cardboard tubes.

PUZZLE

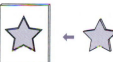

Glue a picture of one simple object on a piece of thick cardboard (use white glue and water mixture to cover the whole picture and cardboard). Cut out the object, making a simple shape. Place the object into the matching frame.

PUPPET

On a child-sized white sock, use a nontoxic waterproof marker to draw a face on one side, hair on the other side.

CAREGIVER STRATEGIES TO ENHANCE DEVELOPMENT

Developmental Profile

Marcel, an eight-month-old, was observed over a three-day period. The Developmental Profile in Figure 12–2 was the outcome. The Child Behaviors from the Prescriptions in Appendix A were used to make estimates of Marcel's skills in each major area of development. His highest estimate is 11 months in locomotion, and the lowest estimate is five months in the teeth category. This range may suggest significant strengths and weaknesses in Marcel's development at this time.

Within the Physical Area (I), Marcel exhibits strength in his muscle control and locomotion. Estimates of 10 and 11 months are based on his skills for climbing on furniture, walking, and standing without assistance. The low score in "teeth" (five months) came about because Marcel is having pain and a hard time teething. This is also affecting his eating and sleeping patterns and his temperament (six months). Estimates in Area II (Emotional) are at age level in "types of feelings" (eight months) and slightly below age in "control of feelings" (seven months). His difficulty teething causes him to be cranky and lose control of his feelings more easily. Marcel exhibits development in the Social (III) and Cognitive/Language (IV) areas near his age level with no significant strengths or weaknesses being observed.

In summary, Marcel exhibits strengths in his physical development and problems with sleeping, eating, and emotional control as the result of teething problems. While these problems are temporary, the caregiver should design activities and tasks to help with these problems, including discussing solutions with Marcel's family members and pediatrician.

Physical Development

Infants of this age are rapidly developing muscular control. They learn to sit alone. They crawl, stand with support, and walk with help. Creeping evolves into **crawling,** where the arms and legs are used in opposition. On hands and knees the infant first slowly moves one limb and then another. With increased control, crawling can become a very fast and efficient means of locomotion, providing the infant with a new world of possible experiences. Quickly after learning to crawl infants begin to pull themselves up and stand with the assistance of objects and people. When infants have gained stability in standing upright, they can turn their efforts toward moving forward (walking). Many months of movement precede the actual accomplishment of walking. Shirley (1931) identified four stages.

1. an early period of stepping, in which slight forward progress is made (3–6 months)
2. a period of standing with help (6–10 months)
3. a period of walking when led (9–12 months)
4. a period of walking alone (12–15 months).

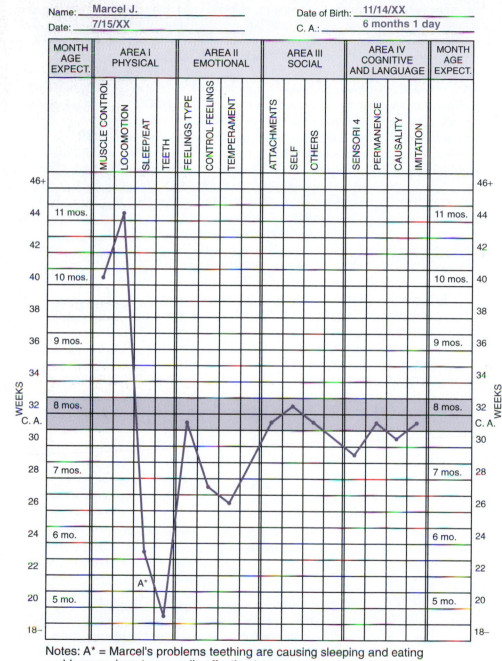

Name: Marcel J.   Date of Birth: 11/14/XX
Date: 7/15/XX   C. A.: 6 months 1 day

Notes: A* = Marcel's problems teething are causing sleeping and eating problems and are temporarily affecting temperament.

FIGURE 12–2   Developmental profile for Marcel J.

All infants proceed through this sequence of locomotion, though the age varies among infants. A formerly low active baby may show a sudden spurt of activity during this time.

Ryan is standing next to a chair watching a bright toy on the floor sparkle in the sunshine. He leans toward it and reaches for it, but he cannot reach it. He takes one step away from the chair while still holding on to the chair. He still cannot reach it. He takes another step, and his hand slips off the chair. He is now on his own. He takes another step, stops, weaves, takes another step, and then falls down. Ryan is beginning to walk. His first attempts at locomotion are filled with standing, stepping, weaving, sitting or falling down, pushing himself back up to standing, and trying again.

A dynamic systems framework helps us to understand that multiple layers of child-environment interaction influence both the long-term and short-term changes that infants experience in their movements and actions (Newell, Liu, & Mayer-Kress, 2001). Ryan will repeat this cycle thousands of times, a process that strengthens his muscles and develops his coordination. Infants quickly, within the first month of walking, move from making short steps from a wide-base stance with feet pointed outward to longer steps made from a smaller base with feet pointed forward (Adolph, Vereijken, & Shrout, 2003). These authors believe that the experience of walking over and over again is what assists infants with developing the more adult-like walk. To accomplish this developmental task Ryan needs open floor space, where he can walk without bumping into furniture or having to step on or over toys on the floor.

To promote the optimal development of gross motor skills, infants need adequate floor space where they can roll, crawl, climb, reach, stand, and walk. Caregivers should be cautious about the equipment they provide. Playpens can very easily become prisons that restrict movement. Wheeled walkers or stationary jumpers can put undue strain on the infant's back, restricting the development and coordination of head, neck, arm, chest, back, leg, and foot muscles, while putting too much emphasis on leg movement.

In the following paragraphs, we will turn our attention to fine motor control, where the development of capabilities is just as impressive between eight and twelve months.

> Although the baby starts practicing muscle control almost immediately, integrating reflex motor movements into controlled patterns takes a long time. The baby needs many things to see and to touch with body, mouth and hands. At first the infant's movements seem random, but as he gets the feel of his own body in space, connections build . . . to help the child organize his muscles around independent plans of action. (Healy, 2004, p. 43)

Infants of this age often hold a finger straight and poke at themselves and objects around them. They push and pull and may keep repeating their actions. In addition, they use their thumb and fingers to grasp objects, perfecting the **pincer grasp.** Using this skill often, they continue to develop their finger muscles and eye-hand coordination. Because they do not have good control of the strength of the pinch, they may sometimes pinch another child hard enough to hurt.

These infants are also developing control of their arms; now they can clap and bring both hands to mid-body repeatedly. Their hands can grasp some objects, so they may bang objects together. They can hold crayons and make marks with them (refer to Appendix A, Developmental Prescription: Muscle, Hand). By the end of this time period, infants are gaining enough control of their arm and hand movements to be able to touch lightly or stroke objects.

Infants eight months to one year old are also beginning to use each hand for different tasks. They may pick up a toy with one hand, transfer it to the other hand to hold, and then pick up another toy. They may reach out and stack one block, transfer the other toy to that hand, and stack the second block.

Advances in motor control, both fine and gross, assist infants with eating. They often use both fingers or a spoon to eat and may even use them at the same time. Infants want to get the food into their mouths, and they use every way they can to accomplish this task. So be prepared for spills, dropped food, and other messes by carefully planning the eating environment. Because infants use their new teeth to bite anything put into their mouths, caution should be used when selecting eating utensils. Plastic, disposable utensils often cannot withstand the infants' biting. Infants should be skilled at holding their own bottles and may be beginning to use a cup. Allow them to complete these skills independently or provide only the necessary amount of assistance.

Sleep patterns continue to change gradually. At this age infants take a morning and afternoon nap but have more time awake in which to be alert and play. Each infant has a personal sleep schedule that is affected by the child's own body needs for sleep, as well as by the sleep routines at home. If the infant is awakened at 5:00 a.m. to get ready to come to child care, that child may need a morning nap earlier than an infant who was allowed to sleep until 7:00 a.m.

Crawling, indoors and outdoors, enables the infant to explore a wide new world.

SUGGESTIONS FOR IMPLEMENTING CURRICULUM—PHYSICAL DEVELOPMENT

CHILD BEHAVIOR	MATERIALS	EXAMPLES OF CAREGIVER STRATEGIES
Muscular Control		
TRUNK, LEG		
Raises self to sitting position	flat surface	Keep area clear of objects that would hurt the infant if child falls on them.
Sits alone		Provide a short time to sit. Infant may tire soon.
Stands holding on to furniture or hand	sturdy chair, bench, table	Remove furniture that could tip over on infant.
Stands without assistance	flat surface	Allow infant to stand alone.
Sits from standing		Keep area clear of objects that could hurt infant. Infant often falls down when trying to sit down from standing.
Squats and stands		Watch sharp-cornered furniture. Pad corners as needed. Infant often stands up underneath furniture (tables) and bumps head.
LOCOMOTION		
Crawls	obstacle-free space	Allow infant to crawl. Play with infant to stimulate crawling. Place toys slightly beyond reach to stimulate crawling.
Steps forward	obstacle-free space	Hold infant's hand; provide furniture to lean on for support when stepping forward.
Crawls up steps	low two- to four-step equipment	Allow infant to crawl up steps. Watch so you can assist infant in getting back down safely. Barricade any steps you do not want the infant to use.
Steps sideways	equipment, furniture	Allow infant to stand and step around to hold on to furniture. Keep chairs, toys away from path.
Walks with help	obstacle-free area	Hold infant's hand(s). Slowly walk around, allowing infant to step and balance as needed. Infant's swaying body will give you clues for stopping and starting.
Climbs on furniture	low, sturdy furniture	Infant can climb but has not learned how much space his or her body takes up so may climb into areas where he or she does not fit. Watch, caution, and assist when necessary.
HAND		
Uses thumb and forefinger	toys, dolls	Provide objects small enough to pinch and lift.
Uses thumb and two fingers	toys, dolls	Provide objects small enough to pinch and lift.
Brings both hands to middle of body	banging objects, foil pie pans, blocks	Play clapping, banging games with infant. Play pat-a-cake.
Uses finger to poke	pillow, ball, small box	Provide soft objects to poke into. Watch carefully because infant may poke other children's face, eyes, and so on.

CHILD BEHAVIOR	MATERIALS	EXAMPLES OF CAREGIVER STRATEGIES
Carries objects in hands	attractive objects small enough to grasp but too big to swallow	Provide objects that can be carried.
Holds and uses pen, crayon	flat surface, fat felt marker, fat crayon, paper	Provide materials and space. Demonstrate where marks go (on paper, not floor or table). Remain with infant when child is using marker or crayon. Allow child to make the kind and number of marks he or she wants to. Praise child for the interest and effort. Put materials away when child decides he or she is finished.
Reaches, touches, strokes object	textured objects	Provide objects of different textures. Infants can stroke, not just grasp and pinch. Demonstrate gentle stroking. Describe the texture, e.g., "the feather is soft." Allow infant to gently stroke many objects.
Uses one hand to hold object, one hand to reach and explore	objects small enough to grasp	Provide several objects at once that stimulate infant's interest.
Stacks blocks with dominant hand	blocks, small objects	Allow infant to choose which hand to use in stacking objects.
Takes off clothes	own clothes with big buttonholes, zippers	Infant's fingers are beginning to handle buttons, zippers. Allow infant to play with these. Infant does not understand when to undress and when to keep clothes on. Discourage undressing when you want infant to stay clothed.
Sleeping		
May have trouble sleeping	calming music, musical toy	Provide adequate time to spend with infant preparing for sleep. Rock, sing and talk to, and stroke infant. Respond immediately if infant awakens during regular sleep time. Rub child's back, talk quietly as you attempt to help infant go to sleep again.
Takes morning nap and afternoon nap	quiet, dim, clean sleeping space	Determine infant's preferences for going to sleep. Feed, hold and rock, rub infant's back, hum and sing to help get the infant to sleep.
Seeks parent or caregiver presence		Primary caregiver should prepare infant for sleep, put infant to bed, respond if sleep is interrupted, and get infant up from nap.
Eating		
Holds bottle	bottle	Allow infant to hold bottle while you hold infant.
Holds cup	cup with special cover	Allow infant to hold own cup. Assist when necessary, e.g., the spout is at infant's nose rather than mouth.

(Continued)

CHILD BEHAVIOR	MATERIALS	EXAMPLES OF CAREGIVER STRATEGIES
Holds and uses spoon	child-size spoon	Provide food that can fit on spoon. Allow infant to use spoon to feed self. Assist when necessary with difficult food. Praise infant's efforts and successes. Child will hold spoon in one hand and eat with fingers of other hand.
Uses fingers to eat most food	finger food	Wash hands and face *before* eating. Allow infant to use fingers to pick up food. Wash hands, face, chair, and whole area after eating time.
Starts establishing food preferences		Identify and record infant's food likes and dislikes. Plan a balanced diet for child, emphasizing foods child likes. Do not force foods child does not like.
May eat less		Do not force eating. Infant's body may need less. Children make adjustments in the amount they eat. Be sure children have food available they like so they can make choices about *amount* rather than *kinds* of foods.
Teeth		
Begins to get teeth	teething ring; cold, hard objects to bite; bib	Provide objects safe to bite. Cold soothes the gums. Change bib as needed since drooling increases.

Emotional Development

Positive interactions with caregivers help infants develop good feelings about themselves. Infants express their happiness in many ways. Anger is expressed more often during this time period. Infants can now conceive of goals or desires and actively pursue them. For example, when Tomas does not want his father to leave at drop-off time, he might crawl over and cling to his leg. Or he might crawl to the door and bang on it once his father has left. Tomas is clearly communicating his desire to keep his dad near and anger (and sadness) at not being able to do so. Teachers must help infants and family members create rituals for coping with the emotions that stem from being separated on a daily basis (Balaban, 2006). Infants will express their anxiety and fears in a multitude of ways and teachers must learn to crack the message encoded in their behaviors (Marion, 2007).

Out of fear, uncertainty, and/or changes in family characteristics an infant may regress temporarily to an earlier stage. Understanding this **regression** helps the caregiver to be aware that the child may need more reassurance than is given to a younger infant. The caregiver should be alert and notice when the child is feeling confident once more and able to function at age level again.

At this age infants are developing preferences. Providing toys they like not only adds to their pleasure in playing with the toys but also enhances their feelings of asserting some control over their world.

At this age infants are often uncertain—sometimes fearful—of new experiences and people.

As discussed previously, developing physical skills also make infants more independent in feeding and dressing themselves. Allowing them to accomplish as many tasks as possible on their own helps them strengthen their sense of independence.

External influences like a verbal "no" or a firm look may sometimes cause infants to limit or change their behavior. Follow up your restrictive words or looks with an explanation. For example, when an infant throws food on the floor, the caregiver can say, "No. You need the carrots up here in your dish. Let's see you put a carrot in your mouth." Sometimes infants will stop their own negative action. You may see them pick up food or a toy, start to throw, and then stop their arm movement and put the object down carefully. This early self-restriction may be caused by distraction rather than self-control. Nevertheless, encourage such actions to reinforce acceptable behavior.

As soon as the child has a modicum of verbal skills, promoting perspective-taking skills and applying the three As will elicit positive emotions. Remember that the most powerful way to promote positive feelings is to *provide attention for appropriate behavior*. Redirecting negative behaviors to positive or desired behaviors works better than drawing attention to negative ones. Be sure to trust the child's motives. Children are doing the best they can at all times.

The temperaments of infants produce varying responses to experiences. Some infants approach new situations openly. When new solid foods and finger foods are introduced, they try them. They accept and eat many of the foods, and those they reject, they reject with minimal fussing. Other infants are hesitant or resist new situations. Each new food causes these infants to pull back and at first reject the new food. With encouragement, these infants may taste the new food and then determine whether they like it or not. Sometimes they so actively resist a new food that it is difficult to get them to eat enough of it to develop an acceptance of it.

Variation in intensity of response often shows up when infants are pulling themselves up and falling down. Falling down, whether toppling forward or sitting down hard on their bottoms, always surprises infants and can sometimes be painful. One infant will scream and cry loudly. Another may cry quietly or whimper or perhaps look surprised and upset but will not verbalize his or her discomfort.

Persistence at trying to stand upright and step forward leads toward walking. Very persistent infants will try again and again to stand or step. Falling down becomes a

SUGGESTIONS FOR IMPLEMENTING CURRICULUM—EMOTIONAL DEVELOPMENT

CHILD BEHAVIOR	MATERIALS	EXAMPLES OF CAREGIVER STRATEGIES
Types of Emotions and Feelings		
Shows happiness, joy, pleasure		Share infant's feelings. Return smile, use a positive tone of voice, hug and pat the child.
Shows anxiety		Use calm, quiet talking, singing. Cuddle and stroke the child. Remove from situation if necessary.
Shows fear		Determine and remove cause of fear if possible. Use calm, quiet talking to describe the feeling. Sing, cuddle, and stroke to calm.
Shows anger, frustration; has tantrums		Determine and remove cause if possible. Use calm talking about child's goal and other ways to pursue it. May sometimes hold and soothe infant. Help infant start a new activity. Keep child safe, but ignore a tantrum.
Rejects items, situations		Allow infant to make choices. Figure out alternative choices for situations he or she needs to experience, e.g., time or place choices.
Develops preferences with toys, people		Identify and record infant's preferences. Make sure these toys are available frequently.
Shows independence— helps with feeding and dressing self	cup, spoon, clothes child can manipulate	Allow infant to help feed and dress self. This takes much time and patience. Lengthen eating time to adjust to self-feeding skills.
Shows affection		Accept and return affection with smile, hug, cuddle.
Begins developing self-esteem		Provide positive affirmation of infant through your tone of voice, looks, touch.
Control of Emotions and Feelings		
Begins to learn to obey "No"		Use "no" sparingly so infants can determine important situations when they must control their behavior. Use firm, not angry, voice. Use firm, not smiling, look on face.
Sometimes inhibits own behavior		Praise infant for self-control; e.g., infant raises arm to throw something, but puts it down on table.
Obeys commands: "No-no"; "Stop"		Use commands sparingly. Praise infants when they obey.

deterrent only after many tries. Other infants persist only a few times, then stop their efforts and change to some new task or interest.

Social Development

Interactions with others are increasing. The mobility infants now have enables them to encounter different people or to move away from them. These infants initiate interactions with others and respond to others' interactions with them.

The infant's egocentric perspective is evident. Infants at this age do not clearly separate others' desires and needs from their own. Therefore, they are often fearful and uncertain and occasionally clingy. They are very possessive of materials and people. Such materials and people still seem part of the infant, not completely separate, and thus they seem to belong to the infant.

The primary caregiver is familiar to the infant and fosters a sense of security. The infant therefore tries to keep the caregiver in sight, reinforcing his or her feelings of security (Figure 12–3).

FIGURE 12–3 Trusted caregivers are used as a secure base for exploring. When the infant wanders too far or encounters someone new, he returns for comfort.

SUGGESTIONS FOR IMPLEMENTING CURRICULUM—SOCIAL DEVELOPMENT

CHILD BEHAVIOR	MATERIALS	EXAMPLES OF CAREGIVER STRATEGIES
Others		
Initiates interactions with others		Respond to infant's behavior. Talk, play with infant. Allow infant access to other children and adults.
Responds		Initiate talking and playing with infant.
May fear strangers		Keep strangers from forcing themselves on infant, who may not want to be held by stranger.
Keeps parent or caregiver in sight		Allow infant to follow you around. Arrange room so infant can see you from different areas of the room.
Initiates play		Respond and play infant's game, e.g., pat-a-cake.
Becomes assertive; initiates action to fill needs		Encourage infant's assertiveness. Observe to determine whether infant is getting aggressive and will need cautions.
Wants own pleasure; may not consider others		Verbalize limits and help infant choose other activities, materials.
Initiates play		Play games with infant, e.g., "Can you do this?" Wave hand, clap hands, etc.
Is possessive of people		Verbally assure infant you will be here and will come back to talk and play with infant again.
Is possessive of materials	many toys	Provide enough toys and materials so infant does not need to share.
May become shy, clinging		Hold, hug, pat; allow infant to remain close; verbally assure infant you are here.
May demand attention		Provide positive verbal attention even though you may be busy with another child.

Cognitive and Language Development

Cognitive Development

Assimilation and accommodation begin to operate independently (refer to Chapter 2 for definitions of these terms). Infants of this age are beginning to separate their thinking about what they want to accomplish from how they can accomplish it.

The establishment of **object permanence** is the major development during this age range. The infants remember events, people, and objects for increasingly longer periods. Awareness of object permanence forms the basis for rapid development of representations in play and language.

These infants are constructing a concept of self separate from all other entities, but have not completed it. People and toys are eventually perceived as real entities that continue to exist even when the infants cannot see them. With this concept, infants now actively search visually and manually for people or objects that are no longer visible. These infants are mentally constructing a representation of the person or object. This mental representation of the real entity forms the foundation for increasingly complex forms of representation.

Along with thinking about other people as separate from themselves, infants of this age also begin to determine that others can cause actions. They will incorporate others' actions into their own play.

At this stage infants imitate people and things that are not present. They have established **deferred imitation**, which requires sufficient cognitive skills to remember and reproduce things they have seen and heard: ". . . early imitation serves a learning function, that is, infants imitate to advance their comprehension and mastery of behaviors that interest them" (Anisfeld, 1984, p. 44).

SUGGESTIONS FOR IMPLEMENTING CURRICULUM—COGNITIVE DEVELOPMENT

CHILD BEHAVIOR	MATERIALS	EXAMPLES OF CAREGIVER STRATEGIES
Piaget's Substages of Sensorimotor Development		
SUBSTAGE 4 (Coordination)		
Differentiates goals; can focus on reaching and on a particular toy	toys, visually attractive objects	Place objects near infant.
Piaget's Concept of Object Permanence		
Establishes object permanence, that object exists when it is no longer visible, e.g., child seeks toy that rolls behind box		Play hiding games, e.g., hide the doll under the blanket; place the block behind you.
Causality		
Learns that others cause actions		Verbalize caregiver's own actions, e.g., "I put the ball behind me."
Imitation and Play		
Imitates other's actions; uses actions as play		Introduce new copying games. Allow time and space for infant to play.

Language Development

Infants, around one year of age, typically speak their first recognizable words and use a combination of sounds, babbling, and single words to communicate with themselves and others (McDevitt & Ormrod, 2007). "Just as the sensorimotor exploration of objects lays the groundwork for object representation, so the sensorimotor exploration of speech lays the groundwork for speech representation" (Anisfeld, 1984, p. 224).

Newborns are born with the capacity for distinguishing frequency and pitch (Healy, 2004), and develop finer auditory discrimination during the first year. Just as we provide infants with a well-balanced diet, we should also provide a well-balanced auditory environment, as "soothing, pleasant and interesting sounds inspire curiosity and a receptive attitude" toward language (p. 46). Sing and talk often with the infants. However, because too much noise, noises that are too loud, or non-stop noise can cause confusion and be detrimental to development (Healy, 2004), monitor background sounds and discuss this issue with family members.

Anisfeld identified levels of meaning, characterizing the first level as pre-symbolic use of words. "The early words have a sign character. . . . They are **context bound**" (1984, p. 67). Infants learn to associate a word with a particular object or action. They respond to the word in that context but cannot identify it in other contexts. For example, each day the caregiver says "Sit in your chair" as she gets the infants ready for lunch. When told to "sit in your chair," Beverly looks at her chair. She does not look at other chairs around the room. *Chair* relates to a specific chair, not to a class of objects called *chairs*. ". . . [C]hildren's early words are nonsymbolic because they function primarily as responses to specific stimulus contexts" (p. 69). An infant says the word in association with the context in which it was learned: ". . . the context-boundness of the first level results from a conceptual limitation. The child does not automatically conceive of words as independent of the specific contexts of their use" (p. 70).

Reading aloud to infants facilitates their ability to visually focus, reinforces basic concepts, stimulates imagination, and develops and enhances language development and listening skills (Zeece & Churchill, 2001). As infants experience multiple readings of the same book, they begin to join in the reading, identifying objects in illustrations by either pointing to or verbally acknowledging an object (Zeece & Churchill, 2001). Linda Lamme (1985) extends this idea when she states in *Growing Up Reading* that

> Pointing to things in pictures and labeling them orally is especially important in the first year when your infant, though not yet talking, is acquiring so much language. Relate what is in the book to your infant's experience. "You have a ball just like that one!" Repetition is important also. After seeing a page several times, your infant will begin to recognize the pictures. You'll quickly come to realize your infant has distinct book preferences.
>
> The last guideline is: The earlier you begin to read aloud, the better. If your child can become used to having stories read aloud before he or she starts walking, reading-aloud sessions can be sustained during those mobile, early walking times. Children who are learning to walk have a hard time sitting still to listen to a story if they have not previously become hooked on book reading (p. 51).

Makin (2006) researched shared book readings between ten mother-infant pairs. She discovered that they showed varying patterns of language use, conversation structure, and use of nonverbal communication strategies such as facial expressions, tempo, and gestures. This variation highlights how children acquire different types of knowledge in their homes. Some family cultures are more expressive, while others are more reserved in how they demonstrate emotions. Neither approach is inherently right or wrong. Teachers should not judge, but rather come to understand these differences so that bridges between home and school can be built; literature is a powerful tool for building bridges and routines for helping children transition from home to school (Lawhon & Cobb, 2002; Zeece, Harris, & Hayes, 2006).

Scribbling is related to the language/reading/writing processes the infant is developing. In her earlier work on infants, *Growing Up Writing*, Lamme (1984) wrote the following:

> Well before his first birthday, your child is ready to make marks on paper or chalkboard. Those first marks will be random scribbles. Your child won't even be watching as he is making the mark and will not see the connection between the mark on paper and the writing tool in his hand. The first stage of development is called "uncontrolled scribbling."
>
> The outstanding feature of these early writing attempts is that they are more than random marks; they represent your child's intentions to create something. Scribbling has been termed "gesturing with a pencil." The role of scribbling in writing development has been compared with babbling in oral language development. In each case, there is probably some random sound or scribble made but, in both cases, your child is intending to communicate (p. 38).

SUGGESTIONS FOR IMPLEMENTING CURRICULUM—LANGUAGE DEVELOPMENT

CHILD BEHAVIOR	MATERIALS	EXAMPLES OF CAREGIVER STRATEGIES
Babbles		Respond with talk.
Shouts		Respond to infant's feelings.
Labels sounds	bell, rattle	Name important objects with one word. Then use in a sentence, e.g., "Bell" (while pointing to it). "Ramon has a bell."
Uses names: Mama, Dada		Reinforce by talking about Mama and Dada.
Responds to familiar sounds		Provide familiar music, routine changes. Acknowledge infant's response, e.g., "Tasha heard the spoons being put on the table."
Responds to familiar words		Frequently use names or labels that infant is learning, e.g., ball, shoe, coat.
Responds to own name		Use infant's name when you start talking with that child.
Makes sounds that reflect emotions		Respond to the infant's message about how he or she feels. Name the emotions, e.g., "Garrett is angry."
Repeats syllables, words, e.g., *bye-bye*		Label frequent behaviors and respond to infant's use, e.g., say "bye-bye" and wave; repeat occasionally.
Makes sounds like conversation		Respond verbally to infant's "conversation," e.g., "Holly is talking to her truck."
Repeats, practices word over and over		Allow infant to play with words. Respond and encourage.

(Continued)

CHILD BEHAVIOR	MATERIALS	EXAMPLES OF CAREGIVER STRATEGIES
Connects words with objects, e.g., says "kitty"—points to kitty	familiar toys, objects	Point or touch objects you verbally label.
Chooses books	picture books of familiar objects	Point to picture of object and say name of object. Repeat often.
Scribbles randomly	paper, markers	Provide writing space and materials.

■ KEY TERMS

context bound

crawling

deferred imitation

object permanence

pincer grasp

regression

CASE STUDY   Marcel

Marcel, for being eight months, is advanced in both learning and motor skill development. He has learned to stand, walk, and crawl with balance and coordination. No obstacle seems to stop him. This may be related to the fact that he has a three-and-a-half-year-old brother he plays with and tries to imitate. Marcel's brother encourages and enjoys playing with Marcel.

Marcel enjoys the support and care of two grandmothers and one grandfather besides his father. All three grandparents stay at home and both Marcel and his brother attend half-time child care. At the time of the assessment, Marcel had no evidence of teeth emerging. When he spent one five-day period showing signs that four teeth were about to break through the gums, his happy disposition suddenly changed. It seemed that nothing pleased him, and he refused to stay in one position for any length of time. Marcel's grandmother wanted to put whiskey on his gums, but the family pediatrician convinced her that any product with alcohol was not good for children, recommending a cold washcloth and a hard teething ring instead. Marcel's father works nights, so he takes the afternoon shift

caring for Marcel. Marcel is mature enough to walk, strong enough to squirm away, and quick enough to slip out of a holding grip when a wave of teething pain came over him. Marcel tested the frustration limits of everyone in the household, including his brother. At one point a grandmother started to get angry, shouting at Marcel, and the other grandmother quickly declared that it was her turn to care for Marcel. With help from child care staff, the family decided to move a large bed into the corner of Marcel's room, and an adult lay down with Marcel at night so he could move about as he needed to in safety as he tried to sleep. After a week of the ordeal, all four teeth broke through his gums and Marcel quickly returned to his pleasant and active self.

1. Why would applying alcohol to his gums be bad for Marcel?

2. What would be the effect of becoming angry with a child who is as agitated as Marcel was? Why?

3. What do you think the behavior of a less physically developed child with a similar teething problem would be?

■ QUESTIONS AND EXPERIENCES FOR REFLECTION

1. Observe one infant who is walking with support. Identify the following:
    a. what infant holds onto for support
    b. where infant walks
    c. what you think causes the infant to sit or fall down

2. Use narrative description to record your observations of one caregiver for five minutes. Then categorize the caregiver's behaviors that relate to social development.

Initiating Behavior		Responding Behaviors	
Caregiver's Behavior	Infant's Response	Infant's Initiating Behavior	Caregiver's Response

3. Observe one infant between 8 and 12 months of age. Record the infant's behavior in two five-minute sequences using a narrative, running record (Appendix A). Transfer the descriptions to the Developmental Profile.

4. List five caregiving and teaching strategies that you use with infants between 8 and 12 months of age.

5. Explain the concept of *object permanence* and how it reflects and impacts both social and cognitive development.

■ CHAPTER REVIEW

1. Why is sharing difficult for the infant between 8 and 12 months of age?

2. List five strategies you can use to facilitate the physical development of an infant in this age range, using the format below.

Caregiver Strategy	Specific Physical Development
1.	
2.	
3.	
4.	
5.	

3. An 11-month-old is responding to labels of objects. Describe a game you can play with this child to stimulate the child's understanding and use of language.

4. Identify four ways an infant in this age range asserts independence.

■ REFERENCES

Adolph, K. E., Vereijken, B., & Shrout, P. E. (2003). What changes in infant walking and why. *Child Development,* 74(2), 475–497.

Anisfeld, M. (1984). *Language development from birth to three.* Hillsdale, NJ: Lawrence Erlbaum Associates.

Balaban, N. (2006, November). Easing the separation process for infants, toddlers, and families. *Beyond the Journal: Young Children on the Web.* Retrieved January 16, 2007, from http://www.journal.naeyc.org/btj/200611/pdf/BTJBalaban.pdf

Healy, J. (2004). *Your child's growing mind: A guide to learning and brain development from birth to adolescence*. (3rd ed.). New York: Broadway Books.

Lamme, L. L. (1984). *Growing up writing*. Washington, DC: Acropolis Books.

Lamme, L. L. (1985). *Growing up reading*. Washington, DC: Acropolis Books.

Lawhon, T., & Cobb, J. B. (2002). Routines that build emergent literacy skills in infants, toddlers, and preschoolers. *Early Childhood Education Journal, 30*(2), 113–118.

Makin, L. (2006). Literacy 8-12 months: What are babies learning? *Early Years: Journal of International Research & Development, 26*(3), 267–277.

Marion, M. (2007). *Guidance of young children* (7th ed.). Upper Saddle River, NJ: Prentice Hall.

McDevitt, T. M., & Ormrod, J. E. (2007). *Child development: Educating and working with children and adolescents* (3rd ed.). Upper Saddle River, NJ: Pearson Prentice Hall.

Newell, K. M., Liu, Y., & Mayer-Kress, G. (2001). Time scales in motor learning and development. *Psychological Review, 108*(1), 57–82.

Shirley, M. M. (1931). *The first two years: A study of twenty-five babies. Postural and Locomotor Development*: Vol. 1. Minneapolis: University of Minnesota Press.

Zeece, P. D., & Churchill, S. L. (2001). First stories: Emergent literacy in infants and toddlers. *Early Childhood Education Journal, 29*(2), 101–104.

Zeece, P. D., Harris, B., & Hayes, N. (2006). Building literacy links for young children. *Early Childhood Education Journal, 34*(1), 61–65.

■ ADDITIONAL RESOURCES

Bremner, G., & Fogel, A. (Eds.). (2001) *Blackwell handbook of infant development*. Malden, MA: Blackwell.

Bremner, G., & Slater, A. (2004) (Eds.). *Theories of infant development*. Malden, MA: Blackwell.

Zigler, E., Finn-Stevenson, M., & Hall, N. W. (2002). *The first three years and beyond: Brain development and social policy*. New Haven: Yale University Press.

Heritage Key (catalog containing information on multi-ethnic children's titles) 6102 East Mescal, Scotsdale, AZ 85254. Phone: (602) 483-3313.

■ HELPFUL WEB SITES

Alexian Brothers Medical Center. Life with Baby: Pregnancy and Beyond. Milestones and other articles about babies at 10 to 12 months. http://www.alexian.org/progserv/babies/10to12m/

Beyond the Journal Archive. "Helping Babies Play," two pages of ideas for engaging infants (birth–18 months) in play, is available at http://www.journal.naeyc.org/btj/200305/HelpingBabies_Sawyers.pdf

About.com Baby Parenting. Activities for Infants and Young Toddlers. http://babyparenting.about.com/od/activitiesandplay/

Purdue News. Researchers look at brain and behavior development in infants. http://www.purdue.edu/UNS/html4ever/0007.Corbetta.babybrain.html

Will I grow out of it? Milestones and Warning Signs for Speech Development. http://www.blankees.com/ baby/speech/lan03.htm

For additional infant and toddler resources, visit our Web site at http://www.earlychilded.delmar.com

CHAPTER 13

The Child from Twelve to Eighteen Months of Age

Caregivers of Toddlers

Caregivers or teachers who are in charge of toddler programs strive to be

- empowered facilitators who structure environments to minimize conflicts and maximize explorations.
- practiced in the three As of child care—Attention, Approval, and Attunement.
- skillful, patient observers who help with problem solving and promote a positive perspective.
- organized and imaginative.
- knowledgeable in toddler development so that they may understand toddlers' daily struggles and enjoy their daily triumphs.
- consistent, gentle, yet firm.
- easily amused.
- genuinely fond of toddlers.

The Toddler

Andrea, 15 months old, stands looking around. She walks over to two-year-old Jenny, who is sitting on the sofa. She stands between Jenny's legs and bounces up and down to Hokey Pokey music from the record player. Andrea and Jenny dance around. Jenny lies down on the floor and Andrea crawls on top of her. Jenny moves and Andrea follows. They both lie quietly for a minute. Andrea walks to the toys. She picks up a toy plastic milk bottle and lifts it to her mouth to drink. She sits down and puts three lock blocks in the bottle. Allen, the caregiver, says, "Shake it, Andrea." She shakes the bottle, and it makes a noise. She shakes it again. She puts a pail over her head and walks around peeking under the edge of the pail and "talking." Andrea climbs into a child's rocking chair, turns around to sit down, and starts rocking. She "talks" and rocks and then climbs out of the chair and walks around, following Allen.

Toddlers solve problems on a physical level. Watch toddlers at play for just five minutes and you will see them walk (which looks like wandering), climb, carry things around, drop things, and continually dump whatever they can find. These large-muscle activities are not done to irritate adults—they are the legitimate activity of toddlers (Gonzalez-Mena & Eyers, 2007). As discussed previously, Piaget calls this the sensorimotor stage of development.

MATERIALS AND ACTIVITIES

Walking is a major development for toddlers at this age. They are fascinated with toys to pull or push as they toddle around. They climb over objects. They may ride wheeled toys. They grasp and throw and drop objects again and again. They are moving into imaginative play and need materials that can facilitate their play.

Toddlers need space and equipment that encourage walking, jumping, and other physical activities.

Types of Materials

pull toys
push toys
trucks, cars
low, riding wheel toys
low, three-step stairs to climb
blocks
pail with objects to put in and
    take out
area with water and sand toys

soft objects to throw
mirrors
dolls
puppets
puzzles
picture books and cards
paper, nontoxic markers,
    crayons
audiotapes and CDs

Examples of Homemade Materials

PULL TOY

Use plain or painted empty spools. Thread and knot spools on a length of clothesline rope.

SOUND/SIGHT BOTTLE

Use a clear plastic liter bottle (soft drink). Wash it thoroughly and allow to dry inside. Put in material or objects that will make noise (such as sand, wooden or plastic blocks, metal bottle caps). Add confetti for color interest. Screw on bottle cap and glue securely. Tape over rough edges of cap.

TOSS BOX

Collect several small, soft toys and place in a cardboard box. Show child how to take out objects, stand away from the box, and throw the objects into the box. Paint the inside of the box as a target to attract the child's attention.

EXPLORING TUBS

Place one solid object in a margarine tub. Put lid on. When children shake it, they hear a noise. Encourage the children to take off the lid to discover what is inside. Put lid back on. Have several tubs available with different objects inside, e.g., plastic clothespins, large wooden spools.

PICTURE CARD

Use a square of two- or three-ply cardboard. Place a photograph of a child on the cardboard and cover the whole square (front, back, and sides) with contact paper or laminating film. Also use colorful pictures cut from magazines. Select pictures that are simple and show one object, such as a car, cat, flower, or bird. Select pictures of objects the child is familiar with.

CLOTHING FRAME BOARD

Cover a piece of wood 12" × 12" × 2" with fabric. Glue one piece of fabric to each side of the wooden frame, with fabric opening at center of frame. Sew buttons on one side at center, buttonholes on other side. Or put on large snaps. Or sew in a large-toothed zipper.

CAREGIVER STRATEGIES TO ENHANCE DEVELOPMENT

Developmental Profile

Andrea's Developmental Profile is presented in Figure 13–1. She was observed over a two-week period regarding the child behaviors listed in the Developmental Prescription (Appendix A), and is three months below C. A. in self concept under "Social Development," and three months above expectations in interactions with others. Overall, Andrea shows healthy, normal development.

In terms of areas I and II, Physical and Emotional, Andrea is estimated to be within expected behavior. However, she seems to not focus attention on herself or her needs, and is much more concerned about gaining attention and responding to the needs of others. As a result, she is estimated to be below age in self development (12 months), and above age in interactions with others (18 months). The minor problem of her not considering her needs and being overly concerned about others might be related to a slightly higher "imitation and play" estimate in Cognitive Development and imitating sounds in Language Development (17 months).

In general, Andrea exhibits expected development except for the problems in not considering herself and needing other people to be happy for her to feel secure.

The caregiver should design tasks and activities using materials and caregiver strategies that help Andrea feel special and make her needs more important than the needs of others, when appropriate. Adding these activities to ones designed for all other areas will ensure a balanced program for Andrea.

Physical Development

An expanding world opens up to toddlers as they become mobile. They walk, lurch, run, fall, bump into things, and persist in moving around in their world. They are unstable when they walk. They may topple over from stepping on an object or by leaning too far or walking too fast. They are learning to make adjustments so that they can remain upright. The experience gained from walking results in their walking becoming more stable and adult-like (Adolph, Vereijken, & Shrout, 2003). Falling is a valuable learning experience as well (Joh & Adolph, 2006), so avoid rescuing the child too quickly; let her get back up and try again.

> They toddle about their own environment not necessarily to get from one part of it to another, but because they are up on their feet and it is satisfying to practice walking. Chairs become things to push and carry because pushing and carrying are also newly obtained skills a toddler delights in practicing. Chairs can also be climbed into and later, if the chairs are an appropriate size, two-year-olds may discover they can back up to them and sit down, apparently an exciting achievement when you are just learning how to do it. (Brickmeyer, 1978)

Toddlers learn with their whole bodies—not just their heads. They learn more through their hands than they do through their ears. They learn by doing, not only by thinking. They learn by touching, mouthing, and trying out, not by being told.

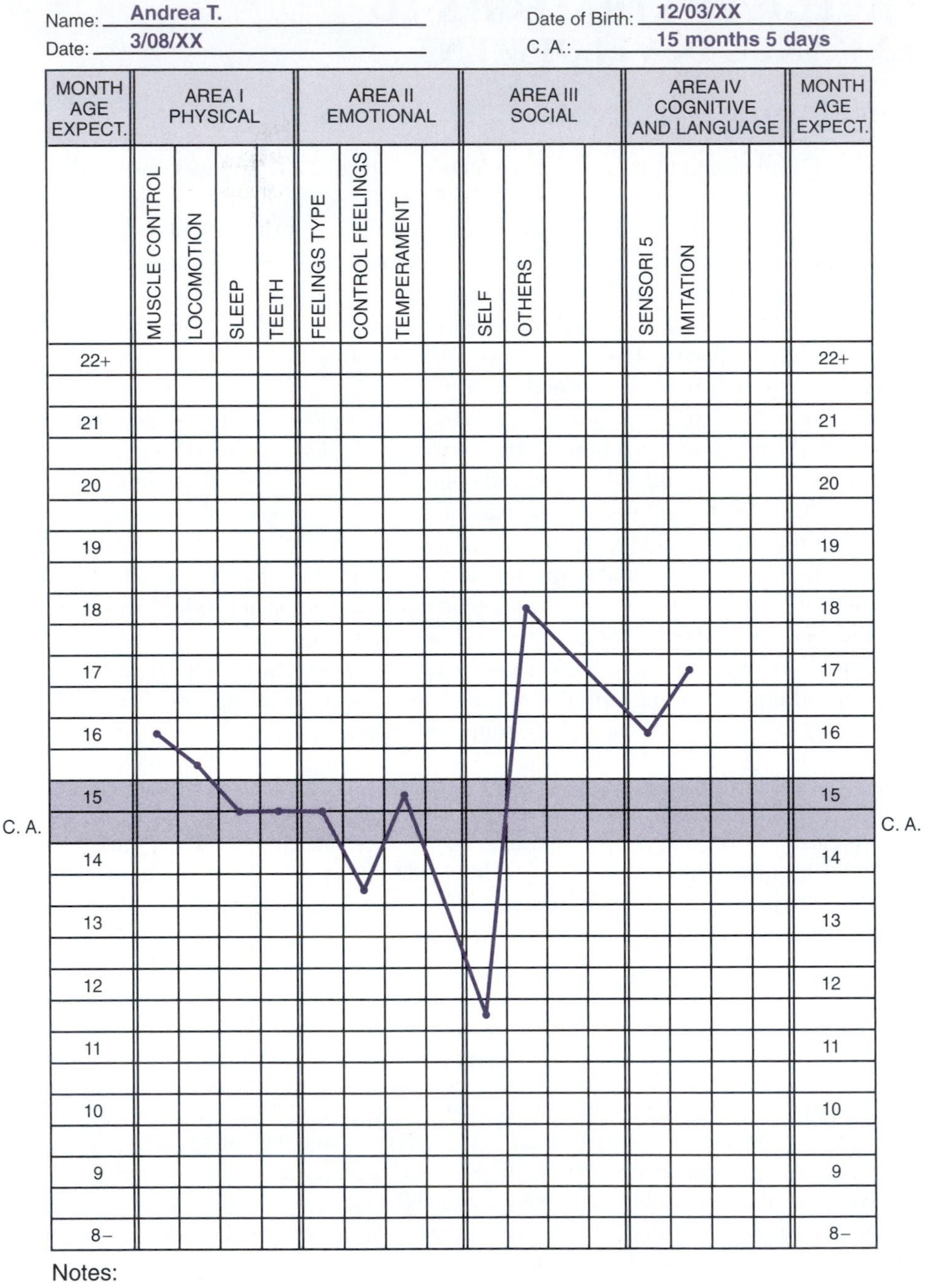

Name: __Andrea T._____   Date of Birth: __12/03/XX_____

Date: __3/08/XX_____   C. A.: _____ 15 months 5 days

MONTH AGE EXPECT.	AREA I PHYSICAL				AREA II EMOTIONAL			AREA III SOCIAL			AREA IV COGNITIVE AND LANGUAGE			MONTH AGE EXPECT.
	MUSCLE CONTROL	LOCOMOTION	SLEEP	TEETH	FEELINGS TYPE	CONTROL FEELINGS	TEMPERAMENT	SELF	OTHERS		SENSORI 5	IMITATION		
22+														22+
21														21
20														20
19														19
18														18
17														17
16														16
15														15
C.A.														C.A.
14														14
13														13
12														12
11														11
10														10
9														9
8–														8–

Notes:

FIGURE 13–1   Developmental profile for Andrea T.

Physical development promotes cognitive development.

Toddlers can become absorbed in discovering the world around them. If you are convinced that toddlers have short attention spans, just watch them with running water and a piece of soap. Hand washing can become the main activity of the morning! Eating is another major activity, as many toddlers switch from very messy to neat in a short time. Filling and dumping are great activities for exercising fine and gross motor skills. Of course, toddlers do put things in containers as part of the process, but they are more likely to end with dumping (Gonzalez-Mena & Eyer, 2007).

Roberto, a fourteen-month-old in a family child care program, likes to combine emptying with transporting things. He finds favorite spots or hiding places: under the bed, in the wastebasket, or even in the sink and toilet bowl. Because he is so engaged with emptying, his teacher provides baskets that can be filled and emptied endlessly (Caplan & Caplan, 1980); rather than trying to limit his behavior.

Piaget's substages 5 and 6 explain the link between cognitive and physical development for toddlers between 12 and 18 months. This stage marks the onset of experimentation. The child begins deliberately to invent new actions she has never tried before and to explore the novel and unique features of objects. She tries to find out what will happen if she uses objects in new ways. She combines objects with other objects to create new ways of doing things and uses trial-and-error approaches to discover new solutions to problems. Newly acquired skills allow the toddler to explore objects in new ways and therefore construct new understandings of the world.

SUGGESTIONS FOR IMPLEMENTING CURRICULUM—PHYSICAL DEVELOPMENT

CHILD BEHAVIOR	MATERIALS	EXAMPLES OF CAREGIVER STRATEGIES
Muscular Control		
TRUNK		
Shows high energy, is active, moves from one activity to another		Provide a variety of materials and activities so the child can often change activities and play objects. These toddlers frequently do not *make* anything or complete an activity. Schedule cleanup and help put away toys at end of playtime.
Raises self to standing	sturdy furniture to grasp; flat surface	Provide space where toddlers can stand up safely. Caution them about standing up under furniture.
LOCOMOTION		
May prefer crawling to walking		Allow toddler to crawl when desired. It is faster than walking when the child is just beginning to walk.
Walks alone		Allow toddler to walk alone when desired. Provide a hand to hold onto when child seeks help.
Climbs up stairs with help	stairs	Provide handrail or your hand to assist child with balance.
Climbs down stairs with help	stairs	Provide handrail *and* your hand. Balance is still poor when walking down stairs.
Climbs over objects	low, sturdy furniture, equipment, boxes	Provide low climbing equipment, furniture, e.g., ottoman, sturdy cardboard boxes, covered foam incline.
HAND		
Uses thumb against fingers	small toys, crayons, pens	Provide materials toddler can grasp.
Shows hand preference		Allow toddler to use whichever hand he or she chooses.
Points with finger	pictures, books, objects	Play pointing game, e.g., open picture book, "Point to the tree."
Throws objects	soft, small objects	Provide a place and target where toddler can throw objects.
Rolls and catches objects	large, small balls	Sit on floor with legs open and outstretched and roll ball back and forth with toddler.
EYE-HAND COORDINATION		
Scribbles	paper, nontoxic markers, crayons	Provide flat surface for toddler to use paper and marker or pen. Admire and describe the marks the toddler makes.
Helps in dressing and undressing	buttons, snaps, zipper, cards, books, clothing frame board, large dolls with clothes	Allow toddler to do as much as possible. Assist when toddler needs help.

CHILD BEHAVIOR	MATERIALS	EXAMPLES OF CAREGIVER STRATEGIES
Sleeping		
Begins to change from morning and afternoon nap to just afternoon nap. May fall asleep during lunch.		Adjust eating and nap schedule so toddler does not miss lunch.
Eating		
Eats three meals and regular snacks		Determine mealtime. Make adjustments for individual children as necessary.
Feeds self: uses cup, spoon, and fingers	food, plate, cup, spoon	Allow toddler to feed self as much as possible. Assist when necessary.
Expresses food likes and dislikes		Record food preferences. Provide foods child likes. Introduce new foods gradually. Combine foods child does not like with ones child does like to provide needed nutrition.
May eat less food		Do not force eating. Make food as attractive as possible.

Emotional Development

Toddlers seek both dependence and independence. Erikson (1963) called this developmental crisis the need to resolve Autonomy versus Shame and Doubt, his second stage of development. For many tasks toddlers need help. The caregiver can provide toddlers with emotional strength and security, accepting toddlers' very real dependence (Wilson, 1987). Toddlers are also trying to become independent. Emotionally they need support that affirms their importance as individuals who can make some choices and accomplish some tasks all by themselves. Their growing sense of achievement enhances their developing positive feelings of self-worth and demonstrates an understanding of cause and effect.

Toddlers experience a wide variety of emotions and sometimes seem to swing wildly between them. One moment they are happy and the next they are fearful. Many fears at this age are learned from adults because our reactions influence the toddler's response. Research showed that higher levels of compliance to clean-up tasks by toddlers was related to both child characteristics (lower levels of anger proneness and social fearfulness) and maternal characteristics (sensitivity and structuring of the task; Lehman, Steier, Guidash, & Wanna, 2002). Hence, adults help children learn to control strong emotions and comply to requests when they use the three As of caregiving—Attention, Approval, and Attunement. Caregivers must take an inventory of themselves and recognize what emotional messages they are conveying to an impressionable toddler. It is the continued responsibility of the caregiver to promote a positive learning environment.

Toddlers feel emotions, express emotions, but do not yet understand emotions. Feeling strong emotions can overwhelm and scare toddlers.

Because toddlers lack the skills to regulate their strong emotions, their anger and frustration may come out as temper tantrums. Adults should prevent temper tantrums whenever possible by attending to and changing the conditions that caused the child's frustrations. Of course, not all sources of frustration and anger can be modified or removed. In those cases, respond to frustration tantrums by quietly talking about the emotion being experienced, the cause of the tantrum, and how scary it feels to be out of control of one's body. Toddlers sometimes have tantrums in order to get their own way. These manipulation tantrums should be ignored, because giving attention during the tantrum may encourage toddlers to use this strategy routinely as a way to get what they want. Instead, the caregiver should make sure that the child is safe and then provide positive attention soon after the tantrum is over.

Toddlers may also express negativism by saying "No!". Their pursuit of independence may carry over into doing the opposite of what was requested or their carrying out their own ideas (not the adult's). Rephrase command statements and refocus attention to something of interest to the toddler. For example, you might rephrase "Put the doll away" to "Mary Jane, where can you find a place to put the doll down?" Providing choices can also assist toddlers in complying with requests and learning to make appropriate choices (Marion, 2007). Children learn concepts of right and wrong from adults. Toddlers are just beginning to use words, and they respond to some labels and commands. But words alone will not control their behavior until they internalize the language and construct concepts of right and wrong.

These concepts are constantly being revised and expanded as the toddlers compare their behavior with adults' reaction to that behavior. At this age toddlers cannot separate themselves from their actions enough to understand the idea, "I like you but I do not like what you are doing." Therefore, caregivers need to find ways to help toddlers discriminate between right and wrong while still accepting each child as a worthy person no matter what his or her behavior.

Use positive guidance strategies. Don't depend on words alone; utilize physical touch or intervention when necessary. For example, prevent a harmful behavior before it occurs by holding back a child's threatening arm before it has a chance to hit. Lead a child by the hand back to the table to clean up after a snack. Don't let children get in trouble and then yell or otherwise express anger toward them. Allowing the child to choose between two positive and equally desirable outcomes helps the child learn to make decisions as well as to have more control over his or her environment (Swim & Marion, 2006). In addition, consistently using the three As of caregiving—Attention, Approval, and Attunement—when the child has behaved correctly will help the child know what is right. If you find yourself saying "I knew that was going to happen," next time don't predict it, *prevent* it (Gonzalez-Mena & Eyer, 2007; Marion, 2007).

Children's responses to a change in routine during this developmental stage are influenced by their temperament. The toddler who is very adaptable may change routines easily or with a little fussing. For example, putting that toddler's chair in a different place in the room may create interest for the child. A toddler who has difficulty adapting to change may react negatively, resisting the moving of the chair by fussing or crying or even having a tantrum. This child may combine resistance to change with negativism.

SUGGESTIONS FOR IMPLEMENTING CURRICULUM—EMOTIONAL DEVELOPMENT

CHILD BEHAVIOR	MATERIALS	EXAMPLES OF CAREGIVER STRATEGIES
Types of Emotions-Feelings		
Expresses emotions in behavior and language		Determine and respond to toddler's emotions.
Recognizes emotions in others		Be consistent in showing emotions, e.g., happiness—smile and laugh; anger—firm voice, no smile.
May fear strangeness		Introduce new people, new experiences to toddler. Caution others not to rush the child. Allow child to approach or withdraw at his or her own rate.
Shows excitement, delight		Respond with similar excitement, e.g., touching a pretty flower, an animal.
Expresses sense of humor		Giggle and laugh with toddler.
Shows affection		Accept and return physical and verbal shows of affection.
Displays negativism		Provide honest, workable choices, e.g., "Do you want to eat at the red or the green table?"

(Continued)

CHILD BEHAVIOR	MATERIALS	EXAMPLES OF CAREGIVER STRATEGIES
Has tantrums		Determine and remove cause if possible. Sometimes ignore. Proceed calmly with involvement with other children, activities.
Uses play to express emotions, resolve conflicts	blocks, dolls, home objects, clothes, toy animals	Provide props for acting out fear, frustration, insecurity, joy.
Seeks dependency, security with parent and caregiver		Provide touching, holding, stroking interactions; respond quickly and consistently to toddler's needs.
Seeks to expand independence		Allow toddler to attempt activities by him- or herself. Do not take over if toddler can be successful without you.
Control of Emotions-Feelings		
Begins to learn right and wrong		Verbalize which behavior is right and which behavior is wrong. Give reasons. Since toddlers are only just beginning to conceptualize right vs. wrong, only occasionally can they apply the concept to control their own behavior.
Reinforces desired behavior		Provide positive feedback when a toddler controls his own behavior.

Social Development

Toddlers are **egocentric**; they see the world from their own point of view or perspective. In the first year and a half of life, their bodies and the objects they play with are perceived to be part of *self*. Gradually, as the concept of object permanence develops, they differentiate *self* from other objects and people, which become *not self*. This major development provides the basis for lifelong expansion of their concept of self and their interactions with others and provides the child with one of his or her earliest experiences with self-image. Caregiver acceptance is extremely important at any stage of development. This acceptance is internalized and becomes part of the child's self.

Toddlers behave differently toward different people. They recognize differences in people and adjust their interactions with them. They may be eager and excited with a familiar caregiver and quiet and withdrawn with a substitute teacher.

Toddlers play with toys and materials and sing and talk usually by themselves in play. They may look at other children and play near them, but they do not interact with them in play. Toddlers now engage in **solitary play** (playing alone) and **parallel play** (playing near but not with other children); they decide what kind of interaction they want with others. At this age the toddler is more adept at dealing with older children and adults than with peers.

Toddlers use familiar games like peekaboo to initiate interactions with caregivers.

SUGGESTIONS FOR IMPLEMENTING CURRICULUM—SOCIAL DEVELOPMENT

CHILD BEHAVIOR	EXAMPLES OF CAREGIVER STRATEGIES
Self	
Has concept of self	Positively reinforce toddler as an individual.
Is egocentric: understands only his or her own viewpoint	Do not expect toddler to feel sorry for someone she has hurt. Toddler assumes everyone thinks and feels the way he or she does.
Others	
Seeks presence of family members or caregiver	Allow toddler to follow you around. Tell child when you are going out of sight.
Initiates and plays games	Play games with toddler. Respond and play child's games.
Occasionally shares	Provide enough materials and equipment so sharing can be encouraged but not required.

(Continued)

CHILD BEHAVIOR	EXAMPLES OF CAREGIVER STRATEGIES
Acts differently toward different people	Expect different responses to different people. Accept toddler's choices.
Uses variety of behaviors to gain attention	Identify toddler's usual behaviors to gain attention. Respond to any of those behaviors as quickly as possible.
May be shy with some people	Do not force toddler to interact with all people. Allow child to keep his or her distance and watch.
Engages in parallel play	Provide materials and space so toddlers can play with own materials but near each other.

Cognitive and Language Development

Cognitive Development

This is a time for learning, so opportunities to learn should be provided, including learning how to learn. Too often adults give children answers to remember rather than problems to solve. This is a grave mistake. "Unless children develop the art of problem solving . . . their brains will remain underdeveloped" (Healy, 2004). Children construct their knowledge and understanding of the world through their experiences with the environment (Elkind, 2003). According to Piaget, however, people engage in **individual constructivism**, in which a single person individually creates new understandings, interpretations, and realities through interactions with materials, equipment, and people in their environment (McDevitt & Ormrod, 2007). Adults must provide developmentally appropriate learning experiences that challenge toddlers' current level of development but are achievable (Bredekamp & Copple, 1997), causing disequilibrium and influencing their development now and in the future. For example, as object permanence becomes more firmly established, toddlers may search for an object they have seen moved and hidden. So playing hiding games such as "Doggie, doggie, where's your bone?" engages and challenges the children.

Toddlers of this age are interested in observing the effects of their own and other's actions; learning about **cause and effect**. Exploration is done using **trial and error**. These little explorers try, probe, and practice activities and observe the results of their actions. A trial-and-error approach to the world can result in guidance encounters with adults as they experiment with new ways to do things. For example, what happens when sand is thrown? Can I go down the slide head first? (Figure 13–2).

Now that toddlers are aware that others cause actions to occur, imitation of others' behaviors becomes a part of their play. They use some play behaviors repeatedly in the same pattern and develop their own ritual play. Researchers have found that stimulating playthings are more important for cognitive development after age one than in earlier months. According to Healy (2004), availability of interesting and challenging play materials in the child's environment after the first year "predict[s] later IQ and school achievement in reading and math" (p. 53).

FIGURE 13–2 Toddlers learn about their physical world by putting themselves in different spaces.

SUGGESTIONS FOR IMPLEMENTING CURRICULUM—COGNITIVE DEVELOPMENT

CHILD BEHAVIOR	MATERIALS	EXAMPLES OF CAREGIVER STRATEGIES
Piaget's Substages of Sensorimotor Development		
SUBSTAGE 5 (Experimentation)		
Object Permanence		
Watches toy being hid and moved. Looks for it where it was moved.		Play game with child. Hide the object while child watches. Let the child watch you move the object to a different place under the blanket. Ask, "Where is it? Can you find it?" Observe and allow child to find the object. Describe their behaviors of watching and thinking.
Causality		
Investigates cause and effect		Allow and encourage child to search to identify the relationship between an action and the effect of it, e.g., "What made the ball go under the table?"
Sees self as causal agent		Verbally identify the child as cause of the action, e.g., "Laquata kicked the ball."
Explores various ways things happen	water toys, water basin	Allow the child time to play with the water and toys to discover different actions of water and of objects in the water.

(Continued)

CHILD BEHAVIOR	MATERIALS	EXAMPLES OF CAREGIVER STRATEGIES
Employs active trial-and-error to solve problems	narrow-neck milk carton, different sizes and shapes of objects	Provide time and materials that stimulate child to think and try out ideas. Ask questions but do not tell answers or show child.
Experiments with objects		Provide open-ended toys and materials that encourage several uses. Encourage child to see how many ways he or she can use them. Ask questions and allow time for the child to experiment; ask "What happens?"
Imitation and Play		
Copies behaviors of others		Encourage child to pretend: to drink from a pretend bottle like baby Gwen, to march like Pearl, to pick up toys. Think about your own behaviors; child will copy what you do. Be sure your actions are the kind of actions you feel comfortable seeing the child copy.
Turns play with imitation into rituals		Allow child to repeat own play and develop own preferences. For example, a child may see you hug a child who comes in the morning and imitate your hugging. The child may repeat this imitation and develop the ritual of hugging the child who has just arrived.

Language Development

Language in toddlers of this age expands, with less reliance on sounds and babbling and more use of recognizable words. A toddler uses many word approximations, which are reinforced and become a usable part of the toddler's expressive vocabulary.

Toddlers may **overgeneralize** or use one word for many different things. *Wawa* may mean anything to drink. *Mama* may mean any woman. Word meaning is usually flexible. The toddler may call anything that is round a *ball*. This is the time the vocabulary of the toddler can be expanded by your use of words to label actions and objects. It is also a time to make them more aware of the world around them by pointing out sounds to listen to and naming what they are. By 18 months toddlers will be asking what things and sounds are as they categorize their world.

Reading and books can provide enjoyable experiences for toddlers as well as promote language and cognitive development. Several different kinds of children's literature interest toddlers.

Point-and-say books have pictures of familiar objects and little text. The object of reading this type of literature is to increase each child's vocabulary, to compare pictures in a book with known items in the environment, to familiarize the child with books, and to show infants and toddlers that books have meaning.

Nursery rhymes, chants, poems, and songs are best chanted or sung throughout the day rather than just presented at read-aloud sessions. Then, at a later time, it can be thrilling to watch infants and toddlers associate the rhymes that he or she already knows with the picture representing that rhyme in a book. Nursery rhymes help them become familiar with the sounds of language. They assist the transition from telegraphic speech, where one to three words represent a sentence, to mature language, where each word is pronounced. (Lamme, 1985, pp. 57–58)

The interrelationships among language, reading, and writing are evident at an early age. Writing can be encouraged by giving children paper and pens or pencils to draw or write on (Lamme, 1984). Toddlers want to represent objects in their world. This is a beginning stage of writing. When you support them as they talk about what they have drawn or written, they connect symbols (mental representations) with language. Furthermore, encouraging children to watch as you write names, labels, and notes models how cultures use written texts to communicate. This modeling helps toddlers to understand that reading and writing serve important purposes.

SUGGESTIONS FOR IMPLEMENTING CURRICULUM—LANGUAGE DEVELOPMENT

CHILD BEHAVIOR	MATERIALS	EXAMPLES OF CAREGIVER STRATEGIES
Uses intonation		Use intonation when you talk to the toddler.
Babbles sentences		Respond to toddler's babbling.
Repeats, practices words		Repeat toddler's word. Occasionally expand it to a sentence, e.g., "gone-gone," "The milk is all gone."
Imitates sounds of other people, objects		Enjoy toddler's sounds. Play sounds game: point to objects and make sound of object, e.g., dog barking.
Responds to word and gesture conversation		Become very familiar with toddler's words and gestures. You often have to guess what the toddler is saying. Make a statement or ask a question to determine if you are interpreting correctly, e.g., "Taylor wants to go outside."
Responds to many questions and commands even if he or she cannot say them		Choose a few questions and commands you can use often and consistently. The toddler will learn what they mean through many experiences, e.g., "Go get your coat."

(Continued)

CHILD BEHAVIOR	MATERIALS	EXAMPLES OF CAREGIVER STRATEGIES
Uses word approximations for some words		Watch the toddler's behavior to help you experience what the child is experiencing. What do you see at the point where the child is looking, pointing, reaching? Say a word or sentence to test whether you are interpreting the word correctly.
Uses words in immediate context		Notice what the toddler is doing, saying, or needing right now. Toddler's talk is about immediate needs and desires, not past or future situations.
Identifies familiar pictures	pictures, picture book	Orally label objects. Ask toddler to point to or name familiar pictures.
Uses markers, chalk	markers, paper, chalk	Provide table space and materials. Write labels and sentences for child.

■ KEY TERMS

cause and effect	overgeneralize	trial and error
egocentric	parallel play	
individual constructivism	solitary play	

CASE STUDY   Andrea

Andrea is a 15-month-old who comes from an upper-middle-class professional family. Both of her parents have successful professions and work full time, so Andrea is in full-time child care. Her Developmental Profile indicates that she has average to above average overall development but is weak in the development of self-interest. This may be because her parents are very busy and Andrea must seek their attention, but she seems to need the attention and approval of other people almost all the time in order to feel secure and happy. When her primary caregiver pays attention to other children, Andrea appears to get upset, withdrawing and pouting.

To help Andrea, the caregivers at her child care center established a Developmental Prescription that analyzed the steps necessary to help Andrea share attention and enjoy time by herself. First, the strategy of "labeling her feelings" was used to assist her with identifying her feelings and her need to be close to others. Then, a meeting was held with her parents to establish a "special time" each day with each of them. The teachers also gave her choices of experiences to engage in alone. Within a short time, Andrea was able to spend time by herself enjoyably and share the attention of her caregivers.

1. Describe how and why each of these strategies would help with Andrea's problem.

2. What other strategies could be used to help children focus on themselves more?

3. What would be the next steps to take if all the strategies didn't help Andrea?

■ QUESTIONS AND EXPERIENCES FOR REFLECTION

1. Interview one caregiver. Ask the caregiver to describe the following:

   a. behaviors of a toddler between 12 and 18 months who is angry

   b. behaviors of the caregiver who is responding to the toddler's angry behavior

   Write the caregiver's descriptions and then put an X beside the descriptions of the behaviors of the toddler and the caregiver that are *physical*.

Behavior of Angry Toddler	Responding Behaviors of Caregiver

2. Listen to one toddler. Make a list of the child's words and "sentences." Watch the child's body language and nonverbal gestures. Then write down the complete sentences you think the child meant (you must think about the context in which the toddler was talking).

Word or Phrase	Meaning
Gone-gone	It is all gone; She went away.

3. Write one lesson plan to use with a toddler to help reinforce a word the toddler uses and to expand the use into sentences. Use the plan with the toddler. Evaluate the toddler's involvement. Evaluate the written lesson plan.

4. Observe one toddler between 12 and 18 months of age. Record the toddler's behavior in two five-minute sequences, using a narrative running record (see Appendix A). Transfer the descriptions to the Developmental Profile (Appendix B).

5. List five strategies to use with toddlers between 12 and 18 months of age.

6. List strategies you need to develop and list ways you intend to develop them.

■ CHAPTER REVIEW

1. If the toddler cannot say the name of an object or person, but you think the child understands the object-name match, how can you find out whether the child has connected the correct name with the correct object or person?

2. Describe something a 16-month-old would do that shows she has developed object permanence.

3. Describe two situations in which a toddler interacts with others. Describe two situations in which a toddler plays alone.

   With others

   a.

   b.

   Alone

   a.

   b.

4. List five safety precautions you need to take with a toddler who is between 12 and 18 months of age. Explain why these precautions must be taken.

5. With the development of eye-hand coordination, what can toddlers do now that they could not do as well several months earlier?

■ REFERENCES

Adolph, K. E., Vereijken, B., & Shrout, P. E. (2003). What changes in infant walking and why. *Child Development, 74*(2), 475–497.

Bredekamp, S., & Copple, C. (Eds.). (1997). *Developmentally appropriate practice in early childhood programs* (Rev. ed.). Washington, DC: National Association for the Education of Young Children.

Brickmeyer, J. (1978). *Guidelines for day care programs for migrant infants and toddlers*. New York: Bankstreet College.

Caplan, F., & Caplan, T. (1980). *The second twelve months of life*. New York: Bantam/Grosset and Dunlap.

Elkind, D. (2003, Winter). Montessori and constructivism. *Montessori Life, 15*(1), 26–29.

Erikson, E. (1963). *Childhood and society* (2nd ed.). New York: Norton.

Gonzalez-Mena, J., & Eyer, D. W. (2007). *Infants, toddlers, and caregivers* (7th ed.). New York: McGraw-Hill.

Healy, J. (2004). *Your child's growing mind: A guide to learning and brain development from birth to adolescence.* (3rd ed.). New York: Broadway Books.

Joh, A. S., & Adolph, K. E. (2006). Learning from falling. *Child Development, 77*(1), 89–102.

Lamme, L. L. (1984). *Growing up writing*. Washington, DC: Acropolis Books.

Lamme, L. L. (1985). *Growing up reading*. Washington, DC: Acropolis Books.

Lehman, E. B., Steier, A. J., Guidash, K. M., & Wanna, S. Y. (2002). Predictors of compliance in toddlers: Child temperament, maternal personality, and emotional availability. *Early Child Development and Care, 172*(3), 301–310.

Marion, M. (2007). *Guidance of young children* (7th ed.). Upper Saddle River, NJ: Prentice Hall.

McDevitt, T. M., & Ormrod, J. E. (2007). *Child development: Educating and working with children and adolescents* (3rd ed.). Upper Saddle River, NJ: Pearson Merrill Prentice Hall.

Swim, T. J., & Marion, M. (2006, November). Terrific toddlers: Good relationships build autonomy, self-regulation, and emotional intelligence. Paper presented at the annual conference of the National Association for the Education of Young Children, Atlanta, GA.

Wilson, L. C. (1987). Mommy, don't go! *Pre-K Today, 2*(1), 38–40.

■ ADDITIONAL RESOURCES

Emde, R. N., & Hewitt, J. K. (Eds.). (2001). *Infancy to early childhood: Genetic and environmental influences on developmental change.* Oxford, UK: Oxford University Press.

Hyson, M. (2004). *The emotional development of young children: Building an emotion-centered curriculum* (2nd ed.). New York: Teachers College Press.

Muir, D., & Slater, A. (Eds.). (2000). *Infant development: The essential readings.* Oxford, UK: Blackwell Publishing.

Roberts, C. (Ed.). (2002). *Johnson's child development: Your toddler from 2 to 3 years.* New York: Dorling Kindersley.

■ HELPFUL WEB SITES

Beyond the Journal Archive. "Helping Babies Play," two pages of ideas for engaging infants (birth–18 months) in play, is available at **http://www.journal.naeyc.org/btj/200305/HelpingBabies_Sawyers.pdf**

Child Development Institute. Information on intellectual and language development. **http://www.childdevelopmentinfo.com**

iVillage Pregnancy & Parenting. The Toddler/Preschooler link takes you to development topics. http://parenting.ivillage.com/

National Network for Child Care. Provides multiple resources regarding the care and education of young children. http://www.nncc.org/

Purdue University Cooperative Extension. The Human Development section provides resources such as newsletters and play kits for infants and toddlers. http://www.ces.purdue.edu/cfs/topics/HD/resources.htm

ZERO TO THREE National Center for Infants, Toddlers, and Families. http://www.zerotothree.org

For additional infant and toddler resources, visit our Web site at
http://www.earlychilded.delmar.com

14

The Child from Eighteen to Twenty-four Months of Age

■ OBJECTIVES

After reading this chapter, you should be able to:

• Identify and record sequences of change in the physical, emotional, social, cognitive, and language development of children from 18 to 24 months of age.

• Select materials appropriate to the development of children at that age level.

• Devise strategies appropriate to children of that age level.

■ CHAPTER OUTLINE

Lennie's Story

Lennie, 23 months old, walks to a child-sized rocking chair, backs up to it and sits down. He rocks and watches the other children. He gets off the chair and sits on his legs to pick up blocks. He picks up a block wagon, stands up, and walks around. He holds the block wagon in his left hand, tries to put in another block with his right hand, and succeeds. He puts the wagon on the floor and pushes it. He takes off one block and then takes off five blocks; he puts them back on. Jasper walks past and Lennie says, "Noooo." Tracey takes the block wagon. Lennie reaches for it but does not get it. He bites Tracey on the arm; when she lets go of the wagon, he picks it up and begins putting blocks in it. He picks up the block wagon and a block bag, gets up and walks around, talking to himself.

MATERIALS AND ACTIVITIES

Walking, climbing, and riding materials and activities are enjoyable for children at this age. As they practice their gross motor skills, they develop increased competence in using them. Their finger and wrist muscles are developing so they can manipulate more complex objects. Their imaginations are expanding as they construct internal representations of their world.

Types of Materials

textures	tunnel
snap toys	riding toys and cycles
large stringing beads	water play equipment
blocks	sand play equipment
toy people	soap paint
caps or lids to twist off containers	finger paint
toys to throw	tempera paint
tools: hammer, broom, shovel	puzzles
cars, trucks	books
zippers	telephones
hairbrush	dolls
toothbrush	stuffed animals
low, wide balance beam	puppets
slide	music: CDs, tapes
pull and push toys	modeling dough
balls	markers, crayons, chalk, pens
low stairs	containers to fill and empty

Examples of Homemade Materials

TUNNEL

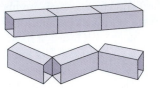

Use a sturdy, long cardboard box large enough for child to crawl through. Cut out ends and tape edges to prevent scraping the child and tearing the box. Place several boxes end to end or in a square or zigzag pattern.

PUPPET

Use a paper plate. The child tears colored paper and yarn and pastes the pieces on the paper plate. These puppets are safer without a wooden stick handle.

TARGET

Use a plastic pail (empty ice cream or peanut butter container). Place tennis balls or yarn balls in the pail. Use a piece of yarn to mark where the child will stand to throw objects into the pail.

MODELING DOUGH
RECIPE

2 cups flour
2 cups water
1 cup salt
3 teaspoons cream of tartar
2 tablespoons oil
food coloring

Combine flour, salt, and cream of tartar. Combine oil, food coloring, and water. Pour liquids into flour-salt mixture in a pot. Stir to get pie dough consistency. Cook, stirring over medium heat until ball forms. Store in a covered container. Shape into a ball, then dip into food coloring, rolling ball back and forth. Watch colors change. Keep manipulating dough to keep it soft. All sorts of shapes can be made, such as a vase (make paper flowers to go in it).

BOOK

Cut three pieces of sturdy cardboard. Select three magazine pictures that make a sequence or that have something in common (e.g., they are all red). Glue one picture on each piece of cardboard. Cover the pictures and cardboard with clear Con-Tact paper. Connect the pieces by punching holes in the side of the cardboard and tying together with yarn.

CAREGIVER STRATEGIES TO ENHANCE DEVELOPMENT

Developmental Profile

Lennie is a 23-month-old; his Developmental Profile is presented in Figure 14–1. Inspection of the profile reveals that Lennie exhibits problems in the Emotional, Social, and Language areas and is within age expectations in other areas.

Specifically, Lennie is estimated at age level in the areas I (Physical) and IV (Cognitive). He is estimated to be significantly below age level in area II (Emotional)—control of feelings (18 months) and the Social area (III)—self-concept (20 months) and interactions with others (18 months). In area IV (Language) he imitates sounds of other people and uses word approximations for some words, so the estimate is 16 months. These estimates reflect the fact that Lennie exhibits an average of two temper tantrums per day and bites other children three to four times per day. Upon closer examination, it appears that Lennie has tantrums in response to being told that he cannot do something by caregivers, and he bites when other children have toys or things he wants. For some children this age, biting is common.

In general, Lennie is a 23-month-old who exhibits normal development except for having temper tantrums and biting behavior. These aggressive and antisocial behaviors must be limited by the caregiver to ensure the safe care of Lennie and the other children. In addition to using the caregiver strategies described below, other techniques that can effectively reduce tantrums and biting behaviors include providing appropriate choices instead of giving a command to do something and offering language scaffolding (i.e., talking for him to the other children). Furthermore, the caregiver can attend to positive behaviors and give approval when Lennie starts to

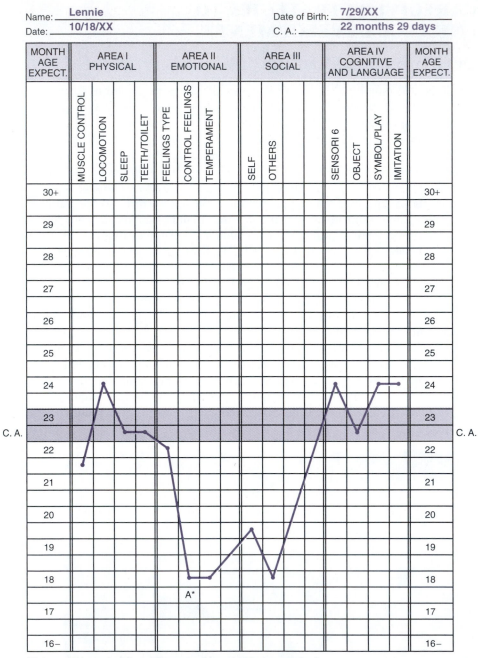

Notes: A* Lennie bites others and has tantrums each day.

FIGURE 14–1   Developmental profile for Lennie.

Caregivers provide a variety of experiences and materials to promote fine motor development.

accept "no" and makes strides toward sharing with others. A specific plan to reduce and eliminate tantrums and biting should be added to the other caregiver strategies to provide Lennie with a comprehensive, balanced program.

Physical Development

Children of this age are gaining much more stability and coordination. They can stand up, squat, reach over, and stand upright again without toppling. They climb on just about everything and, when they are around 18 months old, they try climbing out of their cribs. They will soon succeed. They climb up and down stairs by holding onto a rail or hand to maintain balance, but still do not alternate their feet. These children can now move rapidly, both walking and running, and jump with both feet. They become increasingly more adept at kicking balls. By around 22 months they can pedal cycles such as Big Wheels and they love to push and pull toys and objects. They can throw objects at targets rather than randomly throwing and tossing, though they seldom hit the intended target.

These children's fine motor muscles are developing, so they have increased control of their fingers and wrists. They probe and twist and turn objects. Their muscles relax so they can more easily release the objects they have grasped, allowing them to drop or throw objects when they choose to. They also are more accurate in directing dropped or thrown objects.

Determine each child's dominant hand and allow the child to use it.

At 18 months many children can turn the pages of a book several at a time, but by 24 months they will be able to turn pages one at a time.

Some children may favor one hand over the other. Determine each child's dominant hand and allow the child to use it. The child may occasionally use the other hand when using a spoon, for example; if the child occasionally chooses to do so, this will not be harmful. The caregiver should allow the child to develop and maintain the handedness that is comfortable. Do not attempt to make a left-handed child use utensils and toys with the right hand. That child's neurological patterns have developed with his or her left-handedness. Attempting to change a child's handedness may cause both neurological and muscular stress.

SUGGESTIONS FOR IMPLEMENTING CURRICULUM—PHYSICAL DEVELOPMENT

CHILD BEHAVIOR	MATERIALS	EXAMPLES OF CAREGIVER STRATEGIES
Muscular Control		
LOCOMOTION		
Walks forward	flat floor, ground; clear of toys	Keep area clear of toys or caution child about obstacles.
Walks backward		
Walks sideways	area clear of toys	Play with child: walk sideways, forward, backward.
Runs with stops and starts	clear area	Provide *flat* running space. On incline child may run down too fast and fall on face.

CHILD BEHAVIOR	MATERIALS	EXAMPLES OF CAREGIVER STRATEGIES
Jumps with both feet	low steps, box, block, plastic crate	Keep other children away from jumping spot when one child is jumping to the floor. Sometimes catch child as he or she jumps. Release and steady child so he or she can climb and jump again.
Kicks object	large ball: beach ball, nerf ball, soccer ball, volleyball, rubber ball	Provide space where child can kick the ball and it will not go too far, e.g., into a big cardboard box or into a corner.
Walks up stairs holding railing; walks down stairs holding railing	steps and rail	Provide equipment and time for child to safely walk up and down.
Pushes and pulls objects while walking	small wagon, strollers, pull toys, push toys that make noise, attract visual attention	Provide clear space for walking where pushed and pulled toys have room to move without bumping and catching on equipment, furniture, rug.
Climbs	sturdy box, cubes, footstool, low climbing gym	Provide equipment. Remain close by to assist in getting down if needed.
Pedals cycle	low riding cycle; not high tricycle	Provide space for fast and slow riding, for turning curves and in circles. Keep away children on foot.
ARM		
Throws object at target	bean bag; ball, box, cardboard or wood shape with large holes cut in it	Place target at edge of play area so object is thrown away from children.
HAND		
Grasps and releases with developing finger muscles	small toys, objects, pail, box	Provide objects for game of pick-up-and-drop.
Pulls zippers	zipper board, book, clothes with large zipper with tab	Provide large zipper with tab large enough for small fingers to pinch and pull. Demonstrate where to hold fabric in other hand.
Helps dress and undress self		Allow child to do as much as possible. Plan ahead to provide enough time for child who dresses and undresses slowly.
Scribbles	paper, pens, crayons, markers, pencils, flat hard surface	Provide space and time to scribble.
Increases wrist flexibility; turns wrist to turn object	small objects to twist and turn; jars and screw-on lids	Provide toys that stimulate manipulating, e.g., attractive, textured on several sides. Demonstrate twisting jar lid on and off.

(Continued)

CHILD BEHAVIOR	MATERIALS	EXAMPLES OF CAREGIVER STRATEGIES
Establishes right- or left-handedness		Allow child to pick up objects and use them with hand child chooses. Do not change object into other hand.
Turns book pages	sturdy pages in books	Read to child, carefully turning each page by grasping the upper right-hand corner and moving hand down to middle of page to gently turn the page.
Moves to music	play a CD or other recording	Move with child to the pace of the music.
Digs with tool	shovel, scoop, spoon; sand, dirt	Provide tools which are not sharp and will not bend. Provide space designated for digging. Demonstrate where sand or dirt may and may not go.
Makes individual marks with crayon or pen	paper, pen, crayon, marker	Listen if child talks about his or her marks. Provide feedback about what you see (e.g., colors, shapes) to child.
Sleeping		
May move from crib to bed or cot	firm cot, mattress	Talk about the change *before* it happens. Emphasize child is getting bigger and now can use a *bigger* bed. Demonstrate where shoes go, where blanket is. Provide quiet talk, music, touch familiar to child.
Eating		
Controls cup and spoon better		Emphasize how well child is using cup, spoon. Be patient with spills.
May eat anything, then change to picky eating		Allow child to change eating behavior. Don't fuss at or push child. Child usually will get adequate nutrition if variety of foods are provided.
Teeth		
Has most baby teeth; uses toothbrush	toothbrush, toothpaste, cup of water	Assist when necessary with applying toothpaste and cleaning face afterward.

Emotional Development

Children of this age are continuing to develop positive and negative feelings about themselves. They interpret responses from caregivers and children as reflecting their self-worth. At this stage, children's feelings are hurt by criticism and they are afraid of disapproval or rejection. They become easily frustrated and are able to communicate some feelings and desires. It is important to consciously use the three As at this age of development.

Children's fantasies increase at this age. They are very real and may sometimes be frightening. Improvements in memory and other cognitive skills (e.g., object permanence) result in toddlers expressing more fears and experiencing increased levels of stress due to them. Toddlers may feel fearful of being separated or abandoned by family members, monsters, loud noises, being sucked down the toilet, or of losing control. Teachers can respond to their distress by creating new routines or maintaining existing routines (Simpson & McGuire, 2004). For example, Ms. Linda helps each family to create their own good-bye routines which include hugs, kisses, and waving good-bye from the good-bye window (Balaban, 2006; Herr & Swim, 2002). Because shared reading provides security and calms children's emotional agitation (Rosenkoetter & Barton, 2002), Ms. Linda uses books to calm children after they are separated from their family. She keeps in reach a few favorite books about emotions and being separated from favorite objects or possessions (see Zeece & Churchill, 2001, for book suggestions) that she reads individually to children after they have been dropped off at her family child care center. Ms. Linda also helps families to provide security objects (e.g., blankets, stuffed animals) when a child responds positively to their presence (see, for example, Steir & Lehman, 2000).

Emotions are reflected in intense behaviors. These children can swing between extremes, such as smiling, laughing, followed by screaming, crying. Their basic pattern of intensity of response is affected by their swings into even more intense behaviors. Children who usually respond loudly may now scream and yell or laugh shrilly. Children who have a low intensity of response may use more energy and respond more loudly or actively than usual or they may exhibit even more withdrawn behaviors in response to increases in stress.

As toddlers approach their second birthdays, they become aware that they have a self and that they are separate from the world of other people and things. They now want to act like separate social beings. Becoming a separate psychological being is one of the most complicated tasks a toddler has to face. During the two years starting from birth, the child establishes a very strong attachment to family members and other primary caregivers. When dependence on others begins to diminish, separation follows. The more enjoyable and secure the relationships have been, the easier the separation process (Caplan & Caplan, 1980).

SUGGESTIONS FOR IMPLEMENTING CURRICULUM—EMOTIONAL DEVELOPMENT

CHILD BEHAVIOR	EXAMPLES OF CAREGIVER STRATEGIES
Types of Emotions and Feelings	
Shows one or more emotions at same time	Identify the child's emotions. Respond to the child's needs.
Continues to develop feelings about self	Provide consistent behavior and feedback that helps the child feel good about self; help child know he or she is a worthy person.
Changes feelings about self	Tell child that he or she is still a loved person when child reflects negative or angry feelings about self.

(Continued)

CHILD BEHAVIOR	EXAMPLES OF CAREGIVER STRATEGIES
Seeks approval	Provide verbal and nonverbal approval of child as a person and of child's behavior when it is positive.
May develop new fears	Listen to child's fears. Accept them as real. Comfort child. Reassure child of your concern and of your presence. You may demonstrate that the object, for example a siren toy, is harmless. If you cannot calm the child, remove the toy and introduce again later.
Increases fantasy	Listen to child's fantasies. Accept them as real to the child. Enjoy funny, happy fantasies. Comfort and reassure child of his or her safety when child has scary fantasies, e.g., "There's a monster in the kitchen."
May increase aggressiveness	Remain nearby to caution, remind, and sometimes remove object or child from situation.
Seeks security in routines	Provide consistent routines that child can use by him- or herself as child increases competence and seeks independence.
May become shy again	Allow child to hold back or withdraw. Provide time for child to observe without having to enter into interactions with others.
Sometimes rejects family members or caregiver	Allow child to express rejection in words and behaviors. Continue to express your affection for the child.
Control of Emotions and Feelings	
Uses reactions of others as a controller of own behavior	Use words, facial expressions, gestures to indicate approval and disapproval of child's behavior.
May resist change	Explain change *before* it happens. Provide reason for the change. Motivate by emphasizing the specialness of the child who now is allowed to do something else. Remember that development is a process not a product. Give time for lessons to be learned.
Moves to extremes, from lovable to demanding and stubborn	Allow child to express swings in behavior. Show acceptance of child as a person. Help child work on his or her demands and stubbornness by suggesting alternatives in behavior.

Social Development

Children of this age are continuing to develop a sense of self. They use words that identify them as separate people, such as *I*, *mine*, *me*, *you*. These children are also expanding their relationships with others. They are beginning to recognize other people's feelings and they are working slowly at understanding another person's intentions. Hay, Castle, and Davies (2000) discovered that when toddlers age 18 to 30 months attributed a hostile intent to familiar peers during interactions, they were more likely to use personal force. In other words, if a peer pointed toward or reached for an object that the toddler was using, she was likely to protest, with-draw the object, or physically harm the peer. This pattern of outcomes is particu-larly noteworthy because it suggests that some toddlers may be prone to attributing hostile intent, which may interfere with their ability to form positive relationships with new acquaintances, and that "social misunderstandings and processes of peer rejection might begin even before a child enters formal group care" (p. 465).

Caregivers should help the toddlers to interpret the behaviors of their peers by providing descriptive language. If a toddler reaches for the toy of another, the teacher should describe what he sees and provide an alternative perspective and pos-sible strategies. For example, "Burke, you are watching Libby smash the play dough with the rolling pin. Do you want to roll? Here is another rolling pin for you." You should then involve Libby in the conversation to facilitate her interpretation of Burke's reaching behaviors by saying, "Burke likes the way you are flattening the dough. He was watching you work. He wants to use the rolling pin also. I found one for him." In Chapter 6, we discussed the importance of communicating the intentions and actions of the people involved to assist very young children with beginning to learn perspective taking.

Toddlers are still working on showing ownership and are not yet ready to share. Provide multiple supplies and equipment so that they can engage alongside each other in parallel play.

Toddlers do not share toys easily, so the early childhood teacher should provide enough toys of a similar nature for them to use.

SUGGESTIONS FOR IMPLEMENTING CURRICULUM—SOCIAL DEVELOPMENT

CHILD BEHAVIOR	EXAMPLES OF CAREGIVER STRATEGIES
Self	
Is egocentric, sees things from own point of view	Recognize that child thinks others think and feel the way he or she does. Help child identify own ideas and feelings.
May change identity of self from day to day	Provide feedback to child about self so child can identify consistency within self.
Identifies materials as belonging to self	Recognize and allow ownership of toys.
Uses *I*, *mine*, *me*, *you*	Verbally respond to child's use of pronouns, reinforcing distinction child makes between self and others.
Others	
Demands attention	Both initiate and respond to child to provide attention to child's needs. Share looks, touch, and words with child when you may be busy with another child.
Begins to be aware of others' feelings	Help child identify and verbalize the feelings he has that appear in his behavior, e.g., "Allen is crying; he is sad."
Believes that people have changes in identity—that a change in role changes a person	Identify yourself in your different tasks, e.g., as you sweep and clean, as you cook, as you rock a child.
Expands social relationships	Encourage child to interact with others. Be present and provide your support when child encounters a new child or adult.
Looks to others for help	Consistently provide assistance when needed. Praise child for seeking help with something child would not be able to do for self, e.g., putting on shoe and then seeking help for tying laces instead of fussing and crying.
Imitates tasks of others	Allow and enjoy child's watching you and others. Enjoy the imitations and don't be concerned that the imitation might be incomplete or inaccurate. The child will continue to watch and imitate.
Wants to help, assist with tasks, clean up	Encourage the child to help put toys away, clean up, etc. Work along with child. Child can be a very good helper if he or she sees how you do it.
May do opposite of what is requested	Carefully word your requests. The child's negativism comes out in a frequent "no." Think of different ways to produce desired behavior without saying, "Do this."
Has difficulty sharing	Provide enough toys and materials so child does not have to share. Suggest allowing another child to play with toy when child finishes. Provide alternative toys to the child who must wait for a desired toy.
Engages in parallel play	Provide toys, materials, and space for children to play near each other. You Talk to each of them. Allow them to choose if they want to trade toys or do something else.

Cognitive and Language Development

Cognitive Development

Children of this age are experiencing Piaget's substage 6 or even are transitioning to the preoperational stage of development. This means that they are gradually using mental trial and error. This is much faster than the sensorimotor trial and error, in which children had to manipulate objects. A toddler can now make decisions mentally about how something might work or how he or she might affect an object.

While object permanence is well established, toddlers of this age repeatedly engage in games such as peekaboo. They will explore the hiding locations of objects both on their own or when an adult prompts them. May, Kantor, and Sanderson (2004) described a curriculum project which grew from two children's ritualistic investigation of object permanence. In this project, teachers supported the children's interest by planning activities that provided new or novel opportunities for hiding and promoted development by scaffolding the toddler's learning.

Because of their ability to store and recall mental representations, toddlers are now able to follow one- and sometimes two-step oral directions. In addition, these memory skills help children of this age become skilled at imitating past events. Imitative behaviors often show up in the children's play. For example, the caregiver washing the child's face is imitated later by the child as the child washes a doll's face. Play begins to move from imitative to symbolic during this time period. **Symbolic play** is children's representation of objects or feelings or ideas. They begin to connect past experiences into their current world as they take on simple roles. Infants and toddlers begin symbolic play by imitating actions associated with particular props, learning to substitute one thing for another, and acting as if they are someone else who is familiar to them (Isenberg & Jalongo, 2001; Van Hoorn, Nourot, Scales, & Alward, 2003). Simone might pretend to be a cook and make soup by stirring a spoon in a pot. You might hear Simone say "more salt" just as a cook might say after taste-testing. Symbolic play serves several functions: Children can express conflicts and work them out in the pretend world. They can pretend to be other people or objects, thereby reflecting their understanding of other people or objects as separate from themselves and trying behaviors similar to or different from their own. For those reasons, play is a window for adults to observe and tune into the children's emotional lives (i.e., their worries, fears, and joys; see Honig, 2005). Yet, caution must be exhibited when teachers observe a child's play. While toddlers often imitate a person's behavior, they also put their own spin on the situation by joining together reality and fantasy. For example, a toddler who has never been spanked or hit by a family member might hit a doll. So, for accuracy purposes, teachers should watch play behaviors over a period of time before making interpretations (Marion, 2004).

At around 22 to 24 months, a caregiver can determine what is going on with a child cognitively by **role playing** with puppets or dolls. Often the troubled child explains (verbally or nonverbally) very clearly to the caregiver a situation that might have been disturbing or upsetting. Role playing is also a good way for the child to get feedback in a positive way, a good place to use the three *As*, and a good way to help them solve problems and continue to develop good *self-esteem*.

SUGGESTIONS FOR IMPLEMENTING CURRICULUM—COGNITIVE DEVELOPMENT

CHILD BEHAVIOR	EXAMPLES OF CAREGIVER STRATEGIES
Piaget's Substages of Sensorimotor Development	
SUBSTAGE 6 (Representation)	
Mental trial and error	
Tries out ideas mentally, based on past concrete experiences	Allow child time to figure out solutions. If child seeks assistance, help child think about the problem, e.g., "What can you use to reach that block?"
Object permanence	
Sees object disappear, mentally remembers object, and figures out where it went	Allow the child to think and search for object. Give clues, ask questions only after the child has acted and still needs assistance.
Deferred imitation and symbolization	
Imitates past events	Observe the child's representations. Identify the ideas that seem very important to the child.
Symbolic play	
Resolves conflicts	Allow the child to act out conflict by playing with toys and materials. Observe how the child works out conflict so he or she feels better.
Compensates for unsatisfied needs	Observe child's play. Identify consistent themes in child's play, e.g., child's talk and actions about being a good or a naughty child.
Tries roles	Provide clothes and materials that help child pretend to be someone else.

Language Development

Language throughout life is clearly linked with positive relationships, and it is important to remember that children who get enough cuddling and unconditional love have a better chance at learning language—and everything else (Healy, 2004).

Caregivers must be careful not to criticize children's speech patterns. Good grammatical structure is learned by children when adults set good examples and repeatedly use words correctly. Remember to use the three As when speech is used correctly as well as to encourage children when they have verbalized.

At this age children's vocabulary is expanding rapidly as they label objects that they now recognize as separate entities (Figure 14–2). Children construct the principle that

> words are labels for socially defined classes of objects and events. This achievement is reflected in more systematic and productive extension of words and in accelerated growth of vocabulary. . . . This is the time when children may tire their caregivers by constantly asking for the names of things (e.g., what's this?). They eagerly utter the words they hear and explore their uses. (Anisfeld, 1984, p. 86)

FIGURE 14–2   The caregiver uses familiar objects to play choosing and naming games.

Children use their language to express needs and to direct others. They question as they seek to learn about their world (Wilson, 1988). Toddlers now use nouns, verbs, and pronouns as they combine their words into two- and three-word sentences. These children produce **telegraphic speech**, that is, a sequence of several words that conveys a thought or action but has omitted words. In general, telegraphic speech is almost exclusively made up of lexical words, rather than grammatical words (McDevitt & Ormrod, 2007; see Chapter 11 for the difference between lexical and grammatical words). For example, Cameron says, "Key go car" when he sees his mother take the key ring out of her purse. She responds, "Yes, I have the key. We are going in the car."

There are two broad classes of language functions: "the **cognitive function**—to name, indicate, describe, and comment; and the **instrumental function**—to request, reject, manipulate, and express desires. . . . [W]ords are used for cognitive purposes before they are used for instrumental purposes" (Anisfeld, 1984, p. 91). Caregivers and children use words to classify objects and actions (Figure 14–3). Words help children organize what they see and hear and do. Anisfeld (1984) reported that when adults do the following things they help young children develop proper language:

- The adult speaks to children in short sentences.
- The adult articulates more clearly to young children than to others.
- The adult talks about the situation in which the child is involved.
- The adult expands what the child says ("fills in the missing words as she echoes the child's utterance").
- The adult extends what the child says ("continues a thought started by a child").
- The adult imitates what the child says ("repeats all or part of what the child had said").

FIGURE 14–3 Outdoor activities provide many opportunities to observe, question, label, and describe the toddler's actions.

Pictures, books, and storytelling stimulate language interactions among caregivers and children. Rosenkoetter & Barton (2002) explain how reading to infants and toddlers builds relationships between adults and children as well as between children and books.

> During the early years, reading together is more significant than targeting any specific content or skills. While sitting on a lap, rocking in a chair, or even sprawling side-by-side on the floor with a favorite adult, the toddler builds very positive associations and happy preverbal memories of "reading." . . . With young children, reading times can be very brief, but they must happen every day. Shared reading helps children explore new worlds, laugh across generations, and learn about amazing as well as ordinary things. (p. 34)

As just stated, teachers need to provide opportunities for shared reading frequently—several times during the day, because they tend to be of short duration. Refrain from only reading to a group of toddlers; each child needs time to snuggle up with a primary caregiver and a good book throughout the day. Choose reading materials for young children carefully. Stimulate the toddlers' interests in reading and hearing stories often. Providing a variety of reading materials, such as magazines, board books and picture books, small books and big books, non-fiction and storybooks, assists children with acquiring knowledge as well as a love of reading. In addition, making a flannel board or puppets with characters from familiar stories encourages toddlers to actively engage with the story (Lamme, 1985). Be prepared to read favorite stories again and again or to chant beloved nursery rhymes over and over.

SUGGESTIONS FOR IMPLEMENTING CURRICULUM—LANGUAGE DEVELOPMENT

CHILD BEHAVIOR	MATERIALS	EXAMPLES CAREGIVER STRATEGIES
Uses language to reflect own meaning; expects others to have same meaning		Recognize limited meaning of child's use of words. Be careful not to read extra meaning into what the child says.
Expands vocabulary rapidly, labeling objects		Verbally label objects and actions in child's world. Point to and touch the objects. Also expand the label into a sentence, e.g., "Ball. Michael has a ball."
Points to objects and pictures named by others		Play games, look at pictures, read books; say, "Point to the bird" or "Where is the car?"
Learns social words: *hello, please, thank you*		Consistently use social words in their correct context. Say "please" and "thank you" to the child.
Uses language to express needs, desires		Listen to child's expression of needs. Verbally respond so child knows that his or her words get your attention and you understand them. Use words and actions to meet child's needs or explain why you cannot meet them, e.g., "The milk is all gone."
Uses language to direct others		Listen to child's commands. Respond verbally and with action following child's directions or explain why you are not, e.g., "Here is a napkin" when child asks for one.
Questions; asks "What's that?"		Answer child's frequent and persistent questions. This is how the child learns labels and other information about the world. Provide simple answers, not complicated ones, e.g., "That is a flower" rather than a description of petals, leaves, stem, etc.
Uses nouns, verbs, pronouns		Speak normally with the child so child can hear complete sentence patterns.
Is learning prepositions		Use in natural contexts, e.g., "The ball rolled under the table," "Put the book on the shelf."
Calls self by name		Use the child's name when talking directly to child.
Follows one-step directions		Use simple directions and praise when the child follows them, e.g., "Please put the truck here."
Follows two-step directions		Make sure child is aware that you are giving directions. Use simple directions, e.g., "Please pick up this book and put it on the shelf."
Makes two- and three-word sentences		Use both short and long sentences with the child. Encourage child and respond to child's sentences with elaboration, e.g., Child: "Coat on?" Caregiver: "Yes, you need your coat on."
Looks at books	cloth or paper or cardboard picture books	Read books with child. Demonstrate proper care of books. Allow child to look at books alone.
Listens to stories and rhymes		Tell stories that the child can understand. Use rhymes, poems.
Scribbles	markers, chalk, crayons, paper	Provide writing space and materials. Show interest and approval of scribbling. Share scribbling with others.

Regarding written representations, toddlers experiment with markers, chalk, and crayons as their interest in scribbling continues. Encourage their scribbling by providing time and attention to their use and enjoyment of writing. Avoid asking the child what his scribbles are. The scribbles at this stage may not represent anything. Rather, comment on what you see—lines from top to bottom or across the page, dots, and colors. You might make descriptive comments such as, "I like your orange and brown picture" or "What bold blue lines!" While the focus should be on the process of scribbling rather than the end product, do not forget to display some of the children's work in prominent locations in the environment (Lamme, 1984). This type of documentation assists the toddlers in valuing their own work and models the need to value such developmental milestones to other adults (e.g., family members and colleagues).

■ KEY TERMS

cognitive function	role playing	telegraphic speech
instrumental function	symbolic play	

CASE STUDY   Louise

Louise and her colleagues were very frustrated with Lennie's biting behavior. Not only had he broken the skin on several children's bodies, his daily tantrums caused damage to furniture and equipment. As Lennie's primary caregiver, Louise decided to invite Lennie's parents and the center's director to a conference after the Developmental Profile was completed, to discuss biting and tantrum behavior. She found that Lennie's mother was very defensive and aggressive when questioned about his behavior. Lennie being an only child has apparently made his mother overly defensive about his behavior, although she does not seem to be concerned about Lennie's feelings. Further, she kept referring to how his behavior affects her.

From the conference Louise concluded that a prescription that directly involves the parents is not possible at this time. She and the director analyzed Lennie's biting and tantrum behavior and established a Developmental Prescription for the child care setting. This involves using the following tools: labeling and expressing feelings, self-soothing, emotion management, and setting limits.

After a month of implementing the plan, Lennie's behavior had improved only slightly. It was at this time that his primary caregiver started to notice bruises on Lennie's back and legs. At first, she thought the bruises were the result of his violent tantrums, but one day he came in with a fresh bruise that looked like a hand print. When Lennie was questioned, he became sullen and quiet and withdrew from his caregiver, whom he liked.

1. What steps should Louise take at this point?

2. How would you react emotionally to this situation? How would you deal with and express your feelings?

3. What further steps and strategies could you use to help Lennie and his mother?

4. How may the lack of a reciprocal relationship between Louise and Lennie's mother have affected these outcomes?

■ QUESTIONS AND EXPERIENCES FOR REFLECTION

1. Observe one caregiver for 10 minutes. Use a narrative running record (Appendix A) to write down everything the caregiver does and says. Then categorize the behavior using a format like the following.

Caregiver Behavior (What Caregiver Did)	Caregiver Initiated	With Whom?	Caregiver Responded	To Whom?	Area(s) of Child Development Involved

2. Identify one child's characteristic temperament (by records, caregiver information, or your own observation). Observe how the caregiver makes adjustments in the routine or expectations of the child in response to the situation and how the caregiver helps the child make adjustments. For example, the caregiver may tell a low active child several minutes early that it is time for the child to put on outdoor clothing.

3. Make one toy and allow two children who are 18–24 months old to use it. Observe and write down how they used it, what they said, and your judgment about whether they seemed interested, challenged, or bored using it. Also evaluate the toy's construction.

Toy	How Used	Child's Comments	Interesting/ Challenging/ Boring?	Sturdy, Torn, Broken?
Child 1				
Child 2				

4. Observe one child between 18 and 24 months of age. Observe the child's behavior for two five-minute periods, and write two observations using an anecdotal record (Appendix A). Then transfer the descriptions to the Developmental Profile (Appendix A). Analyze the results and create a project by outlining three or four related learning experiences to support the child's development and interests.

5. List five strategies to use with children between 18 and 24 months of age.

6. Explain the relationship between language development and social relationships for children of this age. Among other things, be sure to address language skills and aggressive acts.

■ CHAPTER REVIEW

1. List three physical changes that enable a child to become more independent.

2. Chris and Marlin both pick up a car and start pulling on it. What can you do and what can you say that shows appropriate understanding of their needs and desires?

3. List three ways symbolic play helps a child.

4. Identify two possible developments in the child's language and state two strategies for each that a caregiver can use to facilitate that development.

Child's Development of Language	Caregiver Strategies
1.	1.
	2.
2.	1.
	2.

■ REFERENCES

Anisfeld, M. (1984). *Language development from birth to three*. Hillsdale, NJ: Lawrence Erlbaum Associates.

Balaban, N. (2006). Easing the separation process for infants, toddlers, and families. *Beyond the Journal: Young Children on the Web*. Retrieved January 16, 2007, from http://www.journal.naeyc.org/btj/200611/pdf/BTJBalaban.pdf

Caplan, F., & Caplan, T. (1980). *The second twelve months of life*. New York: Bantam/Grosset and Dunlap.

Hay, D. F., Castle, J., & Davies, L. (2000). Toddlers' use of force against familiar peers: A precursor of serious aggression? *Child Development, 71*(2), 457–467.

Healy, J. (2004). *Your child's growing mind: A guide to learning and brain development from birth to adolescence*. (3rd ed.). New York: Broadway Books.

Herr, J., & Swim, T. J. (2002). *Creative resources for infants and toddlers* (2nd ed.). Clifton Park, NY: Thomson Delmar Learning.

Honig, A. S. (2005, April). What infants, toddlers, and preschoolers learn from play: A dozen ideas. Paper presented at the American Montessori Society meeting, Chicago, IL.

Isenberg, J. P., & Jalongo, M. R. (2001). *Creative expression and play in early childhood* (3rd ed.). Upper Saddle River, NJ: Merrill Prentice Hall.

Lamme, L. L. (1984). *Growing up writing*. Washington, DC: Acropolis Books.

Lamme, L. L. (1985). *Growing up reading*. Washington, DC: Acropolis Books.

Marion, M. (2004). *Using observation in early childhood education*. Upper Saddle River, NJ: Pearson Prentice Hall.

May, N., Kantor, R., & Sanderson, M. (2004). There it is! Exploring the permanence of objects and the power of self with infants and toddlers. In J. Hendrick (Ed.), *Next steps toward teaching the Reggio way: Accepting the challenge to change* (2nd ed., pp. 164–174). Upper Saddle River, NJ: Prentice Hall.

McDevitt, T. M., & Ormrod, J. E. (2007). *Child development: Educating and working with children and adolescents* (3rd ed.). Upper Saddle River, NJ: Pearson Prentice Hall.

Rosenkoetter, S., & Barton, L. R. (2002). Bridges to literacy: Early routines that promote later school success. *Zero to Three, 22*(4), 33–38.

Simpson, C. G., & McGuire, M. (2004). Are you ready? Supporting children in an uncertain world. *Dimensions of Early Childhood, 32*(3), 35–38.

Steir, A. J., & Lehman, E. B. (2000). Attachment to transitional objects: Role of maternal personality and mother-toddler interaction. *American Journal of Orthopsychiatry, 70*(3), 340–350.

Van Hoorn, J., Nourot, P. M., Scales, B., & Alward, K. R. (2003). *Play at the center of the curriculum*. (3rd ed.). Upper Saddle River, NJ: Merrill Prentice Hall.

Wilson, L. C. (1988). What's in the box? *Pre-K Today, 2*(4), 38–39.

Zeece, P. D., & Churchill, S. L. (2001). First stories: Emergent literacy in infants and toddlers. *Early Childhood Education Journal, 29*(2), 101–104.

■ HELPFUL WEB SITES

Ready Set Read for Caregivers. Helpful articles, including "Talking About Me: Activities for Toddlers (18 to 36 Months Old)." http://www.ed.gov/Family/RSRforCaregvr/

BabyCenter: Your Toddler's Health. Topics include an A-to-Z Guide to Illnesses and Injuries and a safety checklist. http://www.babycenter.com/toddler

FamilyFun **Magazine.** Parenting tips on topics such as "Getting Your Toddler Back to Bed: Overcoming Nighttime Terrors in Two-Year-Olds." http://familyfun.go.com

Parenthood.com Topics A to Z. Articles organized into categories, including Play. http://topics-az.parenthood.com/

U.S. FDA Center for Food Safety and Applied Nutrition. Information for parents with children and toddlers. http://vm.cfsan.fda.gov/~dms/wh-infnt.html

For additional infant and toddler resources, visit our Web site at http://www.earlychilded.delmar.com

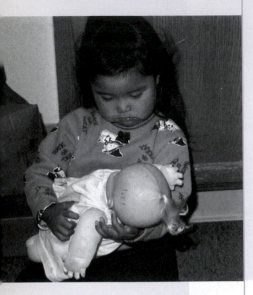

CHAPTER 15

The Child from Twenty-four to Thirty Months of Age

■ **OBJECTIVES**

After reading this chapter, you should be able to:

- Identify and record sequences of change in the physical, emotional, social, and cognitive/language development of children from 24 to 30 months of age.
- Select materials appropriate to the development of children at that age level.
- Devise strategies appropriate to children at that age level.

■ **CHAPTER OUTLINE**

- Materials and Activities
  Types of Materials
  Examples of Homemade Materials
  Activity Ideas
- Caregiver Strategies to Enhance Development
  Developmental Profile
  Physical Development
  Emotional Development
  Social Development
  Cognitive and Language Development
- Case Study: Ming

Ming's Story

Twenty-six-month-old Ming picks up a fire truck and walks up on the porch with it. She pushes it around on the floor, then picks it up and takes it out into the yard. Ms. Tao asks her what she has. Ming responds, "A truck," and smiles. Ms. Tao asks what kind of truck. Ming says, "red," and smiles. Ming picks up a ball and says, "Watch me throw it." She moves the fire truck and tells Ms. Tao, "Can't find ladder." Ms. Tao finds the ladder and starts to put it on the fire truck. Ming requests, "Let me do it." Ming puts a toy fireman in the truck and plays with it. She says to Ms. Tao, "See the truck," and then, "See if it goes?" As Ming plays with the fire truck, the ladder falls off again and she says, "Oh, no," and looks at Ms. Tao. She takes the truck to Ms. Tao to fix the ladder, saying "It fall off" and pointing to the ladder. She watches Ms. Tao fix the ladder and plays with it again. Another child gets the fire truck and begins to play with it. Ming tells the child, "I want the truck, Bill." Bill gives the fire truck back to Ming, who says, "Thank you, Bill."

MATERIALS AND ACTIVITIES

Riding toys are favorites at this age. The children also use climbing and jumping equipment frequently. Kicking and throwing, both more accurate than before, are enjoyed by the children. Finger, hand, and wrist movements, including grasping and

Trikes and other riding toys pose natural challenges for toddlers.

releasing, now coordinate with vision, enabling the children to string beads and to use crayons and other drawing and writing tools with greater accuracy. Children take pleasure in manipulating objects and materials. They focus on the process rather than on producing a product. They respond to and create music. They enjoy symbolic play. Children of this age can find meaning in pictures and books representing ideas with which they are familiar.

Most adults who work with toddlers wonder when and how children begin to be able to look at situations from another person's viewpoint. Some toddlers may seem to behave in an empathetic fashion occasionally or briefly. Such behavior is probably indicative of actions they have observed and reflects an emergent understanding of what someone else is feeling. A toddler may, for example, look concerned if another child cries, may rush over to pat the unhappy one, offer a cracker or toy, or may even burst into tears. Spinrad and Stifter (2006) found that when mothers were more responsive in their interactions with very young children, the toddlers displayed more concerned attention to a crying doll baby and to maternal distress. Logically, teachers who use the three *As* consistently will assist toddlers in learning to be empathetic and to display empathy with peers.

Types of Materials

balance beam	large pegs and boards
climbing equipment	large beads and string
bouncing equipment	markers, crayons, pens, chalk
rocking boat	modeling dough
wagon	construction material: wood,
cycles	styrofoam, glue
wheeled toys	rhythm instruments
items to throw	CDs
balls	audiotapes
blocks	puppets
trucks, cars	dress-up clothes
dolls, people, animals	pictures
jars with twist lids	books
items to put together or pull apart	puzzles
knobs	matching games

Examples of Homemade Materials

BALANCE BEAM

Put masking tape on the floor to indicate a line on which the child can walk.

In the yard partially bury a tree trunk so that several inches remain above ground. Place so that no branch stubs are on the top walking surface.

PEG BOARD

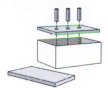

Cut a piece of heavy cardboard to fit in the bottom of a box (such as for shoes or gifts). Cut holes in the cardboard. Cut ½-inch dowel rod into roughly two-inch lengths. Paint if desired. Store cardboard and pegs in the box and use the lid.

MARACAS

Collect gourds in the fall. Allow to dry. The seeds will rattle when the gourd is shaken.

DRUM

Poke a hole in each end of an oatmeal box. Pull a strong string through the box and both ends and extend 12–24 inches (measure on one of your children). Tape the box lid onto one end of the box. Tie a knot or leave the ends loose and tie a bow each time you put it around a child's neck.

SOAP PAINT

Use one part soap flakes, one part water, and food coloring. Beat the mixture with a hand eggbeater. Skim off soap suds to paint on tabletop, shelf paper, or freezer paper.

FINGER PAINT

Use liquid starch, dry tempera paint, and soap flakes. Pour out about a tablespoon of liquid starch on shelf or freezer paper. Sprinkle dry paint on starch. Sprinkle soap flakes on starch. Children mix ingredients as they paint.

TEMPERA PAINT

Mix ½ cup dry tempera paint and ½ cup dry detergent. Add water until mixture is thick but not runny. Keep in covered jar.

PUPPETS

Use paper lunch bags. Child can use crayons or glue on paper to decorate puppet. Help child fit hand in bottom of sack.

CLOTH BOOK

Use pinking shears to cut heavy cloth to make several pieces the same size. Stack the pieces and sew down the middle by machine or by hand. Cut out colored pictures from magazines or greeting cards. Glue one picture per page. Make a theme book, e.g., children riding, or use pictures of different objects or activities.

GROUP BOOK

Have children tear out magazine pictures of objects; the pictures may fit a theme. Glue to pieces of paper. Staple the pages together. Write the title page. Write what children dictate to you for the other pages. (Paper may first be cut into a shape that matches the theme, e.g., pumpkin, leaf.)

PUZZLE

Cut out one uncluttered colored picture from a magazine.

a. Glue it to the center of the cardboard.
b. Cover the picture and cardboard with clear adhesive. Outline three to five sections that are visually recognizable (head, legs, tail) with a pencil. Cut around the picture, being careful to cut only the picture and not the cardboard.
c. Cut the remaining hole in the cardboard slightly larger.
d. Glue a backing onto the remainder of the cardboard with a second piece of cardboard the same size. Fit the puzzle pieces into place. If necessary, trim so the pieces come out easily.

MATCHING GAME

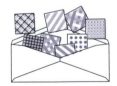

Cut two 2-inch squares from each page of a wallpaper sample book. Make about six pairs, using different pages. Store the pieces in an envelope. To play, mix up the pieces and then select squares that match.

MATCHING GAME

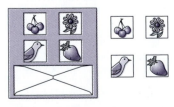

Select four picture pairs of objects that are alike, e.g., two cardinals, two mice, two daisies, two German shepherds. Glue one of each pair onto the bottom of a styrofoam tray. Glue the other four pictures onto cardboard and cut into small squares. Glue part of an envelope in the tray to hold the loose cardboard pieces. Randomly pick pieces that match the pictures on the tray. Ask child to point to matching object.

Activity Ideas

The following are examples of activities that help children construct knowledge, along with some of the items, concepts, and actions involved.

Exploration
Cooking

recipe chart	stir	see
oral language	beat	hear
measure	smell	taste
sift	feel	

Growing Plants

carrot	bean sprouts	observations
sweet potato	food	comparisons
beans	care	charting
lettuce	rate of growth	

Representations
Oral Language

conversation	poetry	singing and rhythms
information gathering	nursery rhymes	dramatic play
storytelling	fingerplays	

Objects

painting rocks, seeds, pine cones
creating prints with potatoes, carrots, celery; footprints, handprints, fingerprints

Pictures

magazines, photographs
art media: crayons, painting, tear and paste

Books

wordless picture books
naming books
books with a story line to read or tell in your own words

CAREGIVER STRATEGIES TO ENHANCE DEVELOPMENT

Developmental Profile

Figure 15–1 shows Ming's Developmental Profile, which is based on a 10-day observation of the child behaviors from the Developmental Prescription in Appendix A.

Ming exhibits a generally low profile in all areas except for the Emotional one, where estimates suggest near age-level expectancies. Within Area I (Physical), Ming

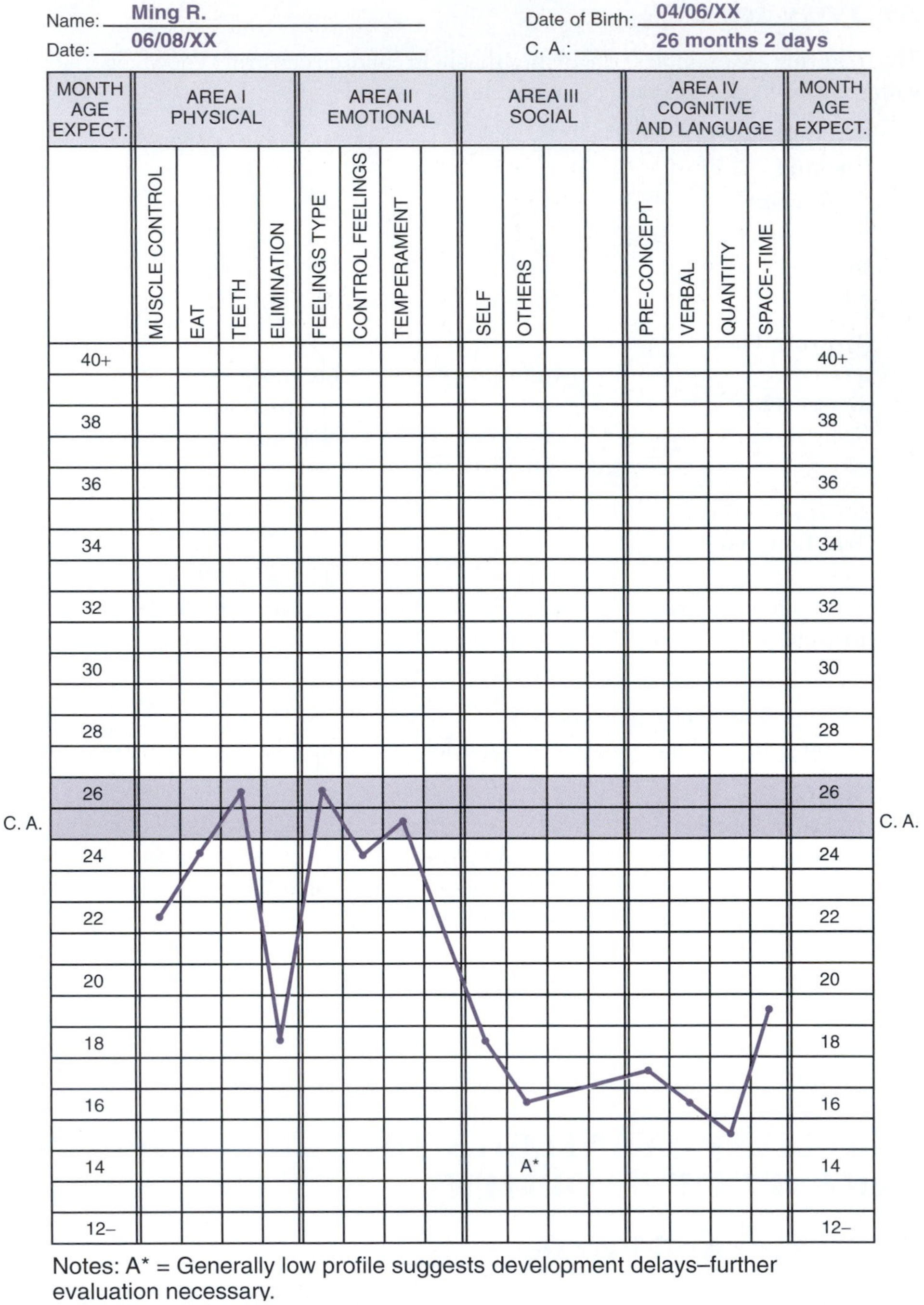

Name: __Ming R.__   Date of Birth: __04/06/XX__

Date: __06/08/XX__   C. A.: __26 months 2 days__

MONTH AGE EXPECT.	AREA I PHYSICAL				AREA II EMOTIONAL			AREA III SOCIAL			AREA IV COGNITIVE AND LANGUAGE				MONTH AGE EXPECT.
	MUSCLE CONTROL	EAT	TEETH	ELIMINATION	FEELINGS TYPE	CONTROL FEELINGS	TEMPERAMENT	SELF	OTHERS		PRE-CONCEPT	VERBAL	QUANTITY	SPACE-TIME	
40+															40+
38															38
36															36
34															34
32															32
30															30
28															28
26															26
24															24
22															22
20															20
18															18
16															16
14									A*						14
12–															12–

C. A. (row at 26)

Notes: A* = Generally low profile suggests development delays–further evaluation necessary.

FIGURE 15–1   Developmental profile for Ming R.

The young child is becoming more coordinated and can balance on smaller surfaces.

is estimated to be four months below C. A. in muscle control because she can't stand on one foot yet and tends to be physically uncoordinated for her age.

Ming has a quiet, accepting temperament, displays positive and negative self-worth, and therefore functions near C. A. in the Emotional Area (II). Socially (Area III), Ming does not realize her skills and abilities and shows emergent independence. She is compliant and polite. As a result, she is estimated to be at the 20-month level socially. Regarding her Cognitive and Language development (Area IV), Ming functions more like an 18-month-old than a 26-month-old. She has trouble classifying, labeling, and understanding concepts such as *up, down, more,* and *now.*

In summary, Ming exhibits general developmental lags in most of the important areas. She is estimated to be almost a year below age expectancy in her cognitive skills. These deficits are considered extreme for her age and are cause for further evaluation. The caregiver should hold a conference with Ming's family to explore whether formal evaluations by a psychologist and her pediatrician should be done to help determine the causes of these lags.

Physical Development

The two-year-old can stand, bend, walk, run, and jump. While riding toys are still favorites at this age, these children also use climbing and jumping equipment frequently. Kicking and throwing are increasingly accurate and enjoyable for the children. Toddlers are more flexible and stable in their movements than before (Adolph, Vereijken, & Shrout, 2003). Their eye-hand coordination is more accurate, so they can reach and grasp objects, but they still have difficulty using hands and fingers independently. They are able to fit objects together and like to put them together and pull them apart.

Toddlers may use either their right or left hand, but most still have not firmly established handedness. These children are visually fascinated with some new items and carefully observe novel objects. They use a spoon when eating and are learning to use a fork. Some children this age have all 20 baby teeth. These children should learn to brush their own teeth. Many children this age exhibit signs of being ready for toilet learning.

SUGGESTIONS FOR IMPLEMENTING CURRICULUM—PHYSICAL DEVELOPMENT

CHILD BEHAVIOR	MATERIALS	EXAMPLES OF CAREGIVER STRATEGIES
Muscular Control		
MOVEMENT		
Bends at waist	objects to drop and pick up: pail and plastic rings	Play game with child. Observe appropriateness of materials, interest of child.
Climbs	low objects: steps up to slide, tires	Select safe materials and safe height.
Jumps	two- to three-step equipment	Keep floor or ground space clear where jumping. Block off higher levels so jump is safe distance for muscles and balance.
Stands on one foot	song for lifting one foot	Make up rhyme or song about standing on one foot. Child will stand on one foot for only a few seconds. Provide feedback and encourage child to repeat or try again.
ARM		
Throws	target: large paper sack or plastic basin; objects: NERF™ ball, yarn ball	Provide space for child to throw objects at target. Decorate target so child is aiming at hoop or door.
HAND		
Touches	textured objects: sandpaper, fur, corduroy, egg carton bottom, juice can	Make feely box. Allow child to pull out objects to touch and see. Label objects and textures for child.
Twists	jars and cans with lids; large plastic nuts and bolts	Provide objects that twist on and off easily.
Eating		
Uses spoon	spoon that fits child's hand	Provide food that can be spooned easily.
Is learning to use fork	fork that fits child's hand	Provide food that will stay on fork.
Uses fingers		Cut solid food in small pieces so it can be picked up with fingers.

CHILD BEHAVIOR	MATERIALS	EXAMPLES OF CAREGIVER STRATEGIES
Teeth		
Has all 20 baby teeth		
Brushes teeth	toothbrush, toothpaste	Assist with toothpaste and water.
Elimination		
May show interest in and readiness for toilet learning	potty chair, training pants; slacks, leggings easy to remove	Show child where potty chair is. Encourage child to use it. Provide feedback to child when he or she does. Avoid pushing child. Many show interest in toileting months before they are ready for actual transition to toilet learning. Review Chapter 3 to understand child who is ready for consistent toilet learning.

Emotional Development

Feelings about the self continue to develop for children between twenty-four and thirty months of age. Emotional development includes positive and negative self-image, competence, and acceptance. Children this age are becoming more independent while simultaneously recognizing their need for help. They attempt to please and show affection. At 24 months they make fewer demands and are better able to express themselves. They can attend for longer and longer periods of time as they fully engage their minds and bodies in learning. However, by 30 months these easier-going children suddenly become more demanding and more possessive about their things. They become frustrated, say "no" to almost everything and have temper tantrums. They may suddenly want help with things they previously could do and want to do things they are not able to do. In quick succession they may be aggressive, then shy, then act like a baby. They cannot handle too many choices and demand sameness and consistency. In fact, meeting their need for sameness may well be the best way to handle the 30-month-old. *Routines* provide children this age with consistency and security. They may be affectionate at one moment and want no affection the next. Here, the caregiver's skills of being well organized, consistent, and flexible (as discussed in earlier chapters) may be challenged. Be sure to use plenty of the three As for your own benefit, as well as directly with the children.

We have tried to point out some of the behavioral components of healthy development in toddlerhood, a stage during which a child works on becoming an autonomous being capable of competently functioning in an environment appropriately geared to his or her needs and abilities. It should be clear that children who are given sufficient opportunities to explore, use their senses, be physically active, use expressive materials, and develop language skills may often—through the very nature of these activities—be destructive, messy, noisy, impudent, and defiant.

Friends show affection for each other.

These behaviors reflect directly the crisis they are experiencing in regard to their identity development: autonomy versus shame and doubt. During these times, early childhood educators must demonstrate respect for the toddler while providing extra helpings of the three As in order to meet the toddlers' developmental needs. Even when frustrated by the toddlers' inconsistent behaviors, teachers should continue to use positive guidance strategies (see Chapter 6), because successfully resolving this emotional crisis is vital for subsequent development.

SUGGESTIONS FOR IMPLEMENTING CURRICULUM—EMOTIONAL DEVELOPMENT

CHILD BEHAVIOR	EXAMPLES OF CAREGIVER STRATEGIES
Types of Emotions and Feelings	
Feels comfortable with self	Provide experiences which appropriately challenge children; when they succeed, they often feel pleased with themselves.
Feels positive self-worth	Give the child positive feedback. Reinforce other people's reflections of the child as a worthy person.
Feels negative self-worth	Be sensitive to the child's frustrations with tasks and with social encounters. Provide reassurance of the child's worth.
Control of Emotions and Feelings	
Expresses emotions	Accept the child's feelings as honest rather than manipulative.

Social Development

Twenty-four-month-olds enjoy the company of other children; they are beginning to interact while playing. Because toddlers still have some difficulty sharing, they continue to engage in parallel play. It is possible to involve children this age in group activities, such as painting individual pictures while sitting at the same table. Facilitating interactions between the toddlers will contribute to the toddlers initiating and engaging in cooperative interactions. By 30 months these children interact with each other, but may often quarrel over possessions rather than participate in a cooperative effort.

Play, according to child development experts, offers children a way to discover who they are and who they can be (Elkind, 2007; Honig, 2005). Toddlers become graceful and coordinated as they dance with scarves, explore gender roles as they play superheroes, and learn to control impulses and persist at difficult tasks through play (Honig, 2005). Children who are given the chance to enjoy a variety of experiences of play—role playing, make-believe play, social play with peers, individual creative and artistic play, dyadic play with an adult—not only develop emotionally, physically, cognitively, and socially but also become self-actualized (Tobin & Davidson, 1989).

With continued assistance, toddlers recognize emotions in others and may help with tasks such as chores. Following a routine may allow the caregiver to gain some cooperation in tasks and cleaning up.

Children of this age are certainly television and video viewers (Weber & Singer, 2004). A parent survey revealed that "By 23 months of age, 100% of the children in the sample watched television and 90% watched videos. . . . [C]hildren typically watched videos for 25 minutes per day and those who watched television programs did so for more than one hour per day" (Weber & Singer, p. 32). While the parents also noted that many of them watched every television program with their child (47 percent), it is unclear what developmental benefits there are for the toddlers. Teachers need to discuss with parents the importance of reading daily with their child. If half an hour or more is devoted to watching television or videos, this time might be more wisely spent on shared reading activities given the developmental and educational outcomes associated with that strategy (Dodici, Draper, & Peterson, 2003; Lawhon & Cobb, 2002; Rosenkoetter & Barton, 2002). In any case, television and videos have no place in an educational setting for infants and toddlers. There is no evidence that "media can be integrated into the lives of very young children in a developmentally appropriate way" (Weber & Singer, 2004, p. 36).

SUGGESTIONS FOR IMPLEMENTING CURRICULUM—SOCIAL DEVELOPMENT

CHILD BEHAVIOR	EXAMPLES OF CAREGIVER STRATEGIES
Self	
Realizes own skills	Provide materials and equipment that child can use to own satisfaction. Provide challenging materials that child can use.
Others	
Shows independence	Allow child to accomplish as many tasks as possible by self. Assist when asked or when you anticipate you are needed.

(Continued)

CHILD BEHAVIOR	EXAMPLES OF CAREGIVER STRATEGIES
Acts to please adult	Provide verbal and nonverbal positive feedback to child. Recognize child's need for your attention and approval. Plan activities child can help you with (e.g., clean-up).
Shows feelings to others	Show feelings to child. Show appropriate actions with feelings, e.g., *happy*: laugh, physical excitement; *sad*: hug, pat, listen. Provide feedback when he or she uses those behaviors.
Recognizes emotions in others	Label children's behaviors. Verbalize about feelings of others. Provide appropriate responses to behaviors. Provide feedback when child identifies or responds to others' emotions.
Understands *mine* and *yours*	Reinforce possession by child and others. It is *mine* while the speaker is using it.
Starts to share	Provide materials and equipment so some sharing is necessary. Provide feedback when child shares. Verbalize reasons for sharing. Recognize, however, that not all children can share yet.
Helps others	Provide opportunities for purposeful helping: clean-up, passing out items, assisting with clothing. Thank child for helping behaviors. Accept toddlers' offers to assist when they volunteer.
Engages in parallel play	Plan space and materials so children can play close to others without having to interact in play.
Engages in cooperative interactions	Engage the toddlers in conversations as they enjoy parallel play. Describe, for example, what each child is doing with materials (how alike and how different).

Cognitive and Language Development

Cognitive Development

Many children between 24 and 30 months are entering Piaget's **preoperational stage** of cognitive development. The first substage of the preoperational stage is **preconceptual**, which occurs from about two to four years of age. These children can mentally sort some objects and actions. The mental symbols are partly detached from experience. Early nonverbal classifications are called *graphic collections*, in which children can focus on figurative properties. These children form some verbal preconcepts, but the meaning of words may fluctuate from one time to another. Verbal reasoning is from the particular to the particular.

Preconceptual children are constructing and organizing knowledge about a wide range of areas in their world. They are beginning to classify objects and to develop very limited ideas of quantity, number, space, and time. Due to their preference for routines and sameness, their sense of time is based more on what happens after an event rather than on an understanding of *later* or minutes of time passage.

The development of the symbolic function occurs in the preconceptual stage. It involves the following mental representations, presented here in increasing order of complexity. In the child's **search for hidden objects** the object remains permanent (does not cease to exist) in the child's thinking even when the child cannot see it. These experiences form the basis for more specific representational thinking. In *deferred imitation* the child imitates another person's behavior even when that person is no longer present. A child engaged in symbolic play may give the caregiver a stone and tell the caregiver to "eat this apple"; the stone represents the real object. The child's *drawings* may be scribbles, experiments with the media, or they may begin to be representations; a child may point to a mark he or she has made on a piece of paper and say his or her own name. **Mental images** are pictures in the mind with which children can carry out action sequences internally. Language is used easily to represent objects or behaviors. As children develop language, they internalize words, meanings, mental images, and thoughts; from a Vygotskian perspective, language plays a critical role in cognitive development. This internalization of thoughts permits toddlers to use private speech to guide and regulate their behaviors (see Chapter 2).

Children at this age are active explorers, seeking information through manipulating and observing their world. As problem solvers, they now move beyond trial and error to mental manipulation of ideas and physical manipulation of objects to construct their reasoning.

When there is only one "right" way to play, opportunities for experimentations and new discovery are limited. Open-ended materials, such as common household objects, recycled items, tools, cooking utensils, and gadgets are particularly fascinating because adults use them. Nesting and stacking objects and containers for dumping and pouring are examples of good mental stimulators. They require active handling and teach about relationships such as top, middle, bottom, small, big, bigger, and biggest. Large hollow and wooden unit blocks of different sizes are the best toys of all (Healy, 2004; Hewitt, 2001).

SUGGESTIONS FOR IMPLEMENTING CURRICULUM—COGNITIVE DEVELOPMENT

CHILD BEHAVIOR	EXAMPLES OF CAREGIVER STRATEGIES
Piaget's Preoperational Stage, Preconceptual Substage	
NONVERBAL CLASSIFICATION	
Makes graphic collections	Allow child to create own classifications.
VERBAL PRECONCEPTS	
Uses words differently at different times	Listen and ask for clarification of words used differently.
Uses words with private meanings	Listen to child's words in context; reword or question to find meaning.
Begins to label classes of objects	Repeat and identify class of object. Extend child's label to include other objects.
Focuses on one attribute	Reinforce classifications. Child has not yet formed stable classes of objects.

(Continued)

CHILD BEHAVIOR	EXAMPLES OF CAREGIVER STRATEGIES
VERBAL REASONING	
Reasons from particular to particular	Understand and accept child's classification of behaviors that seem alike. Ask for clarification if needed.
QUANTITY	
Understands *some, more, gone, big*	Use quantity words in context with objects. Respond and expand on child's use.
NUMBER	
Understands *more*	Use objects to identify *more*.
SPACE	
Understands *up, down, behind, under, over*	Use spatial-position words with actions, e.g., "I will lift you up. I am putting you down on the floor."
TIME	
Understands *now, soon*	Label actions in terms of time, e.g., "Let's wash your hands now."

Language Development

Children of this age are rapidly increasing their vocabulary. Their vocabulary may include as many as two to three hundred words. This is a time for grammatical (e.g., functional or space) words (refer back to Chapter 11).

> . . . more new space words are added to the child's vocabulary in the six month period from two to two-and-a-half than in any other six-month period. . . . The increase in use of two space words combined gives exactness to location: "right home," "way up," "in here," "under the table." (Ames & Ilg, 1980, p. 89)

As toddlers move from telegraphic speech to communicating complete ideas through sentences, they begin to use subject-verb-object sentences and include grammatical or function words, such as *on*, *in*, *a*, and *the*. Anisfeld (1984) says that they *construct* sentences; they do not reproduce sentences from memory. Thus, the child has to think and select words that express his or her ideas in ways others can understand. This may not be smooth, as the toddler has to plan and coordinate all the parts (words) of the sentences. The more words used, the more difficult it is for the toddler to construct a sentence. While toddlers learn to use word order patterns common to their language based on their interactions with more skilled others, they cannot tell you the basic rule or principle of word order they are using. These are abstract principles.

Anisfeld has identified several mental associations that toddlers have to construct in order to effectively engage in verbal conversations:

- **Demonstrative naming:** The first word in a demonstrative naming phrase points out an object, the second names it, e.g., "this ball" or "here spoon."

- **Attribution:** Children give objects a specific attribute, often using an adjective-noun combination, e.g., "blue shoes." The attribute *blue* distinguishes one particular pair of shoes from all other items in a class of things called *shoes*.
- **Possession:** Children make special associations between a person and an object, often using a two-word sentence, e.g., "mommy chair."
- **Action:** **Action sentences** separate the action from the actor and from the object and explore the relations among these three. Children's descriptions of their own or other's actions at this age include sentences like "ride bigwheel" and "I jump."
- **Recurrence:** A recurrence sentence tells of a thing or event that happens again. Children often use "more" to express this, for example, "more juice," "more ride."
- **Negation:** The negative sentences of children this age usually say that something desired or expected is not there or has disappeared or that the child cannot, is not permitted to, or does not want to do something. A child may say, "no car" or "no hit."

Children also extend their construction of language to include two ways of forming new words. They begin to use the plural and the past tense forms of words. By now children understand that there is more than one hand, or eye, or foot. They listen to others talking and learn that the word changes when referring to more than one hand. They then construct their words to include plurals, for example, *hands*, *eyes*, and so forth. However, at this age they apply the same plural rule to all words, making words such as *foots*. Applying the same rule to all of one kind of words is called **overregularization**. When children can distinguish between what is happening now and what has happened previously, they can begin to use some words that are in the past tense, such as "I jumped." They also overregularize past tense forms, constructing words like "goed" and "seed."

Children also have to learn **prosodic patterning** (Figure 15–2) or how to use the appropriate stress and intonation to express their specific ideas. They learn emphasis

FIGURE 15–2   The repetitive lyrics of a song help a child to learn proper word patterns.

and rhythm of word parts, words, and sentences along with the words themselves and syntax. For example, "*my* ball" means something different from "my *ball*."

Books contain language patterns that serve as examples to children who are busily constructing language; therefore, you should read to children often. Children can also tell the story when they have books with pictures. These experiences provide practice in putting thoughts into oral language. Books will soon be selected frequently by toddlers.

Written language is becoming more a part of the children's world. They see print at home, at the grocery store, out the bus window, and in other homes or centers. They look at the print in a book as the caregiver reads the story or tells the story line. They see their own names on each of their own papers. They are eager to make their own marks.

Writing opportunities can be provided to children in several ways. Create a writing center and have recycled paper, printer paper, pencils, pens, crayons, and markers readily available. Toddlers should be able to self-select and self-regulate the use of these materials with your guidance. Provide opportunities to write on an easel or chalkboard. If you do not have a chalkboard available, make your own by painting a section of a low wall with chalkboard paint. Select the location carefully so that it will get a lot of use and is easily cleaned. Thick, soft chalk, while it is messier, makes dark marks more easily. Thin, regular-size chalk breaks easily and can cause frustration (Lamme, 1984).

With repeated practice, some toddlers may begin to do controlled scribbling or even representative drawings. Controlled scribbling has several characteristics.

Gradually, after much playing around with markers, chalk, and crayons, your child's scribbles become more controlled. He begins to see the relationship between the marks he is making on paper and the writing utensil in his hand. His scribbles are more systematic. . . . The lines go up and down . . . or in circles. Dots may surround the picture. . . . He systematically scribbles with each marker in the box. . . . Later, as part of the scribble pattern, circles, triangles, arrows, and squares may emerge. (Lamme, 1984, pp. 39–40)

SUGGESTIONS FOR IMPLEMENTING CURRICULUM—LANGUAGE DEVELOPMENT

CHILD BEHAVIOR	MATERIALS	EXAMPLES CAREGIVER STRATEGIES
Uses demonstrative naming	toys, objects	Point to and label objects, e.g., "a foot," "a hand," "the nose." Extend to sentences: "Mary has a foot. This is a foot."
Uses attribution	toys, objects	Combine labels, e.g., "red car," "big book." Extend to sentences: "Ray has the red car; Twila has the green car."
Uses possession	toys, objects	Identify and label: "Roger's shoe, Jenny's shoe."
Uses action	toys, objects	Identify and label own and child's actions: "Urvi sits on the floor." "Stewart is eating."
Uses recurrence		Use word patterns that indicate repeating or additional, e.g., at snack ask each child if he or she wants *more* apple.

CHILD BEHAVIOR	MATERIALS	EXAMPLES CAREGIVER STRATEGIES
Learns word order		Use proper word order, e.g., "The truck moves." Extend child's "Move truck" to "Yes, the truck moves."
Learns prosodic patterning		Use expression when talking. Accent the proper syllables. The child will imitate you.
Uses subject-verb pattern		Use whole sentences. Expand the child's sentences.
Uses verb-object pattern		Use whole sentences. Expand the child's sentences.
Omits function words		Use whole sentences. Expand the child's sentences.
Selects and uses books	picture books, storybooks	Read aloud. Listen to the child "read."
Controls scribbling	markers, crayons, chalk, chalkboard, paper	Provide materials and space. Write labels and notes to the child. Share the child's scribbling.

■ KEY TERMS

action sentences	negation	preoperational stage
attribution	overregularization	prosodic patterning
demonstrative naming	possession	recurrence
mental images	preconceptual	search for hidden objects

CASE STUDY   Ming

Ming is a sweet 26-month-old who comes from a low-income family. The Department of Social Services provides her child care free of charge because of the severe poverty of her family. She often comes to the program without having eaten and insufficiently dressed for the weather. Her 18-year-old mother is a day laborer with three other small children.

Ming's teacher, Ms. Tao, has known from daily interactions that her mother has limited English proficiency. When the first parent conference was held, she called on the services of another parent who is bilingual. While explaining the Developmental Profile for Ming, she learned that Ming's mother was overwhelmed and lacked education beyond sixth grade. Working

together, though, they created a Developmental Prescription to use in the child care program that will help Ming overcome her general developmental delays.

Imagine that you co-teach with Ms. Tao.

1. List possible causes for Ming's delays in each of the four developmental areas.

2. What would you have suggested to promote Ming's development? Provide at least one example for each of the four developmental areas.

3. What supports at both school and in the home could be provided to help Ming and her family?

■ QUESTIONS AND EXPERIENCES FOR REFLECTION

1. Observe a child 24 to 30 months old for 15 minutes during playtime and record your observations using a running record (Appendix A). Then,

   a. Categorize the child's social behaviors.

   b. List ways in which the child used preconceptual classification.

   c. List the kinds of representations the child used.

2. Make a theme picturebook. Use it with a child. Observe the child's emotional reactions.

   Observe the child's language. Involve the child in rereading the book.

3. Use a commercially prepared puppet to engage a child 24 to 30 months old in pretend play. Record as many observations as you can after the experience.

   a. Analyze the child's responses.

   b. Evaluate the effectiveness of your strategies for facilitating the pretend play.

■ CHAPTER REVIEW

1. List two developing social accomplishments of a child 24 to 30 months old.

2. Describe a situation in which the child is asserting independence.

3. Write an example for each of the following language patterns:

   a. demonstrative naming

   b. attribution

   c. possession

   d. action sentences

   e. recurrence

   f. negation

■ REFERENCES

Adolph, K. E., Vereijken, B., & Shrout, P. E. (2003). What changes in infant walking and why. *Child Development, 74*(2), 475–497.

Ames, L. B., & Ilg, F. L. (1980). *Your two-year-old: Terrible or tender?* New York: Delacorte Press.

Anisfeld, M. (1984). *Language development from birth to three.* Hillsdale, NJ: Lawrence Erlbaum Associates.

Dodici, B. J., Draper, D. C., & Peterson, C. A. (2003). Early parent-child interactions and early literacy development. *Topics in Early Childhood Special Education, 23*(3), 124–36.

Elkind, D. (2007). *The power of play: How spontaneous, imaginative activities lead to happier, healthier children.* Cambridge, MA: Da Capo Press.

Healy, J. (2004). *Your child's growing mind: A guide to learning and brain development from birth to adolescence* (3rd ed.). New York: Broadway Books.

Hewitt, K. (2001). Blocks as a tool for learning: A historical and contemporary perspective. *Young Children, 56*(1), 6–13.

Honig, A. S. (2005, April). What infants, toddlers, and preschoolers learn from play: A dozen ideas. Paper presented at the American Montessori Society meeting, Chicago, IL.

Lamme, L. L. (1984). *Growing up writing.* Washington, DC: Acropolis Books.

Lawhon, T., & Cobb, J. B. (2002). Routines that build emergent literacy skills in infants, toddlers, and preschoolers. *Early Childhood Education Journal, 30*(2), 113–118.

Rosenkoetter, S., & Barton, L. R. (2002). Bridges to literacy: Early routines that promote later school success. *Zero to Three, 22*(4), 33–38.

Spinrad, T., & Stifter, C. A. (2006). Toddlers' empathy-related responding to distress: Predictions from negative emotionality and maternal behavior in infancy. *Infancy, 10*(2), 97–121.

Tobin, W., & Davidson, D. (1989). *Preschool in three cultures.* New Haven, CT: Yale University.

Weber, D. S., & Singer, D. G. (2004). The media habits of infants and toddlers: Findings from a parent survey. *Zero to Three, 25*(1), 30–36.

■ HELPFUL WEB SITES

National Network for Childcare. This article on "Talking with Toddlers and Two-Year-Olds" provides general guidelines for communicating with young children. **http://www.nncc.org/Guidance/dc34_talk.toddlers.html**

USA Today magazine. Are Babies Smarter Than Adults? **http://www.findarticles.com/cf_0/m1272/2655_128/58037920/p1/**

Dr. Greene. Use the search box to look for topics relevant to toddlers, such as temper tantrums. **http://www.drgreene.com/**

Early Childhood Australia. This professional organization provides information about teaching for children's rights as well as full-text articles from *Australian Journal of Early Childhood* and *Every Child.* **http://www.earlychildhoodaustralia.org.au/**

For additional infant and toddler resources, visit our Web site at http://www.earlychilded.delmar.com

CHAPTER **16**

The Child from Thirty to Thirty-six Months of Age

■ OBJECTIVES

After reading this chapter, you should be able to:

- Identify and record sequences of change in the physical, emotional, social, and cognitive/language development of children from 30 to 36 months of age.
- Select materials appropriate to the development of children at that age level.
- Devise strategies appropriate to children at that age level.

■ CHAPTER OUTLINE

- Materials and Activities
  Types of Materials
  Examples of Homemade Materials
  Activity Ideas
- Caregiver Strategies to Enhance Development
  Developmental Profile
  Physical Development
  Emotional Development
  Social Development
  Cognitive and Language Development
- Case Study: Paul
- Summary: Closing Note

Juan's Story

Juan, 35 months old, is playing in the play yard. He sits on a big-wheel tricycle and rolls backward, gets off and runs around with other children, picks at the ground and finds a grub, which he takes to show the caregiver. Juan walks around showing the grub to others, sits on a small trike, takes the grub and puts it by a tree trunk, sits on the ground, climbs a tree, climbs down and runs after a soccer ball, plops down on the big-wheel, gets up and then kicks a soccer ball back and forth with another child. Later he plays with another grub. When asked where the grub is, he stops, puts his hands up in the air and says, "He dead." He finds another grub and shows it to the caregiver, saying, "He sleeping. Wake up, grub." The bug moves and rolls up again. Juan says, "He sleep again."

MATERIALS AND ACTIVITIES

Children this age are active, eager learners. They practice newly acquired skills and develop new ones. They like large muscle activity and are developing their fine muscles for more controlled manipulation of objects. They enjoy imaginative play and exploring their world. Their play incorporates their imagination, their language, and

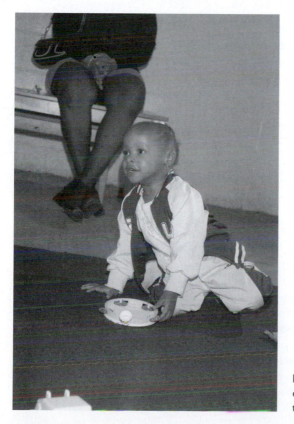

Providing real instruments demonstrates your respect for the capabilities of the toddlers.

their understanding of themselves and others. They construct sentences to share their ideas. They represent their ideas in play and language, and they recognize pictures. They listen to stories and enjoy participating in rhymes, fingerplays, music, and singing.

Types of Materials

riding toys	markers, crayons, chalk, pens
wagon	wooden beads and string
trucks for hauling	rhythm instruments
rocking boat	CDs
tunnel, barrel to crawl through and on	tapes
cardboard blocks	dramatic play props
wooden unit block set	puppets
wooden people	books
wooden animals	materials to explore—feel, measure, use

Examples of Homemade Materials

PROP BOXES

Gather props for a specific story or role. For example, put a stethoscope, white shirt, and small pad of paper in a shoebox for doctor props. In a larger box put a child-size firefighter's hat, boots, and poncho. Gather the materials based on your observations of the children's play. Select items that will enhance and promote development.

PUPPETS

Use cardboard tubes from paper towels. Cut paper to make face. Child uses markers or crayons to make face and clothes features. Glue face on tube.

BOOK: JOURNAL

Sew or staple sheets of unlined paper together. Each morning ask child to identify one toy he or she wants to play with or an activity to do. Write a sentence identifying what the child chose. Allow the child to scribble and draw on the page. Read the sentence to the child. Label journal with the child's name. To promote partnerships with families, send the journal home each Friday. Encourage the family

members to add sentences and illustrations for the days the child is not at school.

WOODEN PEOPLE OR ANIMALS

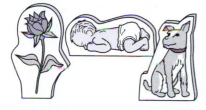

Draw or cut out of a magazine pictures of people: infants, children, adults; firefighter, police officer, doctor; or animals or other objects, such as cars or houses.

Glue pictures on a piece of 1-inch-thick white pine board. With a jigsaw, cut around the outside of the picture on three sides, cutting the bottom straight across. Sand the edges smooth. Apply two coats of nontoxic sealer. The object will stand up by itself.

Activity Ideas

Keeping records of informal observations, besides the records on the Developmental Profiles, will assist you in planning appropriate experiences for each child. Plan for a holistic curriculum. Identify your children's interests. Use these to focus your daily and weekly plans. You will mostly want to plan individual activities, but some short small-group activities may be included, such as reading or telling a story, singing a song, saying a rhyme, or doing a fingerplay. Any small-group activity would also be appropriate for use with individuals.

Children construct physical knowledge by moving objects and observing changes in objects. They observe the effects of their pulling, pushing, rolling, kicking, jumping, blowing, sucking, throwing, swinging, twirling, balancing, and dropping objects. Knowledge about physical events requires inferences drawn from observations. The source of physical knowledge is partly in the object, and the reaction depends on its properties (DeVries, 2000). Offer materials and activities that help children discover the physical characteristics of objects.

Children construct logico-mathematical knowledge by discovering relationships among objects. Comparisons of quantity, number, space, and time are explorations in relating two or more objects or events in a new and abstract way. Children can seek relationships among any kinds of materials. Games and activities that use the invented relationships help stimulate and reinforce their constructions. For example, providing a group of objects to sort and classify might lead a child to notice color relationships.

Children learn social-arbitrary knowledge from other people through various forms of communication (DeVries, 2000). They learn the names of objects, meanings of words, and days of the week, for example, from others. They learn the classroom rules from their caregivers, who bear the major responsibility in the child care program for providing this type of information and helping the child construct social-arbitrary knowledge.

CAREGIVER STRATEGIES TO ENHANCE DEVELOPMENT

Developmental Profile

Juan was observed over a five-day period as he performed the child behaviors of the Developmental Prescription in Appendix A. The resulting Developmental Profile, presented in Figure 16–1, indicates that Juan functions at or above age expectancies in most of the areas.

Specifically, Juan exhibits skills slightly above age expectancies in "muscle control" (36 months) and "sleeping" (40 months) within the Physical Area (I). He also exhibits age-level skills in the Emotional (II), Social (III), and Cognitive (IV) areas. In fact, his cognitive skills in "verbal responding," "classification," and "quality" are slightly above age expectancies. However, Juan exhibits some significant language skill delays. Juan has difficulty expressing himself verbally and discriminating differences between pictures and words.

In summary, Juan is a healthy 35-month-old who functions at or above age level in all areas except language. Juan exhibits significant enough lags in language skills to warrant further evaluation. The caregiver should have a conference with his family to go over the profile and discuss the need for further evaluations in the language area.

A specific program of caregiver strategies to improve language skills should be combined with tasks and activities in all other areas to ensure a balanced program for Juan.

Physical Development

Children of this age are increasing their stability in both fast and slow movements, running and walking. They can walk backward. They run quickly and usually maintain their balance. They can alternate feet going upstairs. They can master a tricycle. They jump up and down, they jump off objects, and they jump forward. They can twist and turn to dress and undress, and they can use their small muscles to hold clothes and begin buttoning, snapping, and zippering. They practice their physical skills. Right- or left-handedness is now established, though children use both hands in many activities (Figure 16–2).

At this age children can establish sleep routines that they can do themselves in the child care setting. Before nap they can go to the bathroom and wash their hands. They can sit on their cots, take their own shoes off, and put the shoes under the cot. They can lie down with their heads near the top of the cot. When they awaken, they can go to the bathroom and return to put on their shoes. If others are still sleeping, they can choose a quiet activity, such as looking at books or listening to a story or music with earphones.

Most children are fully engaged in toilet learning by 36 months of age. They need to wear clothes they can remove quickly and easily. They need easy access to the bathroom, and they need occasional questions and reminders to go to the bathroom.

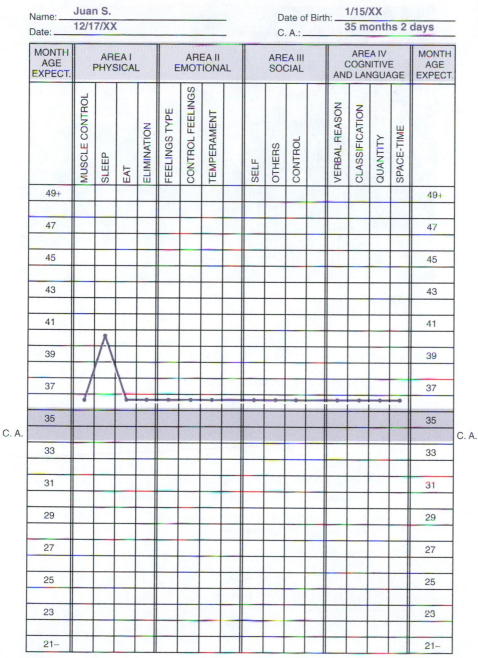

Name: Juan S.

Date: 12/17/XX

Date of Birth: 1/15/XX

C. A.: 35 months 2 days

FIGURE 16–1   Developmental profile for Juan S.

Notes:

FIGURE 16–2   The caregiver allows the child to use crayons in either or both hands even though handedness may be established.

SUGGESTIONS FOR IMPLEMENTING CURRICULUM—PHYSICAL DEVELOPMENT

CHILD BEHAVIOR	EXAMPLES OF CAREGIVER STRATEGIES
Muscular Control	
MOVEMENT AND COORDINATION	
Walks evenly	Provide uncluttered floor space.
Runs	Provide space and games for appropriate running.
Jumps in place and forward	Play games and sing songs that encourage jumping.
Dances to music	Play favorite music and provide scarves for moving rhythmically.
Dresses and undresses self with assistance	Allow time for child to manipulate clothes. Demonstrate how to hold button and buttonholes, zipper and cloth, and so on.
Uses fine motor coordination	Turns one page at a time.
HAND	
Has established handedness	Allow child to select hand to use.
Sleeping	
Assists with preparation routines	Plan time in schedule for children to do as much of the routines as possible. It takes longer for a child to wash and dry hands alone than if you help, but child needs to be independent and to develop skills. Help with tight snaps and so on.
Elimination	
Is in process of or has completed toilet learning	Provide reminders and assistance when needed. Assist with clothes and hand washing when needed. Clean up area. *Wash your hands.*

Emotional Development

Children of this age express their emotions and feelings strongly. They let you know how they feel and then may move beyond their anger or happiness and soon express a wide variety of different feelings. Toddlers, like older children, express negativism in several ways. Sometimes negative behavior is a way of asserting themselves and their independence. They may begin or continue to display physical aggression (Baillargeon et al., 2007; Fagot & Leve, 1998; Tremblay et al., 2004). Their widening world presents many new experiences. Older toddlers may use aggression in their attempts to assert some control over their world.

Because of the link between aggression and concurrent and future mental health issues, child development and early childhood experts are particularly concerned about aggression in toddlers (see, for example, Collins et al., 2003). Much research has been conducted to understand the causes of aggression and patterns of trajectories. Tremblay et al. (2004) found that the best predictors of high, stable physical aggression were maternal variables (e.g., history of antisocial behavior during mother's school years, early childbearing, and coercive parenting behavior) and family variables (e.g., low income and family dysfunction). Similarly, both parent coercion during home observations and marital status predicted externalizing behavior during kindergarten (Fagot & Leve, 1998). These authors also investigated how child characteristics and behaviors predicted outcomes at five years of age; while child playgroup behaviors at 18 months were predictive of later externalizing behaviors, boys' behaviors were also correlated with reports of problems at home and school. Thus, differential patterns of stability and predictability have been found for boys and girls (see also Baillargeon et al., 2007; Gill & Calkins, 2003; Hays, Castle, & Davies, 2000).

The strong display of emotions carries over to children's work in the classroom. Toddlers of this age are enthusiastic learners, enjoying themselves and their discoveries. Their developing mastery of skills enhances their feelings of competence, self-worth, and acceptance of self. Persistence in continuing a task enables these children to discover many things. As they explore, their persistence will probably enable them to accomplish enough so that they have the feeling of "I did it" or "See what I found out." Children generally discover the love of learning when they are offered developmentally appropriate choices and are positively encouraged for their decisions by the caregiver who combines the three As of child care: Attention, Approval, and Attunement. This love of learning is obvious when the child has a long attention span and displays great persistence in finishing a task. A short attention span, however, limits a child's exposure and involvement in many activities. Early childhood educators must devote a great deal of time to observing the children's interests so that experiences can be planned that engage the toddlers. Doing so will assist with the toddlers' abilities to attend and therefore to learn. Optimal learning occurs when children are provided experiences that are hands on, minds on, and feelings on (NAEYC, 1998).

At about 33 months the child will begin to think in terms of her own past and may pretend to be a baby again. This regression may be a need based on her own development or the presence of a new baby in the family. Whatever the cause, these

When young children continually make new discoveries, they become enthusiastic learners.

toddlers need lots of the three As and the time and patience to regain their proper place in their environment. In addition, the ability to focus on the past allows the opportunity for toddlers to reflect on their recent behaviors. For children this age, reflection must be supported by concrete products such as photographs and artifacts such as drawings or sculptures. Holsington (2002) discovered that taking photographs of block play assisted children with asking questions, thinking through problems, and making connections between building experiences.

At around 36 months, depending upon temperament, children's emotional responses become calmer. They become less resistant and use words like *yes* and *will* to replace the earlier *no* and *won't*. The three-year-old is generally a happy, secure and somewhat conforming person. Often you will hear the child repeat back to you the three As that you have given him or her over and over again.

SUGGESTIONS FOR IMPLEMENTING CURRICULUM—EMOTIONAL DEVELOPMENT

CHILD BEHAVIOR	EXAMPLES OF CAREGIVER STRATEGIES
Types of Emotions and Feelings	
Reacts strongly	Accept child's initial response. Help child keep within bounds of appropriate behavior, e.g., let child express anger by vigorously riding a big-wheel for a while or drawing an angry picture.
Acts negatively	Rephrase suggestions to child. Stimulate interest in a different activity. Describe emotions child is feeling.

CHILD BEHAVIOR	EXAMPLES OF CAREGIVER STRATEGIES
Learns enthusiastically	Reinforce child's excitement with learning. Provide opportunities for challenging, developmental, and content-rich experiences.
Masters skills	Provide toys, equipment, and materials that the child needs to use often to master skills.
Control of Emotions and Feelings	
Is physically aggressive	Provide activities for child to work out feelings and the need to control, such as using a puppet for imaginary play or letting the child be a leader in a structured activity. Have the child paint, draw, use clay, dance, or go outdoors to run, jump, and yell.

Social Development

Egocentrism continues to be present in the preconceptual substage. Even though young children can distinguish themselves from others, they are only slowly developing the ideas that follow from this. They are just beginning to understand that others have feelings. They assume that when they speak, everyone understands the exact meaning of their words; they do not realize that others may give different meanings to the same words or experiences.

Young children interpret changes in appearance to mean changes in the basic object or person. "Preconceptual children generally do not see things or people as having a core and consistent identity over time" (Cowan, 1978, p. 133). This fluctuation includes their concepts of self. "They seem to have little idea that their 'self' of a few days ago is relevant to what is happening now, today" (p. 133).

Dramatic play with peers is becoming more prevalent.

Children continue to identify their "selfness" within their world. Their toys are a part of themselves, and they remain very possessive of the toys and materials they are using. However, their strengthening sense of self also provides a foundation for expanding interactions with others. Children this age are increasingly aware of others as individuals. They use adults as resources, seeking assistance from them when they decide they need help. They become directive with others, exerting control over people, animals, and toys as they learn ways to control their world. Children this age sometimes recognize others' needs and may help with tasks or initiate or respond with assistance.

These children's self-control is increasing. Their desire for instant gratification is being restricted, so they sometimes accept delayed gratification. They may take turns occasionally. At times they may decide to share, and they may play cooperatively for short periods of time. The research strongly suggests that what begins to ingrain in that child the deepest sense of these prosocial qualities is the felt experience, over and over and over again, of cooperation; the experience of having an important adult put aside his or her own needs to meet the child's very real needs; the experience of that important adult showing empathy, concern, respect, and nurturance toward the baby or toddler (Wolf, 1986).

SUGGESTIONS FOR IMPLEMENTING CURRICULUM—SOCIAL DEVELOPMENT

CHILD BEHAVIOR	EXAMPLES OF CAREGIVER STRATEGIES
Self	
Acts possessive	Provide enough toys and materials so child can control use of some of them for a time.
Others	
Seeks assistance	Allow child to use you as a resource. Help where needed. Do not take over.
Directs others	Provide opportunities for child to display leadership skills with peers.
Helps others	Praise child's spontaneous helping. Ask for assistance so child can help with routines and so forth.
Control of Self	
Plays cooperatively	Provide toys, materials, and time.
Shares	Encourage by providing opportunities to share, e.g., when eating orange or apple slices.
Takes turns	Use daily routines to help control wasting time, e.g., taking turns to wash hands.

Cognitive and Language Development

Cognitive Development

Children at this age are curious, exploring problem solvers. They are seeking to discover what makes things tick, what objects are made of, and how actions happen. As discussed previously, they use observing, questioning, manipulating, classifying, and measuring to learn about their world.

In the preconceptual stage children may attempt to put objects in an order, like biggest to smallest buttons, but unless the materials present cues, such as fitting together, the children may not be able to determine the logic of ordering. Arranging objects in a

FIGURE 16–3   Blocks, pegs, and other manipulatives provide cues to young children for mathematical concepts such as one-to-one correspondence and sorting.

series, or **seriation**, is guesswork for young children because they do not understand the relationships in a series of objects. However, physical knowledge about the properties of objects develops through their continued interactions with materials (Figure 16–3).

Because toddlers still reason prelogically, adults and children understand experiences differently. Even if both a child and an adult were present during the same experience, each would learn and experience something different. Jane Healy, in her book *Your Child's Growing Mind* (2004), gives several ways to help "bridge the schema" gaps (p. 57), or fill in missing information.

1. As you solve problems together, talk through your own questions. "I wonder how I should start?" "Could I put them together?" "Is it working?" "What's going to happen?" "How did I do?"
2. Ask the child similar questions. Phrase them simply and give the child plenty of time to think and answer.
3. Let the child repeat each solution several times to understand it.
4. Encourage understanding. Ask "Why do you think that happened?" "Why did (or didn't) that work?"

Interacting in this manner not only bridges informational gaps but also, by its very nature, engages toddlers emotionally and intellectually. Older toddlers need curriculum, environments, and interactions that engage them emotionally and intellectually because successfully completing a challenge provide valuable information about their capabilities. Carefully planning learning experiences that give value to the tools of the learning disciplines (e.g., mathematics, social studies) give curriculum intellectual integrity (Bredekamp & Copple, 1997). Toddlers should be given opportunities to investigate scientific topics about which they have questions (e.g., living creatures, microorganisms, gravity; see, for example, Youngquist, 2004) and use scientific tools/ processes such as observing, recording, and testing hypotheses. They should have daily experiences with mathematical concepts such as solving problems, measurement, and geometry. These experiences can be completed separately or integrated into learning experiences and projects (see Chapter 9). An example of an integrated learning experience would be cooking. When caregivers provide opportunities for cooking, toddlers gain cognitive skills (e.g., transformations), mathematics skills (e.g., measuring), literacy skills (e.g., written communication for providing information), and life skills (e.g., making healthy food choices; Colker, 2005; Darbyshire, 2004; Houts, 2002).

A note of caution should be introduced here. In no case should toddlers be forced or required to engage in these activities. These learning experiences should be among the many choices in the environment. Moreover, designing curriculum in this manner ensures that the content is contextualized at all times.

SUGGESTIONS FOR IMPLEMENTING CURRICULUM—COGNITIVE DEVELOPMENT

CHILD BEHAVIOR	EXAMPLES OF CAREGIVER STRATEGIES
Piaget's Preoperational Stage, Preconceptual Substage	
NONVERBAL CLASSIFICATION	
Makes graphic collections	Encourage child to use art media to represent objects, ideas, etc. Listen to child's explanation of his or her own classification system.
VERBAL PRECONCEPTS	
Uses words differently at different times	Observe context of talk. Ask for clarification of meaning if necessary.
Labels objects in one class	Remember that child's meaning may not be as inclusive as yours. Determine exactly what child meant.
VERBAL REASONING	
Thinks one action is like another action	Observe the behavior that precedes a child's talking. Determine how child is drawing relationships among his or her actions.
Reasons from effect to cause	Think backward from action to previous action to understand child's reasoning.
QUANTITY	
Understands *some, more, gone, big*	Use words labeling quantity. They are a part of the daily experiences.
NUMBER	
Understands *more*	Use words labeling number as a comparative. Use daily situations, e.g., "There are more rocks in this pail than in that pail."
SPACE	
Understands *up, down, behind, under, over*	Label child's actions when child is moving into different positions in space, e.g., "Merrilee is behind the box. Ashton is under the box."
TIME	
Understands *now, soon, before, after*	Use time words in daily experiences, e.g., "We wash our hands before we eat." "We go to the bathroom after naptime."

Language Development

Children this age continue to increase their vocabulary. Their daily experiences provide opportunities for them to construct meanings of new objects and to extend previously learned concepts. The labeling process is now part of children's construction of the identity of objects.

Older toddlers continue to overregularize words. However, more and more of their plural words are formed correctly. These children are very gradually constructing concepts of time, and most of their new time words come during this period. The past is still an abstraction they are attempting to understand grammatically. They still overregularize past tense verbs, saying things like, "Jim bited me" and "I bringed these out."

Sentence length increases as children increase their use and familiarity with frequently used vocabulary, word order patterns, and stress and intonation patterns. They speak more complete sentences and are able to express several ideas in a sequence of sentences.

Dramatic play provides opportunities to combine language with imagination. Children of this age can describe their actions and say what they think others might say. They are mastering their language and fitting it into a social context (Honig, 2005).

Books play an increasingly important role. Reading aloud provides examples of language patterns. Reading the pictures encourages self-expression; talking about the story or the pictures facilitates comprehension of the language. Having these experiences fosters larger vocabularies and better storytelling abilities in the children (Figure 16–4).

FIGURE 16–4 Frequent reading of books stimulates the toddlers to re-read and re-tell familiar ones and also create new stories of their own.

The ability to produce or express language during the toddler years has been associated with larger vocabularies and better reading outcomes during the early elementary years (Rescorla, 2002; see also Pullen & Justice, 2003). While the pathways are not completely understood, adult styles of interactions and literacy behaviors at home and at school are believed to play significant roles in literacy outcomes (Britto & Brooks-Gunn, 2001; Dodici, Draper, & Peterson, 2003; Murray & Yingling, 2000; Williams & Rask, 2003). Teachers must develop partnerships with families to support and enhance the language and literacy development of children. While many strategies exist for helping parents read to children at home (Darling & Westberg, 2004), creating literacy bags that contain high-quality children's literature and a guidebook for parents with, for example, questions for discussion has been shown to increase both the quality and frequency of reading books at home for older children (Dever & Burts, 2002). Logically, if parents are helped early on to carve out time daily to read to their infants and toddlers, greater literacy outcomes might be gained (see, for example, Raikes et al., 2006).

Literacy also involves learning to communicate ideas in writing. **Scribbling** continues as the child is involved in the writing process. Each child is developing scribbling at his or her own rate.

> Children are scribblers from the time they hold a writing tool until after they learn to write their names. There is a progression to their scribbles which moves from random scribbling, to controlled scribbling, to the naming of scribbling, to writing mock letters and words, to learning, finally, how to write. It is important not to underestimate the value of scribbling as a foundation for writing. (Lamme, 1984, p. 37)

> You model many uses of writing for children. You write their names, sentences on their artwork papers, and dictated sentences on their pages of scribbling. You write a note to their family members. You write charts about daily experiences, such as the growth steps of beans the children planted. In this way, the children experience meaningful uses of writing.

SUGGESTIONS FOR IMPLEMENTING CURRICULUM—LANGUAGE DEVELOPMENT

CHILD BEHAVIOR	MATERIALS	EXAMPLES OF CAREGIVER STRATEGIES
Increases vocabulary		
Associates word and object		Introduce new objects to see and feel and use. Label objects and actions with single words and use in sentences.
Improves syntax		
Experiments with word order		Repeat child's sentence, using proper word order.
Makes two- and three-word sentences		Respond to child's meaning. Extend the sentence.
Uses longer sentences		Respond to child's meaning. Commend his or her ideas.

CHILD BEHAVIOR	MATERIALS	EXAMPLES OF CAREGIVER STRATEGIES
Improves word forms		
Uses plurals		Use correct plural form. When child says "foots," restate the word, e.g., "See your feet."
Uses past tense		Use correct past tense. When child says "He bited me," restate: "He bit you? Show me where he bit you."
Improves reading skills		
Listens to stories, "reads" pictures and storybooks	recordings, pictures, picture books	Read aloud. Listen to child "read." Use expression. Tell or read story line.
Uses controlled scribbling	markers, chalk, crayons, pencil, paper	Write to child. Write notes to child and others. Label objects. Write dictated sentences.

■ KEY TERMS

dramatic play   scribbling   seriation

CASE STUDY   Paul

Juan has exhibited average or above-average growth in all areas except language. In his home, his parents and four siblings speak only Spanish. After discovering this, Juan's teacher Paul wanted his Developmental Profile to be completed again for his primary language. Rosa, a Spanish-speaking teacher in the program, agreed to assist. The results of this profile differ significantly from the first. His language skills were assessed at the 34-month level, right as expected. Paul and Rosa held a family conference to explain the two Developmental Profiles and work together to establish a Developmental Prescription. Both of his parents were initially concerned about his language delays but were significantly relieved to understand that he is progressing as expected in his home language. They both want attention to be focused on his learning English.

Paul and Rosa designed the Developmental Prescription to support all areas of development, including learning English as his second language.

1. What problems might have been created if Paul did not know that Spanish was the primary language spoken in the home? How might this have significantly altered the development of the Developmental Prescription?

2. Why are assessments, especially those involving language, best conducted in the child's home language?

3. What supports should Paul offer to Juan and his family?

■ QUESTIONS AND EXPERIENCES FOR REFLECTION

1. Observe one child for 10 minutes in a play yard. Write a list of the child's activities. Identify equipment and materials used.

2. Observe a child for 10 minutes in a play yard. Tally the times the child shares a toy or equipment. Tally the times the child plays *with* another child.

3. Observe a caregiver for five minutes. Write down the dialogue the caregiver has with a child or with several children. Categorize the

caregiver's statements that mirror, support, or respond to the child's statements.

4. Observe children at play. List the language and actions that indicate their developing concepts of quantity, number, space, and time.

5. Plan and use one activity with a child to facilitate the child's construction of physical knowledge.

6. Plan and use one activity with a child to facilitate the child's construction of logico-mathematical knowledge.

■ CHAPTER REVIEW

1. List three tasks children this age can complete independently.

2. List four tasks children can assist you with.

3. Describe one way to deal with an angry child.

4. Write one example of a child's statement that uses a word that for the child has a

meaning different from the one adults give the word.

5. Compare how children learn physical knowledge, logico-mathematical knowledge, and social-arbitrary knowledge.

■ REFERENCES

Baillargeon, R. H., Zoccolillo, M., Keenan, K., Cote, S., Perusse, D., Wu, H., Boivin, M., & Tremblay, R. E. (2007). Gender differences in physical aggression: A prospective population-base survey of children before and after 2 years of age. *Developmental Psychology, 43*(1), 13–26.

Bredekamp, S., & Copple, C. (Eds.). (1997). *Developmentally appropriate practice in early childhood programs* (Rev. ed.). Washington, DC: National Association for the Education of Young Children.

Britto, P. R., & Brooks-Gunn, J. (2001). Beyond shared book reading: Dimensions of home literacy and low-income African American preschoolers' skills. *New Directions for Child and Adolescent Development,* (92), 73–89.

Colker, L. (2005). *The cooking book: Fostering young children's learning and delight.* Washington, DC: National Association for the Education of Young Children.

Collins, R., Mascia, J., Kendall, R., Golden, O., Schock, L., & Parlakian, R. (2003). Promoting mental health in child care settings: Caring for the whole child. *Zero to Three, 23*(4), 39–45.

Cowan, P. A. (1978). *Piaget with feeling.* New York: Holt, Rinehart & Winston.

Darbyshire, J. (2004). *Everyday learning: Vol. 2, No. 4. Everyday learning in the kitchen.* S. Wales (Series Ed.) & P. Linke (Vol. Ed.). Watson, ACT: Early Childhood Australia, Inc.

Darling, S., & Westberg, L. (2004). Parent involvement in children's acquisition of reading. *The Reading Teacher, 57*(8), 774–776.

Dever, M. T., & Burts, D. C. (2002). An evaluation of family literacy bags as a vehicle for parent involvement. *Early Child Development and Care, 172*(4), 359–370.

DeVries, R. (2000). Vygotsky, Piaget, and education: A reciprocal assimilation of theories and educational practices [Electronic version]. *New Ideas in Psychology, 18*(2–3), 187–213.

Dodici, B. J., Draper, D. C., & Peterson, C. A. (2003). Early parent-child interactions and early literacy development. *Topics in Early Childhood Special Education, 23*(3), 124–136.

Fagot, B. I., & Leve, L. D. (1998). Teacher ratings of externalizing behavior at school entry for boys and girls: Similar early predictors and different correlates. *Journal of Child Psychology and Psychiatry and Allied Disciplines, 39*(4), 555–566.

Gill, K. L., & Calkins, S. D. (2003). Do aggressive/destructive toddlers lack concern for others? Behavioral and physiological indicators of empathic responding in 2-year-old children. *Developmental and Psychopathology, 15*(1), 55–71.

Hays, D. F., Castle, J., & Davies, L. (2000). Toddlers' use of force against familiar peers: A precursor of serious aggression? *Child Development, 71*(2), 457–467.

Healy, J. (2004). *Your child's growing mind: A guide to learning and brain development from birth to adolescence.* (3rd ed.). New York: Broadway Books.

Holsington, C. (2002). Using photographs to support children's science inquiry. *Young Children, 57*(5), 26–32.

Honig, A. S. (2005, April). What infants, toddlers, and preschoolers learn from play: A dozen ideas. Paper presented at the American Montessori Society meeting, Chicago, IL.

Houts, A. (2002). *Cooking around the calendar with kids: Holiday and seasonal food and fun.* Maryville, MO: Snaptail Press.

Lamme, L. L. (1984). *Growing up writing.* Washington, DC: Acropolis Books.

Murray, A. D., & Yingling, J. L. (2000). Competence in language at 24 months: Relations with attachment security and home stimulation. *Journal of Genetic Psychology, 161*(2), 133–140.

National Association for the Education of Young Children (NAEYC). (1998). *Tools for teaching developmentally appropriate practice* [Video series]. Washington, DC: Author.

Pullen, P. C., & Justice, L. M. (2003). Enhancing phonological awareness, print awareness, and oral language skills in preschool children. *Intervention in School and Clinic, 39*(2), 87–98.

Raikes, H., Pan, B. A., Luze, G., Tamis-LeMonda, C. S., Brooks-Gunn, J., Constantine, J., Tarullo, L. B., Raikes, H. A., & Rodriguez, E. T. (2006). Mother-child bookreading in low-income families: Correlates and outcomes during the first three years of life. *Child Development, 77*(4), 924–953.

Rescorla, L. (2002, April). Language and reading outcomes to age 9 in late-talking toddlers. *Journal of Speech, Language, and Hearing Research, 45*, 360–371.

Tremblay, R. E., Nagin, D. S., Seguin, J. R., Zoccolillo, M., Zelazo, P. D., Boivin, M., Perusse, D., & Japel, C. (2004). Physical aggression during early childhood: Trajectories and predictors. *Pediatrics, 114*(1), e43–e50.

Williams, M., & Rask, H. (2003). Literacy through play: How families with able children support their literacy development. *Early Child Development and Care, 173*(5), 527–533.

Wolf, D. P. (1986). *Connecting: Friendship in the lives of young children and their teachers.* Washington, DC: Exchange Press.

Youngquist, J. (2004). From medicine to microbes: A project investigation of health. *Young Children, 59*(2), 28–32.

■ ADDITIONAL RESOURCES

Hyson, M. (2004). *The emotional development of young children: Building an emotion-centered curriculum* (2nd ed.). New York: Teachers College Press.

■ HELPFUL WEB SITES

Berkeley Parents Network. Provides information about aggressive behavior by toddlers for parents. **http://parents.berkeley.edu/advice/toddler/aggression.html**

KidsHealth. Growth & Development. This provides a wealth of information divided into sections such as Growth, Communication, Learning & Play, and Medical Care. **http://www.kidshealth.org/parent/growth/**

Your Child's Development (Ages 2 to 4). http://parentcenter.babycenter.com/preschooler/pdevelopment/index

Toddlers Today. This Web site has numerous articles about toddlers. Some provide specific strategies for dealing effectively with aggressive behaviors. **http://toddlerstoday.com/resources/articles/aggression.htm**

World Association for Infant Mental Health. The professional organization for professionals concerned with infant mental health issues. This Web site provides links with national and state organizations (e.g., Indiana Association for Infant Mental Health) as well as resources. **http://www.waimh.org/**

SUMMARY: CLOSING NOTE

Even now in the twenty-first century the huge gap between humankind's intellectual development and emotional development is obvious. With the advent of an operational definition and curricula for teaching emotional intelligence and research suggesting only moderate correlation with cognitive intelligence, we now have the knowledge and skills necessary to improve the humanity of the next generation. As a caregiver of infants and toddlers, you have an essential role in ensuring that our youngest citizens learn how to interact humanely and intimately with other people, develop sound mental health and healthy self-esteem, maintain a balance between thinking and feeling, and improve the quality of life.

You are in the unique position to assist education and society in changing from an exclusive emphasis on cognitive and behavioral skills to a greater emphasis on being at ease with ourselves, regardless of environmental circumstances. By placing importance on the emotional and social development of children, as well as the other major areas of physical and cognition, you can significantly help create a social structure in which compassion, understanding, and ethical behavior are valued and practiced.

Caregivers of children from birth through the toddler age are in an ideal position to lay the foundation for emotionally and socially intelligent individuals. Your abilities to practice the three As and sensitively care for young children will determine the development for individuals; in the process, society will truly be affected. Congratulations on your choice of the most important position in society!

For additional infant and toddler resources, visit our Web site at http://www.earlychilded.delmar.com

APPENDIX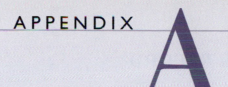

Tools for Observing and Recording

APPENDIX OUTLINE

Running Record

Anecdotal Record

Developmental Prescriptions (Combination of Checklist and Rating Scale)
> *Approximately Birth to Four Months of Age*
> *Approximately Four to Eight Months of Age*
> *Approximately Eight to Twelve Months of Age*
> *Approximately Twelve to Eighteen Months of Age*
> *Approximately Eighteen To Twenty-four Months of Age*
> *Approximately Twenty-four to Thirty Months of Age*
> *Approximately Thirty to Thirty-six Months of Age*

Indoor Safety Checklist

Playground Safety Checklist

RUNNING RECORD

Context	Observations (Behavioral descriptions of what you see and hear)	Analysis/Interpretations/Questions

ANECDOTAL RECORD

Child's Name: Age:
Observer's Name: Date:
Setting:

What actually happened/What I saw:

Reflection/Interpretation/Questions:

Child's Name: Age:
Observer's Name: Date:
Setting:

What actually happened/What I saw:

Reflection/Interpretation/Questions:

DEVELOPMENTAL PRESCRIPTIONS (COMBINATION OF CHECKLIST AND RATING SCALE)

APPROXIMATELY BIRTH TO FOUR MONTHS OF AGE

Child Behavior	Date First Observed	Practicing	Proficient
Physical Development			
MUSCULAR CONTROL			
Reflex			
Grasp reflex			
Startle reflex			
Tonic neck reflex			
Head and neck			
Turns head			
Holds head upright with support			
Lifts head slightly when on stomach			
Holds head to sides and middle			
Holds up head when on back and on stomach			
Holds head without support			
Trunk			
Holds up chest			
Sits with support			
May attempt to raise self			
May fuss if left lying down with little chance to sit up			
Holds up chest and shoulders			
Leg			
Rolls from stomach to back			
Arm			
Moves randomly			
Reaches			

Child Behavior	Date First Observed	Practicing	Proficient
Hand			
Opens and closes			
Keeps hands open			
Plays with hands			
Uses hands to grasp object			
Whole hand and fingers against thumb			
Thumb and forefinger			
Holds and moves object			
Eye-hand coordination			
Moves arm toward object; may miss it			
Reaches hand to object; may grab or miss it			
SEEING			
Focuses eight inches from eyes			
Follows with eyes			
See objects beyond eight inches			
Looks from object to object			
Looks around; focuses on object; then continues visual searching			
HEARING			
Responds to voice and range of sounds			
Reacts to hearing low- and high-pitched sounds			
Locates source of sound			
SLEEPING			
Sleeps much of the day and night			
Takes a long morning nap and a long afternoon nap			
May have irregular sleep habits			

(Continued)

Child Behavior	Date First Observed	Practicing	Proficient
EATING and ELIMINATION			
Establishes regular time for eating and bowel movements			
Emotional Development			
TYPES OF EMOTIONS and FEELINGS			
Shows excitement			
Shows stress			
Shows enjoyment			
Shows anger			
Shows fear			
Protests			
CONTROL OF EMOTIONS and FEELINGS			
Cries			
Increases sounds (talking)			
Reflects sounds (talking)			
Comforted by holding			
TEMPERAMENT (List behaviors to indicate basic approach.)			
Activity level			
Regularity			
Response to new situations: Approach or withdrawal			
Adaptability to change in routine			
Sensory threshold			
Positive or negative mood			
Intensity of response			
Distractibility			
Persistence and attention span			

Child Behavior	Date First Observed	Practicing	Proficient
Social Development			
ATTACHMENT			
Shows special closeness to family members			
Develops familiarity with one primary caregiver			
SELF			
Becomes aware of hands and feet			
Smiles spontaneously			
Smiles at people (social smile)			
INTERACTIONS WITH OTHERS			
Interacts with people			
Laughs			
Initiates talking to others			
Cognitive and Language Development			
SENSORIMOTOR SUBSTAGE 1			
Reflexive actions			
Passive to active search			
SENSORIMOTOR SUBSTAGE 2			
Small, gradual changes come from repetition			
Coordination of behaviors, e.g., looking toward sound			
Puts hand, object in mouth and sucks on it			
Moves hand, object to see it			
Produces a pleasurable motor activity and repeats activity			
OBJECT PERMANENCE			
Follows moving object with eyes until object disappears			
Looks where object disappeared			
Loses interest and turns away			

(Continued)

Child Behavior	Date First Observed	Practicing	Proficient
LANGUAGE INITIATION–RESPONSE			
Initiates making sounds			
Responds vocally to another person			
Makes sound, repeats sound, continues practicing sound and lengthening it			
Imitates a few sounds he or she already knows			
Experiments with sounds			
Coos in vowel-like sounds			
Adds pitch to cooing			
CRYING			
Cries apparently automatically in distress, frustration			
Cries differently to express hunger, discomfort, anger			
Cries less as vocalizing increases			

Additional Observations of Child:

APPROXIMATELY FOUR TO EIGHT MONTHS OF AGE

Child Behavior	Date First Observed	Practicing	Proficient
Physical Development			
MUSCULAR CONTROL			
Head and neck			
Holds head up independently			
Holds head in midline position			
Holds head up when on back, stomach, and sitting			
Trunk			
Holds up chest, shoulders; arches back, hips			
Sits with support			
May attempt to raise self			
May fuss if left lying down with little chance to sit up			
Leans back and forth			
Sits in a chair			
Sits unsupported for short time			
Pushes self to sitting position			
Leg			
Straightens legs when standing			
Stamps feet when standing			
Rolls from back to stomach			
Raises self to hands and knees			
Stands with support			
Pulls self to standing			
Locomotion			
Kicks against surface to move			
Rocks on hands and knees			

(Continued)

Child Behavior	Date First Observed	Practicing	Proficient
Creeps on stomach			
Uses legs to pull, push self when sitting			
Arm			
Visually directs reaching, hitting			
Throws objects			
Hand			
Picks up object with one hand; passes it to the other hand			
Uses objects in both hands			
Grasps and releases objects			
Drops objects			
EATING			
Begins solid foods (new tongue and swallowing technique)			
Drinks from cup (new tongue and swallowing technique)			
Eats at "mealtimes"—solid foods, milk, juice			
Feeds self finger foods			
TEETH			
First teeth emerge: two middle lower, two middle upper			
Emotional Development			
TYPES OF EMOTIONS and FEELINGS			
Shows pleasure in watching others			
Shows pleasure in repetitive play			
Shows depression			
Shows fear: of strangers, of falling down			
Shows frustration with stimulation overload			

Child Behavior	Date First Observed	Practicing	Proficient
Shows happiness, delight, joy, humor			
Shows frustration, anger, and/or rage			
CONTROL OF EMOTIONS and FEELINGS			
Sometimes stops crying when talked to, sung to			
TEMPERAMENT (List behaviors to indicate basic approach.)			
Activity level			
Regularity			
Response to new situations: Approach or withdrawal			
Adaptability to change in routine			
Sensory threshold			
Positive or negative mood			
Intensity of response			
Distractibility			
Persistence and attention span			
Social Development			
ATTACHMENT			
Shows strong attachment to family members			
Differentiates response to family members			
Shows intense pleasure and frustration to person with whom attached			
SELF			
Seeks independence in actions			
Plays self-designed games			
INTERACTIONS WITH OTHERS			
Imitates others			
Plays with people			

(Continued)

Child Behavior	Date First Observed	Practicing	Proficient
Seeks family's and/or caregiver's attention by movement, sounds, smiles, cries			
Follows family members and/or caregiver to be in same room			
Acts shy with some strangers			
Cognitive Development			
SENSORIMOTOR SUBSTAGE 3			
Repeats interesting action			
Refines hand-eye coordination			
Looks for object, reaches for it, and accurately touches it			
Imitates behavior he or she can see or hear			
OBJECT PERMANENCE			
Searches visually (not manually) for short time when object disappears			
Sees part of object; looks for whole object			
Language Development			
Babbles syllable-like sounds			
Responds to talking by cooing, babbling, smiling			
Imitates sounds			
Looks when name is called			
Babbles conversation with others			
Reflects happiness, unhappiness in sounds made			
Babbles two- and three-syllable sounds			
Varies intensity, volume, pitch, and rhythm			

APPROXIMATELY EIGHT TO TWELVE MONTHS OF AGE

Child Behavior	Date First Observed	Practicing	Proficient
Physical Development			
MUSCULAR CONTROL			
Trunk and leg			
Stands holding onto furniture or hand			
Stands without assistance			
Sits from standing			
Squats and stands			
Locomotion			
Crawls			
Steps forward			
Crawls up steps			
Steps sideways			
Walks with help			
Climbs on furniture			
Hand			
Brings both hands to middle of body			
Uses finger to poke			
Carries objects in hands			
Holds and uses pen and crayon			
Uses one hand to hold object, one hand to reach and explore			
Stacks blocks with dominant hand			
Takes off clothes			
EATING			
Holds bottle			
Holds cup			
Holds and uses spoon			
Uses fingers to eat most food			
Starts establishing food preferences			

(Continued)

Child Behavior	Date First Observed	Practicing	Proficient
Emotional Development			
TYPES OF EMOTIONS and FEELINGS			
May have tantrums			
Rejects items, situations			
Develops preferences for toys, people			
Shows independence—helps with feeding and dressing self			
Shows affection			
CONTROL OF EMOTIONS and FEELINGS			
Learning to obey "No"			
Sometimes inhibits own behavior			
Obeys commands: No-No, Stop			
TEMPERAMENT (List behaviors to indicate basic approach.)			
Activity level			
Regularity			
Response to new situations: Approach or withdrawal			
Adaptability to change in routine			
Sensory threshold			
Positive or negative mood			
Intensity of response			
Distractibility			
Persistence and attention span			
Social Development			
OTHERS			
May fear strangers			
Keeps family members or caregiver in sight			

Child Behavior	Date First Observed	Practicing	Proficient
Focuses on own pleasure; may not consider others			
Imitates play			
Shows ownership of people			
Shows ownership of materials			
May become shy, clinging			
May demand attention			
Cognitive Development			
SENSORIMOTOR SUBSTAGE 4			
Differentiates goals			
Can focus on reaching and focus on toy			
Object permanence			
Child knows object exists when it is no longer visible; child seeks toy that rolls behind object			
Causality			
Understands that others cause actions			
Imitation and play			
Imitates others' actions in play			
Language Development			
Shouts			
Labels object sounds			
Uses names: *mama, dada*			
Responds to familiar sounds			
Responds to familiar words			
Repeats syllables, words, e.g., *bye-bye*			
Engages in babble conversations			
Repeats, practices word over and over			
Says one or two words			

APPROXIMATELY TWELVE TO EIGHTEEN MONTHS OF AGE

Child Behavior	Date First Observed	Practicing	Proficient
Physical Development			
MUSCULAR CONTROL			
Locomotion			
May prefer crawling to walking			
Walks alone			
Climbs up stairs with help			
Climbs down stairs with help			
Climbs over objects			
Hand			
Shows hand preference			
Rolls and catches objects			
Eye-hand coordination			
Scribbles			
Helps in dressing, undressing			
Emotional Development			
TYPES OF EMOTIONS and FEELINGS			
Expresses emotions in behavior and language			
Recognizes emotions in others			
Expresses sense of humor			
Displays negativism			
May have tantrums			
Uses play to express emotions, resolve conflicts			
Seeks dependency, security with family and caregiver			
Seeks to expand independence			

Child Behavior	Date First Observed	Practicing	Proficient
CONTROL OF EMOTIONS and FEELINGS			
Begins to understand right and wrong			
Reinforces desired behavior			
TEMPERAMENT (List behaviors to indicate basic approach.)			
Activity level			
Regularity			
Response to new situations: Approach or withdrawal			
Adaptability to change in routine			
Sensory threshold			
Positive or negative mood			
Intensity of response			
Distractibility			
Persistence and attention span			
Social Development			
SELF			
Has concept of self			
Is egocentric: understands only own viewpoint			
OTHERS			
Seeks presence of family or caregiver			
Plays games			
Acts differently toward different people			
Uses variety of behaviors to gain attention			
May be shy with some people			
Engages in parallel play			

(Continued)

Child Behavior	Date First Observed	Practicing	Proficient
Cognitive Development			
SENSORIMOTOR DEVELOPMENT: SUBSTAGE 5			
Object permanence			
Watches toy hidden and moved			
Looks for it where moved			
Causality			
Investigates cause and effect			
Sees self as causal agent			
Explores various ways things happen			
Employs active trial and error to solve problems			
Experiments			
Imitation and play			
Turns play with imitation into rituals			
Language Development			
Imitates sounds of other people, objects			
Responds to word and gesture conversation			
Responds to many questions and commands child cannot say			
Engages in jargon (babbling with a real word inserted)			
Uses word approximation for some words			
Uses words in immediate context			
Looks at board books independently			
Identifies family members in photographs			
Uses markers			

APPROXIMATELY EIGHTEEN TO TWENTY-FOUR MONTHS OF AGE

Child Behavior	Date First Observed	Practicing	Proficient
Physical Development			
MUSCULAR CONTROL			
Locomotion			
Walks backward			
Walks sideways			
Runs with stops and starts			
Jumps with both feet			
Kicks object			
Walks up and down stairs holding railing; both feet to one step			
Pushes and pulls objects while walking			
Climbs			
Pedals cycle			
Arm			
Throws object at target			
Hand			
Grasps and releases with developing finger muscles			
Pulls zippers			
Scribbles			
Increases wrist flexibility, turns wrist to turn object			
Turns book pages			
Digs with tool			
Makes individual marks with crayon or pen			
TEETH			
Uses toothbrush			

(Continued)

Child Behavior	Date First Observed	Practicing	Proficient
Emotional Development			
TYPES OF EMOTIONS and FEELINGS			
Views internal feelings and external behavior as same			
Shows one or more emotions at same time			
Seeks approval			
May develop new fears			
Increases fantasy			
May increase aggressiveness			
Seeks security in routines			
May become shy again			
Sometimes rejects family members or caregivers			
CONTROL OF EMOTIONS and FEELINGS			
Uses reactions of others as a controller of own behavior			
May resist change			
Moves to extremes, from lovable to demanding and stubborn			
TEMPERAMENT (List behaviors to indicate basic approach.)			
Activity level			
Regularity			
Response to new situations: Approach or withdrawal			
Adaptability to change in routine			
Sensory threshold			
Positive or negative mood			
Intensity of response			

Child Behavior	Date First Observed	Practicing	Proficient
Distractibility			
Persistence and attention span			
Social Development			
SELF			
Shows strong ownership by identifying materials as belonging to self			
Uses *I, mine, me, you*			
OTHERS			
Begins to be aware of others' feelings			
Believes people have changes in identity			
Interacts with other children; expands social relationships			
Looks to others for help			
Imitates tasks of others			
Wants to help, assists with tasks			
May do opposite of what is requested			
Engages in parallel play			
Cognitive Development			
SENSORIMOTOR DEVELOPMENT: SUBSTAGE 6			
Mental trial and error			
Tries out ideas mentally, based on past concrete experiences			
Object permanence			
Sees object disappear, remembers object, and figures out where it went			
Deferred imitation and symbolization			
Imitates past events			
Engages in symbolic play			
Uses symbolic play to resolve conflict			
Uses symbolic play to try on roles			

(Continued)

Child Behavior	Date First Observed	Practicing	Proficient
Language Development			
Uses language to reflect own meaning; expects others to have same meaning			
Expands vocabulary rapidly, labeling objects			
Points to objects and pictures named by others			
Learns social words—*hello, please, thank you*			
Uses language to express needs, desires			
Uses language to direct others			
Asks questions			
Uses nouns, verbs, pronouns			
Is learning prepositions			
Calls self by name			
Follows directions of one step or two steps			
Uses telegraphic speech (two- to three-word sentences)			
"Reads" books			
Listens to stories and rhymes			
Scribbles			

APPROXIMATELY TWENTY-FOUR TO THIRTY MONTHS OF AGE

Child Behavior	Date First Observed	Practicing	Proficient
Physical Development			
MUSCULAR CONTROL			
Movement			
Bends at waist			
Climbs			
Jumps			
Stands on one foot			
Is learning to use fork			
ELIMINATION			
May show interest in learning to use toilet			
Emotional Development			
TYPES OF EMOTIONS and FEELINGS			
Self-esteem			
Feels comfortable with self			
Feels positive self-worth			
Feels negative self-worth			
CONTROL OF EMOTIONS and FEELINGS			
Independently expresses many emotions in socially accepted manner			
TEMPERAMENT (List behaviors to indicate basic approach.)			
Activity level			
Regularity			
Response to new situations: Approach or withdrawal			
Adaptability to change in routine			

(Continued)

Child Behavior	Date First Observed	Practicing	Proficient
Sensory threshold			
Positive or negative mood			
Intensity of response			
Distractibility			
Persistence and attention span			
Social Development			
SELF			
Realizes own skills			
Identifies self as boy or girl			
OTHERS			
Acts to please adult			
Recognizes the difference between *mine* and *yours.*			
Shares, but not consistently			
Helps others			
Engages in parallel play			
May engage in brief episodes of cooperative play			
Cognitive Development			
PREOPERATIONAL STAGE: PRECONCEPTUAL			
Nonverbal classification			
Makes graphic collections			
Verbal preconcepts			
Uses words differently at different times			
Uses words with private meanings			
Labels objects in one class			
Focuses on one attribute			

Child Behavior	Date First Observed	Practicing	Proficient
Verbal reasoning			
Reasons from particular to particular			
Quantity			
Understands *some, more, gone, big*			
Number			
Understands *more*			
Space			
Understands up, down, behind, under, over			
Time			
Understands now, soon			
Language Development			
Uses demonstrative naming			
Uses attribution			
Uses possession			
Uses action			
Uses recurrence			
Uses negation			
Learns prosodic patterning			
Uses subject-verb combinations			
Uses verb-object			
May use subject-verb-object			
Selects and reads books			
Uses controlled scribbling			

APPROXIMATELY THIRTY TO THIRTY-SIX MONTHS OF AGE

Child Behavior	Date First Observed	Practicing	Proficient
Physical Development			
MOVEMENT AND COORDINATION			
Runs smoothly			
Jumps in place and forward			
Has firmly established handedness			
ELIMINATION			
Is in process of or has completed toilet learning			
Emotional Development			
TYPES OF EMOTIONS and FEELINGS			
Reacts strongly			
Acts negatively			
Learns enthusiastically			
CONTROL OF EMOTIONS and FEELINGS			
Is physically aggressive			
TEMPERAMENT (List behaviors to indicate basic approach.)			
Activity level			
Regularity			
Response to new situations: Approach or withdrawal			
Adaptability to change in routine			
Sensory threshold			
Positive or negative mood			
Intensity of response			
Distractibility			
Persistence and attention span			
Social Development			
SELF			
Acts possessive			

Child Behavior	Date First Observed	Practicing	Proficient
OTHERS			
Seeks assistance			
Directs others			
Helps others			
CONTROL OF SELF			
Plays cooperatively			
Shares			
Takes turns			
Cognitive Development			
PREOPERATIONAL STAGE: PRECONCEPTUAL			
Nonverbal classification			
Makes graphic collections			
Verbal reasoning			
Thinks one action is like another action			
Reasons from effect to cause			
Time			
Understands *now, soon, before, after*			
Language Development			
Has vocabulary of over 200 words			
Creates longer sentences			
Includes functional words (e.g., *a, an, the*)			
Uses plurals with accuracy and overregularization			
Uses past tense with accuracy and overregularization			
Listens to stories, "reads" pictures, storybooks			

INDOOR SAFETY CHECKLIST

Item	Yes/No	Corrections/ Comments	Date Correction Made
General Environment			
Floors are smooth and have a nonskid surface.			
Pipes and radiators are inaccessible to children or are covered to prevent contact.			
Hot tap water temperature for hand washing is 110°F–115°F or less.			
Electrical cords are out of children's reach and are kept out of doorways and traffic paths.			
Unused electrical outlets are covered by furniture or shock stops.			
Medicines, cleansers, and aerosols are kept in a locked place, where children are unable to see and reach them.			
All windows have screens that stay in place when used; expandable screens are not used.			
Windows can be opened only six inches or less from the bottom.			
Drawers are kept closed to prevent tripping or bumps.			
Trash is covered at all times.			
Walls and ceilings are free of peeling paint and cracked or falling plaster; center has been inspected for lead paint.			
There are no disease-bearing animals, such as turtles, parrots, or cats.			
Children are always supervised.			
There is no friable (crumbly) asbestos releasing into the air.			
Equipment and Toys			
Toys and play equipment are checked often for sharp edges, small parts, and sharp points.			
All toys are painted with lead-free paint.			
Toys are put away when not in use.			
Toy chests have lightweight lids or no lids.			

Item	Yes/No	Corrections/ Comments	Date Correction Made
Art materials are nontoxic, and have either the AP or the CP label.			
Curtains, pillows, blankets, and soft toys are made of flame-resistant material.			
Hallways and Stairs			
Stairs and stairways are free of boxes, toys, and other clutter.			
Stairways are well lit.			
The right-hand railing on the stairs is at child height and does not wobble when held; there is a railing or wall on both sides of stairways.			
Stairway gates are in place when appropriate.			
Closed doorways to unsupervised or unsafe areas are always locked unless this prevents emergency evacuation.			
Staff are able to watch for strangers entering the building.			
Kitchen			
Trash is kept away from areas where food is prepared or stored.			
Trash is stored away from the furnace and water heater.			
Pest strips are *not* used; pesticides for crawling insects are applied by a certified pest control operator.			
Cleansers and other poisonous products are stored in their original containers, away from food and out of children's reach.			
Food preparation surfaces are clean and free of cracks and chips.			
Electrical cords are placed where people will not trip over them or pull them.			
There are no sharp or hazardous cooking utensils within children's reach (e.g., knives).			
Pot handles are always turned in toward the back of the stove during cooking.			
The fire extinguisher can be reached easily in an emergency.			

(Continued)

Item	Yes/No	Corrections/ Comments	Date Correction Made
All staff know how to use the fire extinguisher correctly.			
Bathrooms Stable step stools are available when needed.			
Electrical outlets are covered with shock stops or outlet covers.			
Cleaning products, soap, and disinfectant are stored in a locked place, out of children's reach.			
Floors are smooth and have a nonskid surface.			
The trash container is emptied daily and kept clean.			
Hot water for hand washing is 110°F–115°F.			
Emergency Preparation All staff understand their roles and responsibilities in case of emergency.			
At least one staff person is always present who is certified in first aid and CPR for infants and children.			
The first aid kit is checked regularly for supplies and is kept where it can be reached easily by staff in an emergency.			
Smoke detectors and other alarms are checked regularly to make sure they are working.			
Each room and hallway has a fire escape route posted in clear view.			
Emergency procedures and telephone numbers are posted near each phone in clear view.			
Children's emergency phone numbers are kept near the phone, where they can be reached quickly.			
All exits are clearly marked and are free of clutter.			
Doors open in the direction of all exit travel.			
Cots are placed so that walkways are clear for evacuation in an emergency.			

Source: Statewide Comprehensive Injury Prevention Program (SCIPP), Massachusetts Department of Public Health.

PLAYGROUND SAFETY CHECKLIST

Item	Yes/No	Corrections/ Comments	Date Correction Made
All Equipment			
Nuts, bolts, or screws that stick out are covered with masking tape or sanded down.			
Metal equipment is free from rust or chipping paint.			
Wood equipment is free from splinters or rough surfaces, sharp edges, and pinching/crushing parts.			
Nuts and bolts are tight.			
Anchors for equipment are stable and buried below ground level.			
Equipment is in its proper place and is not bent with use.			
Children who use equipment are of the age/ developmental level for which the equipment was designed.			
Ground Surface			
All play equipment has 8–12 inches of shock-absorbing material underneath (e.g., pea gravel or wood chips).			
Surfaces are raked weekly to prevent them from becoming packed down and to find hidden hazards (e.g., litter, sharp objects, animal feces).			
Stagnant pools of water are not present on the surface.			
There is no exposed concrete where equipment is anchored.			
Spacing			
Swing sets are at least nine feet from other equipment.			
Swings are at least 1½ feet from each other.			
Slides have a 2½- to 3-yard run-off space.			
There is at least eight feet of space between equipment items.			
Boundaries between equipment items are visible to children (e.g., painted lines or low bushes).			

(Continued)

Item	Yes/No	Corrections/ Comments	Date Correction Made
Play areas for bike riding, games, and boxes are separate from other equipment.			
Swing sets are at least six feet from walls and fences, walkways, and other play areas; there is a barrier to prevent children from getting into traffic (e.g., when chasing a ball).			
Slides Slides are six feet in height or less.			
Side rims are at least $2^1/_2$ inches high.			
Slides have an enclosed platform at the top for children to rest and get into position for sliding.			
Slide ladders have handrails on both sides and flat steps.			
There is a flat surface at the bottom of the slide for slowing down.			
Metal slides are shaded to prevent burns.			
Wood slides are waxed, or oiled with linseed oil.			
The slide incline is equal to or less than 30 degrees.			
Steps and rungs are 7–11 inches apart to accommodate children's leg and arm reach.			
Climbing Equipment Ladders of different heights are available for children of different ages and sizes.			
Bars stay in place when grasped.			
The maximum height from which a child can fall is $7^1/_2$ feet.			
Climbers have regularly spaced footholds from top to bottom.			
There is an easy, safe "way out" for children when they reach the top.			
Equipment is dry before children are allowed to use it.			
Rungs are painted in bright or contrasting colors so children will see them.			

Item	Yes/No	Corrections/ Comments	Date Correction Made
Swings Chair swings are available for children under age five.			
Canvas sling and saddle seats are available for older children.			
S-shaped or open-ended hooks have been removed.			
Hanging rings are less than five inches or more than 10 inches in diameter (smaller or larger than child's head).			
The point at which seat and chain meet is exposed.			
Sandboxes Sandboxes are located in a shaded spot; only sterilized sand is used.			
The frame is sanded and smooth, without splinters or rough surfaces.			
The sand is raked at least every two weeks to check for debris and to provide exposure to air and sun.			
The sandbox has proper drainage.			
Poisonous plants and berries are removed from play area.			
There is a source of clean drinking water available in the play area.			
There is shade.			
The entire play area can be seen easily for good supervision.			

Source: Recommendations of Statewide Comprehensive Injury Prevention Program (SCIPP), Massachusetts Department of Public Health.

B

Developmental Profile and Instructions

INSTRUCTIONS

Copy the Developmental Profile form (Figure B–1). Create a profile for each infant and/or toddler in your care by following these instructions.

1. Write the child's name, date(s) of assessment(s), and date of birth (D. O. B.) on the profile. (Use the Sample Developmental Profile in Figure B–2 as an example.)
2. Calculate chronological age (C. A.) using the following method:

		Year	Month	Day
Assessment	=	2007	2	24
D. O. B.	=	2006	2	21
C. A.	=	1 (12 mo.)	0	3

3. Place the C. A. in months in the middle shaded C. A. row on the profile and put one-month intervals at each row for children with chronical ages from 1 to 17 months and two-month intervals for chronical ages from 18 months up (see Figure B–2 for an example).
4. Write the child behaviors assessed from the Developmental Prescription (Appendix A) under each major Developmental Area on the profile (see Sample Profile in Figure B–2).
5. Observe how the child performs on each skill and place an X in the row representing the monthly development for each listed child behavior.
6. Connect the Xs to graphically illustrate the child's development.
7. Write notes on strengths and weaknesses shown by the profile.

FIGURE B–1 Blank Developmental Profile

443

Name: **Juan P.**

Date: **2/24/XX**

Date of Birth: **2/21/XX**

C. A.: **12 months 3 days**

MONTH AGE EXPECT.	AREA I PHYSICAL				AREA II EMOTIONAL			AREA III SOCIAL					AREA IV COGNITIVE AND LANGUAGE					MONTH AGE EXPECT.
	MUSCLE	SLEEP	EAT	TEETH	FEELINGS	CONTROL	TEMPERAMENT	PEERS	YOUNGER	OLDER	ONE TO ONE	GROUP	GOALS	OBJECTS	CAUSALITY	PLAY	LANGUAGE	
18+																		18+
17																		17
16																		16
15																		15
14											B							14
13																		13
C. A. 12																		C. A. 12
11																		11
10																		10
9									A									9
8																		8
7																		7
6–																		6–

Notes: A = Juan has a little problem dealing with a group—sometimes is overwhelmed.
B = He responds very well to one to one adult attention.

FIGURE B–2 Sample of Completed Developmental Profile

444

C

Standards for Infant/Toddler Caregivers

This section provides specific information about standards for practicing or pre-service teachers. Covered in this appendix are the six CDA Competency Areas and five NAEYC Standards for Early Childhood Professional Preparation: Initial Licensure Programs. Table C–1, which was initially provided for you in Chapter 5, is included to remind you of the relationships between these two sets of teacher standards.

Appendix Overview

CDA Competency Standards for Infant/Toddler Caregivers in Center-based Programs
NAEYC Standards for Early Childhood Professional Preparation: Initial Licensure Programs
NAEYC Initial Licensure Standards Summary

CDA COMPETENCY STANDARDS FOR INFANT/TODDLER CAREGIVERS IN CENTER-BASED PROGRAMS

The CDA Competency Standards are the national standards used to evaluate a caregiver's performance with children and families during the CDA assessment process. The Competency Standards are divided into six **competency goals**, which are statements of a general purpose or goal for caregiver behavior. The competency goals are common to all child care settings. The six goals are defined in more detail in 13 **functional areas**, which describe the major tasks or functions that a caregiver must complete in order to carry out the competency goal (see Table C–2).

TABLE C–1. OVERLAP OF THE CDA AND NAEYC STANDARDS

NAEYC Teacher Preparation Standards

CDA Competency Areas	1. Promoting child development and learning	2. Building family and community relationships	3. Observing, documenting, and assessing	4. Teaching and learning	5. Becoming a professional
I. Safe, healthy learning environment	X			X	
II. Advance physical and intellectual competence	X			X	
III. Support social and emotional development; positive guidance	X			X	
IV. Positive and productive relationships with families		X			
V. Well-run, purposeful program			X		
VI. Commitment to professionalism					X

TABLE C–2. CDA COMPETENCY GOALS AND FUNCTIONAL AREAS

I.   To establish and maintain a safe, healthy learning environment.

   1. **Safe:** Candidate provides a safe environment to prevent and reduce injuries.
   2. **Healthy:** Candidate promotes good health and nutrition and provides an environment that contributes to the prevention of illness.
   3. **Learning Environment:** Candidate uses space, relationships, materials, and routines as resources for constructing an interesting, secure, and enjoyable environment that encourages play, exploration, and learning.

II.   To advance physical and intellectual competence.

   4. **Physical:** Candidate provides a variety of equipment, activities, and opportunities to promote the physical development of children.
   5. **Cognitive:** Candidate provides activities and opportunities that encourage curiosity, exploration, and problem solving appropriate to the development levels and learning styles of children.
   6. **Communication:** Candidate actively communicates with children and provides opportunities and support for children to understand, acquire, and use verbal and nonverbal means of communicating thoughts and feelings.
   7. **Creative:** Candidate provides opportunities that stimulate children to play with sound, rhythm, language, materials, space, and ideas in individual ways and to express their creative abilities.

III.   To support social and emotional development and provide positive guidance.

   8. **Self:** Candidate provides physical and emotional security for each child and helps each child to know, accept, and take pride in himself or herself and to develop a sense of independence.
   9. **Social:** Candidate helps each child feel accepted in the group, helps children learn to communicate and get along with others, and encourages feelings of empathy and mutual respect among children and adults.
   10. **Guidance:** Candidate provide a supportive environment in which children can begin to learn and practice appropriate and acceptable behaviors as individuals and as a group.

IV.   To establish positive and productive relationships with families.

   11. **Families:** Candidate maintains an open, friendly, and cooperative relationship with each child's family, encourages their involvement in the program, and supports the child's relationship with his or her family.

V.   To ensure a well-run, purposeful program responsive to particular needs.

   12. **Program Management:** Candidate is a manager who uses all available resources to ensure an effective operation, The Candidate is a competent organizer, planner, record keeper, communicator, and a cooperative coworker.

VI.   To maintain a commitment to professionalism.

   13. **Professionalism:** Candidate makes decisions based on knowledge of early childhood theories and practices. Candidate promotes quality in child care services. Candidate takes advantage of opportunities to improve competence, both for personal and professional growth for the benefit of children and families.

Each functional area is explained by a **developmental context**, which presents a brief overview of child development from birth to three years and provides a rationale for the functional area definition and examples of competent caregiver behavior that follow. Three different developmental levels are identified: young infants (birth–8 months), mobile infants (9–17 months), and toddlers (18–36 months). Children develop at different rates, and descriptions of these levels emphasize the unique characteristics and needs of children at each stage of development.

Each functional area is further explained by a list of sample caregiver behaviors (not included here). These examples describe behavior that demonstrates that a caregiver is acting in a competent way or exhibiting a skill in a particular functional area. During the assessment process, most candidates will exhibit other competent behavior, and a competent candidate might not demonstrate all the examples listed under a functional area. The examples are organized according to developmental stages of children from birth to three years, in order to emphasize the importance of the special skills needed to work with young infants, mobile infants, and toddlers. Special bilingual specialization examples are presented for several functional areas.

The samples of caregiver competency included in the standards should serve as a basis for recognizing other, more specific behaviors that are important to the individual candidate. CDA candidates and individuals conducting or participating in CDA training will be able to think of many different ways to demonstrate skill in the six competency goals and 13 functional areas.

Competent caregivers integrate their work and constantly adapt their skills—always thinking of the development of the whole child. In all functional areas, it is important for competent caregivers to individualize their work with each child while meeting the needs of the group. In every area, too, caregivers must promote multiculturalism, support families with different languages, and meet the needs of children with special needs. And, while demonstrating skills and knowledge, competent caregivers must also demonstrate personal qualities, such as flexibility and a positive style of communicating with young children and working with families.

The Council for Early Childhood Professional Recognition has designed both training and assessment systems for persons interested in the CDA credential. For more information, contact

Council for Professional Recognition
2460 16th St., NW
Washington, DC 20009
Telephone: (202) 265-9090 or (800) 424-4310
Fax: (202) 265-9161
http://www.cdacouncil.org/

NAEYC STANDARDS FOR EARLY CHILDHOOD PROFESSIONAL PREPARATION: INITIAL LICENSURE PROGRAMS

The National Association for the Education of Young Children (NAEYC) has designed standards for teacher preparation programs at the Associate, Initial, and Advanced levels. The NAEYC Standards for Early Childhood Professional Preparation are the national standards used to evaluate teacher preparation programs. This process involves evaluating the pre-service teacher's performance with children and families during annual program reviews. The standards are divided into five categories and, upon occasion, sub-categories.

These standards were created to assist NAEYC with meeting the mission of improving the quality of services for children and families birth through age eight. Teacher preparation standards are just one avenue for tackling this monumental task of helping children learn and develop well. Accreditation standards for early childhood programs, guidelines for developmentally appropriate practices, curriculum content and assessment, teacher preparation standards, and a system for financing early childhood education all work together to create this context.

Because programs educate teachers to participate in a wide range of diverse settings and programs, e.g., private nursery school programs, center- and family-based child care programs, kindergartens, public school programs, early intervention programs including Early Head Start and Head Start, and so on, standards cannot be rigid or "one size fits all."

The following page outlines and summarizes the five Standards for Early Childhood Professional Preparation: Initial Level. Refer to the entire document for more specific guidelines and examples for each standard. More information about each set of standards can be downloaded from the NAEYC website at http://www.naeyc.org/faculty/pdf/2003.pdf (Associate), http://www.naeyc.org/faculty/pdf/2001.pdf (Initial), or http://www.naeyc.org/faculty/pdf/2002.pdf (Advanced).

NAEYC INITIAL LICENSURE STANDARDS SUMMARY

NAEYC Initial Licensure Standards

Standard 1. Promoting Child Development and Learning

Candidates use their understanding of young children's characteristics and needs, and of multiple interacting influences on children's development and learning, to create environments that are healthy, respectful, supportive, and challenging for all children.

Standard 2. Building Family and Community Relationships

Candidates know about, understand, and value the importance and complex characteristics of children's families and communities. They use this understanding to create respectful, reciprocal relationships that support and empower families, and to involve all families in their children's development and learning.

Standard 3. Observing, Documenting, and Assessing to Support Young Children and Families

Candidates know about and understand the goals, benefits, and uses of assessment. They know about and use systematic observations, documentation, and other effective assessment strategies in a responsible way, in partnership with families and other professionals, to positively influence children's development and learning.

Standard 4. Teaching and Learning

Candidates integrate their understanding of and relationships with children and families; their understanding of developmentally effective approaches to teaching and learning; and their knowledge of academic disciplines to design, implement, and evaluate experiences that promote positive development and learning for all children.

Sub-Standard 4a. Connecting with children and families

Candidates know, understand, and use positive relationships and supportive interactions as the foundation for their work with young children.

Sub-Standard 4b. Using developmentally effective approaches

Candidates know, understand, and use a wide array of effective approaches, strategies, and tools to positively influence children's development and learning.

Sub-Standard 4c. Understanding content knowledge in early education

Candidates understand the importance of each content area in young children's learning. They know the essential concepts, inquiry tools, and structure of content areas including academic subjects and can identify resources to deepen their understanding.

Sub-Standard 4d. Building meaningful curriculum

Candidates use their own knowledge and other resources to design, implement, and evaluate meaningful, challenging curriculum that promotes comprehensive developmental and learning outcomes for all young children.

Standard 5. Becoming a Professional

Candidates identify and conduct themselves as members of the early childhood profession. They know and use ethical guidelines and other professional standards related to early childhood practice. They are continuous, collaborative learners who demonstrate knowledgeable, reflective, and critical perspectives on their work, making informed decisions that integrate knowledge from a variety of sources. They are informed advocates for sound educational practices and policies.

Source: NAEYC Standards for Early Childhood Professional Preparation Initial Licensure Programs. © The National Association for the Education of Young Children.

Glossary

A

abstract An idea not existing in the real world; the basis of a concept.

accommodation Piaget's process of changing or altering skills to better fit the requirements of a task.

accreditation Process of demonstrating and validating the presence of indicators of quality as set out by national standards.

action sentence In language development, action sentences separate the action from the actor and object and explore the relations among these three.

active listening The skill required to simply "feed back" the deeper felt message (not words) of the sender in the words of the receiver.

active-dry area An area in the child care center suitable for activities such as large motor activities, construction, and housekeeping.

activity area A space designated for a specific function and a specific age group of children. Size, shape, and utility of space may include tools and equipment necessary to promote the safety and enhance the maturation of children.

adaptation A change in behavior that helps the child survive in his or her environment; described by Piaget as a cognitive skill.

ages and stages A use of chronological age as it relates to functional behavior or a level of development clearly distinguishable from the previous level of development.

alert times Times during the day when a child is attending and attracted to the world around him or her.

anecdotal record A brief narrative account of one event written using descriptive language.

approval one of the three As of child care; feedback that a person is accepted as he or she is.

assessment The process of gathering data about young children, usually through observations, and analyzing it; the results of assessments are used to inform educational decisions.

assimilation Piaget's way of explaining how children refine cognitive structures into schemes.

attachment theory A theory that infants are born needing an emotional attachment to their primary caregiver.

attention One of the three As of child care; focusing sensory modalities (e.g., visual, auditory) on a person or object.

attribution Children give objects a symbol with meaning.

attunement One of the three As of child care; feedback that is *in tune with* or responsive to the behaviors or moods being currently displayed by the infant, toddler, or adult.

avoidant attachment One of the types of attachment between infants and primary caregiver that is related to inconsistent and insensitive caregiver attention.

B

babbling Prelanguage speech with which the baby explores the variety of sounds.

baby signing Nonverbal language using gestures and expressions in infants.

behaviorism School of psychology that studies stimuli, responses, and rewards that influence behavior.

bias A prejudgment concerning the style and forms of a specific culture.

brain plasticity When one part of the brain is damaged, other parts take over the functions of the damaged parts.

C

calibrating Carefully observing the specific behaviors demonstrated by another during an interaction in order to build rapport.

cardiopulmonary resuscitation (CPR) Lifesaving technique of manually starting and maintaining a human heartbeat.

caregiver A person who is educated to provide care and education to another, in our case, an infant or toddler; a person responsible for helping another meet his or her wants and needs.

caring community of learners One of the five guidelines for developmentally appropriate practice that focuses on creating a classroom context that supports the development of caring, inclusive relationships for everyone involved.

cause and effect In sensorimotor development, observation allows a child to identify the relationship between an action and its effect.

center-based care Child care provided away from home for more than six children for some part of the day or night.

certification A form of regulation for professional child care; standards vary by state.

checklist A method for recording observational data that notes the presence of specific, predetermined skills or behaviors.

child-centered The overall goal in the design of the child care center.

Child Development Associate (CDA) A credential provided by the Council for Early Childhood Professional Recognition when a person has provided evidence of meeting the national standards for caregiver performance.

child-directed speech Adjustments adults make in their tone, volume, and speech patterns to capture and sustain focal attention from an infant.

child-proof To ensure a safe environment by removing potential hazards.

choices A guidance technique where the adult provides at least two acceptable options from which the child can choose; minimizes confrontations and helps the child learn to choose wisely.

choke tube Plastic tube used to determine safe sizes of objects for child play.

classical conditioning Association of an unconditioned stimulus with a conditioned stimulus that evokes specific conditioned or unconditioned responses.

cognitive developmental theory Piaget's theory that children construct knowledge and awareness through manipulation and exploration of their environment.

cognitive disequilibrium Piaget's term for children's cognitive reaction when placed in new and unfamiliar situations in which old schemes no longer work well.

cognitive equilibrium Piaget's term for a cognitive state in which a child's schemes work to explain the child's environment.

cognitive functions Refers to a broad class of the functions to name, indicate, describe, and/or comment.

competent caregiver style A style of caregiving that uses appropriate goals and objectives.

consequences The natural and/or logical outcomes of actions.

context bound A characteristic of early language in which an infant only understands a word in the context where it was originally learned.

continuity of care Having the same teachers work with the same group of children and families for more than one year, ideally for three years.

controlling caregiver style A style of caregiving that tends to discount and negate children's feelings and communicate in an insensitive manner, which causes emotional pain.

cooing The second stage of vocalization in infants from birth to four months old, which resembles vowel-like sounds.

CPR See **cardiopulmonary resuscitation.**

crawling Strategy for mobility where the infant or toddler moves on hands and knees while using arms and legs in opposition.

cultural diversity Cultural differences within a group.

culture Values and beliefs held in common by a group of people.

curriculum Everything that occurs during the course of the day with infants and toddlers; planned learning experiences and routine care.

D

daily plans An approach to curriculum in which planned learning experiences are designed daily based on specific observations of the children.

deferred imitation Imitation of another person's behavior even when that person is no longer present.

demand feeding Providing solid or liquid foods when an infant or toddler is hungry.

demonstrative naming In language development, a process in which the first word points out an object and the second names it (e.g., "this ball").

descriptive phrasing A technique for reporting observations, which involves using words or phrases to describe observable behaviors.

detached caregiver style A style that often is not cognitively or emotionally involved enough with children to be aware of their feelings, in that the children tend to become detached or angry with other people.

development Operationally defined as general sequences and patterns of growth and maturity.

developmental perspective Teacher and/or program emphasis, in both home-based care and child care centers, on the developmental needs of children.

developmentally appropriate practice Process of making educational decisions about the well-being and education of young children based on information or knowledge about child development and learning; the needs, interests, and strengths of each individual child in the group; and the social and cultural contexts in which the children live.

disability A condition resulting from a loss of physical functioning; or difficulties in learning and social adjustment that significantly interfere with normal growth and development.

discipline Behavior-limiting steps to reduce harmful behaviors.

discovery The opportunity to find interesting items and examine them closely, to be facilitated as part of environmental design.

disequilibrium An internal mental state which motivates learning because the child is uncomfortable and seeks to make sense of what he or she has observed or experienced.

disorder A disturbance in normal functioning (mental, physical, or psychological).

disoriented attachment A form of attachment between infant and primary caregiver in which the infant has usually been traumatized by severe or prolonged abandonment.

documentation Any activity that generates a performance record with sufficient detail to help others understand the behavior recorded.

documentation panel A visual and written explanation of children's learning displayed to others (parents, children, colleagues, and/or community members).

double substitution Pretend play in which two materials are transformed, within a single act, into something they are not in reality.

dramatic play A form of play that provides opportunities to combine language with imagination.

E

early childhood educator A professional who has been trained to educate young children.

early intervention Comprehensive services for infants and toddlers who have special needs or are at risk of acquiring a disability. Services may include education, health care, and/or social and psychological assistance.

ecological systems theory Bronfenbrenner's theory of nested environmental systems that influence the development and behavior of people.

egocentric Toddlers see the world from their own point of view; in the first year and a half of life their bodies and the objects they play with are perceived to be part of *self*.

elimination The process of excreting urine and feces from the body. Two important caregiver responsibilities are changing diapers frequently and recording the time of and any abnormalities of bowel movements.

emotional detachment A situation arising from physical or emotional abuse in which the infant or toddler fails to create enduring emotional bonds with others.

emotional development The ability in infants to express and regulate pleasure, happiness, fear, and frustration.

emotional intelligence Skills learned early in life that are necessary for healthy ego development, good relationships, and fulfillment in life experiences.

emotional regulation Learning to control and manage strong emotions in a socially and culturally acceptable manner.

empathy Sensitivity to what others feel, need, or want; the fundamental relationship skill present at birth.

equilibration The movement from equilibrium to disequilibrium and back to equilibrium again.

equilibrium A state of homeostasis or balance which reflects how an infant's or toddler's current cognitive schemes work to explain his or her environment.

ethology The study of behavior patterns and character development.

evolutionary theory The theory that child development is genetically determined and happens automatically.

exceptional A term describing any individual whose physical, mental, or behavioral performance deviates so substantially from the average (higher or lower) that additional support is required to meet the individual's needs.

existential self One of the two aspects of the self identified by William James; this type of self is separate from the environment and other people and maintains continuous existence over time.

exosystem Bronfenbrenner's term for the influences that are not a direct part of a child's experience but influence development, such as parent education.

experience-dependent Type of motor neuron pathway that waits for environmental experiences before being activated.

experience-expectant Type of motor neuron pathway that apparently expects specific stimuli at birth.

F

facilitate To help with an activity that someone cannot do by him- or herself at the time.

FAE or fetal alcohol effect Outcomes, though less severe than FAS, for children who were exposed to alcohol during prenatal development.

family-based care Care and education provided to a small group of children in a home setting.

family-caregiver conferences Periodic meetings between family members and caregiver to review documentation and interpretation of each child's developmental progress.

family grouping Method for grouping children where children are of different ages.

FAS or fetal alcohol syndrome Growth delays, facial abnormalities, mental retardation, impulsivity, and behavioral problems resulting from exposure to alcohol during prenatal development.

fear Physical and psychological reaction to threat.

fine motor control A developmental learning skill in which small muscle control is learned.

finger foods Foods that older infants and toddlers can easily feed to themselves such as crackers or dry cereal.

flexibility Component of environment design that reflects changes in response to the individual child and each group of children living in the environment.

G

good touch Term for respectful, sensitive, and pleasurable touch.

goodness of fit The temperamental match between very young children and their caregivers.

grammatical words Function words that have little meaning on their own yet affect the meaning of other words (e.g., articles, prepositions, or conjunctions).

gratification Satisfaction of a need.

gross motor control The control of large muscle activity.

group family child care Care provided for 6 to 12 children in a home setting; usually has two or more caregivers.

guide To direct toward a desirable goal.

H

Head Start programs State-subsidized child care programs for low-income families.

healthy caregiver style A style of caregiving that balances the feelings and needs of the child with those of the caregiver, resulting in a "win-win" rather than a "win-lose" relationship.

hearing Physical and neurological process of bringing sound into the nervous system.

high active Infant temperament type in which infant may kick, wriggle, and jerk, requiring the caregiver to provide more assistance while the infant learns to sit up.

holistic care A type of care that considers the whole child, including physical, emotional, social, language skills, and cognitive development.

home-school journal A notebook or journal in which teachers and family members write notes about key happenings and which they send back and forth on a daily or weekly basis.

home visit A meeting in the child's home providing an opportunity for the professional caregiver to see how the family members and child relate to each other in the home setting.

human immunodeficiency virus (HIV) infection Immune disease that attacks white blood cells and is transmitted through open sores or other bodily fluid sources.

I

identity An infant's or toddler's self-constructed definition of who she is.

I statements Expressions about one's own thoughts and feelings without judging the other person.

image of the child Beliefs about children that teachers hold; these beliefs are examined for how they impact teacher-child interactions, management of the environment, and selection of teaching strategies.

imprinting Term from ethology to explain early critical period for imitating and attaching to a mother figure.

imitation Mimicking or copying; in development, a normal stage of play.

individual constructivism Piaget's belief that each person individually creates new understandings, interpretations, and realities through interactions with materials, equipment, and people in their environment.

in-home care Child care that takes place in the child's home.

infant A child from birth to walking.

inserimento A period of gradual "settling in" or "transition and adjustment" that includes strategies for building relationships and community among adults and children when the child is first entering a Reggio Emilia–inspired child care program.

instrumental function In language development for 18- to 24-month-olds, refers to the broad class of functions to request, reject, manipulate, and comment.

interactional synchrony A sensitively tuned "emotional dance," in which interactions are mutually rewarding to caregiver and infant.

interpretive phrasing A form of reporting that makes judgments without providing observable data to justify the conclusions.

intersubjectivity Vygotsky's term to explain how children and adults come to understand each other by adjusting perceptions to fit the other person's map of the world.

J

jargon Language term which refers to the mixing of one real word with strings of babble.

L

labeling Providing labels for objects for association and language development.

language Visual and auditory symbols representing objects and ideas.

language development Acquisition of one's first language; during 8 to 12 months of age, an infant's use of combinations of sounds, babbling, and words to converse with self and others.

latency stage Freud's psychosexual stage occurring between 6 and 11 years of age when social values and contacts outside the home become important.

learning Processing information in such a way that internal and external behavior is changed and a new response is elicited.

learning center An environment or part of a child care setting that is organized to promote and encourage learning.

lexical words Words that have a concrete or abstract connection to objects or events (e.g., nouns, verbs, and adverbs).

licensing regulations Official rules on teacher-child ratios, safety, health, and zoning that an individual or organization must follow to be granted a license.

limits Positively worded statements about desired or acceptable behavior that help children acquire appropriate behaviors for the setting.

locomotion The attempt to gain stability when moving forward or upwards (e.g., crawling and walking) against the force of gravity.

locus of control The extent to which a person perceives his or her life as within his or her own control.

logico-mathematical knowledge Knowledge that is individually constructed by each child and involves identifying relationships between objects.

low active Infant temperament style of little movement; caregivers may leave the baby in one position longer than they do with infants who are high active.

M

macrosystem Bronfenbrenner's term for influences on development from the general culture, including laws and customs.

make-believe play Vygotsky's term for using imagination to act out internal concepts of how the world functions and how rules are formed.

manipulation Includes reaching, grasping, and releasing objects; in the first year of development the control of objects moves from reflexive to voluntary.

maturation Naturally unfolding course of growth and development.

medically fragile A new subgroup of health disorders for individuals who are at risk for medical emergencies and often require specialized support (e.g., feeding tubes).

memory the process of storing and recalling stimuli at a later time.

mental images Pictures in the mind with which children can carry out action sequences internally.

mesosystem Bronfenbrenner's term for the second level of influence for the child that involves interactions among microsystems, such as a teacher in a child care center and family members.

metacognition Awareness of one's own thought processes.

microsystem Bronfenbrenner's term for the innermost level of influence found in the immediate surrounding of the child, such as parents or an early childhood educator.

milestones Specific behaviors common to an entire population that are used to track development and are observed when they are first or consistently manifested.

mirroring A communication technique of repeating exactly what is said without adding or interpreting any of the speaker's words.

modeling In development, one way a child learns how to act like an adult.

motivate To stimulate someone to action.

movement An activity for children involving creative moving to music and dancing.

movements In newborns from birth to four months, movements are reflexive; they occur without the infant's control.

multiple disabilities Children who have more than one identified exceptionality; typically they have severe educational needs that are not easily accommodated with programs designed for just one special need.

muscular control Gaining conscious control over muscles so that behaviors such as reaching, grabbing, and releasing can occur when the infant or toddler wants them to.

N

National Association for Family Child Care (NAFCC) An association offering professional recognition and distinction to family child care providers whose services represent high-quality child care.

National Association for the Education of Young Children (NAEYC) Professional organization that offers professional resources and development for early childhood educators, as well as recognition for programs that represent high-quality care.

National Parenting Scales (NPS) An assessment of essential parenting skills based on CDA competencies.

nature Biological and genetic foundations that influence development and learning.

negation Language strategy used to communicate that something desired or expected is not there or that the child cannot, is not permitted to, or does not want to do something.

negative reinforcers Consequences for a behavior that have the effect of decreasing the frequency or duration of the behavior.

noble savage Rousseau's term for a young child, born without a moral sense of right and wrong.

nonverbal signal Any feedback given visually without the use of auditory stimuli.

normative approach Observing large numbers of children to establish average or normal expectations.

nurture Environmental factors that influence development and learning.

O

object permanence Starting at 8 to 12 months, infants remember events, people, and objects for increasingly longer periods.

observational learning In child development, one of the major ways in which children learn is to observe the behaviors of others.

omnipotent The sense of being unaware of any physical limitations and feeling above physical laws.

operant conditioning theory A theory about the process of increasing or decreasing the frequency or duration of behaviors through association with positive and negative reinforcing stimuli.

ORAOM Acronym for Observe, Record, Assess, Organize, and Manage; necessary skills for early childhood educators.

organization A process of rearranging new sets of information (schemes) and linking them to other established schemes, resulting in an expanded cognitive system.

original sin Belief by Puritans, for example, that infants are born bad and must be tamed by harsh, restrictive child-rearing practices.

overgeneralize The use of one word to mean many different things.

over-regularization Strategy of applying one standard grammatical rule to an irregular word, e.g., "goed" for the past tense of *go*.

P

pacing Matching complementary behavior to that of another person to build rapport.

parallel play Type of play in which older infants and toddlers engage with similar materials and share physical space but do not interact with one another.

parenting styles The caregiving style of a child's parents and other family members.

partnerships Alliances with family and community members to support and enhance the well-being and learning of young children.

passive influences Influences that affect a person without the necessity of interaction, such as television.

perspective-taking Acquiring the skills for recognizing and responding to the perspectives of others; not a skill to be expected of infants and toddlers, but the foundations for skills should be set.

philosophy Set of educational beliefs that guide behaviors and decision making for individual teachers and groups of teachers (e.g., programs).

phonemic features Sounds usually associated with letter symbols.

phonology Understanding the basic sounds of the language and how they are combined to make words.

physical development The acquisition of skills and control of fine and gross motor muscles; occurs rapidly for children age 8 to 18 months as they learn to crawl, stand with support, and walk independently.

physical knowledge Knowledge constructed through the direct interaction with materials.

pincer grasp The physical skill of using the thumb and pointer finger to grasp objects.

planned experiences Curricular experiences designed to enhance and support the individual learning needs, interests, and abilities of the children in an early childhood program.

portfolio Tool for collecting, storing, and documenting what you know about a child and her development and learning.

positive self-talk The internalization of messages we hear about ourselves from others.

positive reinforcer Consequences for behavior that have the effect of increasing the frequency or duration of the behavior.

possession Children make special associations between a person and an object, often using a two-word sentence; e.g., "mommy chair" to indicate possession.

pragmatics An understanding of how to engage in communication with others that is socially acceptable and effective.

preconceptual The first substage of Piaget's preoperational stage of cognitive development, in which children can mentally sort some objects and actions.

preoperational stage Piaget's second stage of cognitive development, during which toddlers and preschoolers reason based on perception.

prescriptive level The highest behavior in a task analysis that a child can successfully perform, the level at which to begin instruction.

pretend other A child's make-believe other person or object.

pretend self Pretend play directed toward self in which pretense is apparent.

primary caregiving system Method of organizing work in which one teacher is primarily responsible for half of the children and the other teacher is primarily responsible for the rest.

private speech Vygotsky's term for internal dialogue that children use for self-guidance and understanding.

progettazione Italian term that is loosely translated as "flexible planning."

project An ongoing investigation which provokes infants, toddlers, and teachers to construct knowledge.

prosodic patterning Communication strategy in which toddlers learn how to use the appropriate stress and intonation to express their specific ideas.

psychoanalytic theory Freud's theory of personality development, including psychosexual stages.

psychosocial theory Erikson's stage theory of development, including trust, autonomy, identity, and intimacy.

R

rapport building Using the strategies of **calibrating** and **pacing** to establish harmonious agreement between two people.

rating scale Method of recording observational data similar to checklists, but that lists frequencies (e.g., never, seldom, always) or qualities of characteristics or activities (e.g., eats using fingers, eats using spoon, eats using fork).

recurrence A language concept about repetition that young children ofen express with *more*, e.g., "more ride."

referral Assisting families with locating agencies or professionals who can provide additional support and/or services.

reflective self William James's term for the self that discriminates itself from others and the environment and is defined by being different from the "other."

regression Temporary movement back to earlier stages of development after higher levels have been accomplished.

relationships The human need for companionship and close emotional bonds; teachers must consider this need when designing learning environments.

representation Methods for telling others what you think or believe including but not limited to storytelling, drawing, painting, sculpting with clay or wire.

resistant attachment A form of connection between infant and primary caregiver in which the infant resists emotionally and physically connecting with the caregiver.

respect A feeling of high regard for someone and a willingness to treat him or her accordingly.

responses Important aspect of behavioral theories; how one reacts to environmental stimuli.

rights of children The belief that children do not just have needs for adults to deal with but rather rights to appropriate care and education.

role playing When children represent their ideas by acting them out using props such as puppets, dolls, or other dramatic play materials.

routine care Strategies for meeting the basic needs (e.g., hunger, cleanliness) of infants and toddlers.

running record A long narrative account of a significant period of time for a child, a group, or an activity written using descriptive language.

S

scaffolding A term describing incremental steps in learning and development from simple to complex.

schemes Piaget's concept to explain cognitive patterns of actions used to learn new information.

scribbling Nonsense writing marks that are a precursor to writing.

search for hidden objects The object remains permanent (does not cease to exist) in the child's thinking even when the child cannot see it.

secure attachment A connection between infant and primary caregiver in which the infant feels safe and responds warmly to the caregiver.

Seeking Educational Equity and Diversity (SEED) National anti-biased curriculum project that facilitates teachers' examination of their beliefs and practices.

self-awareness Sensory-grounded information regarding one's existence; what a person sees, hears, and feels in the body related to self.

self-esteem Respect for one's own abilities.

self-health Focus on the physical, social, emotional, and cognitive factors within oneself; taking good care of oneself.

self-recognition Conscious awareness of self as different from others and the environment; occurs first usually between 9 and 15 months of age.

self-regulation The skills necessary to direct and control one's own behavior in socially and culturally appropriate ways.

self-responsibility Taking over responsibility for fulfilling some of one's own needs.

self-soothing Comforting and making oneself at ease.

selfless caregiver style A style in which the caregiver makes the child's feelings important to the exclusion of the caregiver's own, which often results in children becoming self-absorbed, guilt ridden, and insensitive to the feelings of other people.

semantics The study of meaning in language, including concepts.

sense of agency In development of self, the awareness that the child can affect other people, places, and things.

senses principle The need for an environment to be pleasing to the senses, e.g., offering natural light and appealing art to look at.

sensorimotor stage Piaget's first stage of cognitive development, which is focused on motor activity and coordination of movements.

sensory threshold Individual differences in how children respond to environmental stimuli, such as noise when sleeping.

separation and individuation The process of defining self as separate from others, which starts in infancy and continues throughout childhood.

separation anxiety Fear exhibited at the loss of physical or emotional connection with the primary caregiver.

seriation Ordering items in sequence based on criteria such as color, length, or size (e.g., small, medium, large).

sleep Most newborns sleep between 11 and 21 hours a day. Infant sleep is not a continuous activity.

social-arbitrary knowledge Culturally constructed knowledge (e.g., language, values, rules) that is passed on or transmitted from one person to another through social interactions.

social learning theories A body of theory that adds social influences to behaviorism to explain development.

sociocultural theory Vygotsky's theory on development, which predicts how cultural values, beliefs, and concepts are passed from one generation to the next.

solitary play Playing alone; a child may look at other children and play near them, but children do not yet interact.

special education Specially designed instruction provided to children in all settings (such as the classroom, the home, and hospitals or community agencies).

stability Within the first month, infants can lift their heads; by the third month they are using their arms to push against the floor to raise their heads and chests.

stages Normal patterns of development that most people go through in maturation, first described by Jean-Jacques Rousseau.

stimuli The initial energy behind a need that creates an action.

stranger anxiety Fear exhibited by older toddlers around nine months of age toward people who are different or unknown; demonstrates their growing cognitive abilities.

substitution Using a "meaningless" object in a creative or imaginative manner or using an object in a pretense act in a way that differs from how the child has previously used the object.

sudden infant death syndrome (SIDS) A tragic event in which a young child dies after going to sleep for a nap or at bedtime with no indication of discomfort.

survival of the fittest Darwin's theory that only the best-adapted members of a species are able to continue to thrive.

symbolic play Children's symbolic representations of objects, feelings, or ideas.

synchrony See **interactional synchrony**.

syntax How words combine into understandable phrases and sentences.

T

tabula rasa Locke's term, Latin for "blank slate," which implies that infants are a blank screen at birth and are completely molded by the influences of the environment.

task analysis Analysis of a behavioral goal in which movements are broken down into a step-by-step format and each small step leading to mastering a complex task is taught in sequence.

teaching A process of active instruction and interactions that provides information to others.

teething Begins in infants approximately four to eight months old and refers to teeth breaking through the gums.

telegraphic speech When infants and toddlers combine two or three words into a sentence including only key words (e.g., "go daddy").

temper tantrum Angry emotional outburst and frustrated behavior when a toddler suddenly wants to do things he or she may not do and does not want to do things he or she can do.

temperament Physical, emotional, and social personality traits and characteristics.

toddler A child between 10 and 36 months of age.

toilet learning The developmental process for gaining control of bladder and bowels; complex process involving physical, cognitive, social, emotional, and language skills.

transparency A component of environmental design that allows you to easily supervise because see-through materials (such as fabrics or decorated acrylic) are used to divide spaces.

trial and error An approach to exploration during which the child utilizes a number of strategies and observes the results of their actions.

U

universal precautions Medical term for a series of standard procedures used to keep the patient and staff as healthy and safe as possible during physical care.

W

walking Upright locomotion; initially executed with support from an adult or furniture and then usually occurs without support around the child's first birthday.

weekly plans Approach to curriculum where experiences are planned on a weekly basis based on specific observations of the children.

Y

you statements Sentences that give advice to or judgment about another person, often closing off further communication.

young infant A child between birth and eight months of age.

Z

zone of proximal development Vygotsky's term for a range of tasks that a child is developmentally ready to learn.

Index

Note: Page numbers in italic type indicate figures or tables.